'So late into the night'

BYRON'S LETTERS AND JOURNALS
VOLUME 5
1816–1817

So we'll go no more a-roving
    So late into the night,
Though the heart be still as loving,
    And the moon be still as bright.

For the sword outwears its sheath,
    And the soul wears out the breast,
And the heart must pause to breathe,
    And Love itself have rest. . . .
                    February 28, 1817.

BYRON. Bust by Bertel Thorvaldsen, 1817
(*Photograph: Fay Godwin*)

'So late into the night'

BYRON'S LETTERS AND JOURNALS

Edited by
LESLIE A. MARCHAND

VOLUME 5
1816–1817

*The complete and unexpurgated text of
all the letters available in manuscript and
the full printed version of all others*

THE BELKNAP PRESS OF
HARVARD UNIVERSITY PRESS
CAMBRIDGE, MASSACHUSETTS

1976

ISBN 0-674-08945-6

Library of Congress Catalog
Card Number 73-81853

Printed in the United States
of America

CONTENTS

EDITORIAL NOTE

This volume, containing the letters written during the first year and a half of Byron's self-exile, reveal an increasing maturity and honesty that give them a new flavour. The very best letters are the ones from Italy, particularly those to Hobhouse, Kinnaird, Murray and Moore. Freed from the inhibitions of English society, Byron's spirit seemed to expand and his letters to reflect the *joie de vivre* that, despite his melancholy, was an inherent part of his character.

In an effort to make each volume as self-contained as possible, I am repeating and will repeat in future volumes, the statements on Editorial Principles and Annotation. The appendices contain information useful for readers of this volume, and the index of proper names is intended to serve the reader until the general index and subject index are published in the last volume.

ACKNOWLEDGMENTS. (Volume 5). The untiring interest and attention of my publisher, John Murray, has made the preparation of this volume more of a pleasure than a burden. And the increasing vivacity of Byron's letters from Italy has renewed my own enthusiasm, as I hope it will that of the readers of the volume. Mrs. Doris Langley Moore is always ready with assistance in solving problems of identification and obscure references in the letters. I am indebted again to the National Endowment for the Humanities for a generous Research Grant for assistance in the project of editing the letters, and to the staff of the Division of Research Grants in particular. Dr. Donald H. Reiman, Editor of *Shelley and His Circle* for the Carl H. Pforzheimer Library, and Mrs. Doucet D. Fischer, Co-ordinating Editor, have been most helpful in many ways.

For permission to have photocopies made of letters in their possession and to use them in this volume I wish to thank these libraries and individuals: Beinecke Rare Book and Manuscript Library, Yale University; Henry E. and Albert A. Berg Collection, New York Public Library; Biblioteca Nazionale Centrale, Florence; Bibliothèque Nationale, Paris; British Museum (Department of Manuscripts); Henry E. Huntington Library; Keats House, Hampstead; Lord Kinnaird; the Marquess of Lansdowne; Academy of Sciences of the U.S.S.R., Moscow, 1952; *Literaturnoe Nasledstvo* [*Literary Heritage*]

No. 58; The Earl of Lytton; John S. Mayfield Library, Syracuse University; Pierpont Morgan Library; Mr. John Murray; New York Public Library, Manuscript Division; Roe–Byron Collection, Newstead Abbey; Royal Library, Copenhagen; Mrs. Diana Spearman; Stark Library, University of Texas; Victoria and Albert Museum (John Forster Collection); D. M. S. Watson Library, University College London.

For permission to quote in a note an unpublished portion of Thomas Moore's diary, I am indebted to the Longman Group Limited, holder of the Moore copyrights.

For assistance of various kinds I am grateful to the following: John Buxton; Vera Cacciatore; John Clubbe; Wilfred S. Dowden; Lucy Edwards; Paul Fussell; Prof. Ian Greenlees, Director of the British Institute, Florence; Piero Innocenti, Dept. of MSS., Biblioteca Nazionale Centrale, Florence; John S. Mayfield; Rae Ann Nager; John O'Connor; Prof. E. S. Pearson, University College London; Mrs. Percival, University College London; Cecil Roberts; William St. Clair.

* * * * * *

EDITORIAL PRINCIPLES. With minor exceptions, herein noted, I have tried to reproduce Byron's letters as they were written. The letters are arranged consecutively in chronological order. The name of the addressee is given at the top left in brackets. The source of the text is indicated in the list of letters in the Appendix. If it is a printed text, it is taken from the first printed form of the letter known or presumed to be copied from the original manuscript, or from a more reliable editor, such as Prothero, when he also had access to the manuscript. In this case, as with handwritten or typed copies, or quotations in sale catalogues, the text of this source is given precisely.

When the text is taken from the autograph letter or a photo copy or facsimile of it, the present whereabouts or ownership is given whether it is in a library or a private collection. When the manuscript is the source, no attempt is made to indicate previous publication, if any. Here I have been faithful to the manuscript with the following exceptions:

1. The place and date of writing is invariably placed at the top right in one line if possible to save space, and to follow Byron's general practice. Fortunately Byron dated most of his letters in this way, but occasionally he put the date at the end. Byron's usual custom of putting no punctuation after the year is followed throughout.

2

2. Superior letters such as S^r or 30th have been lowered to Sr. and 30th. The & has been retained, but &^{c} has been printed &c.

3. Byron's spelling has been followed (and generally his spelling is good, though not always consistent), and *sic* has been avoided except in a few instances when an inadvertent misspelling might change the meaning or be ambiguous, as for instance when he spells *there* t-h-e-i-r.

4. Although, like many of his contemporaries. Byron was inconsistent and eccentric in his capitalization, I have felt it was better to let him have his way, to preserve the flavour of his personality and his times. With him the capital letter sometimes indicates the importance he gives to a word in a particular context; but in the very next line it might not be capitalized. If clarity has seemed to demand a modification, I have used square brackets to indicate any departure from the manuscript.

5. Obvious slips of the pen crossed out by the writer have been silently omitted. But crossed out words of any significance to the meaning or emphasis are enclosed in angled brackets ⟨ ⟩.

6. Letters undated, or dated with the day of the week only, have been dated, when possible, in square brackets. If the date is conjectural, it is given with a question mark in brackets. The same practice is followed for letters from printed sources. The post mark date is given, to indicate an approximate date, only when the letter itself is undated.

7. The salutation is put on the same line as the text, separated from it by a dash. The complimentary closing, often on several lines in the manuscript, is given in one line if possible. The P.S., wherever it may be written in the manuscript, follows the signature.

8. Byron's punctuation follows no rules of his own or others' making. He uses dashes and commas freely, but for no apparent reason, other than possibly for natural pause between phrases, or sometimes for emphasis. He is guilty of the "comma splice", and one can seldom be sure where he intended to end a sentence, or whether he recognized the sentence as a unit of expression. He does at certain intervals place a period and a dash, beginning again with a capital letter. These larger divisions sometimes, though not always, represented what in other writers, particularly in writers of today, correspond to paragraphs. He sometimes uses semicolons, but often where we would use commas. Byron himself recognized his lack of knowledge of the logic or the rules of punctuation. He wrote to his publisher John Murray on August 26, 1813: "Do you know anybody who can *stop*—I mean point—commas and so forth, for I am I fear a

3

sad hand at your punctuation." It is not without reason then that most editors, including R. E. Prothero, have imposed sentences and paragraphs on him in line with their interpretation of his intended meaning. It is my feeling, however, that this detracts from the impression of Byronic spontaneity and the onrush of ideas in his letters, without a compensating gain in clarity. In fact, it may often arbitrarily impose a meaning or an emphasis not intended by the writer. I feel that there is less danger of distortion if the reader may see exactly how he punctuated and then determine whether a phrase between commas or dashes belongs to one sentence or another. Byron's punctuation seldom if ever makes the reading difficult or the meaning unclear. In rare instances I have inserted a period, a comma, or a semicolon, but have enclosed it in square brackets to indicate it was mine and not his.

9. Words missing but obvious from the context, such as those lacunae caused by holes in the manuscript, are supplied within square brackets. If they are wholly conjectural, they are followed by a question mark. The same is true of doubtful readings in the manuscript.

Undated letters have been placed within the chronological sequence when from internal or external evidence there are reasonable grounds for a conjectural date. This has seemed more useful than putting them together at the end of the volumes. Where a more precise date cannot be established from the context, these letters are placed at the beginning of the month or year in which they seem most likely to have been written.

ANNOTATION. I have tried to make the footnotes as brief and informative as possible, eschewing, sometimes with reluctance, the leisurely expansiveness of R. E. Prothero, who in his admirable edition of the *Letters and Journals* often gave pages of supplementary biographical information and whole letters *to* Byron, which was possible at a time when book publishing was less expensive, and when the extant and available Byron letters numbered scarcely more than a third of those in the present edition. Needless to say, I have found Prothero's notes of inestimable assistance in the identification of persons and quotations in the letters which he edited, though where possible I have double checked them. And I must say that while I have found some errors, they are rare. With this general acknowledgment I have left the reader to assume that where a source of information in the notes is not given, it comes from Prothero's edition, where additional details may be found.

The footnotes are numbered for each letter. Where the numbers are repeated on a page, the sequence of the letters will make the reference clear.

In an appendix in each volume I have given brief biographical sketches of Byron's principal correspondents first appearing in that volume. These are necessarily very short, and the stress is always on Byron's relations with the subject of the sketch. Identification of less frequent correspondents and other persons mentioned in the letters are given in footnotes as they appear, and the location of these, as well as the biographical sketches in the appendix, will be indicated by italic numbers in the index. Similarly italic indications will refer the reader to the principal biographical notes on persons mentioned in the text of the letters.

With respect to the annotation of literary allusions and quotations in the letters, I have tried to identify all quotations in the text, but have not always been successful in locating Byron's sources in obscure dramas whose phrases, serious or ridiculous, haunted his memory. When I have failed to identify either a quotation or a name, I have frankly said so, instead of letting the reader suppose that I merely passed it by as unimportant or overlooked it. No doubt readers with special knowledge in various fields may be able to enlighten me. If so, I shall try to make amends with notes in later volumes.

I have sometimes omitted the identification of familiar quotations. But since this work will be read on both sides of the Atlantic, I have explained some things that would be perfectly clear to a British reader but not to an American. I trust that English readers will make allowance for this. As Johnson said in the Preface to his edition of Shakespeare: "It is impossible for an expositor not to write too little for some, and too much for others . . . how long soever he may deliberate, [he] will at last explain many lines which the learned will think impossible to be mistaken, and omit many for which the ignorant will want his help. These are censures merely relative, and must be quietly endured."

I have occasionally given cross references, but in the main have left it to the reader to consult the index for names which have been identified in earlier notes.

SPECIAL NOTE. The letters to Thomas Moore, first published by him in his *Letters and Journals of Lord Byron* (1830), were printed with many omissions and the manuscripts have since disappeared. Moore generally indicated omissions by asterisks, here reproduced as in his text.

BYRON CHRONOLOGY

1816 Jan. 15—Lady Byron left London with her daughter Ada to visit her parents at Kirkby Mallory in Leicestershire.

Feb. 2—Byron received Sir Ralph Noel's letter proposing that he agree to an amicable separation from his wife.

Feb. 7—*The Siege of Corinth* and *Parisina* published together.

March 18—Wrote the first draft of "Fare thee well!".

March–April—Claire Clairmont first introduced herself to Byron.

April 5–6—Byron's books sold at auction.

April 14—Said farewell to Augusta who left for Six Mile Bottom.

April 21—Signed deed of separation.

April 23—Left Piccadilly Terrace for Dover.

April 25—Sailed for Ostend accompanied by Fletcher, Rushton, Berger (a Swiss guide) and Dr. Polidori.

April 27—At Bruges.

April 28—At Ghent.

April 30—At Antwerp.

May 1–6—At Brussels—began third canto of *Childe Harold*.

May 4—Visited field of Waterloo.

May 6—Left Brussels for Louvain.

May 8—At Cologne.

May 9—Lady Caroline Lamb's novel *Glenarvon* published.

May 10–16—Journey up the Rhine—Bonn, Coblenz, Castle of Drachenfels, Mannheim.

May 18—Shelley, Mary Godwin and Claire Clairmont arrived at Sécheron (Geneva).

May 16–18—At Karlsruhe—Dr. Polidori ill.

May 20—As Basle.

May 25—Arrived at De Jean's Hôtel d'Angleterre, Sécheron, near Geneva.

May 27—Byron and Shelley first met at Sécheron.

June 10—Moved into the Villa Diodati—the Shelleys a few hundred yards away at Montalègre.

June—Resumed intimate relations with Claire Clairmont.

June 14–18—Told ghost stories at Diodati with Shelleys—origin of Mary Shelley's *Frankenstein*.

June 22—Started on tour of Lake of Geneva with Shelley—Meillerie, Clarens, Vevey, following Rousseau's geography in *La Nouvelle Héloïse*. Visited Chateau de Chillon.

June 27–28—At Ouchy—wrote *The Prisoner of Chillon*—visited Gibbon's house—completed third canto of *Childe Harold*.

July 1—Returned to Diodati.

July 10—Claire finished fair copy of third canto.

July–August—Visited Mme de Staël frequently at Coppet—wrote "The Dream", "Prometheus", "Darkness".

August—Refused to see Claire alone—she was pregnant.

August 14—M. G. Lewis arrived at Diodati.

August 16—Accompanied Lewis to Voltaire's chateau at Ferney.

August 26—J. C. Hobhouse and Scrope Davies arrived.

August 28—Bade farewell to Shelley, Mary and Claire, who were returning to England.

August 29—Left with Hobhouse and Davies for tour to Chamouni and Mont Blanc.

Sept. 1—Back at Diodati.

Sept. 5—Scrope Davies left for England with Robert Rushton.

Sept. 15?—Dismissed Dr. Polidori.

Sept. 17–29—Tour of Bernese Oberland with Hobhouse.

　　　　—Wrote Alpine Journal for Augusta.

Sept.–Oct.—Wrote first two acts of *Manfred*.

Oct. 5—Left with Hobhouse for Italy by Simplon Napoleon road.

Oct. 12.—Arrived in Milan.

Oct. 13—Visited the Ambrosian Library.

Oct.—Met De Breme, Monti, Silvio Pellico and Mr. de Beyle [Stendhal] in Milan.

Nov. 3—Set off with Hobhouse for Venice, via Desenzano, Verona, Vicenza and Padua.

Nov. 10—Arrived in Venice.

Nov. 14—Took lodgings with the Segatis in the Frezzeria.

Nov. 18—Third canto of *Childe Harold* published.

Nov.—In love with Marianna Segati.

　　　　—Studying Armenian at monastery on Island of San Lazzaro.

Dec. 5—*The Prisoner of Chillon and Other Poems* published.

—Hobhouse left with his brother and sister for tour of Italy.

Dec.—Met the Countess Albrizzi and frequented her *conversazioni*.

1817 Jan. 12—Claire Clairmont, in England, gave birth to Byron's illegitimate daughter Allegra.

Jan.-Feb.—Took part in the Venetian Carnival festivities—finished *Manfred*.

March—Ill with fever.

April 17—Left Venice for Rome, via Ferrara, Bologna and Florence.

April 29—Arrived in Rome—at 66 Piazza di Spagna.

—Hobhouse his cicerone.

May 5—Finished rewriting third act of *Manfred*, and *Lament of Tasso*, written during journey.

May—Sat for bust by Thorwaldsen.

May 19—Witnessed public execution by guillotine of three robbers.

May 20—Left·Rome for Venice.

May 28—Arrived in Venice.

June 4—Took six months' lease of the Villa Foscarini at La Mira on the Brenta river.

June 14—Established for summer at La Mira.

June 16—*Manfred* published.

June 26—Began writing fourth canto of *Childe Harold*.

July 1—"Monk" Lewis in Venice—Byron spent a week with him there.

July 29—First draft of fourth canto of *Childe Harold* finished.

July 31—Hobhouse returned from Rome—he and Lewis at La Mira—Marianna Segati with Byron in Villa Foscarini.

August—Met Margarita Cogni (the "Fornarina"), wife of a baker.

August 29—Heard story of a Venetian merchant who returned to find his wife living with a cavalier servente—basis of *Beppo*.

Sept.—Douglas Kinnaird, Lord Kinnaird, W. S. Rose in Venice—introduced Byron to Frere's *Whistlecraft*.

Sept.—Made acquaintance of R. B. Hoppner, British Consul in Venice.

Oct. 23—Announced to Murray the completion of *Beppo*.

9

Nov. 1—Journeyed to Este to visit house he had leased from Hoppner.

Nov. 13—Returned from La Mira to Venice.

Dec. 10—Received news of sale of Newstead estate to Major Thomas Wildman for £94,500.

BYRON'S LETTERS AND JOURNALS

[TO JAMES HOGG] [*1816*]

... Wordsworth—stupendous genius! damned fool! These poets run about their ponds though they cannot fish. I am told there is not one who can angle—damned fools! ....[1]

[TO JOHN MURRAY] *January 2d. 1816*

Dear Sir—Your offer is *liberal* in the extreme—(you see I use the *word to* & *of* you—though I would not consent to your using it of yourself to Mr. H[unt?]) & much more than the two poems can possibly be worth[1]—but I cannot accept it—nor will not.—You are most welcome to them as additions to the collected volumes without any demand or expectation on my part whatever—but I cannot consent to their separate publication.—I do not like to risk my fame (whether merited or not) which I have been favoured with—upon compositions which I do not feel to be at all equal to my own notions of what they should be—(& as I flatter myself some *have been* here & there)—though they may do very well as things without pretension to add to the publication with the lighter pieces.—I am very glad that the handwriting was a favourable omen of the morale of the piece—but you must not trust to that—for my copyist would write out anything I desired in all the ignorance of innocence[2]—I hope however in this instance with no great peril to either.——

yrs. very truly
BYRON

P.S.—I have enclosed your draft *torn* for fear of accidents by the way:—I wish you would not throw temptation in mine—it is not from a disdain of the universal idol—nor from a present superfluity of his treasures—I can assure you—that I refuse to worship him—but what is right is right—& must not yield to circumstances.—

[1] This fragment from one of Byron's letters was quoted to Henry Crabb Robinson by a friend (Cargill) and recorded in his diary of Dec. 1, 1816.

[1] Murray had sent Byron a draft for 1,000 guineas for the copyrights of *The Siege of Corinth* and *Parisina.* Still holding the aristocratic view that a gentleman should not take money for his poetry, and a little uncertain of the reception of the poems, Byron returned the money and gave his publisher the right to place them unobtrusively in the collected works. Murray, however, published them together in a separate volume in 1816, and they were successful.

[2] The copyist was Lady Byron. Byron suggests that his wife was too innocent to detect the danger in the incest theme in *Parisina.*

I hope Mrs. M[oore] is quite re-established.[1] The little girl was born on the 10th of December last: her name is Augusta *Ada*[2] (the second a very antique family name,—I believe not used since the reign of King John). She was, and is, very flourishing and fat, and reckoned very large for her days—squalls and sucks incessantly. Are you answered? Her mother is doing very well, and up again.

I have now been married a year on the second of this month—heigh-ho! I have seen nobody lately much worth noting, except S * * [Sebastiani][3] and another general of the Gauls, once or twice at dinners out of doors. S * * [Sebastiani] is a fine, foreign, villainous-looking, intelligent, and very agreeable man; his compatriot[4] is more of the *petit-maître*, and younger, but I should think not at all of the same intellectual calibre with the Corsican—which S * * [Sebastiani], you know, is, and a cousin of Napoleon's.

Are you never to be expected in town again? To be sure, there is no one here of the 1500 fillers of hot rooms, called the fashionable world. My approaching papa-ship detained us for advice, &c. &c.—though I would as soon be here as any where else on this side of the straits of Gibraltar.

I would gladly—or, rather, sorrowfully—comply with your request of a dirge for the poor girl you mention.[5] But how can I write on one I have never seen or known? Besides, you will do it much better yourself. I could not write upon any thing, without some personal experience and foundation; far less on a theme so peculiar. Now, you have both in this case; and, if you had neither, you have more imagination, and would never fail.

This is but a dull scrawl, and I am but a dull fellow. Just at present, I am absorbed in 500 contradictory contemplations, though with but

[1] Moore's daughter had died in March, 1815. See March 27, 1815, to Moore, note 1.

[2] Byron's daughter.

[3] Count Sebastiani (1772?–1851) a suave-mannered courtier, had served under Napoleon, and later held various posts, diplomatic and ministerial, under the Bourbons.

[4] Sebastiani's companion was another man of good breeding and polished manners, Auguste Charles Joseph, Comte de Flahault (1785–1870), who had been aide-de-camp to Napoleon, and subsequently (after Byron's time) ambassador to Vienna, Berlin and London. On June 20, 1817, he married Margaret Mercer Elphinstone, whom Byron admired and later said he wished he had married.

[5] Moore explains this: "I had mentioned to him, as a subject worthy of his best powers of pathos, a melancholy event which had occurred in my neighborhood, and to which I have myself made allusion in one of the Sacred Melodies, 'Weep not for her'" (Moore, I, 640.)

one object in view—which will probably end in nothing, as most things we wish do. But never mind—as somebody says, "for the blue sky bends over all".[6] I only could be glad, if it bent over me where it is a little bluer; like the "skyish top of blue Olympus", which, by the way, looked very white when I last saw it. Ever, &c.

[TO LADY BYRON]   *January 6th 1816*

When you are disposed to leave London—it would be convenient that a day should be fixed—& (if possible) not a very remote one for that purpose.[1]—Of my opinion upon that subject—you are sufficiently in possession—& of the circumstances which have led to it—as also— to my plans—or rather—intentions—for the future.———When in the country, I will write to you more fully—as Lady Noel has asked you to Kirkby—there you can be for the present—unless you prefer Seaham. ———— As the dismissal of the present establishment is of import- ance to me—the sooner you can fix on the day the better—though of course your convenience & inclination shall be first consulted.—— The child will of course accompany you—there is a more easy and safer carriage than the chariot—(unless you prefer it) which I mentioned before—on that you can do as you please.—

[TO LEIGH HUNT]   *Terrace Piccadilly J[anua]ry 12th. 1816*

Dear Hunt—A day or two ago I sent you a note with a draft en- closed on Hoares my bankers for Mrs. Margarot.[1]—It has since occurred to me that this being sent by the twopenny post—& ad- dressed to you at the office in M[aiden] Lane C[ovent] G[arde]n instead of "the Vale" it may have been refused by your people as not *post paid*—mistaking it for a communication for ye. journal—as is the custom I believe with all the N[ews] P[aper] offices—though I

---

[6] *Christabel*, Part I, line 331.

[1] Byron had urged the necessity of breaking up the expensive household at 13 Piccadilly Terrace because of his debts. There had been some altercation con- cerning his plans (one of which was to go abroad) and he probably wrote this note to avoid a scene. Lady Byron was greatly offended by its tone, but Byron felt that he made it up to her before she left. See Marchand, *Byron: A Biography*, II, 557.

[1] In December, 1815, Hunt's *Examiner* appealed for subscriptions for Mrs. Elizabeth Margarot, widow of Maurice Margarot, one of the Corresponding Society members sentenced in 1793 to transportation for fourteen years to Botany Bay. He returned to England in 1809, but died in 1815. A total of £189. 13 was raised, of which Byron's contribution was £21.

directed to L[eigh] H[unt] Esqre—& not to the Editor.—Will you favour me with a line in answer to this by the post—merely to say if you received the former letter—

> yrs. ever very truly
> [Signature cut out]

[TO SAMUEL ROGERS]   *J[anua]ry 20th. 1816*

Dear Rogers—I wrote to you hastily this morning by Murray to say that I was glad to do as Mac[k]intosh & you suggested about Mr. Godwin.[1]—It occurs to me now that as I have never seen Mr. G[odwin] but once—& consequently have no claim to his acquaintance that you or Sir J[ame]s had better arrange it with him in such a manner as may be least offensive to his feelings[2]—& so as not to have the appearance of officiousness nor obtrusion on my part:—I hope you will be able to do this—as I should be very sorry to do anything by him—that may be deemed indelicate.—The sum Murray offered and offers was & is one thousand & fifty pounds:—this I refused before because I thought it more than the two things were worth to M[urray] & from other objections which are of no consequence. I have however closed with M[urray] in consequence of Sir J's & your suggestion— and propose the sum of six hundred pounds to be transferred to Mr. Godwin in such manner as may seem best to you [words cut out] friend.——The remainder—I think of for other purposes.[3]——As M[urray] offered the money down for the copyrights—it may be done directly—and I am ready to sign & seal immediately:—& perhaps it had better not be delayed.—I shall feel very glad if it can be of any use to Godwin—only don't let him be plagued—nor think himself obliged & all that—which makes people hate one another &c.

> yrs. ever truly
> [signature cut out]

[1] Sir James Mackintosh had suggested to Rogers that, since he had heard that Byron had refused to accept a large sum from Murray for his poems, he might give it to Godwin, who was in dire need. See Jan. 2, 1816, to Murray, note 1.

[2] Byron need not have been concerned about Godwin's feelings with regard to accepting money. He sponged on Shelley and others for many years, without feeling embarrassed or obliged.

[3] Byron intended to divide the remainder of the thousand guineas between Coleridge and Maturin.

[TO JOHN MURRAY]   *Jry. 21st. 1816*

Dear Sir—I have had the enclosed note from Mr. R[ogers]—who
wishes me to pause—which—I will for a day or two—& see you
tomorrow at about three.—If you have not written to Coleridge &
Maturin:—it may be better *not*—till I see you—pray say whether you
have or not?—& return me R[ogers]'s note—

                                                        ever yrs. &c.
                                                        B

[TO JOHN MURRAY]   *Jry. 22nd. 1816*

Dr. Sir—When the sum offered by you—& even *pressed* by you:—
was declined—it was with reference to a *separate* publication—as you
know—& I know.—That it was large I admitted & admit—& *that*
made part of my consideration in refusing it till I knew better what you
were likely to make of it.—With regard to what has passed or is to
pass about Mr. Godwin—the case is in no respect different from the
transfer of former copyrights to Mr. Dallas:—had I taken you at your
word—that is—taken your money—I might have used it as I pleased
—& it could be in no respect different to you—whether I paid it to a
w⟨hore⟩ or a hospital—or assisted a man of talent in distress.[1]——
The truth of the matter seems this—you offered more than the poems
are worth—I *said* so—& I *think* so:—but you know—or at least ought
to know your own business best:—& when you recollect what passed
between you & me upon pecuniary subjects—before this occurred:—
you will acquit me of any wish to take advantage of your imprudence.
——The things in question shall not be published at all—& there's an
end of the matter.—

                                                        yrs. &c.
                                                        B

P.S.—You will oblige me by returning the Manuscripts—by the
bearer and immediately.——

[TO SAMUEL ROGERS]   *J[anua]ry 23d. 1816*

Dear Rogers—I am sorry that I cannot dine with you today:—I
have not lately been very well—and am under sentence of pill &
potion for an attack of liver &c.——You may set your heart at rest

---

[1] See Jan. 2, 1816, to Murray and Jan. 20, 1816, to Rogers.

17

on poor G[odwin]'s business:[1]—Murray when it came to the point demurred—& though not exactly refusing—gave such sort of answers as determine me to take the M.S. away & not publish at all.——With regard to his offer I can only say—that some weeks ago—he even pressed it upon me—so far as (after I had returned his draft) to lay the money on the table if I would consent to a *separate* publication:—this I refused—because the pieces were in my opinion better adapted for and at any rate safer in the collection he had got together—& for *this purpose* I told him he was welcome to them for nothing.—I never said nor meaned to say that if he was permitted to publish *separately*—that the purchase of the copyrights would not be accepted.—When you sent me Mac[k]intosh's letter—I felt inclined to comply with it's suggestion—& sent to Murray—at the same time telling him my reason:—in this at the time he acquiesced—but since on my sending to him that it was thought a smaller sum would do for Mr. G[odwin] &c.—he returns me an answer—which—in short—it is no matter.——I am sorry for the trouble you have had on the occasion—& still more that I have failed in being of any use to G[odwi]n—Pray explain to Sir J[ame]s Mac[k]intosh for me & believe me

ever yrs. most truly
BYRON

[TO JOHN MURRAY]   *Jan[uar]y 25, 1816*

Mr. F.—[1]& his Forum may be damned:—you are not going to be such a goose—as to let him have books for such a purpose:—the fellow sent me a letter of the same kind—to which I have not answered—nor shall:—do you the same.—I enclose you the vagabond's epistle to me.——Take no notice of him.—

[TO LEIGH HUNT]   *January 29th. 1816*

Dear Hunt—I return your extract with thanks for the perusal—& hope you are by this time on the verge of publication. My pencil marks

---

[1] See Jan. 2, 1816, to Murray, Jan. 20, 1816, to Rogers, and Jan. 22, 1816, to Murray.
[1] Unidentified.

on the margin of your former M.S.S.[1] I never thought worth the trouble of decyphering—but I had no such meaning as you imagine for their being witheld from Murray—from whom I differ entirely as to the *terms* of your agreement—nor do I think you asked a piastre too much for the poem.———However I doubt not he will deal fairly by you on the whole:—he is really a very good fellow—& his faults are merely the leaven of his "trade"—"the trade"—the Slave trade of many an unlucky writer.———The said Murray & I are just at present in no good humour with each other [2]—but he is not the worse for that:—I feel sure that he will give your work a fair or a fairer chance in every way than your late publishers—& what he can't do for it—it will do for itself.—Continual laziness—& occasional indisposition have been the causes of my negligence—(for I deny neglect) in not writing to you immediately—these are excuses—I wish they may be more satisfactory to you than they are to me.—I opened my eyes yesterday morning on your compliment of Sunday[3]—if you knew what a hopeless & lethargic den of dullness & drawling our hospital is[4]—during a debate—& what a mass of corruption in it's patients—you would wonder—not that—I very seldom speak—but that I ever attempted it—feeling—as I trust I do—independently.—However—when a proper spirit is manifested "without doors" I will endeavour not to be idle within—do you think such a time is coming? methinks there are gleams of it—my forefathers were of the other side of the question in Charles's days—& the fruit of it was a title & the loss of an enormous property.[5]———If the old struggle comes on—I shall lose the one & shall never regain the other—but—no matter—there are things even in this world—better than either.—

very truly ever yrs.

B

---

[1] Byron had made some comments on the manuscript of Hunt's *The Story of Rimini*.
[2] See Jan. 22, 1816, to Murray and Jan. 23, 1816, to Rogers.
[3] In the *Examiner* for Sunday, Jan. 28, 1816, in an article on "Men of Talent in Parliament", Hunt had paid Byron a compliment but had wondered why he did not speak oftener.
[4] The House of Lords.
[5] Byron's ancestor, Sir John Byron, was made a baron by Charles I for his assistance to the King, but the ancestral home of the Byrons, Newstead Abbey, was sequestered by the Parliament after the overthrow of Charles; it was restored to the Byrons with the restoration of Charles II.

[TO SIR RALPH NOEL] *February 2d. 1816*

Sir—I have received your letter.[1]—To the vague & general charge contained in it I must naturally be at a loss how to answer—I shall therefore confine myself to the tangible fact which you are pleased to alledge as one of the motives for your present proposition.—Lady Byron received no "dismissal" from my house in the sense you have attached to the word—she left London by medical advice—she parted from me in apparent—and on my part—real harmony—though at that particular time rather against my inclination for I begged her to remain with the intention of myself accompanying her when some business necessary to be arranged permitted my departure.———It is true—that previous to this period—I had suggested to her the expediency of a temporary residence with her parents:—my reason for this was very simple & shortly stated—viz—the embarrassment of my circumstances & my inability to maintain our present establishment.—The truth of what is thus stated may be easily ascertained by reference to Lady B[yron]—who is Truth itself—if she denies it—I abide by that denial.———My intention of going abroad originated in the same painful motive—& was postponed from a regard to her supposed feelings on that subject.———During the last year I have had to contend with distress without—& disease within:—upon the former I have little to say—except that I have endeavoured to remove it by every sacrifice in my power—& the latter I should not mention if I had not recent & professional authority for saying—that the disorder which I have to combat—without much impairing my apparent health—is such as to induce a morbid irritability of temper—which—without recurring to external causes—may have rendered me little less disagreeable to others than I am to myself.———I am however ignorant of any particular ill treatment which your daughter has encountered:—she may have seen me gloomy—& at times violent—but she knows the causes too well to attribute such inequalities of disposition to herself—or even to me—if all things be fairly considered.———And now Sir—not for your satisfaction—for I owe you none—but for my own—& in justice to Lady Byron—it is my duty to say that there is no part of her conduct—character—temper—talents—or disposition—which could in my

1 Sir Ralph had written to Byron: ". . . with your opinions it cannot tend to your happiness to continue to live with Lady Byron, and I am yet more forcibly convinced that after her dismissal from your house, and the treatment she experienced whilst in it, those on whose protection she has the strongest natural claims could not feel themselves justified in permitting her return thither." And he proposed that arrangements be made through lawyers for a separation.

20

opinion have been changed for the better—neither in word nor deed—nor (as far as thought can be dived into) thought—can I bring to recollection a fault on her part—& hardly even a failing—She has ever appeared to me as one of the most amiable of beings—& nearer to perfection than I had conceived could belong to Humanity in it's present existence.——Having said thus much—though more in words—less in substance—than I wished to express——I must come to the point—on which subject I must for a few days decline giving a decisive answer. —I will not however detain you longer than I can help—and as it is of some importance to your family as well as mine—and a step which cannot be recalled when taken—you will not attribute my pause to any wish to inflict pain or vexation on you & yours:—although there are parts of your letter—which—I must be permitted to say—arrogate a right which you do not now possess——for the present at least—your daughter is my wife:—she is the mother of my child—& until I have her express sanction of your proceedings—I shall take leave to doubt the propriety of your interference.—This will be soon ascertained—& when it is—I will submit to you my determination—which will depend very materially on hers.——I have the honour to be

yr. most obedt. & very humble Sert.
BYRON

[TO LADY BYRON]   *February 3d. 1816*

I have received a letter from your father proposing a separation between us—to which I cannot give an answer without being more acquainted with your own thoughts & wishes—& from *yourself*:—to vague & general charges & exaggerated statements from others I can give no reply:——it is to *you* that I look—& with *you*—that I can communicate on this subject,——when I permit the interference of relatives—it will be as a courtesy to them—& not the admission of a right.——I feel naturally at a loss how to address you—ignorant as I am—how far the letter I have received—has received your sanction—& in the circumstances into which this precipitation has forced me—whatever I might say would be liable to misconstruction—I am really ignorant to what part of Sir Ralph's letter alludes—will you explain? ——To conclude—I shall eventually abide by your decision—but I request you most earnestly to weigh well the probable consequences—& to pause before you pronounce.——Whatever may occur—it is but justice to you to say—that you are exempt from all fault whatever—&

that neither now nor at any time have I the slightest imputation of any description to charge upon you.————I cannot sign myself other than

yours ever most affectionately

B<small>N</small>

[TO JOHN MURRAY] *F[ebruar]y 3d. 1816*

Dear Sir—I sent for "Marmion" (which I return) because it occurred to me that there might be a resemblance between part of "Parisina"—& a similar scene in Canto 2d. of "Marmion"—I fear there is—though I never thought of it before—& could hardly wish to imitate that which is inimitable.[1]—I wish you would ask Mr. Gifford whether I ought to say anything upon it:—I had completed the story—on the passage from Gibbon—which in fact leads to a like scene naturally—without a thought of the kind—but it comes upon me not very comfortably:——There are a few words & phrases I want to alter in the M.S. & should like to do it—before you print[2]—I will return it in an hour.

yrs. ever

B

[TO LADY BYRON] *February 5th. 1816*

Dearest Bell—No answer from you yet—perhaps it is as well—but do recollect—that all is at stake—the present—the future—& even the colouring of the past:—The whole of my errors—or what harsher name you choose to give them—you know—but I loved you—& will not part from you without your *own* most express & *expressed* refusal to return to or receive me.——Only say the word—that you are still mine in your heart—and "Kate!—I will buckler thee against a million"[1]—

ever yours dearest most

B

---

[1] Byron, who was very sensitive to any suggestion of plagiarism, even unintentional, was disturbed by a vague resemblance of a passage in *Parisina* (stanza XIV) and some lines in Scott's *Marmion* (Canto II, stanza XXI). He did not, however, call it to the attention of readers when the poem was published.

[2] Byron had repented of his pique with Murray and allowed him to publish *Parisina* with *The Siege of Corinth* together in a separate volume, and he did eventually accept payment for the volumes.

[1] *The Taming of the Shrew*, Act. III, scene 2.

[On cover in Byron's hand] Mrs. Fletcher[2] is requested to deliver the enclosed with her *own hands* to Lady Byron.

[TO————]   *Piccadilly Terrace Feb. 7th. 1816*

[In Augusta Leigh's hand—signed by Byron]

Sir—I have the honour to inform you that I have paid the half year's rent to Mr. James [Denen?] whose receipt I have in behalf of the Duchess of Devonshire—and to him I refer you for any further information on the subject as he was the person with whom the taking of the house was negotiated & who made application for the payment of the rent. I presume I was correct in paying it to him. I have the honour to be

Yr obedt humble Sert.

BYRON

[TO SIR RALPH NOEL]   *February 7th. 1816*

Sir—I have read Lady Byron's letter—enclosed by you to Mrs. Leigh—with much surprize & more sorrow.—Lady B[yron] left London without a single hint of such feelings or intentions—neither did they transpire in her letters on the road nor subsequent to her arrival at Kirkby.———In these letters Lady Byron expresses herself to me with that playful confidence & affectionate liveliness which is perhaps a greater proof of attachment than more serious professions; she speaks to her husband of his child—like a wife and a mother:—I am therefore reduced to the melancholy alternative of either believing her capable of a duplicity—very foreign to my opinion of her character—or that she has lately sunk under influence—the admission of which—however respected & respectable heretofore—is not recognized in her vows at the Altar.———My house—while I have one—is open to her—& my heart always—even though I should have no other shelter to offer her.———I cannot suspect Lady B[yron] of making the grounds stated—the pretext for dissolving our connection—with a view to escape from my shattered fortunes—although the time chosen for this proposition—& the manner in which it was made—without enquiry—without appeal—without even a doubt—or an attempt at conciliation might almost excuse such a supposition.—If I address you in strong

2 Ann Rood, Annabella's maid, had married Byron's valet Fletcher just before she left London.

language—Sir—I still wish to temper it with that respect which is required by the very duties you would persuade me to abandon;—& request your candid interpretation of such expressions—as circumstances have compelled me to use.—I may not debase myself to implore as a suppliant the restoration of a reluctant wife—but I will not compromise my rights as a husband—& a father.—I invite Lady Byron's return—I am ready to go to her should she desire or require it—and I deprecate all attempts which have been or may be made to part us.——
I have the honour to be—Sir—with great respect

yr. most obedt. very humble Sert.
BYRON

[TO JOHN CAM HOBHOUSE]   *F[ebruar]y 8th. 1816*

Dear H—I shall be very glad to see you—but it is all vain—& all over.—She has written two letters—one to Mrs. L[eigh] & since—a second to me—quite decisive of her determination on the subject.——However—let me see you—I mean to go abroad the moment packages will permit.——"There is a world beyond Rome"[1]—

ever yrs.
B

[TO LADY BYRON]   *February 8th. 1816*

All I can say seems useless—and all I could say—might be no less unavailing—yet I still cling to the wreck of my hopes—before they sink forever.——Were you then *never* happy with me?—did you never at any time or times express yourself so?—have no marks of affection—of the warmest & most reciprocal attachment passed between us?—or did in fact hardly a day go down without some such on one side and generally on both?—do not mistake me—[two lines crossed out] I have not denied my state of mind—but you know it's causes—& were those deviations from calmness never followed by acknowledgement & repentance?—was not the last which occurred more particularly so?—& had I not—had we not—the days before & on the day when we parted —every reason to believe that we loved each other—that we were to meet again—were not your letters kind?—had I not acknowledged to you all my faults & follies—& assured you that some had not—&

---

[1] Unidentified. Perhaps an adaptation of *Coriolanus*, Act III, scene 3, line 133: "There is a world elsewhere."

would not be repeated?—I do not require these questions to be answered to me—but to your own heart.——The day before I received your father's letter—I had fixed a day for rejoining you—if I did not write lately—Augusta did—and as you had been my proxy in correspondence with her—so did I imagine—she might be the same for me to you.—Upon your letter to me—this day—I surely may remark—that it's expressions imply a treatment which I am incapable of inflicting—& you of imputing to me—if aware of their latitude—& the extent of the inferences to be drawn from them.—This is not just——but I have no reproaches—nor the wish to find cause for them.——Will you see me?—when & where you please—in whose presence you please:—the interview shall pledge you to nothing—& I will say & do nothing to agitate either—it is torture to correspond thus—& there are things to be settled & said which cannot be written.——You say "it is my disposition to deem what I *have worthless*"—did I deem *you* so?—did I ever so express myself to you—or of you—to others?——You are much changed within these twenty days or you would never have thus poisoned your own better feelings—and trampled upon mine.——

ever yrs. most truly & affectionately

B

[TO SAMUEL ROGERS]   *February 8, 1816*

Dear Rogers—Do not mistake me—I really returned your book for the reason assigned & no other—it is too good for so careless a fellow —I have parted with all my own books—and positively won't deprive you of so valuable "a drop of that immortal man."[1] I shall be very glad to see you—if you like to call as you intended:—though I am at present contending with "the slings and arrows of outrageous Fortune"[2] some of which have struck at me from a quarter whence I did not indeed expect them.—But no matter—"there is a world elsewhere" & I will cut my way through this as I can:—if you write to Moore—will you tell him that I will answer his letter the moment I can muster time and spirits?

ever yrs.
BYRON

[1] Unidentified.
[2] *Hamlet*, Act III, scene 1.

25

[TO SIR JAMES BLAND BURGES[1]]   *Fy. 11th. 1816*

My dear Sir James—All attempts at conciliation or explanation
have hitherto been unsuccessful:———but nothing decisive has taken
place on my part.—Your support & evidence as far as consistent with
truth & justice—(& more you know me too well to think I should insult you by expecting) will indeed be important.—Whenever you
wish to see me I am at your service—

> ever yr. obliged & faithful Servt.
> BYRON

[TO JOHN HANSON]   *Fy. 12th. 1816*

Dear Sir—It shall be done.—You & Mr. F[arquhar?][1] can come at
your own hour for the purpose. I have heard nothing further—except
all kinds of vague & exaggerated rumours from different quarters.—
It seems a little unfair,—that the parties should furnish all the world
with their charges—except the person against whom they are directed.
———Are you sure that Sir S[amuel] R[omilly] is retained for me?[2]

> yrs. ever
> B

[TO LADY BYRON]   *Fy. 15th. 1816*

I know not what to say—every step taken appears to bear you further
from me—and to widen "the great Gulph between thee and me"[1] if it
cannot be crossed I will at least perish in it's depth.———Two letters
have been written by me to you—but I have not sent them—& I know
not well why I write this or whether I shall send it or no.———How far
your conduct is reconcileable to your duties & affections as a wife and a
mother—must be a question for your own reflection—the trial has not

---

[1] Lady Noel's brother-in-law and Annabella's uncle. See April 22, 1815, to
Burges, note 1. (Vol. 4, p. 288).

[1] James Farquhar, an Aberdeen lawyer who had represented Mrs. Byron's interests in London at the time her son inherited the title and the Newstead estate.
He was a friend of Hanson.

[2] Sir Samuel Romilly had in fact already been employed by the Noels and Lady
Byron, although he had a general retainer for Byron, a fact which caused Byron to
develop an undying enmity for him.

[1] *Luke*, XVI, 26.

been very long—a year—I grant you—of distress—distemper—and misfortune—but these fall chiefly on me—& bitter as the recollection is to me of what I have felt—it is much more so to have made you a partaker in my desolation.—On the charges to be preferred against me—I have *twice* been refused any information by your father & his advisers:—it is now a fortnight—which has been passed in suspense— in humiliation—in obloquy—exposed to the most black & blighting calumnies of every kind:—without even the power of contradicting conjecture & vulgar assertion as to the accusations—because I am denied the knowledge of all or any particulars, from the only quarter that can afford them—in the mean time I hope your ears are gratified by the general rumours.—I have invited your return—it has been refused—I have entreated to see you—it is refused—I have requested to know with what I am charged—it is refused—is this mercy—or justice?——We shall see.——And now—Bell—dearest Bell—whatever may be the event of this calamitous difference—whether you are restored to—or torn from me—I can only say in the truth of affliction— & without hope—motive—or end in again saying what I have lately but vainly repeated—that I love you:—bad or good—mad or rational —miserable or content—I love you—& shall do to the dregs of my memory & existence.—If I can feel thus for you now—under every possible aggravation & exasperating circumstance that can corrode the heart—& inflame the brain—perhaps you may one day know—or think at least—that I was not all you have persuaded yourself to believe me—but that's nothing—nothing can touch me further.——I have hitherto avoided naming my child—but as this was a feeling you never doubted in me—I must ask of it's welfare—I have heard of it's beauty—& it's playfulness—and I request—not from you—but through any other channel—Augusta's—if you please—some occasional news of it's well being.——

I am yours &c. &c.

B

P.S.—If there are any explanations—I can give—pray require them. —From some parts of your letters I am led to believe that you may have heard exaggerated or imaginary reports with regard to me since our last interview—either now or at our meeting I will not shrink from any question which you or yours may think it requisite to ask me—I will not pretend to deserve—but at least I will never deceive you.—

Dear Sir—I thank you for the account of Mr & Lady F[rances] W[ebster]'s triumph—you see by it—the exceeding advantage of unimpeachable virtue & uniform correctness of conduct &c. &c.[1]— They tell me you called on me a day or two ago—if you have good news to tell—it will not be unwelcome—if any bad—you need not be afraid—I am pretty well seasoned to all extremes.—Have you carried on "the Siege"[2] tolerably?—I suppose you begin to think with Lintot in "the Narrative of Jno. Dennis's Phrenzy"—expressed in Pope's dialogue between the bookseller—physician—Nurse & patient——"I believe the fellow is really mad—& if he is—who the devil will buy the remarks?—I wish he had been————before I meddled with the remarks."[3]——Have you got your picture from Phillips?[4]—

yrs. &c. &c.

B

Dear Sir—[Six lines crossed out] To return to *our* business—your epistles are vastly agreeable.—With regard to the observations on

[1] In the Court of Common Pleas on February 16, 1816, James Wedderburn Webster obtained a judgment of £2000 damages against a Mr. Baldwin for a libel charging Webster's wife Lady Frances and the Duke of Wellington with adultery. Lady Frances, like Lady Caroline Lamb and many other English ladies, followed the victorious generals to Brussels and Paris after the defeat of Napoleon. Byron was inclined to be sceptical of the virtue of Lady Frances after he had "spared" her, following his flirtation of 1813. It was at this time that he wrote his verses to her beginning "When we two parted". When Moore later met Lady Frances Webster, he recorded in his diary of January 5, 1819, that the conversation was chiefly about Byron "whom she talked of, as if nothing had happened—and (if I may believe Scroope Davies) nothing ever did—but B. certainly gave me to think otherwise, and her letters (which I saw) showed, at least, that she was (or fancied herself) much in love with him—His head was full of her, when he wrote the Bride. . . . I should pronounce her cold-blooded & vain to an excess—& I believe her great ambition is to attract people of celebrity—if so, she must have been gratified—as the first Poet [Byron] & first Captain [Wellington] of the age have been among her lovers—the latter liaison was, at all events, not altogether spiritual—[See Sept. 4 and Sept. 18, 1815, to Webster, Vol. 4, pp. 310–311, 312–313] at least the character of the man makes such platonism not very probable—her manner to me very flattering & the eyes played off most skillfully—but this is evidently her habit—the fishing always going on, whether whales or sprats are to be caught—"

[2] *The Siege of Corinth* was published with *Parisina* on Feb. 7, 1816.

[3] See Pope, *Works*, ed. Courthope, Vol. X, p. 457.

[4] Byron presented his publisher with one of the Phillips portraits, the one that now hangs over the mantel in the Byron Room at John Murray's.

carelessness &c.—I think with all humility—that the gentle reader has considered a rather uncommon & designedly irregular versification for haste & negligence—the measure is not that of any of the other poems —which (I believe) were allowed to be tolerably correct according to Byshe[1] & the fingers—or ears—by which bards write & readers reckon—great part of "the Siege" is in (I think) what the learned call Anapests (though I am not sure, being heinously forgetful of my metres & my "Gradus") and many of the lines intentionally longer or shorter than it's rhyming companion—& the rhyme also recurring at greater or lesser intervals of caprice or convenience—I mean not to say that this is right—or good—but merely—that I could have been smoother had it appeared to me of advantage—& that I was not otherwise without being aware of the deviation—though I now feel sorry for it—as I would undoubtedly rather please than not: my wish has been to try at something different from my former efforts—as I endeavoured to make them differ from each other—the versification of "the Corsair" is not that of "Lara" nor the "Giaour" that of "the Bride"—Childe H[arol]d is again varied from these—& I strove to vary the last—somewhat from *all* of the others.—Excuse all this damned nonsense—& egotism—the fact is that I am rather trying to think on the subject of this note—than really thinking on it.—I did not know you had called—you are always admitted & welcome when you choose.

yrs. &c. &c.

B

P.S.—You need not be in any apprehension or grief on my account:[2] —were I to be beaten down by the world & it's inheritors—I should have succumbed to many things—years ago—you must not mistake my *not* bullying for dejection:—nor imagine that because I feel I am to faint—but enough—for the present.—I am sorry for Sotheby's row[3]—what the devil is it about? I thought it all settled—& if I can do anything about him or Ivan still—I am ready & willing.—I do not

[1] Edward Bysshe's *The Art of English Poetry* (1702) was then the standard work on versification, rhyme, etc.

[2] Murray had expressed concern for Byron's state of mind apropos of the separation and the rumours connected with it.

[3] William Sotheby's quarrels with the actors and managers finally caused Drury Lane to reject his tragedy *Ivan*, which Byron had recommended to the Committee in September, 1815.

think it proper for me just now to be much behind the scenes[4]—but I will see the Committee & M[anagers?] upon it—if S[otheby] likes.— If you see Mr. Sotheby—will you tell him that I wrote to Mr. Coleridge on getting Mr. S[otheby]'s note—& have I hope done what Mr. S[otheby] wished on that subject.——

[TO LADY BYRON]   *February 21st. 1816*

The enclosed was received today. My name was signed to your acknowledgement of Mr. Bainbridge's[1] legacy—(or some requisite paper) several days ago.—The last time I saw it was in Mr. Hanson's hands & I understood that it was to be returned to Mr. Wharton. As I do not know Mr. or Mrs. Ellis[2]—perhaps the answer had better be from yourself—I am also without information on the subject more than I have stated.—I hope my little Ada is well—& that you are better

ever yrs. most affectly.

B

[TO LORD HOLLAND]   *February 23d. 1816*

My dear Lord—There is no subject—however unpleasant—which would not become less so—by your taking the trouble to be the organ of communication:—the present one has been so public & violent a topic of discussion[1] (if my information be correct) that there need be no hesitation on the score of delicacy in mentioning it to me or any one else—least of all by you—from whom I have never experienced any thing which could be attributed to other motives than kindness.—If I have never alluded to the subject of your note in my late conversations with you—it was only because I thought you must be sick of it already —from other & various quarters.——I will see you upon it tomorrow or any other morning or rather afternoon—after 3 o clock—which you are pleased to name.——It is perhaps proper I should tell you— that I have already twice declined acceding to the proposition of the other parties—who have refused me *all explanation* or copy of the

---

[4] During the separation proceedings false rumours were circulated concerning Byron and the beautiful actress Mrs. Mardyn, and he didn't want to encourage them by visiting the green room.

[1] Unidentified.

[2] Unidentified.

[1] Dr. Stephen Lushington, Lady Byron's counsellor, appealed to Lord Holland to act as an intermediary in trying to get Byron to accede to a separation.

charge or charges which I am to encounter.—the father writes me two or three bullying letters—for which (though I cannot quarrel with old women) I have a little & but a little resentment against him or his wife: & then wonders that I don't fall down & worship him.—In the mean time every kind of abuse & calumny is permitted if not sanctioned in the circulation by these venerable persons & a confidential housekeeper (a Mrs. Clermont[2] who was once Lady Noel's maid then her—God knows what—& now—it seems though I can't tell how—a most important personage in the family)—and at the same time all specific statements again & again refused to my repeated request—& no answer returned but a positive demand of what Sir Ralph calls an *"amicable separation"* a phrase which I don't quite understand—but which means I suppose something the same as a hostile alliance.— — In short—they are violent—& I am stubborn—& in these amiable tempers matters stand at present.—They think to drive me by menacing with legal measures—let them go into court—they shall be met there.— —After what has been already said—they cannot be more anxious for investigation than myself.— —With regard to the consequences which must be disagreeable in any case—where the exposure of private conversation & every unguarded word and movement is liable to question & examination— —all that is unpleasant—but it is to be borne—& if it were even to be attended with utter destruction to me & mine and all generations lineal & collateral—I will go through it—before I permit accusers to become judges.—I have one word—& but one word to say of Lady B[yron]—whatever may become of this business or me in consequence of it—I can attach no blame to *her*— where there is wrong it may be fairly divided—between her relatives & myself & where there is right she has the monopoly.— —They have presumed on the difference in the esteem of the world for Lady B[yron] & her Lord—to take an ungenerous advantage—knowing that where there was a dissention—all would naturally be with her.—I stop this scrawl—(private of course)

ever yrs most truly
B

P.S.—I need not add that you have my full approbation & sanction to say whatever you please on this subject to me—either from yourself or any other person.

[2] Mary Anne Clermont was Lady Noel's trusted maid, who had been with her at the time of Annabella's birth and after, and then returned as governess and confidante. Byron, probably not wrongly, ascribed to her Lady Byron's intransigence during the separation and afterward.

Dear Hunt—Your letter would have been answered before—had I not thought it probable—that as you were in town for a day or so—I should have seen you—I don't mean this as a hint at reproach for not calling—but merely that of course I should have been very glad if you had called on your way home or abroad—as I always would have been —and always shall be.—With regard to the circumstance to which you allude—there is no reason why you should not speak openly to me upon a subject already sufficiently rife in the mouths & minds of what is called "the World":—of the "fifty reports" it follows that forty nine must have more or less error & exaggeration—but I am sorry to say— that on the main & essential point of an intended—&—it may be—an inevitable separation—I can contradict none.———At present I shall say no more—but this is not from want of confidence.———In the mean time I shall merely request a suspension of opinion.—Your prefatory letter to "Rimini"[1] I accepted as it was meant as a public compliment & a private kindness—I am only sorry that it may perhaps operate against you—as an inducement & with some a pretext—for attack— on the part of the political & personal enemies of both:—not that this can be of much consequence—for in the end the work must be judged by it's merits—& in that respect you are well armed.—Murray tells me it is going on well—& you may depend upon it there is a sub-stratum of poetry which is a foundation for solid & durable fame.— The objections (*if* there be objections—for this is a *pre*sumption & not an *as*sumption) will be merely as to the mechanical part—& such as I stated before—the usual consequence of either novelty or revival.—— I desired Murray to forward to you a pamphlet with two things of mine in it[2]—the most part of both of them—& of one in particular—*written* before *others* of my composing—which have preceded them in *publica-tion*:—they are neither of them of much pretension—nor intended for it—you will perhaps wonder at my dwelling so much & so frequently on former subjects & *scenes*—but the fact is that I found them fading fast from my memory—& I was at the same time so partial to their *place* (& events connected with it) that I have stamped them while I could —in such colours as I could trust to *now*—but might have confused & misapplied hereafter—had I longer delayed the attempted delineation.[3]

[1] Hunt's *The Story of Rimini*, published by Murray in 1816, had a rather familiar dedicatory letter to Byron, addressing him as his friend.

[2] *The Siege of Corinth* and *Parisina.*

[3] The Victoria and Albert MS. ends here. The remainder of the letter is in the Murray collection.

——I am very well in health now—though I was a good deal indisposed about a fortnight back—with *liver* &c. I have scrawled a longer letter than I intended—& yet not upon the topics which I meant to touch upon.—I will add only a word or two—& that is—to be under no uneasiness on my account—I have that within me—which whether good or bad— will I think support me (at least has hitherto supported me in many & difficult circumstances)—through every thing—I do not mean to say that I do not feel—but it is one thing to suffer—& another to shrink.——I cannot however in this case much blame any one but myself:—& least of all the person who—could I divide any wrong which may belong to it—would be the probable participator.

ever yrs. most truly
B

[TO LADY BYRON]   *February 26th. 1816*

Dearest Pip—I wish you would make it up—for I am dreadfully sick of all this—& cannot foresee any good that can come of it.—If you will—I am ready to make any penitential speech or speeches you please—& will be very good & tractable for the rest of my days—& very sorry for all that have gone before.—At any rate—if you won't comply with this proposition—I beg you to keep this note to yourself —& neither show it to Doctors Bailey[1] nor Lushington[2] nor Commons[3]—nor any other of your present Cabinet—at least the professional part of it.—I am very sure *you* will not mistake it for anything but what it is meant to be—& I am terribly tired of the stately style of our late letters & obliged to take refuge in that which I was used to

yrs. ever & truly
B

Private—

[TO JAMES PERRY]   *February 26th. 1816*

If you *dare* publish the enclosed—that is—if it is worth publishing— & will not bring you into any scrape—print it *as a translation* from

---

[1] Dr. Matthew Baillie was consulted by Lady Byron when she thought Byron's actions were caused by mental derangement.

[2] Dr. Stephen Lushington, Lady Byron's chief Counsellor during the separation negotiations.

[3] Allusions to Doctors' Commons usually had the connotations of divorce proceedings which were handled there.

some recent *French poetry*—but *keep* my *secret*[1]—for obvious reasons. At any rate favour me with an answer as soon as convenient.—It would not be bad fun to call it Chateaubriand's[2] provided it be not detrimental to you or too unfair to him—the dog deserves no quarter, and of course no one would *seriously* suppose it to be of his writing. At all events, don't let it appear with the (real) translator's name on any account—because—besides other reasons—half the cream of these things is in the uncertainty of the real Author. If you can venture upon it with safety I would request you as a favour to be particular in correcting the proofs—as the handwriting is very indifferent and it also may want better punctuation. [He wishes Perry to deliberate and to be quite sure that the poem will not bring him into "the tender mercies of the Inquisition."][3]

Of course if it did I would avow myself much rather than that it should fall upon you—but in any case it is better to be on firm ground —and therefore take a cautious survey and be wary.

[TO LADY NOEL]   *February 27th. 1816*

Dear Lady Noel—Augusta has communicated your account of my little girl.—I am glad to hear that it is so fine a child—& I hoped that I could have contrived another for you still finer—had it so pleased Lady Byron (& yourself) to have continued encreasing our antient & respectable families—

yrs. very truly
Bₙ

[TO JOHN HANSON]   *Fy. 29th. 1816*

Dear Sir—I hear they have got *Romilly*;[1]—pray ascertain that point

---

[1] Byron's pretended translation, "Ode from the French" appeared in the *Morning Chronicle*, March 15, 1816.

[2] This note accompanied the poem when it appeared in the *Morning Chronicle*: "We have received the following poetical version of a poem, the original of which is circulating in Paris, and which is ascribed (we know not with what justice) to the Muse of M. de Chateaubriand." The ironical ascription was aimed at the turncoat character of Chateaubriand, who had been a supporter of Napoleon, but who on the day the allies entered Paris published a pamphlet in support of the Bourbons and legitimacy, and subsequently accepted various posts under Louis XVIII. The poem is libertarian, praising freedom and damning "tyrants".

[3] Catalogue summary of part of letter.

[1] See Feb. 12, 1816, to Hanson, note 2.

34

because he may have forgotten that he has a retainer for *us*——& do not delay in it as it may lead to awkward mistakes on both sides—

yrs. ever

B

[TO THOMAS MOORE] *Feb. 29th. 1816*

I have not answered your letter for a time;[1] and, at present, the reply to part of it might extend to such a length, that I shall delay it till it can be made in person, and then I will shorten it as much as I can.

In the mean time, I am at war "with all the world and his wife;" or rather, "all the world and *my* wife" are at war with me, and have not yet crushed me,—whatever they *may* do. I don't know that in the course of a hair-breadth existence I was ever, at home or abroad, in a situation so completely uprooting of present pleasure, or rational hope for the future, as this same. I say this, because I think so, and feel it. But I shall not sink under it the more for that mode of considering the question—I have made up my mind.

By the way, however, you must not believe all you hear on the subject; and don't attempt to defend me. If you succeeded in that, it would be a mortal, or an immortal, offence—who can bear refutation? I have but a very short answer for those whom it concerns; and all the activity of myself and some vigorous friends have not yet fixed on any tangible ground or personage, on which or with whom I can discuss matters, in a summary way, with a fair pretext;—though I nearly had *nailed one* yesterday, but he evaded by—what was judged by others—a satisfactory explanation. I speak of *circulators*—against whom I have no enmity, though I must act according to the common code of usage, when I hit upon those of the serious order.

Now for other matters—Poesy, for instance. Leigh Hunt's poem is a devilish good one—quaint, here and there, but with the substratum of originality, and with poetry about it, that will stand the test. I do not say this because he has inscribed it to me, which I am sorry for, as I should otherwise have begged you to review it in the Edinburgh. It is really deserving of much praise, and a favourable critique in the E[dinburgh] R[eview] would but do it justice, and set it up before the public eye where it ought to be.

How are you? and where? I have not the most distant idea what I am going to do myself, or with myself—or where—or what. I had, a few

---

1 Moore had heard rumours of the separation and wanted Byron's version of it.

weeks ago, some things to say, that would have made you laugh; but they tell me now that I must not laugh, and so I have been very serious —and am.

I have not been very well—with a *liver* complaint—but am much better within the last fortnight, though still under Iatrical advice. I have latterly seen little of * * * * * * * * * * * * *

I must go and dress to dine. My little girl is in the country, and, they tell me, is a very fine child, and now nearly three months old. Lady Noel (my mother-in-law, or, rather, *at* law) is at present over-looking it. Her daughter (Miss Milbanke that was) is, I believe, in London with her father. A Mrs. C[lermont][2] (now a kind of house-keeper and spy of Lady N[oel]) who, in her better days, was a washer-woman, is supposed to be—by the learned—very much the occult cause of our late domestic discrepancies.

In all this business, I am the sorriest for Sir Ralph. He and I are equally punished, though *magis pares quem similes* in our affliction. Yet it is hard for both to suffer for the fault of one, and so it is—I shall be separated from my wife; he will retain his.

Ever, &c.

[TO JOHN MURRAY (*a*)]   [*March, 1816?*]

Books Missing[1]—

Petronius (Quarto old dutch E[ditio]n)[2]
Tibullus Catullus Propertius—in vellum (old E[ditio]n)
Ld. *Carlisle's* poems—
Tyrnhill's Aristotle's poetics—(I would not lose this—it was my last prize book at Harrow)

————

These & some others must be searched out—I am very uncomfortable in not finding them—

B

3 Swords &c. &c.
There are others also for which I refer you to the Catalogue—

[2] See Feb. 23, 1816, to Lord Holland, note 2.
[1] Byron was preparing to sell his books before going abroad.
[2] This book was listed in the catalogue of the auction of Byron's books by Evans, April 6, 1816: "Petronius Arbiter, Variorum, *Amst.* 1669.

Dear Sir/—Missing besides the former list

    Hayley's Cowper (Russia)
    Hobhouse's Albania—
    The Cosmopolite—

    ————

These & the others must really be found—

                                    yrs. truly
                                        B

[TO JAMES HOGG]

                    13 Terrace, Piccadilly, March 1st. 1816

Dear Sir/—I never was offended with you—& never had cause.— —
At the time I received your last letters—I was "marrying & being
given in marriage"; & since that period—have been occupied or in-
dolent—and am at best a very ungracious or ungrateful correspondent, & hardly ever write letters but by fits & starts.— —At
this moment my conscience smites me with an unanswered letter of
Mr. W. Scott's—on a subject which may seem to him to require
an answer—as it was on something relative to a friend of his—for
whose talents I have a sincere admiration.[1]— —My family about three
months ago was increased by a little girl—who is reckoned a fine
child—I believe—though I feel loth to trust to my own partialities.—
She is now in the country.— —I will mention your wishes on the score
of collection & publication to Murray—but I have not much weight
with him—what I have I will use.—As far as my approval of your intention may please you—you have it—& I should think Mr. Scott's
liking to your plan—very ominous of its success.[2]— —The objections
you mention to the two things of mine lately published—are very
just & true not only with regard to these but to all their predecessors—
some more & some less.— —With regard to the quarter from which
you anticipate a probable & public censure on such points—I can only
say—that I am very sure there will be no severity but what is *deserved*—
& were there ever so much it could not obliterate a particle of the

----

[1] Probably Maturin, whom Scott recommended to furnish a drama for Drury
Lane.

[2] Hogg was projecting a volume of the most distinguished poets of the day, and
Byron had promised him something, but the project fell through. Hogg later pub-
lished *The Poetic Mirror*, in which he parodied contemporary poets, including
Byron.

obligation which I am already too much under to that journal[3] & it's conductors—(as the Grocer says to his customers) "for past favours".— —And so—you want to come to London—it is a damned place—to be sure—but the only one in the world—(at least in the English world) for fun—though I have seen parts of the Globe that I like better—still upon the whole it is the completest either to help one in feeling oneself alive—or forgetting that one is so.— —I am interrupted but will write again soon—

yrs. very truly
BYRON

P.S.—I forgot to thank you for liking &c. &c.—but am much obliged to you—as well as for a former compliment in the inscription of your "Pilgrims of the Sun".[4]

[TO LADY BYRON]   *March 1st. 1816*

Dearest Bell/—Although you have announced to others and by others—the recommendation of "legal advisers" to hold no communication with that dangerous terrace in Piccadilly—& your adoption of this exquisite maxim of matrimonial jurisprudence:—I must again urge my often repeated request that you would grant me an interview —Pray do.— —Yesterday Mr. Davison[1] called upon me—& I begged him to repeat my request—which I can see no great harm in granting: —let your father—or whoever you please—be present if you desire it.— —I have not attempted to see you—(further than by so often requesting your permission) because I have no wish to agitate or intrude upon you by my sudden & unwelcome apparition—if my presence should still be important enough in your eyes to occasion such a feeling.—I have still & have always had throughout this business—the most sincere & heartfelt wish for your reconciliation to me—& there is no step I am not willing to take to effect it:— —but — —this failing—my determination is equally taken as to the course I shall pursue:—this will be found the case at the proper time.

[3] *The Edinburgh Review.*
[4] Hogg had dedicated his *Pilgrims of the Sun* (1815) to Byron:
> ". . . 'tis thy bold and native energy;
> Thy soul that dares each bound to overfly,
> Ranging thro' Nature on erratic wing—
> These do I honour . . . ."
[1] A friend of the Noels. See Elwin, *Lord Byron's Wife*, pp. 57, 313.

——I do not say this from any notion or wish or thought of intimidation:—nor am I ignorant of the firmness of your disposition:—I merely state the fact—that I am prepared to meet your "legal advisors" and to try what force there is "in the decrees of Venice." ——I presume it is in vain to expect any answer from you or yours— except through your speaking trumpets—and perhaps not even through them:—yet I do hope that you will see me—and am very sure that we should agree—in any case much better by our discussion of the subject than through the sagest of interpreters.—I hope that you are well—I am much better than I was a short time ago—but am now pestered with a rheumatism in my left arm—which has come on since yesterday—I verily believe it is a remnant of that long passage at the Gallery of Halnaby.——They tell me young Pip. is well & shews marvellous indications of acquaintance with her nurse & her Grandmother:—it is perhaps time that she should begin to recognize another of her relations.—G[eorge] Byron is about to be married[2]—I wish him as much luck & as little law as possible—The Lady is said to be a distant relative of the Noels—she is pretty—& agreeable—& I think they have a very good chance of going on very well.— Dearest Bell.

yrs. ever most affectly.
BYRON

P.S.—I hope you will not think me flippant or unfeeling—for really I do not mean it—but in this as in many things—one must either laugh or cry—& I prefer the former (while I can) even if it should be Sardonically.——

[TO LORD HOLLAND]   *March 2d. 1816*

My dear Lord—Not having received any answer to what you had the goodness to say on my part to the other party:—I must now declare *off* even from *that*—& can only say that I consider that the time allotted has been sufficient for their decision—& as they have formed none I have made mine.[1] I will now not only sign no separation —but agree to none—not even to a verbal permission for Lady B[yron]'s absence——I feel much obliged by any trouble you have had

---

2 George Anson Byron, first cousin of the poet, and after his death the 7th Lord Byron, married in 1816 Elizabeth Mary, daughter of Sacheverell Chandos Pole, of Radbourne, Derbyshire.
1 See Feb. 23, 1816, to Lord Holland, note 1.

in this unpleasant business—& however I may regret what may occur—or has occurred—believe me

ever yrs. most truly
B

[TO LORD HOLLAND] *March 3d. 1816*

My dear Lord—I answer *No.* At the same time you may assure Dr. L[ushington] from me—that I am far from imputing any undue motive to him—& that his explanation of the delay is satisfactory.—With regard to "amicable arrangement" I am open to the *most* amicable of arrangements—I am willing & desirous to become reconciled to Lady B[yron] & her friends—ready to make any advance or even sacrifice for that purpose——to dismiss all & any irritation from my mind which may have arisen on this subject—to be forgiven where I may have offended—& in some points—it may be—to forgive.—— But I will sign no separations.——And now—my dear Lord—I must beg you even more to excuse whatever trouble this business may have occasioned to you—& am

ever yrs. most truly
BYRON

[TO LADY BYRON (*a*)] *March 4th. 1816*

Dearest—If I did not believe that you are sacrificing your own happiness—as much—as I know—you are destroying mine:—if I were not convinced—that some rash determination—& it may be—promise —is the root of the bitter fruits we are now at the same time devouring & detesting—I would & could address you no more.——Did I not love you—were I not sure that you still love me—I should not have endured what I have already. I have rejected all propositions of separation—as I would spurn an adder—and from the same motive. ——If you or yours conceive that I am activated by mercenary motives—I appeal to the tenor of my past life in such respects—I appeal to my conduct with regard to settlements previous to your marriage—I appeal to all who know me—or who ever will know.— Whatever I may have felt—(& what I feel—I often shew—) in moments of pressure and distress—they were not the privations of Misfortune from which I recoiled—but it's indignities.—I look upon the *manner* & statement of the proposals lately transmitted to me—as

40

the greatest insult I have received from your family—in this struggle for moral existence,—I will not trust myself with the subject.—I desire to see you—I request to be reconciled with you:———recollect I have done all that human being can in such circumstances to effect this object for your sake—for my child's—for mine—even for those who endeavour to prevent it—I will persevere in it—while the shadow of a hope can be distinguished—and when even that is effaced —I shall regret the sufferings—which to more than *one*—or *two*—will be inevitable—there is that which will recoil upon some who may deem themselves secure.—

yrs. ever most attachedly

B

[TO LADY BYRON (*b*)]   *March 4th. 1816*

I know of no offence—not merely from man to wife—nor of one human being to another—but of any being almost to God himself— which we are not taught to believe would be expiated by the repeated atonement which I have offered even for the *unknown* faults (for to me till stated they are unknown—to any extent which can justify such persevering rejections) I may have been supposed to commit—or can have committed against you.—But since all hope is over—& instead of the duties of a wife—& the mother of my child—I am to encounter accusation & implacability—I have nothing more to say—but shall act according to circumstances—though not even injury can alter the love with which (Though I shall do my best to repel attack) I must ever be yours

B

I am told that you say *you* drew up the *proposal* of separation—if so— I regret to hear it—it appeared to me to be a kind of appeal to the supposed mercenary feelings of the person to whom it was made "if you part with &c. you will gain *so much now*—& so much—at the death of &c."———a matter of pounds shillings & pence!—no allusion to my child—a hard—dry—attorney's paper:—Oh—Bell—to see you thus stifling and destroying all feeling all affections—all duties—(for they are your first duties—those of a wife & mother) is far more bitter than any possible consequences to me.——

41

[TO JOHN HANSON] *March 4th. 1816*

Dear Sir/—Before *we cite*—it will be better to ascertain (if possible) whether *they really* mean to go into court—because—if they do not—or *she* does not—this measure on our part may be a pretext for them to urge & induce her to go on—by saying that we have set the example —and that it is [mere?] self defence & so forth.—I wish this to be considered & will see you upon it this evening when you like—Mrs. L[eig]h will call upon you & fix an hour.—

yrs. truly
B

[TO JOHN MURRAY] *March 6th. 1816*

Dear Sir—I have received the enclosed—& beg you to send the writer immediately anything of mine—coming under the description of his request—except "the Curse of Minerva"[1]—(which I disown as stolen & published in the miserable & villainous copy in the Mag[azine]) it was not & is not meant for publication.—I sent to you today—for this reason.—The books you purchased—are again seized—and as matters stand—had much better be sold at once by public auction[2]—I wish to see you tomorrow to return your bill for them—which—thank heaven—is neither due nor paid—*that* part as far as *you* are concerned—being settled—(which can be & shall be when I see you tomorrow) I have no further delicacy about the matter—this is about the tenth execution in as many months—so I am pretty well hardened—but it is fit I should pay the forfeit of my forefathers' extravagances & my own—& whatever my faults may be—I suppose they will be pretty well expiated in time—or eternity.—

ever yrs. very truly
B

---

1 *The Curse of Minerva* was written in Athens in the spring of 1811. Byron had suppressed it in 1812 before it was published, but a quarto edition had been printed by Murray's printer T. Davison for private circulation. From this it was published in a pirated edition in Philadelphia by De Silver and Co. in 1815.

2 When executions were pending Byron had determined to sell his books in November, 1815, and he employed Messrs. Armstrong and Crooke, who valued them at £450. Murray sent him a draft for £500 as a temporary accommodation, but the books were traced and attached by the Sheriff. Byron managed to pay off the debt, and the books were finally sold at public auction by R. H. Evans on April 5–6, 1816. Murray bought many of them and also the well-known screen with pictures of prize fighters and actors on it.

P.S.—I need hardly say that I knew nothing till this *day* of the new *seizure*—(I had released them from former ones) and thought when you took them—that they were yours——you shall have your bill again tomorrow.——

March 6th. 1816

Sir/—I feel truly sorry for any disappointment or delay that may have been occasioned by the circumstances you mention—& only fear that you overrate the importance of any communication I could have made or can make.——When you wrote to me last year—the unpublished songs of the H[ebrew] Melodies—were much at your service—had your work been sent forth at that time[2]—but in the interim the Musical publishers printed the words—& Mr. Murray inserted them in his collection—& I could only regret that they had not first appeared in your volumes.——The other day—I particularly desired Mr. Murray to forward to your bookseller any things of mine in his care—*not* already published—from those already published—you are welcome to make any selection or extracts you like—though I fear this will not suit you.—The Monthly magazine poem attributed to me—I *disavow* in the form in that miscellany—it is a miserable & mutilated piracy from a *privately* printed thing of mine *never* intended for publication[3]—& I trust & request that you will not disgrace your pages with copying such *trash*—(as a moment's inspection would convince you that the pretended extract is) into your own volume.—I enclose the only things I have by me in M.S.—which I do not think worth your insertion—(even if they are legible which I doubt)—and I will speak again to Mr. Murray to send any others which may happen to be in his hands—I have the honour to [be]

yr. very obedt. & very humble Sert.

BYRON

[1] Richard Alfred Davenport (1777?–1852) was a miscellaneous writer and editor, who later wrote a history of the Bastille (1838), and *A Dictionary of Biography* (1831) besides editing editions of various British poets.
[2] Byron had made an offer of some of the *Hebrew Melodies* to the Editor of the *Poetical Register* on Feb. 7, 1815.
[3] See March 6, 1816, to Murray, note 1.

An Interview—

———

If not an interview a disclosure to you of the circumstances on which she acts

————

Of anything said to Mrs. L[eigh] by Lady B[yron] on this subject Ld. B[yron] promises on his honour to take no advantage.——

[TO THOMAS MOORE]   *March 8th. 1816*

I rejoice in your promotion as Chairman and Charitable Steward, &c. &c. These be dignities which await only the virtuous. But then, recollect you are *six* and *thirty* (I speak this enviously—not of your age, but the "honour—love—obedience—troops of friends,"[1] which accompany it), and I have eight years good to run before I arrive at such hoary perfection; by which time,—if I *am* at all,—it will probably be in a state of grace or progressing merits.

I must set you right in one point, however, The fault was *not*—no, nor even the misfortune—in my "choice" (unless in *choosing at all*)— for I do not believe—and I must say it, in the very dregs of all this bitter business—that there ever was a better, or even a brighter, a kinder, or a more amiable and agreeable being than Lady B[yron]. I never had, nor can have, any reproach to make her, while with me. Where there is blame, it belongs to myself, and, if I cannot redeem, I must bear it.

Her nearest relatives are a * * * *—my circumstances have been and are in a state of great confusion—my health has been a good deal dis-ordered, and my mind ill at ease for a considerable period. Such are the causes (I do not name them as excuses) which have frequently driven me into excess, and disqualified my temper for comfort. Something also may be attributed to the strange and desultory habits which, becoming my own master at an early age, and scrambling about, over and through the world, may have induced. I still, however, think that, if I had a fair chance, by being placed in even a tolerable situation, I

---

[1] *Macbeth*, Act. V, scene 3.

44

might have gone on fairly. But that seems hopeless,—and there is nothing more to be said. At present—except my health, which is better (it is odd, but agitation or contest of any kind gives a rebound to my spirits and sets me up for the time)—I have to battle with all kinds of unpleasantness, including private and pecuniary difficulties, &c. &c.

I believe I may have said this before to you,—but I risk repeating it. It is nothing to bear the *privations* of adversity, or, more properly, ill fortune; but my pride recoils from its *indignities*. However, I have no quarrel with that same pride, which will, I think, buckler me through every thing. If my heart could have been broken, it would have been so years ago, and by events more afflicting than these.

I agree with you (to turn from this topic to our shop) that I have written too much. The last things were, however, published very reluctantly by me, and for reasons I will explain when we meet. I know not why I have dwelt so much on the same scenes, except that I find them fading, or *confusing* (if such a word may be) in my memory, in the midst of present turbulence and pressure, and I felt anxious to stamp before the die was worn out. I now break it. With those countries, and events connected with them, all my really poetical feelings begin and end. Were I to try, I could make nothing of any other subject,—and that I have apparently exhausted. "Woe to him," says Voltaire, "who says all he could say on any subject." There are some on which, perhaps, I could have said still more: but I leave them all, and not too soon.

Do you remember the lines I sent you early last year, which you still have? I don't wish (like Mr. Fitzgerald, in the Morning Post) to claim the character of "Vates" in all its translations, but were they not a little prophetic? I mean those beginning "There's not a joy the world can,"[2] &c. &c. on which I rather pique myself as being the truest, though the most melancholy, I ever wrote.

What a scrawl I have sent you! You say nothing of yourself, except that you are a Lancastrian churchwarden, and an encourager of mendicants. When are you out? and how is your family? My child is very well and flourishing, I hear; but I must see also. I feel no disposition to resign it to the contagion of its grandmother's society, though I am unwilling to take it from the mother. It is weaned, however, and something about it must be decided.

Ever, &c.

[2] See March 2, 1815, to Moore, note 1 (Vol. 4, p. 277).

Dear Sir/—I will call this evening at half past 7 or 8 o clock—& [meet?] you upon this subject.—

yrs. very truly

B

[TO LADY BYRON] *March 11th. 1816*

There is one point on which it is proper you should be set right— however my motive may be misconstrued—as almost every thing I have said has lately been.—You told Mrs. Leigh that "I had menaced you with legal measures as if you were to be intimidated by these" this is a misapprehension on your part—or a misstatement on hers.— The words "legal measures" were first used by your father in a letter to me (ready for production when necessary) and all that has ever been said or done by me since that threat amounted & amounts only to my determination to resist such proceedings by such lawful defences as truth & justice permit & prescribe to the accused as well as the accuser.—These measures have not been of my seeking—& whatever the results may be—I am not aware of any impropriety in declaring that I shall defend myself from attacks which strike at the root of every tie—& connection—of hope—& character—of my child's welfare—& it may be—even of your own.———I am prepared on such points—& being so should not have alluded to them—had I not con- ceived that you have either misconceived—or been too [ready?] to misconceive me—by attributing to me "legal menaces" which I merely resolved to resist.———As a negociation has partly commenced —I will state to you that as far as our present circumstances & fortunes are concerned—I have no objection to proceed.—But the Wentworth property is no part of present consideration—it may never be the subject of consideration at all:—*you* may survive me (I hope you will) Lady Noel may survive you—or both—if I survive you—it ceases to me:—when the time comes—if it does come—I will do what is right—you have no reason—at least no just one—to doubt me on such points—when I married you I settled all I could & about all I had upon you—& though strongly advised & justified in demanding a settlement of yr. father's dispensable property—I would not & did not —solely from delicacy to you—& to your family.—If however you doubt me—in the event of the succession to the W[entworth] Estates —you will *then* have the means of redress should I seem to you reluctant in making proper arrangements:—but in the present case—whatever your success might be in the probable cause which may ensue—*possessions* & not *reversions* are under the cognizance of the Courts. ——At all events—I shall not submit to such measures as may lead to further misconstructions of my conduct:—& if your real object & that of your friends is a fair & equal separation—with no ultimate view of another nature—you will be satisfied with arrangements proportioned to the present relative circumstances of the parties.——If the W[entworth] property ever falls in—I will make what shall be fully allowed to be fair & liberal arrangements—but I will not be menaced —nor forced into any present stipulations:—nor deprived of the pleasure of acting of my own accord towards yourself—at least as liberally as the law would [decree?] for you—*supposing* (for it is but a supposition) that you carried all before you.—

yrs ever

B

P.S.—As I do not write with a lawyer at my elbow—I must request a fair construction of what I have written.

[TO ROBERT WILMOT[1]]   *March 11th. 1816*

Lord Byron presents his compliments to Mr. Wilmot:—Ld. Byron considered & considers himself no further bound by any project of separation submitted to Ld. B's inspection than *not* to make use of Lady B's disavowal of specified imputations—should the subject become that of discussion in a court of law.—Such was the impression on Lord Byron's mind—on the point of arrangements Ld. B. conceived himself as having acceded to the *principle* of a separation—but on the terms that he had still the use of his own discretion—subject to the advice of his friends & legal advisers—but to no positive stipulations and upon understanding the full drift of the proposal as to the contingency of the York property Ld. B. declined—& declares that he will not now nor at any time previous to the death of Lady Noel enter upon any legal agreement whatever with regard to that reversion.——

1 Robert John Wilmot (1784–1841) was Byron's first cousin, being the son of Byron's father's sister Juliana. He married Anne Horton, a Derbyshire heiress whose beauty inspired Byron's "She walks in beauty like the night." He was tactless and far from impartial as a mediator in the separation, and he later had a hand in burning Byron's Memoirs after his death.

Ld. Byron presents his compliments to Mr. Wilmot.

Lord Byron assented to the *principle* of a separation.

Lord Byron himself submitted the paper to Mr. Hanson for consideration after having previously discussed the points it contained with his friends—but having come to no definitive conclusion upon them.—Lord Byron did say to Mr. Wilmot that dispatch was desirable —but never entertained an idea that an instrument was to be drawn up & signed without further consideration with friends or legal advisers. —Ld. Byron saw Mr. Wilmot (he believes) shake hands with Mr. H[obhouse]—or Mr. H[obhouse] with him—and Lord Byron did speak of an intention of visiting Greece by way of Dalmatia—but does not understand that this was to be a part of the articles of separation.— Mr. Wilmot was requested by Lord Byron to wait on Lady Byron with a view to comply with her wish to open a negotiation—& he was selected from a wish to consult her feelings as being at the same time a relative of Ld. B's and a person who was more likely to be impartial & agreeable to herself & friends than other & more intimate connections of Ld. Byron's—Lord Byron's "own proposition" was a promise (which he has no objection to renew) to do what should be deemed fair & liberal by Lady B—in the event of the Noel property falling in— Lady B—may insist on what "legal instrument" she pleases—that was a subject for *consideration*—& Ld. B—neither did—could—would —nor will give unqualified assent to any such proposition—either from Lady B—or any person or persons whatsoever.——

Mr. Wilmot's paper was & is considered by Lord Byron as submitting certain points for discussion to Lord B—& his advisers—but whether for assent or dissent—Ld. B—conceives that Mr. W. is not the person who has the right to determine.—

Ld. Byron "positively assented" to nothing but acquiescence in *not* using Lady B's disavowal in the event of a trial.—This disavowal was left in Mr. W's hands for this very reason—that it was not improbable that the business might still come into court.—

Lastly—Lord B—begs leave to observe that he never could be considered as bound by an unsigned paper drawn up by another person or persons.—

And with regard to the proposition from Lady B's advisers of "arbitrators—&c." Lord B—on the fullest consideration—& advice of friends & legal advisers—again declares it to be inadmissible—& in the point of view in which it has been placed before him—he looks upon it as

a most unjust & unjustifiable demand on the part of Lady B—& her family—& her advisers—legal or otherwise.——
Ld. B—is surprised that Mr. W. should describe Mr. Davies as giving "assent" on questions of property as Mr. D. always declined giving an opinion upon such points at all.—

[TO ROBERT WILMOT (*a*)]   *March 12th. 1816*

Sir—Although the tone & temper of your last letter to me would have justified me in refusing any reply to it—I have answered it—& as temperately as such circumstances could admit.—I have now to add that whatever differences may arise or have arisen—I consider *myself* (& *myself only*) as the responsible person to you—& as such I hold myself at your disposal—should you regard yourself as injured in this business——I must also add that I cannot but look upon the style you have used towards me as improper & unusual & that I by no means acquiesce in your right to hold such language.——I have the honour to be

yr. very obedt. humble servt.
BYRON

[TO ROBERT WILMOT (*b*)]   *March 12th. 1816*

Sir—My last communication referred to those "queries" or rather to the manner in which they were put—and on this point I have already expressed my opinion to you which I see no reason to revoke.——
You cannot regret more than I do my selection of you as a mediator though not perhaps for the same reason:——I feel very sorry for any disquiet that it may have occasioned to you—and the misconceptions on all sides—though obliged to you for undertaking the thankless office—and attributing to you every good motive in the attempt.—
I beg leave to add that whatever may have appeared "extraordinary & unexpected" in my recent manner of addressing you—has arisen entirely from what I conceive to be a harsh & hasty mode of expression in your letter to myself.——

I am very truly yr. obedt. Sert.
BYRON

P.S.—The impression made by the tone of yr. letter on my mind & the mind of others—was that you had a wish to quarrel with *one* of us

—and as the person principally concerned in the business—I thought I had a right to the preference—and at all events did not choose that my responsibility should fall but on him who had incurred it—that is on me.—

[TO ROBERT WILMOT]   *March 14th. 1816*

I do not quite understand the drift of your note of this day—but this is no time for cavils—neither do I feel disposed to imagine blame to anyone beyond myself.——If you did not misconceive me—then I misconceived you—it must be one—and it might be both—the impression on my mind with regard to the transaction you have already heard—and as far as *you* have had trouble and uneasiness in this cursed business which blisters all it touches—I am much more sorry than I could be for any consequences to me.——
I never bore you any enmity—even at the moment when I thought that circumstances would force us into dissention—and I have to remember much kindness from you at times when I valued kindness more than I can do now.—

Ever yrs. very truly
B

[TO LEIGH HUNT]   *March 14th. 1816*

Dear Hunt—I send you six Orchestra tickets for D[rury] L[ane] (countersigned by me which makes the admission *free*—which I explain—that the door keeper may not impose upon you) they are for the best place in the house—but can only be used *one* at a time—I have left the *dates unfilled* and you can *take* your own nights which I should suppose would be Kean's —the seat is in the Orchestra. —I have inserted the name of Mr. H[azlitt?] a friend of yours in case you like to transfer to him—do not forget to fill up the date for such days as you choose to select.—

yrs. ever truly
BYRON

[TO SIR SAMUEL ROMILLY]   *13 Piccadilly—March 15, 1816*

If Sir Samuel Romilly is willing to accept of the sole and final arrangement of the affair between Lord & Lady Byron—his Lordship declares that he will abide by Sir Samuel's decision, and that he empowers Mr. Hobhouse to convey this communication.

B YRON

[In Hobhouse's hand—signed by Byron]

[TO JOHN HANSON]   *March 19th. 1816*

Dear Sir/—Mr. Hobhouse has the copy of the agreement—& he is now at his father's—Whitton nr. Hounslow—I have no copy whatever,—nor know where to get one unless from Mr. Hobhouse.—I will show him your correspondence with R[omilly] when I see him.—

yrs. very truly
B YRON

[TO JOHN CAM HOBHOUSE]   *March 19th. 1816*

Dear H.—I am asked by Hanson particularly for a copy of that damned agreement which seems as troublesome as the other—though I shall abide by it—Pray send it to *him per post*—

ever yrs. most truly
B

To Mr. Hanson
29, Bloomsbury Square.—

[TO MESSRS. ARMSTRONG & CROOKE]   *March 20th. 1816*

Messrs Armstrong & Crooke are desired [to] deliver to Mr. Murray or order the books & Screen which he has bought of Ld. Byron[1]—

B YRON

[TO LADY BYRON]   *[March 20–25? 1816]*

Dearest Bell—I send you the first verses that ever I attempted to write upon you, and perhaps the last that I may ever write at all.[1]

[1] See March 6, 1816, to Murray, note 2.
[1] Byron's verses "Fare Thee Well", a first draft of which he dated March 18, 1816. See *Shelley and His Circle*, ed. by Kenneth Neill Cameron, (1970), Vol. IV, pp. 655–657, which gives a facsimile of the first draft, with its many corrections.

This at such a moment may look like affectation, but it is not so. The language of all nations nearest to a state of nature is said to be Poetry. I know not how this may be; but this I know.

You know that the lover, the lunatic, and the poet are "of imagination all compact."[2] I am afraid you have hitherto seen me only as the two first, but I would fain hope there is nothing in the last to add to any grievances you may have against the former. [Substance of note, as he recollected it, recorded by Hobhouse, which Byron sent to Lady Byron with "Fare Thee Well."]

[TO JOHN HANSON]   *Thursday [March 21, 1816]*

Dear Sir—The sum now due from Sir R[alph] Noel—is—*three* quarters of a year's interest on the *2d* of *this month*—and I hope you will impress on Mr. Wharton[1] the propriety of it's being paid up:— as I conceive that it can have nothing to do with the subjects of present discussion—

yrs. very truly
B

[TO JOHN CAM HOBHOUSE]   *March 22d. 1816*

Dear H—Did not you take old Joe's earthquake epistle[1] with you?— if you did I think you might make an amusing extract from it for *Perry*[2]—& (if it be true which I take to be the case) it is a circumstance worth notice in the geological way among the fashionable vanities of the day.—I hope you will take care of the letter—for I want it again— pray bring it with you tomorrow.

yrs. very truly
B

[TO JOHN MURRAY]   *March 22d. 1816*

Dear Sir/—I was in hope that I should have seen yourself or Clerk this day for the final arrangement of the book-business—since being

---

[2] *Midsummer Night's Dream*, Act. V. scene 1.
[1] Sir Ralph Noel's business agent.
[1] Joe Murray, the old servant at Newstead Abbey, must have written an amusingly illiterate account of an earthquake that shook the Abbey.
[2] Proprietor of the *Morning Chronicle.*

given to you the sum due on the levy—I conceived there could be no further delay nor difficulty—& it is highly expedient that whatever arrangements I may have to make should be now completed.————The few prints—& silver cup which I sent to you this morning were intended by me to be additional articles in the proposed sale—with the screen————and (if you had no objections) to be so accounted for —though they cannot make much difference.—I wish—if possible—to have this off my mind—& the sooner the better—I am not aware of any further protest on the part of Ar[mstron]g & C[rook]e for the non-delivery of the books:1—

yrs. very truly
BYRON

March 23d. 1816

Dear Lady Holland/—I am truly obliged by the kindness of your trouble in sending me the letters.1—Any others from you or Lord Holland will be no less welcome.—It is my intention to proceed by way of Geneva—but to make no great delay in Switzerland—as my wish is to get to Rome & see as much of the the rest of Italy as I can.—Paris I should be sorry to see *now*.————I am merely waiting to complete a few previous arrangements—& have the hope of leaving England early in April—at any rate in the second week of that month.————In the late little earthquake of the midland counties—I hear—that Newstead has had a shake rather formidable to a building of such decrepitude:2—so that my "house is dividing against itself" not only according to the figure in the New Testament but in reality.————It is not my plan to be very long abroad—but my stay may depend on circumstances which I can neither foresee nor control—& it does not much matter.—In all times & places I shall preserve the recollection of your kindness & that of your Lord.—

ever yr. very truly & obliged
BYRON

1 See March 6, 1816, to Murray, note 2.
1 To allay rumours that were then circulating, Byron was seeking letters from his friends attesting that he had never spoken ill of Lady Byron.
2 See March 22, 1816, to Hobhouse, note 1.

Dear Lady Byron—I am truly sorry to hear that you have been informed & falsely informed that—since the commencement of the proceedings which are presumed to be drawing towards a conclusion —I have spoken of you harshly or lightly.—Neither are true—and no such terms—if such have been used—have originated from me—or have been sanctioned by me.—I have been out but little—indeed hardly at all—have seen no one with very few exceptions—but my own immediate relatives or connections—and to all these I can & do appeal—for confirmation or refutation of what is here advanced. I might indeed assert—& could prove—(but it matters little)—that the contrary has been the case.——If in the violence & outrageous latitude of accusation which has been indulged beyond all example and all excuse in the present case by those who from friendship to you or aversion from me—or both—have thought proper to proclaim themselves assailants in your cause—any few—(and few they must have been) of those who have known me & judged less severely of me— have been provoked to repel accusation by imputation—and have endeavoured to find a defence for me—in crimination of you—I disavow their conduct—and disclaim themselves.——I have interfered in no such proceedings—I have raised no party—nor even attempted it—neither should I have succeeded in such an attempt— the World has been with you throughout—the contest has been as unequal to me as it was undesired—and my name has been as completely blasted as if it were branded on my forehead:—this may appear to you exaggeration—it is not so—there are reports which once circulated not even falsehood—or their most admitted & acknowledged falsehood—can neutralize—which no contradiction can obliterate— nor conduct cancel:—— such have since your separation been busy with my name—you are understood to say—"that you are not responsible for these—that they existed previous to my marriage—and at most were only *revived* by our differences"—Lady Byron they did not exist—but even if they had—does their *revival* give you no feeling?— are you calm in the contemplation of having (however undesignedly) raised up that which you can never allay?—& which but for you might have never arisen?—is it with perfect apathy you quietly look upon this resurrection of Infamy?—To return to what is the object of my present intrusion upon you—I have little to add—except that I am & have been very much hurt to hear that you could give credit to my having recourse to such unworthy means of defence as recrimination on you:—my first letter to your father is in itself sufficient to have rendered abortive such attempts had I been willing to use them— Few people have attempted to blame you to me—& those who have will not venture to say that they have met with encouragement.—— Before I close this—I have a word to say of *Wilmot*[1]—it is this—he should not have attempted the office of mediator—after being biassed on one side—which he subsequently admitted that he was—before Mr. Hobhouse & a person said to be acting for you:—to this may be attributed much of the subsequent awkwardness of his situation:— any one acting for *two* should at least incline to *neither.*—This by the way is a parenthesis.——Of whomever & whatever I have spoken—I have never blamed you—never attempted to condemn you.—The utmost I may have said—is—that I looked upon the proceedings as extreme and that I had no great faith in your affection for me.—This however was only repeated by me to Augusta:—and it was the conviction of *more* than myself—though *not* of *her*—on the contrary—she always combated the impression.—It is not very wonderful—that such a belief confirmed by events should exist in any mind—even in mine.—

ever yrs. most affectly.

B

P.S.—If you will name the person or persons who have attributed to me—abuse of you—you will do an act of justice—& so will I.— I shall at least know whom to avoid—surely—there was bitterness enough in my portion without this addition.—

[TO SAMUEL ROGERS]   *March 25th. 1816*

Dear Rogers—You are one of the few persons with whom I have lived in what is called intimacy—and have heard me at times conversing on the untoward topic of my recent family disquietudes. Will you have the goodness to say to me at once—whether you ever heard me speak of her with disrespect—with unkindness—or defending myself at *her* expence by any *serious* imputation of any description against *her*? Did you never hear me say "that when there was a right or a wrong, she had the *right?*"—The reason I put these questions to you or other of my friends—is because I am said—by her and hers— to have resorted to such means of exculpation. Ever truly yours,

B

---

[1] See March 11, 1816, to Wilmot, note 1.

Enclosed are three letters of which I request an attentive perusal. ——Mr. Hobhouse & Mr. Davies are not in London—(when they arrive I shall make them a like appeal) and to *these* alone in addition to the writers of the letters—with my sister—Sir J[ame]s Burges—& legal or medical advisers—have I ever spoken confidentially & without reserve on recent events—or discussed any topic connected with your name.——The only levity almost with which I can charge myself is a trick upon Mrs. Clermont—in sending to her *"a friendly hint"* with the address of a female author (writer of "the Bravo of Bohemia" for the stage) whom she mistook—as I foresaw she would—for a female something else—& put herself or you to some expence in advertisements (which have been *carefully preserved* for the Nonce)—to obtain further intelligence.—In the present poisoned state of your mind towards me—this may perhaps appear a heinous offence against that excellent woman Mrs. *Clermount* "Honest—Honest—Iago" but time will perhaps teach you that there was no great harm in making the person ridiculous who was endeavouring to make me wretched—I mean the woman mentioned—the person who was an attendant of your mother's—& subsequently your governess—then a spy—and subsequently a *false*-witness—I say *false*—as having misstated the evidence of another.——The letters I enclose are to vindicate me on one score—that of abusing you which they must do to one not totally unjust—it can be with little other view—as from all I have heard or seen—the most remote hope of a reunion at any period (to which I clung while it was possible even when considering present separation as unavoidable) appears to be madness.—Be it so.—⟨To her it is so God be with you!⟩

yrs. &c. &c.

Dear Lady B—I sent you yesterday a letter—& to-day another containing *3* from Ld. Holland & other persons—containing—a refutation of reports spread with regard to my having spoken ill of you.—I wish to know if these were delivered to *you*—as it is essential for me to know this—& also to have them again when you have perused them.——One word in reply to say that in themselves—they were or

were not satisfactory in this respect—would be a satisfaction to me—
& surely not too much for you to award.—

BYRON

P.S.—If these letters have been witheld—(& I am told that they
were taken from my servant by your father)—I beg leave to say that I
conceive such a proceeding will justify me in putting a stop to all
proceedings—for a final arrangement—to which as far as it has gone
—I regard myself as strictly adherent—& bound to adhere.———

[TO JOHN HANSON]   *March 27th. 1816*

Dear Sir—The letters have reached their destination—you may
therefore proceed with all dispatch—It is also proper that Mr.
Wharton or Sir R[alph] should be required to pay the interest due—as
but a short time remains—& Sir R[alph] is on the point of leaving
London.—

yrs. very truly
B

[TO JOHN MURRAY]   *March 29th. 1816*

Dear Sir—I did imagine—and perhaps you will find it so by a
reference to accounts—that my *book bill* with you was paid up to a much
later period than is specified by the account which begins in *January
1813*—and some parts of my Banker's book appear to refer to this—
though I cannot take upon me to assert it till my receipts have been
examined—but that a payment & clearance on the score of books was
made in that year, or early in 1814 I am very certain.—I perceive that
the sum total is 346 pounds—that is about a hundred and four less than
the valuation of the whole—including about as many as I had purchased
previously in the course of some years at other markets—and though
I am not aware of many lost or mislaid—I am sure that the cost was a
much greater sum in the previous purchases than the valuation of the
present whole—& the bill due to you for a part put together.———
Under these circumstances and the further consideration that the sale
of the later publications has not answered expectation—I beg leave to
decline any negotiation whatever on the subject—& return you your
bills—accordingly—and the papers concerning the copyrights.—I
must remain your debtor for the present on the book account—and will

take my chance from Evans's sale—returning you your note which is not due till the 12th. of April—& which I will reclaim tomorrow from my bankers.[1]—

I am yr. very obedt. &c. &c.

BYRON

March 30th. 1816

Dear Sir/—Will you send me copies (tomorrow) of the several agreements which have hitherto passed on the copyright score:—you shall have them again when you please.—

yrs. very truly

B

[TO JOHN MURRAY (b)]   [*March 30, 1816?*]

Dear Sir/I send you my last night's dream[1]—and request to have 50 copies (for *private distribution*) struck off—and a proof tomorrow if possible—I wish Mr. Gifford to look at them—they are from life.—

yrs. &c.

B

[TO LEIGH HUNT]   [*March–April? 1816*]

[Two fragments of letters]

... good of "Rimini"—Sir Henry Englefield[1] (a mighty man in the *blue* circles & a very clever man any where) sent to Murray in terms of the highest eulogy:—and with regard to the common reader—my *sister* and *cousin* (who are now all my family—and the last gone since away to be married) were in fixed perusal & delight with it—& they

[1] See March 6, 1816, to Murray, note 2.

[1] "A Sketch" was a bitter satire on Mrs. Clermont, "Born in the garret, in the kitchen bred." Byron distributed the 50 copies to friends, and this poem, together with "Fare Thee Well", found its way into the newspapers, first in the *Sun*, and subsequently in other papers. This was the cause of widespread attacks on Byron in the press. He was defended in the *Morning Chronicle*, the *Examiner* and a few other papers. This publicity did much to undermine Byron's popularity before he went abroad.

[1] Sir Henry Charles Englefield (1752–1822), antiquary and miscellaneous writer. He directed the issue of engravings of English cathedrals and churches for the Society of Arts.

are "not critical" but fair—natural—unaffected—& understanding persons.——Frere[2]—and all the Arch-literati—I hear—are also very unanimous in a high opinion of the poem—"I hear this by the way —but I will send."—

————————

When you come up put some linen in your pocket & stay here for a day or two——I will try for Hobhouse. . . .Asia once more.—I can give you here bachelor's fare—& room—& welcome—& shall expect you on Mon-. . . .

[TO "G.C.B." (CLAIRE CLAIRMONT) (*a*)]   [*March–April? 1816*]

Ld.B. is not aware of any "importance" which can be attached by any person to an interview with him—& more particularly by one with whom it does not appear that he has the honour of being acquainted. —————He will however be at home at the hour mentioned.

[TO CLAIRE CLAIRMONT? (*b*)]   [*March–April? 1816*]

Certainly—but don't go away—in the meantime look at the Morning Post & the measured motion which will amuse you.— [In another hand] God bless you—I *never* was so happy!—[1]

[TO JOHN MURRAY]   [*April, 1816*]

Dear Sir/—I have waited to see you which I very much wish.—I must request you to postpone at any rate—*publishing* anything *new* of mine—for a few weeks at least—I will give you the reasons when I see you—which I wish this evening if possible.

yrs. ever
B

2 John Hookham Frere, diplomatist, friend of Canning, and author. He had been a contributor of clever satires to the *Anti-Jacobin*, and later his "Whistlecraft" gave Byron a model for the mock-heroic style of *Beppo* and *Don Juan*.
1 This is a curious note. The handwriting at the bottom seems to be that of Claire Clairmont. It must have been written about the time that she was besieging Byron and thrusting herself upon him when he was making preparations to go abroad. This would seem to justify the statement in one of her early letters: ". . . I am quite often surprised at your gentleness and kindness, and feel most entirely grateful."

Dear H[obhouse?]—All true to the letter—[Berger?][1] being drunk can't attest—I sent you a letter this morning—which read—

yrs. ever

B

[TO JOHN MURRAY (*a*)] *April 2d. 1816*

Dear Sir—I send back the catalogue—and the proof of the "Sketch"[.] I doubt about "*weltering*" but the dictionary should decide—look at it—we say "weltering in blood"—but do not they also use "weltering in the wind" "weltering on a gibbet"—there is no dictionary so look or ask.—In the mean time I have put "festering" which perhaps in any case is the best word of the two—Shakespeare has it often—& I do not think it too strong for the figure in this thing.

yrs. &c. &c.

B

P.S.—Be *quick.*——

[TO JOHN MURRAY (*b*)] *April 2d. 1816*

You will think me a great bore—but I have one alteration to make where there is an ambiguity—the second of the two last lines of the second paragraph must run thus

"Foe to all Vice—yet hardly Virtue's friend—
For Virtue pardons those she would amend.[1]

pray attend to this—and excuse all this trouble from

yrs. very truly

BYRON

[TO JOHN MURRAY (*c*)] *April 2d. 1816*

Look to your *printer*—and don't let him make the same blunders over again—I have corrected hastily—and if you can keep him

---

[1] Berger was a Swiss whom Byron took as a servant and guide before he left England, and who was with him during the summer of 1816, accompanying him on his tour with Hobhouse in September and apparently going with him as far as Venice. See Dec. 19, 1816, to Hobhouse, note 8.

[1] *A Sketch*, lines 35–36.

correct—you may strike off the *50.*——*Number the lines.*——
Recollect—it is *"blight"* & not *light* twice over.——Let me see you
when you can as I have something to say—

yrs. very truly

B

I am not sure whether I shall not print the "fare thee well" with
these—as a relief to the shade—what think you?—

[TO JOHN CAM HOBHOUSE]   *April 2d. 1816*

Dear H—It is not only convenient but very agreeable.—Hunt dines
with me—so pray be up by *four* at furthest—as he dines early to return
to Hampstead.—

ever yrs most truly

B

[TO AUGUSTA LEIGH]   *April 3d. 1816*

Dearest A—As Lady B[yron] is much better—you must write
immediately about the trustees and request as a personal favour to me
that *Doyle*[1] be *not* nominated one for the reasons I gave & am prepared
to give.—I do not say this as an excuse to make impediments—as I am
prepared to sign the articles in any case—but I beg to have this request
urged—& *now* urged—it is very odd you have had no answer by Mr.
W[ilmot].[2]

yrs. very truly

B

[TO LADY BYRON]   [*April 3, 1816*]

[Enclosing Annabella Milbanke's letter of November 8, 1814, with
those comments:]
[Annabella had written: "I shall be too happy—there will be no
reverse whilst you love me there cannot." Byron underscored "there

---

[1] A friend of the Noels and of Annabella, Col. Francis Hastings Doyle acted as
a chief adviser to them in the separation negotiations. His sister Selina Doyle was
one of Annabella's confidantes during the period.

[2] See March 11, 1816, to Wilmot, note 1.

will be no reverse" and commented: "Prediction fulfilled February—1816.—"]

[At the end of the letter Byron wrote]:

"Or non tu sai com' è fátta la dónna?

——————————

——————————

Avviluppa promésse—giuramenti;
Che tutti spargon poí per l'aria i vénti.—"

[TO SELINA DOYLE[1]]   *April 6th. 1816*

Ld. Byron has this morning found the enclosed papers—which he presumes that Lady Byron had forgotten to take with her.—They appear to be letters addressed to Miss Doyle—to whom Ld. B[yron] now forwards them & hopes that they will be found complete as she left them:—they were lying in an open drawer.—

[TO JOHN MURRAY]   *April 6th. 1816*

Dear Sir/—I beg to be understood about the books.—You took them at a fair valuation—& whatever little profit there may be on the sale is yours[1]—& yours it must remain—for by God—I can have nothing to do with it—such a thing would be a sort of swindling—more particularly with an account still owing to you.—So there's an end of that matter——besides you bought many of the dearest bargains yourself.——Your bill for these is due on the 12th.—& the duplicate of it—I shall put in the fire when I see you on Monday.——With regard to the account—perhaps you will let it stand over for the present—& I will not allow it to remain longer than I can help—as I have some hopes of being able to put my affairs in a train for liquidation.—

yrs. very truly
B

[TO LADY BYRON]   *April 10th. 1816[1]*

I have received a letter sealed with one of your seals & apparently written under your sanction—signed "M.A.Clermont":—with it's

[1] See April 3, 1816, to Augusta Leigh, note 1.
[1] See March 6, 1816, to Murray, note 2.
[1] Hobhouse says that Byron's friends advised him not to send this letter (see Broughton, *Recollections*, Vol. II, page 328). But there is a copy of the letter at John Murray's in Lady Byron's handwriting.

contents you are probably acquainted as they must have arisen from a communication from me to yourself in which that person is mentioned —& which it appears you have imparted to her—*recently* I presume— as the interval which has elapsed since I wrote to you enclosing Ld. Holland's & other letters—has been nearly a fortnight.—as well as I can remember.—With yourself or your relatives I choose to communicate:—it is to you that I address what I have to say on that subject.—Enclosed is an extract from Rood's[2] deposition or examination—or whatever it is technically to be called:—from this it will appear that Mrs. C[lermont] did misstate to Lady Noel what Mrs. R. had said—or rather attributed to Mrs. R words which she did not say—but which Mrs. Cl[ermo]nt *herself* had used:—words of doubled falsehood—false as attributed to Mrs. R.—false in point of fact whoever asserted them.—You—Lady Byron—know——& I know— that you never were in "peril of your life" from me—that in the extremest withering of mind which distemper of body—distress of circumstance—and exasperation of stimulus singly or united struck through me—you never thought so—never were so:—no violence was ever even contemplated by me—from the first day of our connection to that of your desertion—towards *you* nor anyone near to you—except myself—& when I look on what is around us—on what we were—on what we are—and live—I feel that I am neither what I have been—nor what I should be to endure it.——Of the woman alluded to—you recollect that she came into this house uninvited by me—that she was neither relative—nor domestic—nor had any business here—except what appears to have been the business of her life.——But she was *your* guest—& as such treated by me with every attention & proper consideration:—she was *your* stranger—and I made her our inmate—she came as a guest—she remained as a spy— she departed as an informer—& reappeared as an evidence—if false— she belied— if true—she betrayed me——the worst of treacheries—a "bread and salt traitress" she ate & drank & slept & awoke to sting me.——The curse of my Soul light upon her & hers forever!—may my Spirit be deep upon her in her life—& in her death—may her thirst be unquenchable—& her wretchedness irrevocable—may she see *herself* only & eternally[3]—may the fulfilment of her wishes become the destruction of her hopes—may she dwell in the darkness of her own

---

[2] Ann Rood was Annabella's maid. She married Byron's valet William Fletcher and was apparently loyal to Byron, for she made a deposition to aid him in case the matters came to court.

[3] The manuscript ends here. The rest is from a copy at John Murray's.

heart & shudder—now & for existence.———Her last food will be the bread of her enemies.———I have said it.———To you dearest Bell—I am as ever

very truly
BYRON

[TO MARGARET MERCER ELPHINSTONE] *April 11th. 1816*

Dear Miss Mercer/—I thank you truly for yr. kind acceptance of my memorial[1]—more particularly as I felt a little apprehensive that I was taking a liberty of which you might disapprove.———A more useless friend you could not have—but still a very sincere and by no means a new one—although from circumstances you never knew—(nor would it have pleased you to know)—how much.—These having long ceased to exist—I breathe more freely on this point—because *now* no motive can be attributed to me with regard to you of a selfish nature—at least I hope not.———I know not why I venture to talk thus—unless it be— that the time is come—when whatever I may say—can not be of importance enough to give offence—& that neither my vanity nor my wishes ever induced me at any time to suppose that I could by any chance have become more to you than I now am.———This may account to you for that which—however little worth accounting for— must otherwise appear inexplicable in our former acquaintance—I mean—those "intermittents" at which you used to laugh—as I did too—although they caused me many a serious reflection.———But this is foolish—perhaps improper———yet it is—or rather—was the truth —and has been a silent one while it could have been supposed to proceed from hope or presumption:—I am now as far removed from both by irrevocable circumstances as I always was by my own opinion & by yours—& I soon shall be still further if further be possible—by distance.———I cannot conclude without wishing you a much happier destiny—not than *mine is*—for that is nothing—but than mine ever could have been—with a little common sense & prudence on my

---

[1] The Countess Guiccioli (*My Recollections of Lord Byron*, p. 184) says that Byron gave a book to Scrope Davies at Dover as he was leaving England to be delivered to Miss Mercer Elphinstone with this message: "Tell her that had I been fortunate enough to marry a woman like her, I should not now be obliged to exile myself from my country." But she probably garbled the account. This "memorial" was probably delivered to her soon after she had been kind to him at Lady Jersey's ball, when all the other ladies cut him and Augusta. See Hazlitt's account of this in his *Conversations of James Northcote*, No. 15.

part:———no one else has been to blame—it may seem superfluous to wish *you* all this—& it would be so if our happiness always depended on ourselves—but it does not—a truth which I fear I have taught rather than learned however unintentionally.—

ever most truly yrs.
BYRON

P.S.—This letter was intended as an answer to your note—which however required none—will you excuse it for the sake of the *paper* on which it is written? it is part of the spoils of Malmaison & the imperial bureau[2]—(as it was told me) and for this reason you will perhaps have the kindness to accept the few sheets of it which accompany this—their stamp is the Eagle.—Adieu——

[TO JOHN HANSON]   *Sunday.—14 Apl. 1816*

Dear Sir/—The sooner the deed is ready for signature the better[1]— I shall be at home on any afternoon at three to sign it.——Wharton has written to me to request the naming of a day.—Mr. Hobhouse has written to you—merely to enter on record *his* opinion as to the *meaning* of the paper—which he drew up—but of course I abide by the Solicitor General's present pronunciation upon it.——Pray let us finish this as soon as need be—& believe me

yrs. very truly
BYRON

P.S.—I want Lady B[yron]'s letter from Kirkby—*the letter*[2]—*before* this business—

[TO SAMUEL ROGERS]   *[April 14, 1816?]*

My sister is now with me, and leaves town tomorrow; we shall not meet again for some time, at all events—if ever; and, under these circumstances, I trust to stand excused to you and Mr. Sheridan for being unable to wait upon him this evening.

---

[2] This was probably one of the relics that Hobhouse brought back from Paris.
[1] The deed of separation, which Byron finally signed on April 21, 1816.
[2] This was the playful letter beginning "Dearest Duck", giving no indication of an impending separation.

"More last words"—not many—and such as you will attend to—answer I do not expect—nor does it import—but you will hear me.——I have just parted from Augusta—almost the last being you had left me to part with—& the only unshattered tie of my existence—wherever I may go—& I am going far—you & I can never meet again in this world—nor in the next—let this content or atone.—If any accident occurs to me—be kind to *her*.——if she is then nothing—to her children:——some time ago—I informed you that with the knowledge that any child of ours was already provided for by other & better means—I had made my will in favour of her & her children—as prior to my marriage:—this was not done in prejudice to you for we had not then differed—& even this is useless during your life by the settlements—I say therefore—be kind to her & hers—for never has she acted or spoken otherwise towards you—she has ever been your friend—this may seem valueless to one who has now so many:——be kind to her—however—& recollect that though it may be advantage to you to have lost your husband—it is sorrow to her to have the waters now—or the earth hereafter—between her & her brother.—She is gone—I need hardly add that of this request she knows nothing—your late compliances have not been so extensive—as to render this an encroachment:—I repeat it—(for deep resentments have but *half* recollections) that you once did promise me thus much—do not forget it—nor deem it cancelled it was not a vow.——Mr. Wharton has sent me a letter with a question—& two pieces of intelligence—to the question I answer that the carriage is yours—& as it has only carried us to Halnaby—& London—& you to Kirkby—I hope it will take you many a more propitious journey.——The receipts can remain—unless troublesome, if so—they can be sent to Augusta—& through her I would also hear of my little daughter—my address will be left for Mrs. Leigh.—The ring is of no lapidary value—but it contains the hair of a king and an ancestor—which I should wish to preserve to Miss Byron.—To a subsequent letter of Mr. Wharton's I have to reply that it is the "law's delay" not mine—& that when he & Mr. H[anson] have adjusted the tenor of the bond—I am ready to sign,

yrs. ever very truly
BYRON

3 vol—of Milton's prose works 1 vol. of Swift—left at Seaham—to be sent to Mr. Murray

The Annexed Comedy sent to me by Mr. Raymond[1] appears . . . a good acting Play, & as such I would recommend it to the other gentlemen of the [Drury] L[ane] Committee.

[TO AUGUSTA LEIGH]   *April 15th. 1816*

Dearest A—Enclosed is a letter from George—*who* is "Dr. Middleton"[1] & what is all this about him &c.?—G[eorge]'s affairs or mine?— —I trust you got home *safe*—& are well—I am sadly without you—but I won't complain—I will write more soon—ever thine—dearest A

most truly

B

turn over—

P.S.—I can't bear to send you a short letter—& my heart is too full for a long one— —don't think me unkind or ungrateful—dearest A— —& tell me how is Georgey & *Do*—& you & *tip*[2]—& all the *tips* on four *legs* or *two*—ever & again—& for ever

thine

"P.P. Clerk of this parish"[3]

[TO JOHN MURRAY]   *April 15th. 1816*

Dear Sir/—I wished to have seen you to *scold you*—really you must not send anything of mine to Lady C[aroline] L[amb]—I have often sufficiently warned you on this topic—you do not know what mischief you do by this.— —Of the copies of late things written by me—I wish more particularly the *last* not to be circulated—at present—(you know

---

[1] Stage manager of Drury Lane Theatre.

[1] Unidentified.

[2] Georgiana was Augusta's oldest child, Elizabeth Medora (Do) her fourth, and Tip was her dog.

[3] A playful signature which Byron used on occasion, taken from Pope's *Memoirs of P. P., Clerk of this Parish*, a supposed satire on Bishop Burnet's *History of My Own Times*.

which I mean—those to A[ugusta])[1] & there was a short epigram some time ago—of which I trust you have given no copies as it never was intended for publication at all.———

ever yrs.

B

[TO JAMES WEDDERBURN WEBSTER]　　　　　*April 16th. 1816*

Dear Webster/—I have no desire to dun or to distress you—but I was surprized at your silence—more especially hearing that you were purchasing lands & tenements.—Hearing this I naturally thought you were in a state of disentanglement—& my own affairs being at present in a very poetical posture—I stated to you my expectation that you would take steps towards the payment—for which I can hardly be considered as very importunate—as it is now the third year without allusion to the subject[1]—nor had it been made now—were I not about to leave England—& anxious to settle my affairs previously.———I now write to mention—that it being inconvenient to you—I will say no more on the subject—you must be aware that it could be no pleasure to me to receive that which it would be disturbing to you to pay:—& as I lent it with a view to prevent difficulties I shall not now render any little advantage it may have been to you useless by plunging you into new ones.—I should & shall of course neither take nor authorize any measure that may be disagreeable to you.—Kinnaird (the Hon[oura]ble D[ougla]s) is kind enough to act for me while I am abroad & I will direct him not to molest you:—I write in the greatest hurry with packages—passports—&c.—but shall not be off for a day or two.—

ever yrs. most truly

BYRON

[TO ISAAC NATHAN]

Piccadilly, Tuesday Evening [April 16 or 23? 1816]

My dear Nathan,—I have to acknowledge the receipt of your very

---

[1] Caroline Lamb wrote to Byron in an undated letter, probably April, 1816, of Murray's showing her "some beautiful verses of yours", and added "I do implore you for God sake not to publish them . . . Of course, I cannot say to Murray what I think of those verses, but to you, to you alone, I will say I think they will prove your ruin." (*LJ*, II, 450) These were the "Stanzas to Augusta" beginning: "When all around grew drear and dark." Caroline was aware of the rumours going around concerning Byron and his sister.

[1] Byron had made a loan of £1,000 to Webster in 1813. See Oct. 10, 1813, to Hanson (*b*) (Vol. 3, p. 138).

seasonable bequest, which I duly appreciate; the unleavened bread shall certainly accompany me in my pilgrimage; and, with a full reliance on their efficacy, the *Motsas* shall be to me a charm against the destroying Angel wherever I may sojourn; his serene highness, however will, I hope, be polite enough to keep at a desirable distance from my person, without the necessity of besmearing my *door posts or upper lintels* with the blood of any animal. With many thanks for your kind attention, believe me, My dear Nathan,

Yours very truly,
BYRON

[TO JOHN HANSON]   *April 17th. 1816*

Dear Sir/—It is a question for you & Mr. Wharton & the Solicitor General—settle it amongst you—I am ready to sign[1]—only let it be soon—for I go on Sunday——pray—conclude—& believe me,

ever yrs. very truly,
BYRON

P.S.—I am sorry to hear you have been ill——when you and Wharton are ready—I am at home every day till 4 in the afternoon.— —Col. Doyle—might as well have repeated the *whole* as well as "part" of Mr. H[obhouse]'s letter—it contained (I believe for I did not see it) a repetition of Mr. H[obhouse]'s interpretation of the paper when drawn up.——

[TO AUGUSTA LEIGH]   *April 22d. 1816*

My own Sweet Sis—The deeds are signed—so that is over.—All I have now to beg or desire on the subject is—that you will never mention nor allude to Lady Byron's name again in any shape—or on any occasion—except indispensable business.—Of the child you will inform me & write about poor little dear *Da*[1]—& see it whenever you can.—I am all in the *hurries*—we set off tomorrow—but I will write from Dover.—My own dearest—kindest—best Sis—

ever & ever thine
B

---

[1] The deed of separation was finally signed by Byron on April 21, 1816 (Sunday), and he left London for Dover on the 23rd (Tuesday).
[1] His daughter Ada.

Dear Sir/—Denen[?] has distrained on the effects left at the house in Piccadilly terrace for the half year's rent:—I know not if this be lawful *without* a *previous action*—This *you* know best—if it be—there is one trunk of wood with papers—letters &c.—also some *shoes*—and another thing or two which I could wish redeemed from the wreck.——They have seized all the *servants' things* Fletcher's & his wife's &c.—I hope you will see to these poor creatures having *their* property secured—as for *mine* it must be sold. I wish Mr. Hobhouse to confer with you upon it.——Many thanks for yr. good wishes:——I sail tonight for Ostend—my address had best be (for the present)—A—Milord Byron—Poste—Restante—*à Genève.*—I hope that you will not forget —to seize an early opportunity of bringing Rochdale & Newstead to the hammer—or private contract.——I wish you for yourself & family every possible good—& beg my remembrances to all— particularly Lady P[ortsmout]h & Charles——I am with great sincerity

yrs. very affectly.

BYRON

P.S.—Send me some news of my *child*—every now & then—I beg as a favour not to hear a word of the rest of *that branch* of the family.— Of course I do not mean my *own* immediate relatives.——

My dearest Augusta,—We sail tonight for Ostend[1], and I seize this moment to say two or three words.

I met last night with an old Schoolfellow (Wildman[2] by name), a Waterloo Aid-de-camp of Lord Uxbridge's. He tells me poor Fred. Howard[3] was *not* mangled, nor in the hands of the French; he was shot through the body charging a party of infantry, and died (*not* on the field) half an hour afterwards at some house not far off, and in no great pain.

I thought this might make his friends easier, as they had heard that

---

[1] See Feb. 7, 1816, to [?].

[1] The wind was contrary and he spent the night at the Ship Inn and sailed the next morning, April 25th.

[2] Thomas Wildman, a classmate of Byron at Harrow, later (in 1818) bought Newstead Abbey.

[3] Frederick Howard, youngest son of Lord Carlisle, was killed at the battle of Waterloo.

he was a sufferer by falling into the enemy's hands. Capt. Wildman was near him at the time, and I believe saw him again shortly before his death, and after his wound.

We left town early yesterday morning, that is, *rose* early and *set* off late, after all the usual bustle and confusion.

Address to me—à Genève *Poste Restante*, and (when you hear) tell me how little *Da* is, and . . .

[The rest of the letter is missing]

[TO JOHN CAM HOBHOUSE]   *Ostend.—April 27th. [26th.?] 1816*[1]

My dear Hobhouse—We got in last night very well—though it blew freshly & contrary all the way—but we tacked & tided in about midnight.—All are—and every thing is—landed—& tonight we design for Ghent.—As a veteran I stomached the sea pretty well—till a damned "Merchant of Bruges" capsized his breakfast close by me— & made me sick by contagion:—but I soon got well—& we were landed at least ten hours sooner than expected—and our Inn (the *"Cure* imperial" as Fletcher calls it—) furnished us with beds & a "flaggon of Rhenish"—which by the blessing of Scrope's absence— the only blessing his absence could confer—was not indulged in to the extent of the "light wine" of our parting potations.——Don't forget the Cundums—and will you tell Manton that he has put a very bad brush into the pistol case—& to send me *two* good new ones by your servant (when you come) for cleaning the *locks* of my pistols.——*You* are in town by this time—having dined at Canterbury or Sitting-bourne—pitying us "poor mariners that sail upon the seas"—we are in the agonies of furnishing Berger with [stivilli?][2] to march en Courier before us—& the last I saw of Fletcher was with two eggs in his mouth.——The sick Dutchman set off per packet for Bruges this morning:——the custom house was very polite—and all things very fair—I don't know why you vituperated Ostend:—it seems a very tolerable town—better than Dover—better than the Spanish & Portuguese ordinary towns—or any of our Oriental—at least in the Caravansera department.—I shall lay to for you at Geneva[3]——you have perhaps examined my late Piccadilly premises—and I hope

---

[1] Byron left Dover on the morning of April 25 and supposedly arrived in Ostend about midnight. According to Polidori, they left Ostend at 3 o'clock on the 26th.
[2] Stivale? (boots).
[3] Hobhouse expected to join Byron shortly in Geneva, but he was delayed and did not arrive there until August 26.

recovered your personals.——My best luck—or rather his own—to Scrope—all remembrances to Kinnaird & the rest of "us youth" and ever

yrs. most truly
BYRON

P.S.—If you hear anything of my little daughter tell it me—good I hope.—As to the rest—as the Irishman said in the Dublin Theatre when Wellesley Pole[4] was there—"Here's three times three for Lord Wellington and *Silence* for the rest of the family."—Tell Scrope that Mr. Levi did us about the Ducats—by *ninepence* each—I will thrash him as I come back.—Mind you write—& fix a time for coming—or'Sdeath and Pin money!—I shall be very indignant.—

[TO JOHN CAM HOBHOUSE]   *Bruxelles—May 1st. 1816*

My dear H[obhous]e—You will be surprized that we are not more "en avant" and so am I—but Mr. Baxter's[1] wheels and springs have not done their duty—for which I beg that you will abuse him like a pickpocket (that is—*He*—the said *Baxter* being the *pickpocket*) and say that I expect a deduction—having been obliged to come out of the way to this place—which was not in my route—for repairs—which however I hope to have accomplished so as to put us in motion in a day or two.——We passed through Ghent—Antwerp—and Mechlin —& thence diverged here—having seen all the sights—pictures— docks—basins—& having climbed up steeples &c. & so forth——the first thing—after the flatness & fertility of the country which struck me—was the beauty of the towns—Bruges first—where you may tell Douglas Kinnaird—on entering at Sunset—I overtook a crew of beggarly looking gentlemen not unlike Oxberry[2]—headed by a Monarch with a Staff the very facsimile of King Clause in the said D[ouglas] K[innaird]'s revived drama.——We lost our way in the dark—or rather twilight—not far from Ghent—by the stupidity of the postilion (*one* only by the way to 4 horses) which produced an alarm of intended robbery among the uninitiated—whom I could not convince —that four or five well-armed people were not immediately to be

---

4 Wellesley Pole was a wastrel nephew of the Duke of Wellington.

1 Byron had ordered from Baxter the coachmaker a huge Napoleonic travelling coach before he left England at a cost of £500 (still unpaid).

2 William Oxberry (1784–1824) was an actor who had made his debut at Covent Garden and was for some time manager of the Olympic Theatre. In 1816 he played the part of Moses in Sheridan's *School for Scandal* at Drury Lane.

plundered and anatomized by a single person fortified with a horse-whip to be sure—but nevertheless a little encumbered with large jack boots—and a tight jacket that did not fit him—The way was found again without loss of life or limb:——I thought the learned Fletcher at least would have known better after our Turkish expeditions—and defiles—and banditti—& guards &c. &c. than to have been so valourously alert without at least a better pretext for his superfluous courage. I don't mean to say that they were *frightened* but they were vastly suspicious without any cause.—At Ghent we stared at pictures —& climbed up a steeple 450 steps in altitude—from which I had a good view & notion of these "paese bassi."——Next day we broke down—by a damned wheel (on which Baxter should be broken) pertinaciously refusing it's stipulated rotation—this becalmed us at Lo-Kristi—(2 leagues from Ghent)—& obliged us to return for repairs—At Lo Kristi I came to anchor in the house of a Flemish Blacksmith (who was ill of a fever for which Dr. Dori[3] physicked him —I dare say he is dead by now) and saw somewhat of Lo-Kristi— Low-country—low life—which regaled us much—besides it being a Sunday—all the world were in their way to Mass—& I had the pleasure of seeing a number of very ordinary women in extraordinary garments:—we found the "Contadini" however very goodnatured & obliging though not at all useful.——At Antwerp we pictured— churched—and steepled again—but the principal Street and *bason* pleased me most—poor dear Bonaparte!!!—and the foundries &c.— as for Rubens—I was glad to see his tomb on account of that ridiculous description (in Smollet's P[eregrine] Pickle) of Pallet's absurdity at his monument—but as for his works—and his superb "tableaux"—he seems to me (who by the way know nothing of the matter) the most glaring—flaring—staring—harlotry imposter that ever passed a trick upon the senses of mankind—it is not nature—it is not art—with the exception of some linen (which hangs over the cross in one of his pictures) which to do it justice looked like a very handsome table cloth —I never saw such an assemblage of florid night-mares as his canvas contains—his portraits seem clothed in pulpit cushions.——On the way to Mechlin—a wheel—& a *spring* too gave way—that is—the one went—& the other would not go—so we came off here to get into dock—I hope we shall sail shortly.——On to Geneva.—Will you have the goodness—to get at my account at Hoares—(my bankers) I believe there must be a balance in my favour—as I did not draw a

[3] Dr. John William Polidori, whom Byron had hired as a personal physician. See Appendix IV.

great deal previously to going:—whatever there may be over the two thousand five hundred—they can send by you to me in a further credit when you come out:—I wish you to enquire (for fear any tricks might be played with my drafts) my bankers books left with you— will show you exactly what I have drawn—and you can let them have the book to make out the remainder of the account. All I have to urge to Hanson—or to our friend Douglas K[innaird]—is to *sell* if possible. ——All kind things to Scrope—and the rest—

ever yrs. most truly & obligedly
B

P.S.—If you hear of my child—let me know any good of her health —& well doing.—Will you bring out πασανιας[4] (Taylor's ditto) when you come—I shall bring to for you at Geneva—don't forget to urge Scrope into our crew—we will buy females and found a colony— provided Scrope does not find those ossified barriers to "the fore-fended place"—which cost him such a siege at Brighthelmstone— write at your leisure—or "ipse veni".——

[TO AUGUSTA LEIGH]   *Bruxelles—May 1st. 1816*

My Heart——We are detained here for some petty carriage re-pairs—having come out of our way to the Rhine on purpose—after passing through Ghent—Antwerp—and Mechlin.——I have written to you twice—once from Ostend—and again from Ghent—I hope most truly that you will receive my letters—not as important in themselves—but because you wish it—& so do I.—It would be difficult for me to write anything amusing—this country has been so frequently described—& has so little for description—though a good deal for observation—that I know not what to say of it—& one don't like talking only of oneself.—We saw at Antwerp the famous basons of Bonaparte for his navy—which are very superb—as all his under-takings were—& as for churches—& pictures—I have stared at them till my brains are like a guide-book:—the last (though it is heresy to say so) don't please me at all—I think Rubens a very great dauber— and prefer Vandyke a hundred times over—(but then I know nothing about the matter) Rubens' women have all red gowns and red shoulders—to say nothing of necks—of which they are more liberal than charming—it may all be very fine—and I suppose it must be

---

4 Pausanias's *Description of Greece* was one of the books listed as among Byron's possessions when he died in Missolonghi.

Art—for—I'll swear—'tis not Nature.——As the low Countries did not make part of my plan (except as a route) I feel a little anxious to get out of them—level roads don't suit me—as thou knowest—it must be up hill or down —& then I am more au fait.—Imagine to yourself a succession of avenues with a Dutch Spire at the end of each—and you see the road;—an accompaniment of highly cultivated farms on each side intersected with small canals or ditches—and sprinkled with very neat & clean cottages—a village every two miles—and you see the country——not a rise from Ostend to Antwerp—a molehill would make the inhabitants think that the Alps had come here on a visit—it is a perpetuity of plain & an eternity of *pavement* (on the *road*) but it is a country of great apparent comfort—and of singular though *tame* beauty—and were it not out of my way—I should like to survey it less cursorily.—The towns are wonderfully fine.——The approach to Brussels is beautiful—and there is a fine palace to the right in coming¹ . . . .

[TO JOHN CAM HOBHOUSE]   *Brussels—May 2d. 1816*

My dear H[obhous]e—I sent you a long epistle yesterday from this place—and merely write today to request you to supply an omission of mine—by giving a character (for me & from me) to my late Coachman & footman—*Everett* & *Bayman* by name—they lived with me more than four years & discharged their duties honestly & faithfully— the Coachman came a few months before the other—both left me at the same time—they were discharged with the rest of my establishment on my leaving England.——I believe that I mentioned this to Douglas K[innaird]—(to whom & to Mrs. K. I beg my remembrances) & referred the servants to him in my absence to give their characters— I can only say—that I believe they both deserve very good ones—& I hope they will get places—or at any rate not be left out of them owing to my forgetfulness in not having written out a "charta of bon Servizio"—as the Sieur Demetrio used to break it into English.—Will you have the goodness to excuse all this trouble from

yrs. ever—
BYRON

P.S.—For particulars of journey &c. I refer you to my yesterday's epistle—today all the same—& very well—I have written to you twice: once from Ostend—once from hence—*this scrawl* is the third—

¹ The manuscript ends here at the end of the page. One or more pages seem to be missing.

but that's nothing.—We hope to set out for Switzerland in a day or two. Don't be long for I should [like] to get to Rome or Venice before the Autumn.———

My dear Hobhouse/—We are this far by the Rhenish route on our way to Switzerland—where I shall wait to hear of your intentions as to junction before I go to Italy.———I have written to you three times— and mention the number—in case of any non-arrival of epistles.—We were obliged to diverge from Anvers & Mechlin to Brussels—for some wheel repairs—& in course seized the opportunity to visit Mont St. Jean &c. where I had a gallop over the field on a Cossac horse (left by some of the Don gentlemen at Brussels) and after a tolerably minute investigation—returned by Soignies—having purchased a quantity of helmets sabres &c all of which are consigned to the care of a Mr. Gordon at B[russe]ls (an old acquaintance) who desired to forward them to Mr. Murray—in whose keeping I hope to find them safe some day or other.———Our route by the Rhine has been beautiful—& much surpassing my expectation—though very much answering in it's outlines to my previous conceptions.———The Plain at Waterloo is a fine one—but not much after Marathon & Troy—Cheronea—& Platea.———Perhaps there is something of prejudice in this—but I detest the cause & the victors—& the victory—including Blucher & the Bourbons.———From Bonn to Coblenz—& Coblenz again to Bingen & Mayence—nothing can exceed the prospects at every point —not even—any of the old scenes—though this is in a different style: —what it most reminded me of were parts of Cintra—& the valley which leads from Delvinachi—by Libochabo and Argyrocastro (on the opposite mountains) to Tepaleni—the last resemblance struck even the learned Fletcher—who seems to thrive upon his present expedition & is full of comparisons & preferences of the present to the last— particularly in the articles of provision & Caravanseras.———Poor Polidori is devilish ill—I do not know with what—nor does he—but he seems to have a slight constitution—& is seriously laid up—if he does not get well soon—he will be totally unfit for travelling—his com- plaints are headaches & feverishness:—all the rest are well—for the present—nor has he had any patients except a Belgian Blacksmith (at Lo Kristi a village where our wheels stuck) and himself.—At Cologne I had a ludicrous adventure—the host of our hotel mistook a German Chambermaid—whose red cheeks & white teeth had made me venture upon her carnally—for his wife—& stood swearing at the door like a Squadron of Cavalry—to the amusement of consternation of all his audience—till the mystery was developed by his wife walking out of her own room—& the girl out of mine.—We have seen all the sights—churches & so forth—& at Coblentz crossed the Rhine—and scrambled up the fortress of Ehrenbreitstein now a ruin—we also saw on the road the sepulchres—& monuments of Generals Marceau & Hoche & went up to examine them—they are simple & striking—but now much neglected if not to say defaced by the change of times & this cursed after-crop of rectilignes & legitimacy.—At Manheim we crossed the Rhine & keep on this side to avoid the French segment of Territory at Strasburg—as we have not French passports—& no desire to view a degraded country—& oppressed people.—This town (a very pretty one) is the seat of the court of the Grand Duke of Baden:—tomorrow I mean to proceed (if Polidori is well enough) on our journey.—At Geneva I expect to hear from you—tell me of Scrope and his intentions—and of all or any things or persons—saving and except *one* subject—which I particularly beg never to have mentioned again—unless as far as regards my *child*—& my *child only*.——If Scrope comes out—tell him there are some "light wines" which will bring to his recollection "the day of Pentecost" & other branches of his vinous thirty nine articles.—I have solaced myself moderately with such "flaggons of Rhenish" as have fallen in my way—but without our Yorick—they are nothing.—I hope your book of letters[1] is not slack in sale—and I can't see why Ridgway should not pay "a few paouands" for the 2d. Edition unless it be that I did not pay him his bill & that he thinks therefore *you* should.——I trust that you will give *Spooney* a jog as to selling & so forth—& tell my Potestas (Kinnaird) to come the committee over him.—I suppose poor K[innaird] will be devilishly bothered with his Drury Lane speech this year—how does Mathurin's play go on —or rather go off—of course the prologue has fallen to your lot—& the Comedy eh?—I hope you executed the ten thousand petty commissions I saddled you withal——pray remember me to all the remembering—& not less to the superb Murray—who is now enjoying inglorious ease at his green table—& wishing for somebody to keep him in hot water.——Wishing you all prosperity—I am ever

yrs. most truly
BYRON

---

[1] Hobhouse had published in 1815 his *Letters by an Englishman Resident at Paris during the Last Reign of Napoleon* (2 vols.).

My dear Hobhouse/—*No* letter from *you*—is this miscarriage by the way?—or are you coming?—Never mind which—as there is no remedy —but I shall wait here till I hear from you:—All the other epistles I expected have arrived.—There is an epistle from Hoares who tell me they have given in an account to you of my banking concerns:—I hope you saw or will see (as I believe I locked up my draft book in my desk & you cannot get to it) the *drafts* at Hoares—which I drew immediately previous to my departure—as the holders might possibly take advantage of my absence to alter or play tricks with them—they being Servants or tradesmen—& not much used to resist temptation— I put this as a possibility—which it is best to ascertain and avoid—& you & I know of human nature & so forth—not to trust to anything but one's optics & *these only* in very *clear* weather.——Hoares will shew you them—as they always keep them in case of accidents—& it would be a satisfaction to me to know you have looked over them—as I could not do so myself——Perhaps you have written to me by way of France—& *there* letters are rather more carefully investigated than delivered.——I wrote to you three times from Flanders—& once from Bonn—and once from Carlsruhe—the Rhine from Bonn to Mayence is the perfection of *mixed* Beauty;—from Basle to Geneva we were five days—arriving here last night—Nothing has disappointed me on my way or out of it—except not hearing from you—but I trust to see you & the "forefender" Scrope according to compact—and do not like to begin my Alpine scrambles without you.——We went over the site of Aventicum—where there is some beautiful Mosaic of some extent & preservation—a few inscriptions—a column or two *down*—several scattered shafts—& one solitary pillar in the midst of a field—the last of its family—besides extensive traces of wall & amphitheatre.—From Morat I brought away the leg and wing of a Burgundian:—the descendants of the vanquished—when last here in the service of France buried or carried away the greater part of the heap—except what the Swiss had made into *knife-handles*—but there are still a few left—and with some of these relics I made free though for a less sordid purpose.——I do not like boring you with descriptions of what I hope you will see—and shall only say that all my expectations have been gratified—& there are things—not inferior to what we have seen elsewhere—& one or two superior—such as Mont Blanc—& the Rhine.——Polidori has been ill—but is much better—a little experience will make him a very good traveller—if his health can stand it.—In the hope of seeing you soon—I shall scribble no further—I believe the best way is to write frequently & briefly—both on account of *weight*—& the *chance* of letters reaching their destination—*you* must excuse repetitions (as uncertainty induces them) and amongst others the *repetition* of my being

very much & ever yrs.
BYRON

P.S.—Remembrances to all—particularly to Kinn[air]d—Hunt—& Davies.— P.S. I have written to Mrs. Leigh—but pray let her know when you hear—as she will be glad of it.———

[TO JOHN CAM HOBHOUSE]   *Geneva—May 27th. 1816*

My dear Hobhouse—I have written to you several times & merely wish to say that I have not had a line since we parted—from you in return:—but that I shall stay here some time in the expectation of seeing or hearing from you.——I have had an agreeable journey—& no disappointments in point of scenery &c. Mrs. Rawdon[1] is here whom I mean to request to take this part of the way for me—as I doubt the French posts are very negligent—or even interceptive of English letters—even those not of a political aspect—which Heaven knows— mine are not disposed to be.——I see by the French papers that Mathurin's tragedy has been successful—I am truly glad of it—as any one must be who desires to see merit rise in "these costermonger days.".——I have written to you so frequently & fully—that I will not tire you with any further repetitions than that of my being ever truly yrs.

affectly.
B

[TO MRS. RAWDON]   *May 27th. [1816]*

Ld. Byron presents his compliments to Mrs. Rawdon.—He took the liberty of requesting permission to wait upon her for the purpose (after paying his respects) of asking the favour of Mrs. R[awdon] to convey a letter part of the way to England—to a friend of his—Mr. Hobhouse—for the fate of which by the common post (though it contains no politics) he has some apprehension.—If this request is too

---

[1] Byron had met the Rawdons, mother and daughter, in Cheltenham in September, 1812. See Sept. 28, 1812, to Lady Melbourne (Vol. 2, p. 216).

great a presumption on former acquaintance—Ld. B—will of course feel sorry in having made it—& still more so should it appear to occasion the least trouble to Mrs. Rawdon.—Lord Byron hopes that Mrs. & Miss Rawdon are both well.—

[TO PRYCE GORDON]   [*Geneva, June? 1816*]

...I cannot tell you what a treat your gift of Casti[1] has been to me; I have almost got him by heart. I had read his 'Animali Parlanti,' but I think these 'Novelle' much better. I long to go to Venice to see the manners so admirably described....

[TO JOHN CAM HOBHOUSE]   *Evian—June 23d. 1816*

My dear H[obhous]e/—Despite of this date—address as usual to the Genevese Poste—which awaits your answers as I await your arrival— with that of Scrope—whose pocket appears (by your late letter of revolutions at the Union) to have become as "light" as his "wines"— though I suppose on the whole he is still worth at least 50-000 pds— being what is called here a "Millionaire" that is in Francs & such Lilliputian coinage. I have taken a very pretty villa in a vineyard— with the Alps behind—& Mt. Jura and the Lake before—it is called Diodati—from the name of the Proprietor—who is a descendant of the critical & illustrissimi Diodati—and has an agreeable house which he lets at a reasonable rate per season or annum as suits the lessée— when you come out—don't go to an Inn—not even to Secheron—but come on to head-quarters—where I have rooms ready for you—and Scrope—and all "appliances & means to boot".—Bring with you also for me some bottles of *Calcined Magnesia*—a new *Sword cane*—pro-cured by Jackson—he alone knows the sort—(my last tumbled into this lake—) some of Waite's *red* tooth-powder—& tooth-brushes—a Taylor's *Pawrsanias*—and—I forget the other things.—Tell Murray I have a 3d. Canto of Childe Harold finished—it is the longest of the three—being one hundred & eleven Stanzas—I shall send it by the first plausible conveyance.—At the present writing I am on my way on a water-tour round the Lake Leman[1]—and am thus far proceeded

[1] Gordon had given Byron in Brussels the *Novelle Amorose* of Casti.
[1] Although he doesn't mention it, Byron was accompanied by Shelley on this trip, which inspired his *Prisoner of Chillon* and the stanzas on Rousseau in the third canto of *Childe Harold*.

in a pretty open boat which I bought & navigate—it is an English one & was brought lately from Bordeaux—I am on shore for the Night—and have just had a row with the Syndic of this town who wanted my passports which I left at Diodati—not thinking they would be wanted except in grand route—but it seems this is Savoy and the dominion of his Cagliari Majesty whom we saw at his own Opera—in his own city—in 1809—however by dint of references to Geneva—& other corroborations—together with being in a very ill humour—Truth has prevailed—wonderful to relate they actually take one's word for a fact—although it is credible and indubitable.—Tomorrow we go to Meillerei—& Clarens—& Vevey—with Rousseau in hand—to see his scenery—according to his delineation in his Heloise now before me.— The views have hitherto been very fine—but I should conceive less so than those of the remainder of the lake.——All your letters (that is *two*) have arrived—thanks & greetings:—what—& who—the devil is "Glenarvon". I know nothing—nor ever heard of such a person—and what do you mean by a brother in India?—you have none in India—it is *Scrope* who has a brother in India.—my remembrances to Kinnaird— & Mrs. Kinn[air]d—to all & every body—& Hunt in particular—& Scrope—& Mr. Murray—and believe me

yrs ever most truly

B

P.S.—I left the Doctor at Diodati—he sprained his ancle. P.S. Will you particularly remember to bring me a largish bottle of the strongest *Pot Ash*—as before—Mr. Le Man[n] will furnish it—that Child and Childish Dr. Pollydolly contrived to find it broken, or to break it at Carlsruhe—so that I am in a fuss—the Genevese make it badly—it effervesces in the Sulphuric acid, and it ought not—bring me some of a more quiescent character.

[TO JOHN MURRAY]   *Ouchy nr. Lausanne—June 27th. 1816*

Dear Sir—I am thus far (kept by stress of weather) on my way back to Diodati (near Geneva) from a voyage in my boat round the lake—& I enclose you a sprig of *Gibbon's Acacia* & some rose leaves from his garden—which with part of his house I have just seen—you will find honourable mention in his life made of this "Acacia" when he walked out on the night of concluding his history.—The garden—& *summer house* where he composed are neglected—& the last utterly decayed—but they still show it as his "Cabinet" & seem perfectly aware of his memory.—My route—through Flanders—& by the

Rhine to Switzerland was all I expected & more.————I have traversed all Rousseau's ground—with the Heloise before me—& am struck to a degree with the force & accuracy of his descriptions—& the beauty of their reality:—Meillerie—Clarens—& Vevey—& the Chateau de Chillon are places of which I shall say little—because all I could say must fall short of the impressions they stamp.———Three days ago— we were most nearly wrecked in a Squall off Meillerie—& driven to shore—I ran no risk being so near the rocks and a good swimmer— but our party were wet—& incommoded a good deal:—the wind was strong enough to blow down some trees as we found at landing— however all is righted & right—& we are thus far on return.———Dr. Polidori is not here—but at Diodati—left behind in hospital with a sprained ancle acquired in tumbling from a wall—he can't jump.——— I shall be glad to hear you are well—& have received for me certain helms & swords sent from Waterloo—which I rode over with pain & pleasure.———I have finished a third Canto of Childe Harold (consisting of one hundred & seventeen stanzas (longer than either of the two former)—& in some parts—it may be—better—but of course on that *I* cannot determine.—I shall send it by the first safe-looking opportunity.—

ever very truly yrs.

B

[TO DOUGLAS KINNAIRD]   *Diodati—Geneva—July 20th. 1816*

Dear Kinnaird/—I send you—not what you want—but all I can give—and such as it is I give it with good will.[1]———It may be too long & if so—whatever may be cut in speaking—at least let it be published *entire*—as it is written so as not very well to condone curtailment without the sense suffering also.—Let Miss *Somerville*[2]— (& none else) deliver it—if she has *energy* that's the woman I want— I mean for spouting.—I protest against Mrs. Davison[3]—I protest

---

[1] This was Byron's "Monody on the Death of the Right Hon. R. B. Sheridan", written at the request of Douglas Kinnaird to be read at Drury Lane Theatre. Sheridan died on July 7, 1816.

[2] Miss Somerville was a young actress who made her debut at Drury Lane in the part of Imogine in Maturin's *Bertram.*

[3] Maria Rebecca Davison (1780?–1858) had played Lady Teazle and Rosalind at Drury Lane. Contrary to Byron's wish, she did recite his "Monody" at the opening of Drury Lane on Sept. 7, 1816, and played the part of Lady Teazle in Sheridan's *The School for Scandal.* Kinnaird had offered the reading of the Monody to Kean who refused. See Peter J. Manning, "Edmund Kean and Byron's Plays". *Keats-Shelley Journal,* XXI–XXII (1972–1973), 188–206.

against the *temple*—or anything but an Urn on the scene—and above all I protest against the "Comic Muse in Mourning."—If she is *Comic*—she should not be in *Mourning*—if she is in *mourning*—she ought not to be in Mourning—but should she be *comic* & in *mourning* too—the verses & Sheridan's memory (for *that* occasion at least) will go to the devil together.———No—I say an Urn (not a tea urn) and Miss Somerville with a little teaching as to "Energy" I have spiced it with Cayenne all through—except a small infusion of the pathetic at starting.—I send the lines (118 in Number) in a separate sheet by the post—& will send a duplicate in a day or two—for fear of your not receiving this copy in time.—Tragedy—I have none,—an act—a first act of one—I had nearly finished some time before my departure from England—when events occurred which furnished me with so many real passions for time to come—that I had no attention for fictitious ones:— The scenes I had scrawled are thrown with other papers & sketches into one of my trunks now in England—but into which I know not— nor care not—except that I should have been glad to have done anything you wished in my power,—but I have no power nor will to recommence—& surely—*Maturin* is your man—not I:—of what has passed in England I know but little—& have no desire to know more— except that you & any other friends are well. I have written a third Canto of Childe Harold (of 118 Stanzas) and a (not long) poem on the Castle of Chillon—both of which I mean to send to England soon for publication—during which I could wish to ask you to *correct* the *proofs* and arrange with Murray for me:—I merely wait a good opportunity to convey these to your care—if you can afford leisure & patience— perhaps G[eorge] Lamb—or some other good natured fellow would halve it with you—though I have hardly the conscience to ask either them or you.——I have now answered you and arrived at my Sheet's end—with my best remembrances to Mrs. K—(whose silk kerchief is as precious as Othello's) believe me

ever yrs.

ß

[TO DOUGLAS KINNAIRD]   *Diodati nr. Geneva.—July 22d. 1816*

Dear Kinnaird—A few days ago I answered your letter and sent in a separate cover the lines you requested—which—whether they answer the purpose or not—will at least prove my attention to your request— & my respect for the memory of Sheridan.—Perhaps the author's name had better be made secret—at least I should prefer this—for the present.— —I now send you a Duplicate—a corrected & correct one— of the same—to "make assurance double sure" in case the former letter and copy should not arrive.—I fear the postage will be heavy— as the letters are so—but that you must excuse—part I have paid—& would willingly pay the rest—(as I am out of the country of Franking for you) but I can only pay to a certain distance.— —Pray send me a few lines acknowledging the receipt of one—or both of these dispatches—& believe me

yrs. ever most truly
B

P.S.—Miss *Somerville* should be your declaimer.— —I have not put the "Stagepoints" you wot of—because *that* is [a] *trick* & below the subject and unfit for it—we should be as sad & simple as possible.

[TO JOHN MURRAY]   *Diodati—nr. Geneva. July 22d. 1816*

Dear Sir—I wrote to you a few weeks ago—and Dr. P[olidori] received your letter—but ye. packet has not made its appearance nor ye. epistle of which you gave notice therein.—I enclose you an advertisement—which was copied by Dr. P[olidori]—& which appears to be about the most impudent imposition that ever issued from Grub Street.—I need hardly say that I know nothing of all this trash—nor whence it may spring—"Odes to St. Helena—Farewells to England— &c. &c."—and if it can be disavowed—or is worth disavowing you have full authority to do so.—I never wrote nor conceived a line of any thing of the kind—any more than of two other things with which I was saddled—something about "Gaul" and another about "Mrs. La Valette"—and as to the "Lily of France" I should as soon think of celebrating a turnip.— —On the "morning of my Daughter's birth" I had other things to think of than verses—and should never have dreamed of such an invention—till Mr. Johnston and his pamphlet's advertisement broke in upon me with a new light on the Crafts & subtilties of the Demon of printing—or rather publishing.— — I did hope that some succeeding lies would have superseded the thousand and one which were accumulated during last winter—I can forgive whatever may be said of or against me—but not what they make me say or sing for myself—it is enough to answer for what I have written —but it were too much for Job himself to bear what one has not—I suspect that when the Arab Patriarch wished that "his Enemy had written a book"[1] he did not anticipate his own name on the title page.——I feel quite as much bored with this foolery as it deserves—and more than I should be—if I had not a headache.——Of Glenarvon[2]—Madame de Stael told me (ten days ago at Copet) marvellous & grievous things—but I have seen nothing of it but the Motto—which promises amiably "For us & for our tragedy"[3]—if such be the posy what should the ring be? "a name to all succeeding &c."[4]—the generous moment selected for the publication is probably its kindest accompaniment—and truth to say—the time was well chosen,—I have not even a guess at the contents—except for the very vague accounts I have heard—and I know but one thing which a woman can say to the purpose on such occasions and that she might as well for her own sake keep to herself—which by the way they very rarely can—that old reproach against their admirers of "kiss and tell" bad as it is—is surely somewhat less than ———and *publish*.—I ought to be ashamed of the Egotism of this letter—it is not my fault altogether—and I shall be but too happy to drop the subject when others will allow me.—I am in tolerable plight—and in my last letters told you what I had done in the way of all rhyme—I trust that you prosper—and that your authors are in good condition—I should suppose your Stud has received some increase—by what I hear—Bertram[5] must be a good horse—does he run next meeting? and does the Quarterly cover still at so much the mare and the groom? I hope you will beat the Row—

yrs. alway & [truly?]

[TO SAMUEL ROGERS]   *Diodati—nr. Geneva July 29th. 1816*

Dear Rogers—Do you recollect a book? Mathison's letters[1]—which you lent me—which I have still—& yet hope to return to your

---

[1] "Oh . . . that mine adversary had written a book." *Job*, XXXI: 35.

[2] *Glenarvon*, Lady Caroline Lamb's novel, first appeared in June, shortly after Byron left England. The hero–villain, Glenarvon, is obviously modelled on Byron.

[3] *Hamlet*, Act III, scene 2.

[4] Lady Caroline Lamb changed the motto with each edition. The Motto Byron refers to was from the *Corsair* (slightly altered):

"He left a name to all succeeding times,
Link'd with one virtue and a thousand crimes."

[5] Maturin's *Bertram*, which Byron had recommended to *Drury Lane*, was first produced May 9, 1816, and had a successful run. Murray published the play which reached a seventh edition in 1816.

[1] Friedrich von Matthisson (1761–1831), a German poet.

library?—well—I have encountered at Copet and elsewhere Gray's Correspondent (in it's Appendix) that same Bonstetten[2]—(to whom I lent ye translation of his Correspondent's epistles for a few days)—but all he could remember of Gray amounts to little—except that he was the most "melancholy and gentlemanlike" of all possible poets.—Bonstetten himself is a fine & very lively old man—and much esteemed by his Compatriots—he is also a litterateur of good repute—and all his friends have a mania of addressing to him volumes of letters—Mathison—Muller[3] the historian &c. &c. He is a good deal at Copet[4]—where I have met him a few times.—All there are well—except Rocca[5]—who I am sorry to say—looks in a very bad state of health—the Duchess[6] seems grown taller—but—as yet—no rounder since her marriage—Schlegel[7] is in high force—and Madame as brilliant as ever.——I came here by the Netherlands—and the Rhine Route—& Basle—Berne—Morat—& Lausanne—I have circumnavigated the lake—and shall go to Chamouni—with the first fair weather—but really we have had lately such stupid mists—fogs—rains—and perpetual density—that one would think Castlereagh had the foreign affairs of the kingdom of Heaven also—upon his hands.——I need say nothing to you of these parts—you having traversed them already—I do not think of Italy before September.——I have read "Glenarvon"

> "From furious Sappho scarce a milder fate
> ———by her love—or libelled by her hate."[8]

& have also seen Ben. Constant's Adolphe[9]—and his preface denying the real people—it is a work which leaves an unpleasant impression—

[2] Charles Victor de Bonstetten (1745–1832), a Swiss man of letters, met Thomas Gray in England in 1769, and had an extended correspondence with him.
[3] Johann von Müller (1752–1809), author of a *History of the Helvetic Con-. federation*, was a lifelong friend and correspondent of Bonstetten.
[4] Coppet was the home of Madame de Staël on the north shore of the Lake of Geneva. Byron visited her there frequently during the summer of 1816.
[5] Madame de Staël married in 1811, as her second husband, a young French officer, M. de Rocca.
[6] Madame de Staël's daughter Albertine married in February 1816 the Duc de Broglie.
[7] August Wilhelm von Schlegel (1767–1845), a protégé of Madame de Staël, lived at Coppet and formed part of her brilliant circle. His egotism caused Byron to dislike him.
[8] From Pope's *Horace Imitated*, first satire of the second book, lines 83–84: "From furious Sappho scarce a milder fate,/P—xed by her love, or libell'd by her hate." The dash is in Byron's manuscript letter.
[9] Benjamin Constant's novel *Adolphe* pictured with rather cruel detail (imperfectly camouflaged) his cooling passion for Madame de Staël.

but very consistent with the consequences of not being in love—which is perhaps as disagreeable as anything—except being so—I doubt however whether all such "liens" (as he calls them) terminate so wretchedly as his hero & heroine's.——There is a third Canto (a longer than either of the former) of Ch[il]de Har[ol]d finished—and some smaller things—among them a story on the "Chateau de Chillon"—I only wait a good opportunity to transmit them to the Grand Murray—who—I hope—flourishes. —Where is Moore?— why aint he out?—my love to him—and my perfect consideration & remembrances to all—particularly to Lord & Lady Holland—& to your Duchess of Somers[e]t.[10]—

ever yrs. very truly

P.S.—I send you a fac simile—a note of Bonstetten's thinking you might like to see the hand of Gray's Correspondent.

[TO ——————]   *Diodati.—July 30th. 1816*

Dear Sir—I feel truly obliged by the details with regard to Bonnivard which you have been good enough to send me—and have only to regret that I did not possess them before—though I feel that any thing that I could say would fall very far short of the subject.——On Sunday I sent a servant over to Coppet with the M.S.S.—which the Baroness had expressed a wish to read—and I hope that she received them in safety.—I will not detain your messenger longer than to say how much I have ye honour to be

yr. obliged and most obedt. humble Sert.
BYRON

P.S.—Do me the favour to present my best compliments.—

[TO MADAME DE STAËL]   *August 24th. 1816*

Dear Madam—It was my intention to address you at some length— but my subject has too many thoughts for words.——The intelligence you mentioned came upon me unexpectedly—as my Correspondents in England are forbidden by me to name or allude to any branch of that family except my daughter. To say that I am merely *sorry* to hear of

---

[10] Lady Charlotte Hamilton, first wife of Edward Adolphus, 11th Duke of Somerset.

Lady B[yron]'s illness is to say nothing—but she has herself deprived me of the right to express more.—The separation may have been *my fault*—but it was *her* choice.———I tried all means to prevent—and would do as much & more to end it,—a word would do so—but it does not rest with me to pronounce it.———You asked me if I thought that Lady B[yron] was attached to me—to that I can only answer that I love her.—I am utterly unable to add a word more upon the subject and if I were to say ten thousand they could only come to the same conclusion—and be as unavailing as sincere.—

Bn[1]

I cannot conclude without thanking you once more for your kind disposition towards me on this—as on other occasions—and by begging you to believe me ever so faithfully

your obliged and affectionate servant
BYRON

[TO MADAME DE STAËL]   *August 25th. 1816*

Dear Madam—My letter is at your disposal—but it will be useless: —it contains however the truth of my wishes and my feelings on that subject———and as they have been doubted—I am willing to put them to the proof.—I will take my chance of finding you at home some morning in the ensuing week.———I received the work of Mr. Schlegel —which I presume is the book to which you allude—and will take great care of it.—Your messenger waits and I will not now take up more of your time than to assure you how much I am ever & truly

yr. obliged & faith[fu]l Sert.
BYRON

[TO AUGUSTA LEIGH]   *Diodati Aug[us]t 27th. 1816*

[First line scratched out]

Your confidential letter is safe, and all the others. This one has cut me to the heart because I have made you uneasy. Still I think all these apprehensions—very groundless. Who can care for such a wretch as

---

[1] The letter ends here in the manuscript in the Murray collection. The last sentence is added from the manuscript of the letter by V. de Pange in an unpublished dissertation in the Bodleian Library. Since de Pange had access to manuscript letters in the Broglie Collection, this may suggest that the Murray MS. is a first draft.

C[arolin]e, or believe such a seventy times convicted liar? and in the next place, whatever she may suppose or assert—I never "committed" any one to her but *myself*. And as to her fancies—she fancies any thing—and every body—Lady M[elbourne] &c. &c. Really this is starting at shadows. You distress me with—no—it is not *you*. But I have heard that Lady B[yron] is ill, & am so sorry—but it's of no use—do not mention her again—but I shall not forget her kindness to you.

I am going to Chamouni (to leave my card with Mont Blanc) and I mean to buy some pretty granite & spar playthings for children (which abound there) for my daughter—and my nieces—you will forward what I select to little Da—& divide the rest among your own. I shall send them by Scrope; this goes by another person. I shall write more and longer soon.

do not be uneasy—and do not "hate yourself" if you hate either let it be *me*—but do not—it would kill me; we are the last persons in the world—who ought—or could cease to love one another.

Ever dearest thine

+ B

P.S.—I send a note to Georgiana. I do not understand all your mysteries about "the verses"[1] & the Asterisks; but if the name is not put asterisks always are, & I see nothing remarkable in this. I have heard nothing but praises of those lines.

[TO JOHN HANSON]   *Geneva. August 28th. 1816*

My dear Sir—Your letter and the enclosed are safely arrived.— Many thanks.——Claughton I doubt—will never be able to resume the purchase.—I thought the reversion of [Hafod] was to set all smooth with him.—Pray do not forget to reinstate *Joe Murray's wages* and *board wages*—my Sister tells me they are cut off—but I hope there is at least *rent enough* on the estate to defray his expences—poor old Man— and I particularly request that you will have the goodness to see to him—I shall not feel easy till I hear he is so.———Of "*Mr. Bernard Byron*" (as he calls himself) I know nothing—nor ever heard from nor of such a person—nor can I conjecture his business with me—I once had a short correspondence (on literary subjects) with a *Mr. Bernard Barton*—are you sure *that* is not the name?—You had better

[1] Probably the verses to Augusta published with the *Prisoner of Chillon* with the title "Stanzas to * * * *".

write to him again—and say that "as you and Mr. D[ougla]s Kinnaird act for me during my absence—all business had best be addressed to one or both (if he chooses) of you—or—that—if that is not convenient—letters addressed to me here will find me or be forwarded. —["] At any rate write to him again for an explanation (if he has any) in case he should have business—though I know nothing of it— nor of him.——Many thanks to you and yours for your kind enquiries——I am in tolerable health—and may perhaps be in England next spring—though in my present state of affairs—I do not see what good I could do.——Letters addressed to Geneva will be forwarded when I pass the Alps—so you can still address to this place.—My residence is not in the town but on the borders of the lake—in a very prettily situated country house.—When you see my daughter—tell me how she is—and how she looks—but do not mention to me nor allude to any other branch of that family.——I shall be very glad to hear from you—believe me—with best remembrances to you & yours.—

ever truly & affectly. yrs.

BYRON

[TO JOHN MURRAY]   *Diodati.—August 28th. 1816*

Dear Sir—The Manuscript (containing the third Canto of Childe Harold—the Castle of Chillon &c. &c.) is consigned to the care of my friend Mr. Shelley—who will deliver this letter along with it.—Mr. Gifford will perhaps be kind enough to read it over;—I know not well to whom to consign the correction of the proofs—nor indeed who would be good natured enough to overlook it in its progress—as I feel very anxious that it should be published with as few errata as possible.——Perhaps—my friend Mr. Moore (if in town) would do this.——If not—Mr. S[helley] will take it upon himself,—and in any case—he is authorized to act for me in treating with you &c. &c. on this subject.——You talked of a letter—which was to be sent by you to me—but I have received none—before—or since—one by Mr. Browne.—As that Gentleman returned by Brussels—which is the longest route—I declined troubling him with the care of this packet.— —Believe me very truly yours.

BYRON

P.S.—There is in the volume—an epistle to Mrs. Leigh—on which I should wish her to have her opinion consulted—before the publication—if she objects—of course—*omit* it.[1]——I have been very glad to hear you are well—& well-doing—and that you stopped Master Cawthorne in his foolish attempts to republish the E[nglish] B[ards] & S[cotch] R[eviewers].—I wish you all good things.——

[TO AUGUSTA LEIGH]   *[Diodati—Geneva Sept. 8th. 1816]*

My dearest Augusta—By two opportunities of private conveyance— I have sent answers to your letter delivered by Mr. H[obhouse].—— S[crope] is on his return to England—& may probably arrive before this.—He is charged with a few packets of seals—necklaces—balls &c.—& I know not what—formed of Chrystals—Agates—and other stones—*all of* & *from Mont Blanc* bought & brought by me on & from the spot—expressly for you to divide among yourself and the children—including also your niece Ada, for whom I selected a ball (of Granite—a soft substance by the way—but the only one there) wherewithall to roll & play—when she is old enough—and mischievous enough—and moreover a Chrystal necklace—and anything else you may like to add for her—the Love!——The rest are for you— & the Nursery—but particularly Georgiana—who has sent me a very nice letter.—I hope Scrope will carry them all safely—as he promised ——There are seals & all kinds of fooleries—pray—like them— for they come from a very curious place (nothing like it hardly in all I ever saw)—to say nothing of the giver.——And so—Lady B[yron] has been "kind to you" you tell me—"very kind"—umph—it is as well she should be kind to some of us—and I am glad she has the heart & the discernment to be still *your* friend—you was ever so to her.—I heard the other day—that she was very unwell—I was shocked enough—and sorry enough—God knows—but never mind;— H[obhouse] tells me however that she is *not* ill—that she *had* been indisposed—but is better & well to do.—this is a relief.——As for me I am in good health—& fair—though very unequal—spirits—but for all that—she—or rather—the Separation—has broken my heart— I feel as if an Elephant had trodden on it—I am convinced I shall never get over it—but I try.——I had enough before I ever knew her and more than enough—but time & agitation had done something for me; but this last wreck has affected me very differently,—if it were *acutely*—it would not signify—but it is not that,—I breathe lead.——

[1] This was Byron's "Epistle to Augusta". Mrs. Leigh did object and it was not published until 1830 in Moore's life of Byron (Moore, II, 38–41).

While the storm lasted & you were all pressing & comforting me with condemnation in Piccadilly—it was bad enough—& violent enough—but it is worse now.—I have neither strength nor spirits—nor inclination to carry me through anything which will clear my brain or lighten my heart.—I mean to cross the Alps at the end of this month—and go—God knows where—by Dalmatia—up to the Arnauts again—if nothing better can be done;—I have still a world before me—this—or the next.———H[obhouse] has told me all the strange stories in circulation of me & mine;—*not* true,—I have been in some danger on the lake—(near Meillerie) but nothing to speak of; and as to all these "mistresses"—Lord help me[1]—I have had but one.—Now—don't scold—but what could I do?—a foolish girl—in spite of all I could say or do—would come after me—or rather went before me—for I found her here—and I have had all the plague possible to persuade her to go back again—but at last she went.—Now—dearest—I do most truly tell thee—that I could not help this—that I did all I could to prevent it—& have at last put an end to it.—I am not in love—nor have any love left for any,—but I could not exactly play the Stoic with a woman—who had scrambled eight hundred miles to unphilosophize me—besides I had been regaled of late with so many "two courses and a *desert*" (Alas!) of aversion—that I was fain to take a little love (if pressed particularly) by way of novelty.———And now you know all that I know of that matter—& it is over. Pray—write—I have heard nothing since your last—at least a month or five weeks ago.——I go out very little—except into the *air*—and on journeys—and on the water—and to Coppet—where Me. de Stael has been particularly kind & friendly towards me—& (I hear) fought battles without number in my very indifferent cause.—It has (they say) made quite as much noise on this as the other side of "La Manche"—Heaven knows why—but I seem destined to set people by the ears.——Don't hate me—but believe me ever

yrs. most affectly.
B

[TO AUGUSTA LEIGH] *Sept. 14th. 1816*

My dearest Augusta—The paper with the initials came safely with your letter, but the hair was either omitted or had slipt out. You may be sure I looked everywhere carefully, but I suppose you in your hurry

---

[1] The Murray MS. ends here; the remainder is from the Lytton MS.

forgot it. Pray send (or save for me) two or three—but tie them with a *thread*—or wrap them in a manner more liable to security.

I have written to you lately *thrice*, twice by private conveyance & once by post. This is the fourth since the letter you mention.

Your having seen my daughter is to me a great satisfaction; it is as if I had seen her myself. Next to you—dearest—she is nearly all I have to look forward to with hope or pleasure in this world. Perhaps she also may disappoint & distress me, but I will not think so; in any case she will at least love me—or my memory.

By Mr. Davies I sent you for yourself—little Da—& my nieces, a variety of Chrystal & other trinkets from Mont Blanc & Chamouni, which I got upon the spot for you all. I hope they will arrive safely.

In my last letter I mentioned to you the origin of the stories about "mistresses." As to "pages"—there be none such—nor any body else. Such assertations and reports find their own remedy sooner or later.

If I understand you rightly, you seem to have been apprehensive— or menaced (like every one else) by that infamous Bedlamite [erased] [Caroline Lamb]—If she stirs against you, neither her folly nor her falsehood should or shall protect her. Such a monster as that *has no sex*, and should live no longer.

But till such an event should occur, you may rely that I shall remain as quiet as the most unbounded Contempt of her, and my affection for you & regard for your feelings can make me. I should never think of her nor her infamies, but that they seem (I know not why) to make you uneasy. What 'tis she may tell or what she may know or pretend to know—is to me indifferent. You know I suppose that Lady B[yro]n *secretly opened my letter trunks before she left Town, and that* she *has also been* (*during* or since the separation) in *correspondence with* that self-avowed libeller & strumpet [erased] wife. This you may depend upon though I did not know it till recently.

Upon such conduct I am utterly at a loss to make a single comment— beyond every expression of astonishment. I am past indignation.

There is perhaps a chance of your seeing me in Spring, as I said before I left England; but it is useless to form plans, and most of all for me to do so. I may say (as Whitbread said to me of his own a short time before his decease), that "none of mine ever succeeded."

We purpose making a short tour to the Berne Alps next week, and then to return here and cross the Simplon to Milan. Your letters had better be always directed to *Geneva Poste Restante* and my banker (Mr. Hentsch, a very attentive and good man), will take care to forward them, wherever I may be.

I have answered Georgiana's letter & am very glad she likes her little cousin. How come Ada's hair *fair?*———she will be like her mother and torture me. However if she is kind to you—and when the time comes—if she will continue so, it is enough.

I do not write to you in good spirits, and I cannot pretend to be so, but I have no *near* nor *immediate* cause of being thus, but as [so?] it is; I only request you will say nothing of this to Hobhouse by letter or message, as I wish to wear as quiet an appearance with him as possible; —besides I am in good health & well without.

The Jerseys are here; I am to see them soon. Made. de Staël still very kind & hospitable, but Rocca (to whom she is privately married) is not well, with some old wounds badly cured.

If I see anything very striking in the Mountains I will tell thee. To Scrope I leave the details of Chamouni & the Glaciers & the sources of the Aveiron. This country is altogether the Paradise of Wilderness —I wish you were in it with me—& every one else out of it—Love me, A., ever thine—

B

[TO "LE PASTEUR DE COLOGNY"]   *Diodati Septr. 16th. [1816]*

Sir—In answer to your request—I have enclosed a draft on *Monsieur Hentsch & Co.*—for the sum of three hundred francs—and I should feel obliged by an answer merely that I may know that you have received this note and the enclosure.[1]—I send it as you direct to Monr. Diodati's by his Governor.—I have the honour to be

yr. most obedt. very humble Sert.
BYRON

[TO AUGUSTA LEIGH]   *Ouchy. Sept. 17. 1816*

My dearest Augusta,—I am thus far on my way to the Bernese Alps & the Grindenwald, and the *Yungfrau* (that is the "Wild woman" being interpreted—as it is so perverse a mountain that no other sex would suit it), which journey may occupy me eight days or so, and then it is my intention to return to Geneva, preparatory to passing the Simplon—

Continue to direct as usual to Geneva. I have lately written to you

[1] The pastor of Coligny, the village in which Diodati was situated, asked Byron for a donation for the poor of the village. This was his response.

several letters (3 or 4 by post and two by hand) and I have received all yours very safely. I rejoice to have heard that you are well. You have been in London too lately, & H[obhouse] tells me that at your levée he generally found Ld. F. Bentinck[1]—pray why is that fool so often a visitor? is he in love with you? I have recently broken through my resolution of not speaking to you of Lady B[yron]—but do not on that account name her to me. It is a relief—a partial relief to me to talk of her sometimes to you—but it would be none to hear of her. *Of* her you are to judge for yourself, but do not altogether forget that she has destroyed your brother. Whatever my faults might or may have been—*She*—was not the person marked out by providence to be their avenger. One day or another her conduct will recoil on her own head; *not* through *me*, for my feelings towards her are not those of Vengeance, but—mark—if she does not end miserably *tot ou tard*. She may think— talk—or act as she will, and by any process of cold reasoning and jargon of "duty & acting for the best" &c., &c., impose upon her own feelings & those of others for a time—but woe unto her—the wretchedness she has brought upon the man to whom she has been everything evil ⟨except in one respect⟩ will flow back into its fountain. I may thank the strength of my constitution that has enabled me to bear all this, but those who bear the longest and the most do not suffer the least. I do not think a human being could endure more mental torture than that woman has directly & indirectly inflicted upon me—within the present year.

She has (for a time at least) separated me from my child—& from you—but I turn from the subject for the present.

To-morrow I repass Clarens & Vevey; if in the new & more extended tour I am making, anything that I think may please you occurs, I will detail it.

Scrope has by this time arrived with my little presents for you and yours & Ada. I still hope to be able to see you next Spring, perhaps you & one or two of the children could be spared some time next year for a little tour *here* or in France with me for a month or two. I think I could make it pleasing to you, & it should be no expense to L[eigh] or to yourself. Pray think of this hint. You have no idea how very beautiful great part of this country is—and *women* and *children* traverse it with ease and expedition. I would return from any distance at any time to see you, and come to England for you; and when you consider

---

[1] Lord Frederick Bentinck, a friend of Charles Fox, was, like Augusta's husband, an ardent follower of horse racing.

the chances against our—but I won't relapse into the dismals and anticipate long absences—

The great obstacle would be that you are so admirably yoked—and necessary as a housekeeper—and a letter writer—& a place-hunter to that very helpless gentleman your Cousin, that I suppose the usual self-love of an elderly person would interfere between you & any scheme of recreation or relaxation, for however short a period.

What a fool I was to marry—and *you* not very wise—my dear—we might have lived so single and so happy—as old maids and bachelors; I shall never find any one like you—nor you (vain as it may seem) like me. We are just formed to pass our lives together, and therefore—we—at least—I—am by a crowd of circumstances removed from the only being who could ever have loved me, or whom I can unmixedly feel attached to.

Had you been a Nun—and I a Monk—that we might have talked through a grate instead of across the sea—no matter—my voice and my heart are

ever thine—
B

[TO AUGUSTA LEIGH]   *Clarens. Septr. 18th. 1816*

Alpine Journal

Yesterday September 17th. 1816—I set out (with H[obhouse]) on an excursion of some days to the Mountains.—I shall keep a short journal of each day's progress for my Sister Augusta—

Sept. 17th.—

Rose at 5.—left Diodati about seven—in one of the country carriages—(a Charaban)—our servants on horseback—weather very fine—the Lake calm and clear—Mont Blanc—and the Aiguille of Argentière both very distinct—the borders of the Lake beautiful—reached Lausanne before Sunset—stopped & slept at Ouchy.—H[obhouse] went to dine with a Mr. Okeden—I remained at our Caravansera (though invited to the house of H's friend—too lazy or tired—or something else to go) and wrote a letter to Augusta—Went to bed at nine—sheets damp—swore and stripped them off & flung them—Heaven knows where—wrapt myself up in the blankets—and slept like a Child of a month's existence—till 5 o Clock of

Septr. 18th.

Called by Berger (my Courier who acts as Valet for a day or two—the learned Fletcher being left in charge of Chattels at Diodati) got up— H[obhouse] walked on before—a mile from Lausanne—the road overflowed by the lake—got on horseback & rode—till within a mile of Vevey—the Colt young but went very well—overtook H. & resumed the carriage which is an open one—stopped at Vevey two hours (the second time I have visited it) walked to the Church—view from the Churchyard superb—within it General Ludlow (the Regicide's) monument[1]—black marble—long inscription—Latin—but simple— particularly the latter part—in which his wife (Margaret de Thomas) records her long—her tried—and unshaken affection—he was an Exile *two and thirty years*—one of the King's (Charles's) Judges—a fine fellow.—I remember reading his memoirs in January 1815 (at Halnaby—) the first part of them very amusing—the latter less so,— I little thought at the time of their perusal by me of seeing his tomb— near him Broughton (who read King Charles's sentence to Charles Stuart)—is buried with a *queer* and rather *canting*—but still a Republican epitaph——Ludlow's house shown—it retains still his inscription "Omne Solum forte patria"—Walked down to the Lake side—servants—Carriage—saddle horses—all set off and left us plantés la by some mistake—and we walked on after them towards Clarens—*H[obhouse]* ran on before and overtook them at last —arrived the second time (1st time was by water) at Clarens beautiful Clarens!—went to Chillon through Scenery worthy of I know not whom—went over the Castle of Chillon again—on our return met an English party in a carriage—a lady in it fast asleep!— fast asleep in the most anti-narcotic spot in the world—excellent—I remember at Chamouni—in the very eyes of Mont Blanc—hearing another woman—English also—exclaim to her party—"did you ever see any thing more *rural*"—as if it was Highgate or Hampstead—or Brompton—or Hayes.—"*Rural*" quotha!—Rocks—pines—torrents— Glaciers—Clouds—and Summits of eternal snow far above them— and "*Rural!*" I did not know the thus exclaiming fair one—but she was a—very good kind of a woman.——After a slight & short dinner— we visited the Chateau de Clarens—an English woman has rented it recently—(it was not let when I saw it first) the roses are gone with their Summer—the family out—but the servants desired us to walk over the interior—saw on the table of the saloon—Blair's sermons— and somebody else's (I forgot who's—) sermons—and a set of noisy

[1] Edmund Ludlow, the Regicide's monument is in St. Martin's Church, Vevey, where he spent his exile, wrote his memoirs, and died.

children—saw all worth seeing and then descended to the "Bosquet de Julie" &c. &c.—our Guide full of *Rousseau*—whom he is eternally confounding with *St. Preux*—and mixing the man and the book—on the steps of a cottage in the village—I saw a young *paysanne*—beautiful as Julie herself—went again as far as Chillon to revisit the little torrent from the hill behind it—Sunset—reflected in the lake—have to get up at 5 tomorrow to cross the mountains on horseback—carriage to be sent round—lodged at my old Cottage—hospitable & comfortable—tired with a longish ride—on the Colt—and the subsequent jolting of the Charaban—and my scramble in the hot sun—shall go to bed—thinking of you dearest Augusta.——Mem.—The Corporal who showed the wonders of Chillon was as drunk as Blucher[2] —and (to my mind) as great a man.—He was *deaf* also—and thinking every one else so—roared out the legends of the Castle so fearfully that H[obhouse] got out of humour—however we saw all things from the Gallows to the Dungeon (the *Potence* & the *Cachets*) and returned to Clarens with more freedom than belonged to the 15th. Century.——At Clarens—the only book (except the Bible) a translation of *"Cecilia"* (Miss Burney's *Cecilia*) and the owner of the Cottage had also called her dog (a fat Pug *ten* years old—and hideous as *Tip*)[3] after Cecilia's (or rather Delville's) dog—Fidde—

Septr. 19th.

Rose at 5—ordered the carriage round.—Crossed the mountains to Montbovon on horseback—and on Mules—and by dint of scrambling on foot also,—the whole route beautiful as a *Dream* and now to me almost as indistinct,—I am so tired—for though healthy I have not the strength I possessed but a few years ago.—At Mont Davant we breakfasted—afterwards on a steep ascent—dismounted—tumbled down & cut a finger open—the baggage also got loose and fell down a ravine, till stopped by a large tree—swore—recovered baggage—horse tired & dropping—mounted Mule—at the approach of the summit of Dent Jamant—dismounted again with H. & all the party.—Arrived at a lake in the very nipple of the bosom of the Mountain.—left our quadrupeds with a Shepherd—& ascended further—came to some snow in patches—upon which my forehead's perspiration fell like rain making the same dints as in a sieve—the chill of the wind & the snow turned me giddy—but I scrambled on & upwards— *H.* went to the highest *pinnacle*—I did not—but paused within a few

[2] Byron had observed, or been told of, the drunkenness of Blücher when he visited England during "the summer of the Sovereigns", in 1814.

[3] Tip was Augusta's dog.

yards (at an opening of the Cliff)—in coming down the Guide tumbled three times—I fell a laughing & tumbled too—the descent luckily soft though steep & slippery—H. also fell—but nobody hurt. The whole of the Mountain superb—the shepherd on a very steep & high cliff playing upon his *pipe*—very different from Arcadia—(where I saw the pastors with a long Musquet instead of a Crook—and pistols in their Girdles)—our Swiss Shepherd's pipe was sweet—& his time agreeable—saw a cow strayed—told that they often break their necks on & over the crags—descended to Montbovon—pretty scraggy village with a wild river—and a wooden bridge.—H. went to fish—caught one—our carriage not come—our horses—mules &c. knocked up—ourselves fatigued—(but so much the better—I shall sleep). The view from the highest point of today's journey comprized on one side the greatest part of Lake Leman—on the other—the valleys & mountains of the Canton Fribourg—and an immense plain with the Lakes of Neufchatel & Morat—and all which the borders of these and of the Lake of Geneva inherit—we had both sides of the Jura before us in one point of view, with Alps in plenty.—In passing a ravine—the Guide recommended strenuously a quickening of pace—as the stones fall with great rapidity & occasional damage—the advice is excellent—but like most good advice impracticable—the road being so rough in this precise point—that neither mules nor mankind—nor horses—can make any violent progress.—Passed without any fractures or menace thereof.—The music of the Cows' bells (for their wealth like the Patriarchs is cattle) in the pastures (which reach to a height far above any mountains in Britain—) and the Shepherds' shouting to us from crag to crag & playing on their reeds where the steeps appeared almost inaccessible, with the surrounding scenery—realized all that I have ever heard or imagined of a pastoral existence[4]—much more so than Greece or Asia Minor—for there we are a little too much of the sabre & musquet order—and if there is a Crook in one hand, you are sure to see a gun in the other—but this was pure and unmixed—solitary—savage and patriarchal—the effect I cannot describe—as we went they played the "Ranz des Vaches" and other airs by way of farewell.— I have lately repeopled my mind with Nature.

Septr. 20th.

Up at 6—off at 8—the whole of this days journey at an average of between from two thousand seven hundred to three thousand feet

[4] This scene is one of several described in the Journal which Byron used in the descriptions of the Alpine background in *Manfred*. See Act I, scene 2: "The natural music of the mountain reed. . . ."

above the level of the Sea. This valley the longest—narrowest—& considered one of the finest of the Alps——little traversed by travellers—saw the Bridge of La Roche—the bed of the river very low & deep between immense rocks & rapid as anger—a man & mule said to have tumbled over without damage—(the mule was lucky at any rate—unless I knew the *man* I should be loth to pronounce *him* fortunate).—The people looked free & happy and *rich* (which last implies neither of the former) the cows superb—a Bull nearly leapt into the Charaban—"agreeable companion in a postchaise"—Goats & Sheep very thriving—a mountain with enormous Glaciers to the right —the Kletsgerberg—further on—the Hockthorn—nice names—so soft—Hockthorn I believe very lofty & craggy—patched with snow only—no Glaciers on it—but some good epaulettes of clouds.—Past the boundaries—out of Vaud—& into Bern Canton—French exchanged for a bad German—the district famous for Cheese— liberty—property—& no taxes.—H. went to fish—caught none— strolled to river—saw a boy [and] a kid—kid followed him like a dog —kid could not get over a fence & bleated piteously—tried myself to help kid—but nearly overset both self & kid into the river.—Arrived here about six in the evening—nine o clock—going to bed—H. in next room—knocked his head against the door—and exclaimed of course against doors—not tired today—but hope to sleep nevertheless —women gabbling below—read a French translation of Schiller— Good Night—Dearest Augusta.——

Septr. 21st.

Off early—the valley of Simmenthal as before—entrance to the plain of Thoun very narrow—high rocks—wooded to the top—river—new mountains—with fine Glaciers—Lake of Thoun—extensive plain with a girdle of Alps—walked down to the Chateau de Schadau— view along the lake—crossed the river in a boat rowed by women— *women* [went?] right for the first time in my recollection.—Thoun a pretty town—the whole day's journey Alpine & proud.—

Septr. 22d.

Left Thoun in a boat which carried us the length of the lake in three hours—the lake small—but the banks fine—rocks down to the water's edge.—Landed at Neuhause—passed Interlachen—entered upon a range of scenes beyond all description—or previous conception.— Passed a rock—inscription—2 brothers—one murdered the other— just the place fit for it.—After a variety of windings came to an enormous rock—Girl with fruit—very pretty—blue eyes—good teeth—very fair—long but good features—reminded me of Fy.[1] bought some of her pears—and patted her upon the cheek—the expression of her face very mild—but good—and not at all coquettish. —Arrived at the foot of the Mountain (the Yung-frau—i.e. the Maiden) Glaciers—torrents—one of these torrents *nine hundred feet* in height of visible descent—lodge at the Curate's—set out to see the Valley—heard an Avalanche fall—like thunder—saw Glacier— enormous—Storm came on—thunder—lightning—hail—all in per- fection—and beautiful—I was on horseback—Guide wanted to carry my cane—I was going to give it him when I recollected that it was a Swordstick and I thought that the lightning might be attracted towards him—kept it myself—a good deal encumbered with it & my cloak— as it was too heavy for a whip—and the horse was stupid—& stood still every other peal. Got in—not very wet—the Cloak being staunch —H. wet through—H. took refuge in cottage—sent man—umbrella— & cloak (from the Curate's when I arrived—) after him.—Swiss Curate's house—very good indeed—much better than most English Vicarages—it is immediately opposite the torrent I spoke of—the torrent is in shape curving over the rock—like the *tail* of a white horse streaming in the wind—such as it might be conceived would be that of the *"pale* horse" on which *Death* is mounted in the Apocalypse.—It is neither mist nor water but a something between both—it's immense height (nine hundred feet) gives it a wave—a curve—a spreading here—a condensation there—wonderful—& indescribable.—I think upon the whole—that this day has been better than any of this present excursion.—

Septr. 23d.

Before ascending the mountain—went to the torrent (7 in the morn- ing) again—the Sun upon it forming a *rainbow* of the lower part of all colours—but principally purple and gold—the bow moving as you move —I never saw anything like this—it is only in the Sunshine.——As- cended the Wengren [sic] Mountain.——at noon reached a valley near the summit—left the horses—took off my coat & went to the summit— 7000 feet (English feet) above the level of the *sea*—and about 5000 above the valley we left in the morning—on one side our view com- prized the *Yung frau* with all her glaciers—then the *Dent d'Argent*— shining like truth—then the *little Giant* (the Kleiner EIgher) & the great Giant (the Grosser EIgher) and last not least—the Wetterhorn. —The height of the Yung frau is 13000 feet above the sea—and 11000 above the valley—she is the highest of this range,—heard the

[1] Fanny [Frances] Webster?

101

Avalanches falling every five minutes nearly—as if God was pelting the Devil down from Heaven with snow balls—from where we stood on the *Wengren* [sic] Alp—we had all these in view on one side—on the other the clouds rose from the opposite valley curling up perpendicular precipices—like the foam of the Ocean of Hell during a Springtide— it was white & sulphery—and immeasurably deep in appearance— the side we ascended was (of course) not of so precipitous a nature— but on arriving at the summit we looked down the other side upon a boiling sea of cloud—dashing against the crags on which we stood (these crags on one side quite perpendicular);—staid a quarter of an hour—began to descend—quite clear from cloud on that side of the mountain—in passing the masses of snow—I made a snowball & pelted H. with it—got down to our horses again—eat something— remounted—heard the Avalanches still—came to a morass—H. dismounted—H. got well over—I tried to pass my horse over—the horse sunk up [to] the chin—& of course he & I were in the mud together— bemired all over—but not hurt—laughed & rode on.—Arrived at the Grindenwald—dined—mounted again & rode to the higher Glacier— twilight—but distinct—very fine Glacier—like a *frozen hurricane*— Starlight—beautiful—but a devil of a path—never mind—got safe in—a little lightning—but the whole of the day as fine in point of weather—as the day on which Paradise was made.—Passed *whole woods of withered pines—all withered*—trunks stripped & barkless— branches lifeless—done by a single winter—their appearance reminded me of me & my family.—

Septr. 24th.

Set out at seven—up at five—passed the black Glacier—the Mountain Wetterhorn on the right—crossed the Scheideck mountain—came to the Rose Glacier—said to be the largest & finest in Switzerland.—*I* think the Bossons Glacier at Chamouni—as fine—H. does not—came to the Reichenback waterfall—two hundred feet high—halted to rest the horses—arrived in the valley of Oberhasli—rain came on— drenched a little—only 4 hours rain however in 8 days—came to Lake of Brientz—then to town of Brientz—changed—H. hurt his head against door.—In the evening four Swiss Peasant Girls of Oberhasli came & sang the airs of their country—two of the voices beautiful— the tunes also—they sing too that *Tyrolese air* & song which you love— Augusta—because I love it—& I love because you love it— they are still singing—Dearest—you do not know how I should have liked this—were you with me—the airs are so wild & original & at the same time of great sweetness.——The singing is over—but below

102

stairs I hear the notes of a Fiddle which bode no good to my nights rest.—The Lord help us!—I shall go down & see the dancing.—

Septr. 25th.

The whole town of Brientz were apparently gathered together in the rooms below—pretty music—& excellent Waltzing—none but peasants—the dancing much better than in England—the English can't Waltz—never could—nor ever will.—One man with his pipe in his mouth—but danced as well as the others—some other dances in pairs—and in fours—and very good.——I went to bed but the revelry continued below late & early.—Brientz but a village.——Rose early.—Embarked on the Lake of Brientz.—Rowed by women in a long boat—one very young & very pretty—seated myself by her—& began to row also—presently we put to shore & another woman jumped in—it seems it is the custom here for the boats to be *manned by women*—for of five men & three women in our bark—all the women took an oar—and but one man.——Got to Interlachen in three hours—pretty Lake—not so large as that of Thoun.—Dined at Interlachen—Girl gave me some flowers—& made me a speech in German—of which I know nothing—I do not know whether the speech was pretty but as the woman was—I hope so.—Saw another—very pretty too—and *tall* which I prefer—I hate short women—for more reasons than one.—Reembarked on the Lake of Thoun—fell asleep part of the way—sent our horses round—found people on the shore blowing up a rock with gunpowder—they blew it up near our boat—only telling us a minute before—mere stupidity—but they might have broke our noddles.—Got to Thoun in the Evening—the weather has been tolerable the whole day—but as the wild part of our tour is finished, it don't matter to us—in all the desirable part—we have been most lucky in warmth & clearness of Atmosphere—for which "Praise we the Lord."——

Septr. 26th.

Being out of the mountains my journal must be as flat as my journey.——From Thoun to Bern good road—hedges—villages—industry—prosperity—and all sorts of tokens of insipid civilization.——From Bern to Fribourg.—Different Canton—Catholics—passed a field of Battle—Swiss beat the French—in one of the late wars against the French Republic.—Bought a dog—a very ugly dog—but *"tres mechant"*. this was his great recommendation in the owner's eyes & mine—for I mean him to watch the carriage—he hath no tail—& is called "Mutz"—which signifies "*Short-tail*"—he is apparently of the

103

Shepherd dog genus!—The greater part of this tour has been on horse-back—on foot—and on mule;—the Filly (which is one of two young horses I bought of the Baron de Vincy) carried me very well—she is young and as quiet as anything of her sex can be—very goodtempered —and perpetually neighing—when she wants any thing—which is every five minutes—I have called her *Biche*—because her manners are not unlike a little dog's—but she is a very tame—pretty childish quadruped.—

Septr. 28th. [27th.]

Saw the tree planted in honour of the battle of Morat—340 years old—a good deal decayed.—Left Fribourg—but first saw the Cathedral—high tower—overtook the baggage of the Nuns of La Trappe who are removing to Normandy from their late abode in the Canton of Fribourg—afterwards a coach with a quantity of Nuns in it—Nuns old—proceeded along the banks of the Lake of Neufchatel—very pleasing & soft—but not so mountainous—at least the Jura not appearing so—after the Bernese Alps—reached Yverdun in the dusk —a long line of large trees on the border of the lake—fine & sombre—the Auberge nearly full—with a German Princess & suite—got rooms—we hope to reach Diodati the day after tomorrow—and I wish for a letter from you my own dearest Sis—May your sleep be soft and your dreams of me.—I am going to bed—good night.—

Septr. 29th. [28th.]

Passed through a fine & flourishing country—but not mountainous—in the evening reached Aubonne (the entrance & bridge something like that of Durham) which commands by far the fairest view of the Lake of Geneva—twilight—the Moon on the Lake—a grove on the height—and of very noble trees.—Here Tavernier (the Eastern traveller) bought (or built) the Chateau because the site resembled and equalled that of *Erivan* (a frontier city of Persia) here he finished his voyages—and I this little excursion—for I am within a few hours of Diodati—& have little more to see—& no more to say.—In the weather for this tour (of 13 days) I have been very fortunate—fortunate in a companion (Mr. H[obhous]e) fortunate in our pros-pects—and exempt from even the little petty accidents & delays which often render journeys in a less wild country—disappointing.—I was disposed to be pleased—I am a lover of Nature—and an Admirer of Beauty—I can bear fatigue—& welcome privation—and have seen some of the noblest views in the world.—But in all this—the recol-lections of bitterness—& more especially of recent & more home

104

desolation—which must accompany me through life—have preyed upon me here—and neither the music of the Shepherd—the crashing of the Avalanche—nor the torrent—the mountain—the Glacier—the Forest—nor the Cloud—have for one moment—lightened the weight upon my heart—nor enabled me to lose my own wretched identity in the majesty & the power and the Glory—around—above—& beneath me.—I am past reproaches—and there is a time for all things—I am past the wish of vengeance—and I know of none like for what I have suffered—but the hour will come—when what I feel must be felt—& the——but enough.——To you—dearest Augusta—I send—and *for* you—I have kept this record of what I have seen & felt.—Love me as you are beloved by me.——

[TO WILLIAM FLETCHER]   *Thoun [September 21–22? 1816]*

I forgot to tell you to desire Springhetti (the Italian whose horses are engaged by us to Italy) on his arrival—to wait for my return.——Do not forget to have the *Caléche* repaired;—and also the *shoes.*—Enquire for letters at the post.——Keep a look out on the things—lock up the shoe-trunk—and recollect that there [several words illegible] Napoleons.—[Let?] the Governor or one of the men sleep in the house during my absence—and let Stevens—be in the upper room while you are in mine.—

&c. &c.
BYRON

P.S.—I expect to return in about a week.—

[TO JOHN MURRAY]   *Diodati. Septr. 29th. 1816*

My Dear Sir—I am very much flattered by Mr. Gifford's good opinion of the M.S.S.[1]—& shall be still more so if it answers your expectations—& justifies his kindness.—I liked it myself—but that must go for nothing—the feelings with which much of it was written need not be envied me.—With regard to the price—*I* fixed *none* but

[1] Murray had written to Byron on September 12 that he had carried the manuscript of the third canto of *Childe Harold* to Gifford, "trembling with auspicious hope about it." Although Gifford was suffering from jaundice, he sat up until he had finished the whole of it and was "infinitely delighted." "He says that what you have heretofore published is nothing to this effort. He says also, besides its being the most original and interesting, it is the most finished of your writings; and he has undertaken to correct the press for you." (Smiles, I, 365.)

left it to Mr. Kinnaird—& Mr. Shelley & yourself to arrange—of course they would do their best—and as to yourself—I know you would make no difficulties.—But I agree with Mr. K. perfectly that the concluding *five hundred* should be only *conditional*—and for my own sake I wish it to be added only in case of your selling a certain number —*that number* to be fixed by *yourself*—I hope this is fair—in every thing of this kind—there must be risk—and till that be past in one way or the other—I would not willingly add to it—particularly in times like the present—and pray always recollect that nothing could mortify me more—no failure on my own part—than having made you lose by any purchase from me.———The Monody was written by request of Mr. K. for the theatre—I did as well as I could—but where I have not my choice—I pretend to answer for nothing.—Mr. H. & myself are just returned from a journey of lakes & mountains—we have been to the Grindenwald—& the Jung-frau—& stood on the summit of the Wengeren Alp—and seen torrents of nine hundred feet in fall—& Glaciers of all dimensions—we have heard Shepherds' pipes—and Avalanches—and looked on the clouds foaming up from the valleys below us—like the spray of the ocean of hell.———Chamouni and that which it inherits—we saw a month ago—but (though Mont Blanc is higher) it is not equal in wildness to the Jung-frau—the Eighers—the Shreckhorn—& the Rose Glacier.———We set off for Italy next week —the road is within this month infested with Bandits—but we must take our chance & such precautions as are requisite.——

ever yrs. very truly
BYRON

P.S.—My best remembrances to Mr. G[ifford]—pray say all that can be said from me to him.——I am sorry that Mr. M. did not like Phillips picture—I thought it was reckoned a good one—if he had made the speech on the original—perhaps he would have been more readily forgiven by the proprietor & the painter of the portrait.—Do not forget to consult Mrs. Leigh on the lines to her—they must not be published without her full consent & approbation.——

[TO DOUGLAS KINNAIRD] *Diodati. Septr. 29th. 1816*

My Dear Kinnaird.—I have written to Mr. Murray to say that I agree with you that the concluding £500 should only be paid in case of the sale of a certain number to be fixed by Murray himself—I hope this is fair—I would not on any account have him a loser—nor hard driven in a bargain on my account.——I do not feel pressed—having funds sufficient for a good half year or perhaps a year in circular notes —and therefore will not accept your kind offer nor anticipate Murray's bills—but when they are cashed I will draw for them as it may happen —let them lie at your house (Morlands) & when they are money place them to my account—only letting me know the dates & the amount.— You had better address to me still at *Geneva*—for the present— when you write—& my bankers (Messrs Hentsch) will forward the letters wherever I may happen to be.—— H[obhouse] & myself are just returned from our excursion over the mountains——He is well & desires all remembrances—I shall be very glad to hear of your success in all matters—dramatic—&c. &c. and I hope to be one of the "numerous crowded—brilliant—overflowing—& enraptured audiences—["] who applaud Miss Keppel.[1] We hear Exmouth hath beaten the Algerines[2]—but why do I ask this?—I hope you will do the same by Arnold.[3]—Pray continue to like Shelley—he is a very good —very clever—but a very singular man—he was a great comfort to me here by his intelligence & good nature.—

ever yrs. most truly
BYRON

[TO JOHN MURRAY] *Diodati. Septr. 30th. 1816*

My dear Sir—I answered your obliging letters yesterday. Today the Monody arrived—with it's *title page*—which is I presume a separate publication.—"The request of a Friend"—

"Obliged by Hunger and request of friends."[1]

I will request you to expunge that same—unless you please to add "by a person of quality—or of wit and honour about town"—merely say—written to be spoken at D[rury] L[ane].—Tomorrow I dine at Coppet—Saturday I strike tents for Italy—this evening on the lake

---

[1] Miss Keppel was Kinnaird's wife, a singer who had gone back to the stage under her maiden name.

[2] Sir Edward Pellew, 1st Baronet and 1st Viscount Exmouth (1757–1833), an admiral who won distinction in the war against the French, bombarded Algiers in 1816 on the refusal of the bey to abolish Christian slavery.

[3] Samuel James Arnold (1774–1852), dramatist, produced at Drury Lane and elsewhere many original musical plays. One of his plays, *The Prior Claim*, was written in conjunction with Henry James Pye, the Poet Laureate, whom Byron had ridiculed in *English Bards and Scotch Reviewers*. Kinnaird was apparently adapting a play which he hoped to have produced at Drury Lane.

[1] Pope's *Epistle to Dr. Arbuthnot*, Line 44.

in my boat with Mr. Hobhouse—the pole which sustains the mainsail slipped in tacking & struck me so violently on one of my legs (the *worst* luckily) as to make me do a foolish thing—viz. to *faint*—a downright swoon—the thing must have jarred some nerve or other—for the bone is not injured—& hardly painful (it is six hours since) and cost Mr. H[obhouse] some apprehension and much sprinkling of water to recover me;—the sensation was a very odd one—I never had but two such before—one from a cut on the head from a stone several years ago—and once (long ago also) in falling into a great wreath of snow——a sort of gray giddiness first—then nothingness—and a total loss of memory on beginning to recover—the last part is not disagreeable—if one did not find it again.——You want the original M.S.S—Mr. Davies has the first fair copy in my own hand—& I have the rough composition here—and will send or save it for you since you wish it.——With regard to your new literary project[2]—if any thing falls in the way which will—to the best of my judgment—suit you—I will send you what I can.—At present I must lay by a little—having pretty well exhausted myself in what I have sent you.—Italy or Dalmatia & another summer may or may not set me off again—I have no plans—& am nearly as indifferent what may come—as where I go. I shall take Felicia Hemans' "restoration &c."[3] with me—it is a good poem—very.——Pray repeat my best thanks & remembrances to Mr. Gifford for all his trouble & good nature towards me. Do not fancy me laid up from the beginning of this scrawl—I tell you the accident for want of better to say;—but it is over—and I am only wondering what the deuce was the matter with me——I have lately been all over the Bernese Alps—& their lakes—I think many of the scenes—(some of which were not usually frequented by the English—) finer than Chamouni—which I visited some time before.——I have been to Clarens again—& crossed the mountains behind it—of this tour I kept a short journal for Mrs. Leigh which I sent yesterday in three letters—it is not at all for perusal—but if you like to hear about the romantic part—she will I dare say show you what touches upon the rocks &c.—but it has not—nor can have anything to do with publication.——"Christabel"—I won't have you sneer at Christabel —it is a fine wild poem.—Mr. H[obhouse] tells me you employed the power of Attorney to some purpose against Cawthorn;—he deserved

[2] Murray had announced that he was seriously thinking of starting a new monthly literary journal.
[3] Felicia Hemans published in 1816 a poem called *The Restoration of the Works of Art to Italy*.

no better—& had fair notice—I regret having made anyone suffer—but it was his own choice. Keep a watch over him still.——M[adam]e de Stael wishes to see the Antiquary & I am going to take it to her tomorrow;—she has made Coppet as agreeable as society and talent can make any place on earth

yrs. ever
B

[TO AUGUSTA LEIGH]   *Diodati. October 1st. 1816*

My dearest Augusta—Two days ago I sent you in three letter-covers a journal of a mountain-excursion lately made by me & Mr. H[obhouse] in the Bernese Alps.—I kept it on purpose for you thinking it might amuse you.——Since my return here—I have heard by an indirect Channel—that Lady B[yron] is better—or well.—It is also said that she has some intention of passing the winter on the Continent. Upon this subject I must [say?] a word or two—and as you are—I understand —on terms of acquaintance with her again—you will be the properest channel of communication from me to her.—It regards my child.—It is far from my intention now or at any future period—(without misconduct on her part which I should be grieved to anticipate) to attempt to withdraw my child from it's mother—I think it would be harsh—& though it is a very deep privation to me to be withdrawn from the contemplation & company of my little girl—still I would not purchase even this so very dearly;—but I must strongly protest against my daughter's leaving England—to be taken over the Continent at so early a time of life—& subjected to many unavoidable risks of health & comfort;—more especially in so unsettled a state as we know the greater part of Europe to be in at this moment—I do not choose that my girl should be educated like Lord Yarmouths son[1]—(or run the chance of it which a war would produce) and I make it my personal & particular request to Lady Byron—that—in the event of her quitting England—the child should be left in the care of proper persons—I have no objection to it's remaining with Lady Noel—& Sir Ralph— (who would naturally be fond of it) but my distress of mind would be

---

[1] Francis Charles, 6th Marquess of Hertford and 18th Earl of Yarmouth (1777–1842) was a diplomatist and a person of note (and notoriety for his dissipations and pomp) at the court of the Prince Regent. He was the model for Thackeray's "Marquess of Steyne" in *Vanity Fair* and "Marquess of Monmouth" in Disraeli's *Coningsby*. His son was largely educated abroad and followed his father in a diplomatic career.

very much augmented if my daughter quitted England—without my consent or approbation.———I beg that you will lose no time in making this known to Lady B[yron]—and I hope you will say something to enforce my request,—I have no wish to trouble her more than can be helped.———My whole hope—and prospect of a quiet evening (if I reach it) are wrapt up in that little creature Ada—and you must forgive my anxiety in all which regards her even to minuteness.———My journal will have told you all my recent wanderings—I am very well—though I had a little accident yesterday—being in my boat in the evening—the pole of the mainsail slipped in wearing round—& struck me on a nerve of one of my legs so violently—as to make me faint away—Mr. H[obhous]e & cold water brought me to myself—but there was no damage done—no bone hurt—and I have no pain whatever—some nerve or tendon was jarred—for a moment—& that was all.—Today I dine at Coppet—the Jerseys are I believe to be there.— Believe me ever & truly my own dearest Sis. most affectionately and entirely yours

Bn

[TO JOHN MURRAY (a)]   *Diodati. Octr. 5th. 1816*

Dear Sir—I have received a letter from Mrs. L[eigh] in which she tells me that she has decided on the omission of the lines entitled "an Epistle &c."———Upon this point—her option will be followed.— You will of course remember that these lines are the only ones in the volume which I will allow to be omitted—& that the "Monody on S[heridan]" is to be included in the publication—& united with the rest.—As I have no copy of the "epistle to Mrs. L[eigh]"—I request that you will preserve one for me in M.S. for I never can remember a line of that nor any other composition of mine.—I am a good deal surprized that Mr. Davies has not arrived—he has several small commissions—amongst other the original (fair copy) M.S. of the volume you have received.—The rough original—I have sent this evening to my Banker's (Mr. Hentsch of Geneva) who will forward it by Mr. St. Aubyn[1] to England—it is in a box containing letters &c.

---

[1] J. H. St. Aubyn. Byron later identified him as of the University of Oxford, son of Sir John St. Aubyn. See Jan. 24, 1817, to Murray. He later apparently wrote a poem called *Mazza*, modelled on Byron's *The Corsair*. See *Maria Gisborne & Edward E. Williams, Shelley's Friends, Their Journals and Letters*, ed. by Frederick L. Jones, 1951, p. 112. (Jones has read the name of the poem as "Magya", which Williams called "a Venetian tale in imitation of the Corsair".) Trelawny was staying with St. Aubyn in Geneva before going to Pisa in 1822 to meet Shelley and Byron.

and addressed to Mrs. Leigh at her house in the country.——The parcel containing the *Morat Bones* is addressed to you—take care of them for me.—Recollect—do not omit a line of the M.S. sent you except "the epistle".——It is too late for me to start at Shadows.—— If you like to have the original—Mrs. L[eigh] will I dare say send them to you—they are all in the box.——Tomorrow I am for Italy— Milan first—address to Geneva—I do not want to see proofs—if Mr. G[ifford] will have the goodness to look over them—I have written to you twice—yrs. in haste

ever & truly
B

P.S.—Remember me particularly to Mr. Gifford & Mr. Moore— if you see the latter.—I have been twice at Coppet this week— Madame is very well & particularly agreeable—her daughter (the Duchess) is with child.—There were the Duchess of Ragusa & a Prince of—I forget the name—but it was of fifty consonants—German of course—there—both very worthy & pleasing personages.—I have read the last E[dinburgh] R[eview] they are very severe on the Germans[2]—and their Idol Goethe—I have also read Wedderburne Webster—and Ilderim—and the Pamphleteer.[3]——

[TO JOHN MURRAY (*b*)]   *Diodati Octr. 5th. 1816*

Save me a copy of "Bucks Richard 3d."[1] republished by Longman— but do not send out more books—I have too many.——The "Monody" is in too many paragraphs—which makes it unintelligible to me—if anyone else understands it in the present form they are wiser—however —as it cannot be rectified till my return & has been already published —even publish it on in the collection—it will fill up the place of the omitted epistle.——Strike out "by request of a friend"—which is sad trash & must have been done to make it ridiculous.——Be careful in the printing the Stanzas beginning—

"Though the day of my destiny's &c."

[2] The *Edinburgh Review* for June, 1816, reviewed Goethe's *Aus meinem Leben, Dichtung und Wahrheit.*

[3] Wedderburn Webster published *Waterloo and other Poems* in 1816; *Ilderim: A Syrian Tale* was by H. Gally Knight; *The Pamphleteer* was a contemporary periodical which Byron quoted later in his letters to Bowles on the Pope controversy.

[1] Sir George Buc's *History of the Life and Reigne of Richard the Third*, first published in 1646 as the work of George Buck, Esq.

which I think well of as a composition.——"The Antiquary"[2] is not the best of the three—but much above all the last twenty years—saving it's elder brothers.—Holcroft's memoirs[3] are valuable as showing strength of endurance in the man—which is worth more than all the talent in the world.—And so you have been publishing "Margaret of Anjou—" and an Assyrian tale—and refusing W.W.'s Waterloo——and the "Hue & Cry"[4]—I know not which most to admire your rejections or acceptances.——I believe that *prose* is—after all—the most reputable—for certes—if one could foresee—but I wont go on—that is with this sentence——but poetry is—I fear—incurable—God help me—if I proceed in this scribbling—I shall have frittered away my mind before I am thirty.—but it is at times a real relief to me.——For the present—Good Evening.—

> [Yours very truly,
> B][5]

[TO CHARLES HENTSCH[1]]   *Diodati. Octr. 5th. 1816*

Dear Sir—I send you the boat—which is not—I fear—in very good order—but I can recommend it as a very safe one—having tried it over the whole of the Lake—without any accident.——For the many marks of your kindness and attention during my stay in your beautiful country—and not less for your parting compliment I thank you very sincerely—& have the honour to be yr very

> faithful & obliged Sert.
> BYRON

P.S.—There are 4 oars—and all the sails with the boat—I mention this that the people may deliver them accurately.—I have also sent the boxes—you were kind enough to offer to take care of for me—they contain papers—& the Morat bones.—Mr. St. Aubyn is going to England & has promised to take charge of them—in that case—you

---

[2] Scott's *Antiquary* (1816) followed *Waverley* (1814) and *Guy Mannering* (1815).

[3] Holcroft's *Memoirs* (1816) were written partly by himself and partly by Hazlitt.

[4] *Margaret of Anjou*, a poem by Margaret Holford; *Ilderim, A Syrian Tale*, by H. Gally Knight; *Waterloo and Other Poems*, by Wedderburn Webster; "Hue and Cry", unidentified.

[5] Not in M.S. Supplied from *LJ*, III, 372.

[1] Byron's banker at Geneva who, like his other bankers and his publisher, performed many services for him.

will have the goodness to deliver them to him. Once more accept my thanks and—Adieu.— —

[TO JOHN MURRAY] *Martigny. Octr. 9th. 1816*

Dear Sir—Thus far on my way to Italy.—We have just passed the "Pisse-Vache—" (one of the finest torrents in Switzerland)—in time to view the Iris—which the Sun flings along it—before Noon.— —I have written to you twice lately—Mr. Davies I hear is arrived—he brings the original M.S. which you wished to see.—Recollect that the printing is to be from that which Mr. Shelley brought—& recollect also that the concluding stanzas of C[hilde] H[arold]—(those to my *daughter*) which I had not made up my mind whether to publish or not when they were *first* written (as you will see marked on the margin of ye 1st. Copy) I had (& have) fully determined to publish with the rest of the Canto—as in the copy which you received by Mr. Shelley—before I sent it to England.—Our weather is very fine— which is more than the Summer has been;—at Milan I shall expect to hear from you—address either to Milan poste restante—or by way of Geneva—to the care of Monsr. Hentsch Banquier.—I write these few lines in case my other letter should not reach you—I trust one of them will—

yrs. ever truly
B

P.S.—My best respects & regards to Mr. G[ifford]—will you tell him—it may perhaps be as well to put a short note to that part relating to *Clarens*—merely to say—that of course the description does not refer to that particular spot so much as to the *command* of scenery round it—I do not know that this is necessary—& leave it to Mr. G's choice—as my Editor—if he will allow me to call him so at this distance.— —

[TO AUGUSTA LEIGH] *Milan.—Octr. 13th. 1816*

My dearest Augusta—You see I have got to Milan.—We came by the Simplon—escaping all perils of precipices and robbers—of which last there was some talk & apprehension—a chain of English carriages having been stopped near Cesto a few weeks ago—& handsomely pilfered of various chattels.—We were not molested.— —The

113

Simplon as you know—is the most superb of all possible routes;—so I shall not describe it—I also navigated the Lago Maggiore—and went over the Borromean Islands—the latter are fine but too artificial—the lake itself is beautiful—as indeed is the whole country from Geneva hither—and the Alpine part most magnificent.——Close to Milan is the beginning of an unfinished triumphal arch—for Napoleon—so beautiful as to make one regret it's non-completion.—As we only reached Milan last night—I can say little about it—but will write again in a few days.—The Jerseys are here—Made. de Stael is gone to Paris (or going) from Coppet.—I was more there than elsewhere during my stay at Diodati—and she has been particularly kind & friendly towards me the whole time.—When you write—address to *Geneva*—still—Poste *restante*—and my banker—(Monsr. Hentsch) will forward your letters.—I have written to you so often lately—that you will not regret the brevity of this.—I hope that you received safely my presents for the children (by Scrope) and that you also have (by the post) a little journal of a journey in & on the Alps which I sent you early this month—having kept it on purpose for *you*.—

ever my own dearest yrs. most

B

[TO AUGUSTA LEIGH]   *Milan Octr. 15. 1816*

My dearest Augusta—I have been at Churches, Theatres, libraries, and picture galleries. The Cathedral is noble, the theatre grand, the library excellent, and the galleries I know nothing about—except as far as liking one picture out of a thousand. What has delighted me most is a manuscript collection (preserved in the Ambrosian library), of original love-letters and verses of Lucretia de Borgia & Cardinal Bembo; and a lock of hair—so long—and fair & beautiful—and the letters so pretty & so loving that it makes one wretched not to have been born sooner to have at least seen her. And pray what do you think is one of her *signatures?*—why this + a Cross—which she says "is to stand for her name &c." Is not this amusing?[1] I suppose you know that she was a famous beauty, & famous for the use she made of it; & that she was the love of this same Cardinal Bembo (besides a story about her papa Pope Alexander & her brother Cæsar Borgia—which some people don't believe—& others do), and that after all she

[1] The cross was a secret love symbol used frequently in Byron's letters to Augusta, and sometimes in hers to him.

114

ended with being Duchess of Ferrara, and an excellent mother & wife also; so good as to be quite an example. All this may or may not be, but the hair & the letters are so beautiful that I have done nothing but pore over them, & have made the librarian promise me a copy of some of them; and I mean to get some of the hair if I can. The verses are Spanish—the letters Italian—some signed—others with a cross—but all in her own hand-writing.

I am so hurried, & so sleepy, but so anxious to send you even a few lines my dearest Augusta, that you will forgive me troubling you so often; and I shall write again soon; but I have sent you so much lately, that you will have too many perhaps. *A thousand loves* to *you* from *me*—which is very generous for I only ask *one* in return

Ever dearest thine
B

[TO JOHN MURRAY]   *Milan Octr. 15th. 1816*

Dear Sir—I hear that Mr. Davies has arrived in England—but that of some letters &c. committed to his care by Mr. H[obhouse] only *half* have been delivered—This intelligence naturally makes me feel a little anxious for mine—and amongst them for the M.S. which I wished to have compared with the one sent by me through the hands of Mr. Sh[elle]y—I trust that it has arrived safely—and indeed not less so—that some little chrystals &c. from Mont Blanc—for my daughter —and my nieces—have reached their address.—Pray have the goodness to ascertain from Mr. Davies that no accident (by customhouse—or loss) has befallen them—& satisfy me on this point at your earliest convenience.——If I recollect rightly—you told me that Mr. Gifford had kindly undertaken to correct the press (at my request) during my absence—at least I hope so—it will add to my many obligations to that Gentleman.——I wrote to you on my way here—a short note—dated Martinach [*sic*].—Mr. Hobhouse & myself arrived here four days ago—by the Simplon—& Lago Maggiore route—of course we visited the Borromean Islands—which are fine—but too artificial. —The Simplon is magnificent in its nature and it's art—both God & Man have done wonders—to say nothing of the Devil—who must certainly have had a hand (or a hoof) in some of the rocks & ravines through & over which the works are carried.——Milan is striking— the Cathedral superb—the city altogether reminds me of Seville—but a little inferior.——We had heard divers bruits, & took precautions on the road near the frontier against some "many worthy fellows (i.e. felons) that were out"[1]—and had ransacked some preceding travellers a few weeks ago near Sesto or Cesto—I forget which—of cash & raiment—besides putting them in bodily fear—and lodging about twenty slugs in the retreating part of a Courier belonging to Mr. Hope[2];—but we were not molested—and—I do not think in any danger—except of making mistakes in the way of cocking & priming whenever we saw an old house—or an ill-looking thicket—and now & then suspecting the "true men" who have very much the appearance of the thieves of other countries.—What the thieves may look like—I know not—nor desire to know—for—it seems—they come upon you in bodies of thirty ("in buckram & Kendal green"[3]) at a time—so that voyagers have no great chance—it is something like poor dear Turkey in that respect but not so good—for there you can have as great a body of rogues to match the regular banditti—but here the gens d'armes are said to be no great things—and as for one's own people—one can't carry them about like Robinson Crusoe with a gun on each shoulder.— I have been to the Ambrosian library—it is a fine collection—full of M.S.S. edited & unedited—I enclose you a little list of the former recently published.—These are matters for your literati—for me in my simple way—I have been most delighted with a correspondence of letters all original and amatory between *Lucretia Borgia* & *Cardinal Bembo*—(preserved there)[4] I have pored over them and a lock of her hair—the prettiest and finest imaginable—I never saw fairer—and shall go repeatedly to read the epistles over and over—and if I can obtain some of the hair by fair means—I shall try—I have already persuaded the librarian to promise me copies of the letters——& I hope he will not disappoint me.—They are short—but very simple sweet & to the purpose—there are some copies of verses in Spanish also by her;—the tress of her hair is long and as I said before— beautiful. The Brera Gallery of paintings has some fine pictures;—but nothing of a collection—of painting I know nothing—but I like the Guercino[5]—a picture of Abraham putting away Hagar—& Ishmael— which seems to me natural & goodly.—The Flemish School such as I

---

[1] *Macbeth*, Act. IV, scene 3.

[2] Thomas Hope, virtuoso and author?

[3] *Henry IV*, Part I, Act II, scene 4.

[4] The letters, seven in Italian, and two in Spanish, were first published by Baldassare Oltrocchi at Milan in 1859: *Lettere di Lucrezia Borgia a Messer Pietro Bembo, dagli autografi conservati in un codice della Biblioteca Ambrosiana.*

[5] Giovanni Francesco Barbieri, nicknamed from his squint il Guercino (1590–1666).

saw it in Flanders—I utterly detested despised & abhorred—it might be painting—but was not nature;—the Italian is pleasing—& their *Ideal*—very noble.——The Italians I have encountered here are very intelligent & agreeable—in a few days I am to meet Monti.[6]——By the way I have just heard an anecdote of Beccaria[7] who published such admirable things against the punishment of death:—as soon as his book was out—his Servant (having read it I presume) stole his watch —and his Master while correcting the proofs of a second edition did all he could to have him hanged by way of advertisement.——I forgot to mention the triumphal Arch begun by Napoleon as a gate to this city—it is unfinished—but the part completed——worthy of another age—and the same country. The Society here is very oddly carried on —at the theatre—and the theatre only—which answers to our Opera. —People meet there as at a rout—but in very small circles.—From Milan I shall go to Venice.—If you write to Geneva as before—the letter will be forwarded

yrs. ever

Bn

[TO MR. TREVANION[1]]   *Milan Oct. 15th. 1816*

Dear Trevannion—We arrived here a few days ago after a tedious but undisturbed journey—and many others having passed before & since I believe the road may be accounted tolerably safe.—Near the frontier—or rather on passing Cesto—it may be as well to take a couple of Gens d'armes though perhaps even this is superfluous— nobody having been stopped since the affair of Hope's courier.—The Simplon is in very fair order and a most magnificent route it forms— you can also see the Borromean Isles; the road leading along the Lago Maggiore—they are worth the voyage—which is only a few hours.— Of the inns here I can only speak from report—*none* very *good,*—our own indifferent—but it is not the best by any means—the Vetturino brought us to it—& here we shall remain for the fortnight previous to our setting out for Venice. I think you will like Milan—the town is

6 Vincenzo Monti (1754–1828) the distinguished Italian poet. Byron was impressed with him at first but later found his chameleon politics less than admirable. Monti had flattered Napoleon with his *Mascheroniana* and then celebrated the return of the Austrians in several poems.

7 Cesare Bonesana, Marchese di Beccaria (1738–1794), published his *Dei Delitti e delle Pene* in 1764.

1 Trevanion was a distant cousin of Byron. Sophia Trevanion of Carhays, Cornwall, married Byron's grandfather, Admiral Byron.

117

fine and reminds me of Seville which however is the finer of the two.
If you arrive before our departure I hope to see you,

ever yrs. very truly
BYRON

[AUTOGRAPH NOTE]   *Oct. 17, 1816*

"And Beauty draws us by a single Hair".[1] The Hair contained in
this paper belonged to Lucretia Borgia and was obtained by me from
a lock of it which is preserved in the Ambrosian Library[2]. . .

[TO AUGUSTA LEIGH]   *Milan Octr. 26th. 1816*

My dearest Augusta—It is a month since the date of your last
letter—but you are not to suppose that your letters do not arrive—all
the assertions of the post being impeded—are (I believe) false—and
the faults of their non-arrival are in those who write—(or rather do not
write) not in the conveyance.—I have hitherto written to you very
regularly—indeed, rather perhaps too often—but I now tell you that
I will not write again at all—if I wait so long for my answers.—I have
received no less than three letters from one person—all dated within
this month of Octr. so that it cannot be the fault of the post—and—as
to the address—I particularly stated *Geneva* as usual post restante—
or to the care of Monsr. Hentsch Banquier Geneva—perhaps the latter
is the safest.——I mention all this—not from any wish to plague you
—but because ⟨my unfortunate⟩ circumstances perhaps make me feel
more keenly anything which looks like neglect—and as among my
many faults towards you—*that* at least—has not been one—even in
that in which I am often negligent—viz. letter writing—pray do not
set me the example—lest I follow it.——I have written twice since my
arrival at Milan—and once before I left Geneva—my Diodati letter
contained some directions about my daughter Ada—and I hope you
received that letter & fulfilled my request as far as regards my child.—
I wish also to know—if Scrope delivered the things entrusted to him
by me—as I have no news of that illustrious personage.—Milan has
been an agreeable residence to me—but we prepare going on to
Venice next week—you will address however as usual (to my bankers)

[1] Pope, *The Rape of the Lock*, Canto II, line 28: "And beauty draws us with a single hair."
[2] See Oct. 15, 1816, to Murray.

118

at Geneva.——I have found a good many of the noble as well as literary classes of society intelligent—& very kind & attentive to strangers.—I have seen all the sights—& last night among others—heard an Improvisatore recite—a very celebrated one—named Sgricchi[1]—it is not an amusing though a curious effort of human powers.——I enclose you a letter of Monti (who is here & whom I know) the most famous Italian poet now living—as a specimen of his handwriting—if there are any of your acquaintance fond of collecting such things you may give it to them—it is not addressed to me.—— I shall write again before I set out—believe me ever & truly

yrs.

B

[TO AUGUSTA LEIGH]   Octr. 28th. 1816

My dearest Augusta—Two days ago I wrote you the enclosed but the arrival of your letter of the 12th. has revived me a little, so pray forgive the apparent *"humeur"* of the other, which I do not tear up—from laziness—and the hurry of the post as I have hardly time to write another at present.

I really do not & cannot understand all the mysteries & alarms in your letters & more particularly in the last. All I know is—that no human power short of destruction—shall prevent me from seeing you when—where—& how—I may please—according to time & circumstance; that you are the only comfort (except the remote possibility of my daughter's being so) left me in prospect in existence, and that I can bear the rest—so that you remain; but anything which is to divide us would drive me quite out of my senses; Miss Milbanke appears in all respects to have been formed for my destruction; I have thus far—as you know—regarded her without feelings of personal bitterness towards her, but if directly or indirectly—but why do I say this?—You know she is the cause of all—whether intentionally or not is little to the purpose——You surely do not mean to say that if I come to England in Spring, that you & I shall not meet? If so I will never return to it—though I must for many reasons—business &c &c—But I quit this topic for the present.

My health is good, but I have now & then fits of giddiness, & deafness, which make me think like Swift—that I shall be like him &

[1] Tommaso Sgricci (1789–1836), a celebrated *improvvisatore*, whom Byron saw again in Venice.

the *withered* tree he saw—which occasioned the reflection and "die at top" first. My hair is growing grey, & *not* thicker; & my teeth are sometimes *looseish* though still white & sound. Would not one think I was sixty instead of not quite nine & twenty? To talk thus—Never mind—either this must end—or I must end—but I repeat it again & again—*that woman* has destroyed me.

Milan has been made agreeable by much attention and kindness from many of the natives; but the whole tone of Italian society is so different from yours in England; that I have not time to describe it, tho' I am not sure that I do not prefer it. Direct as usual to Geneva— hope the best—& love me the most—as I ever must love you.

B

[TO LADY BYRON]   *Milan. Novr. 1st. 1816*

Before I left Diodati—I wrote to Augusta to transmit a request from me to you on the subject of Ada our daughter—and also a little present which I purchased for her on Mont Blanc. Some time ago I heard that you were unwell—they have since told me you are better—my information in both instances was casual and indirect—as—I cannot (though I sometimes mention you myself) without great pain—hear from others upon any subject connected with you—since our separa-tion.——Do not mistake this feeling for resentment—I bear you none.—I do not say that I have *not* deserved it—I do not say that you intended it—for it could not *be* in your nature—but I do not think a human being ever suffered a greater degree of mental torture than I have undergone since & during our separation:—if it has not des-troyed my health with my peace—it is because I have a great capacity of suffering—and that my constitution appears to be so predisposed as to endure agitation rather than repose,—upon this only can I account for my having borne and bearing what I feel and sustain.—— You will not relieve me—you will not even believe me—but I loved and love you most entirely;—things which you know—and things which you did not know—made me what I was—or rather appeared to you—and amongst others—a want of confidence—had I trusted you—as I had almost resolved soon after our marriage—all would have been better—perhaps well.——However I am paying the penalty of my evils—and eating my heart.——Do not write to me—do not destroy whatever slender or remote hope I may still cling to—but believe me when I protest to you with the most sincere & solemn truth to you and before God—that if there were a means of becoming reunited to you I would embrace it—and that I am very wretched.—Be assured also that I am past the sensation of resentment.——The day after tomorrow—we (that is Mr. H[obhouse] & myself) set off for Venice.——In the Spring I may perhaps be in England—I wish it—but perhaps not.—Let me at least find my daughter there.—I will never willingly do more to distress you—and least I should do so now—I stop—

ever & most truly and affectionately yrs.

B

[TO JOHN MURRAY]   *Milan. Novr. 1st. 1816*

Dear Sir—I have recently written to you rather frequently—but without any late answer.—It is of no great importance.—Mr. Hobhouse & myself set out for Venice in a few days—but you had better still address to me at Mr. Hentsch's Banquier Geneva—he will forward your letters.——I do not know whether I mentioned to you some time ago—that I had parted with the Dr. Polidori—a few weeks previous to my leaving Diodati. I know no great harm of him—but he had an alacrity of getting into scrapes—& was too young and heedless—and having enough to attend to in my own concerns—without time to become his tutor—I thought it much better to give him his Congé.—He arrived at Milan some weeks before Mr. H. & myself.—About a week ago—in consequence of a quarrel at the theatre with an Austrian Officer—in which he was exceedingly in the wrong—he has contrived to get sent out of the territory and is gone to Florence.——I was not present—the pit having been the scene of altercation—but on being sent for from the Cavalier Brema's box where I was quietly staring at the Ballet—I found the man of medicine begirt with grenadiers—arrested by the guard—conveyed into the guard-room—where there was much swearing in several languages.——They were going to keep him there for the night—but on my giving my name—and answering for his apparition the next morning —he was permitted to egress.—Next day—he had an order from the government to be gone in 24 hours—and accordingly gone he is some days ago—we did what we could for him—but to no purpose—and indeed he brought it upon himself—as far as I could learn—for I was not present at the squabble itself.—I believe this is the real state of his case—and I tell it you because I believe things sometimes reach

121

you in England—in a false or exaggerated form. We found Milan very polite and hospitable and have the same hopes of Verona & Venice.—I have filled my paper

> ever yrs.
> BYRON

[TO AUGUSTA LEIGH (a)]   *Milan. Novr. 2d. 1816*

Dearest Augusta—Will you take particular care that Lady B[yron] receives the enclosed letter—I wrote to you twice lately—& will again soon—ever dearest yrs.

> B

[TO AUGUSTA LEIGH (b)]   *Milan. Novr. 2d. 1816*

My dearest Augusta—I wrote to you the other day—& I now do so to send a few lines—and to request you to take particular care that Lady B[yron] receives a letter sent in another enclosure. I feel so miserable that I must write to her—however useless.——In a day or two we set off for Venice. I have seen a good deal of Milanese society but nothing to make me forget others—or forgive myself.—— Dr. Polidori—(whom I dismissed some time before I left Geneva—as I had no use for him & his temper & habits were not good) had been in Milan some time before—but getting into a scrape & a quarrel with some Austrians—has been sent by the Government out of the territory.—*I* had nothing to do with his squabble—& was not even present—though—when he sent for me—I tried of course to get him out of it—as well as Mr. Hobhouse—who tried also for him—but to no purpose. I tell you all this because in England—by some kind mistake—his squabbles may be set down to me—and now (if this should be the case) you have it in your power to contradict it.——It happened about a week ago.——I shall probably write to you on my road to Venice—from Verona—or elsewhere—

> ever my dearest thine
> B

[TO THOMAS MOORE]   *Verona, November 6th, 1816*

My Dear Moore,—Your letter, written before my departure from England, and addressed to me in London, only reached me recently.

Since that period, I have been over a portion of that part of Europe which I had not already seen. About a month since, I crossed the Alps from Switzerland to Milan, which I left a few days ago, and am thus far on my way to Venice, where I shall probably winter. Yesterday I was on the shores of the Benacus, with his *fluctibus et fremitu*.[1] Catullus's Sirmium[2] has still its name and site, and is remembered for his sake: but the very heavy autumnal rains and mists prevented our quitting our route, (that is, Hobhouse and myself, who are at present voyaging together), as it was better not to see it at all than to a great disadvantage.

I found on the Benacus the same tradition of a city still visible in calm weather below the waters, which you have preserved of Lough Neagh, "When the clear, cold eve's declining."[3] I do not know that it is authorised by records; but they tell you such a story, and say that the city was swallowed up by an earthquake. We moved to-day over the frontier to Verona, by a road suspected of thieves,—"the wise *convey* it call,"[4]—but without molestation. I shall remain here a day or two to gape at the usual marvels,—amphitheatre, paintings, and all that time-tax of travel—though Catullus, Claudian, and Shakespeare have done more for Verona than it ever did for itself. They still pretend to show, I believe, the "tomb of all the Capulets"—we shall see.

Among many things at Milan, one pleased me particularly, viz. the correspondence (in the prettiest love-letters in the world) of Lucretia Borgia with Cardinal Bembo, (who, *you say*, made a very good cardinal,) and a lock of her hair, and some Spanish verses of hers,— the lock very fair and beautiful. I took one single hair of it as a relic, and wished sorely to get a copy of one or two of the letters; but it is prohibited; *that* I don't mind; but it was impracticable; and so I only got some of them by heart. They are kept in the Ambrosian Library, which I often visited to look them over—to the scandal of the librarian, who wanted to enlighten me with sundry valuable MSS., classical, philosophical, and pious. But I stick to the Pope's daughter, and wish myself a cardinal.

I have seen the finest parts of Switzerland, the Rhine, the Rhone, and the Swiss and Italian lakes; for the beauties of which I refer you

1 Benacus was the Latin name of the Lago di Garda. See Virgil, *Georgics*, II, line 160: "Fluctibus et fremitu assurgens, Benace, marino."
2 Catullus's "Sirmio" was the peninsula on the Lago di Garda now known as Sirmione.
3 From an Irish melody.
4 *Merry Wives of Windsor*, Act I, scene 3.

to the Guide-book. The north of Italy is tolerably free from the English; but the south swarms with them, I am told. Madame de Stael I saw frequently at Copet, which she renders remarkably pleasant. She has been particularly kind to me. I was for some months her neighbour, in a country house called Diodati, which I had on the Lake of Geneva. My plans are very uncertain; but it is probable that you will see me in England in the spring. I have some business there. If you write to me, will you address to the care of Mons. Hentsch, Banquier, Geneva, who receives and forwards my letters. Remember me to Rogers, who wrote to me lately, with a short account of your poem, which, I trust, is near the light.[5] He speaks of it most highly.

My health is very endurable, except that I am subject to casual giddiness and faintnesses, which is so like a fine lady, that I am rather ashamed of the disorder. When I sailed, I had a physician with me, whom, after some months of patience, I found it expedient to part with, before I left Geneva some time. On arriving at Milan, I found this gentleman in very good society, where he prospered for some weeks; but, at length, at the theatre, he quarrelled with an Austrian officer, and was sent out by the government in twenty-four hours. I was not present at his squabble; but, on hearing that he was put under arrest, I went and got him out of his confinement, but could not prevent his being sent off, which, indeed, he partly deserved, being quite in the wrong, and having begun a row for row's sake. I had preceded the Austrian government some weeks myself, in giving him his congé from Geneva. He is not a bad fellow, but very young and hot-headed, and more likely to incur diseases than to cure them. Hobhouse and myself found it useless to intercede for him. This happened some time before we left Milan. He is gone to Florence.

At Milan I saw, and was visited by, Monti, the most celebrated of the living Italian poets. He seems near sixty; in face he is like the late Cooke the actor. His frequent changes in politics have made him very unpopular as a man. I saw many more of their literati; but none whose names are well known in England, except Acerbi.[6] I lived much with the Italians, particularly with the Marquis of Breme's family, who are very able and intelligent men, especially the Abate.[7] There was a

[5] Moore's *Lalla Rookh* was finished but was not published until 1817.

[6] Giuseppe Acerbi (1773–1846) was a literary man closely associated with Monti.

[7] The Marchese di Breme (1754–1828) was a man of some power and influence in Italian affairs. His second son Luigi (or Ludivico), the Abbate, a man of literary taste, was attached to the romantic school and to liberal views. Byron had met him at Coppet.

famous improvvisatore[8] who held forth while I was there. His fluency astonished me; but, although I understand Italian, and speak it (with more readiness than accuracy), I could only carry off a few very common-place mythological images, and one line about Artemisia, and another about Algiers, with sixty words of an entire tragedy about Eteocles and Polynices. Some of the Italians liked him—others called his performance "seccatura" (a devilish good word, by the way)[9] and all Milan was in controversy about him.

The state of morals in these parts is in some sort lax. A mother and son were pointed out at the theatre, as being pronounced by the Milanese world to be of the Theban dynasty—but this was all. The narrator (one of the first men in Milan) seemed to be not sufficiently scandalised by the taste or the tie. All society in Milan is carried on at the opera: they have private boxes, where they play cards, or talk, or any thing else; but (except at the Cassino) there are no open houses, or balls, &c., &c. *

The peasant girls have all very fine dark eyes, and many of them are beautiful. There are also two dead bodies in fine preservation—one Saint Carlo Boromeo at Milan;[10] the other not a saint, but a chief, named Visconti, at Monza[11]—both of which appeared very agreeable. In one of the Boromean isles (the Isola bella), there is a large laurel— the largest known—on which Buonaparte, staying there just before the battle of Marengo, carved with his knife the word "Battaglia". I saw the letters, now half worn out and partly erased.

Excuse this tedious letter. To be tiresome is the privilege of old age and absence; I avail myself of the latter, and the former I have anticipated. If I do not speak to you of my own affairs, it is not from want of confidence, but to spare you and myself. My day is over— what then?—I have had it. To be sure, I have shortened it; and if I had done as much by this letter, it would have been as well. But you will forgive that, if not the other faults of

Yours ever and most affectionately,

B

---

[8] Tommaso Sgricci.
[9] Byron used the word in *Beppo*, stanza 31.
[10] Carlo Borromeo (1538–1584), canonized in 1610, lies in a subterranean chapel in front of the altar at Milan Cathedral.
[11] The body of Ettore Visconti is in a building adjoining the Cathedral at Monza.

I have been over Verona. The amphitheatre is wonderful—beats even Greece. Of the truth of Juliet's story, they seem tenacious to a degree, insisting on the fact—giving a date (1303), and showing a tomb. It is a plain, open, and partly decayed sarcophagus, with withered leaves in it, in a wild and desolate conventual garden, once a cemetery, now ruined to the very graves. The situation struck me as very appropriate to the legend, being blighted as their love. I have brought away a few pieces of the granite, to give to my daughter and my nieces. Of the other marvels of this city, paintings, antiquities, &c., excepting the tombs of the Scaliger princes,[12] I have no pretensions to judge. The gothic monuments of the Scaligers pleased me, but "a poor virtuoso am I,"[13] and

Ever yours.

[TO AUGUSTA LEIGH]   *Verona Novr. 6th. 1816*

My dearest Augusta—I am thus far on my way to Venice—and shall stay here a day to see the place—the paintings—the "tomb of all the Capulets" which they show—(at least a tomb they call so after the story—from which Shakespeare drew the plot of his play) and all the sights & so forths at which it is usual to gape in passing.—I left Milan on Sunday & have travelled but slowly—over some celebrated ground—but Lombardy is not a beautiful country at least in autumn—excepting however the Lago di Garda & it's outlines which are mountainous on one side—and it is a very fine stormy lake throughout—never quiet—and I had the pleasure of seeing it in all its vexation—foaming like a little Sea—as Virgil has described it—but (thank God) you are not a blue-stocking—and I wont inflict the appropriate bit of Latin upon you—my own dearest Sis.——I wrote you a few scraps of *letterets* (I may call them they were so short) from Milan—just to keep you out of (or *in*) a fuss about baby B.—Dr. Polidori—whom I parted with before I left Geneva—(not for any great harm—but because he was always in squabbles—& had no kind of conduct)—contrived at Milan—which he reached before me—to get into a quarrel with an Austrian—& to be ordered out of the city by the government.———*I did not even see his adventure*—nor had anything

[12] The tombs of the Della Scala family near the church of Santa Maria Antica.
[13] A line from Moore's poem "To Mrs———" in *The Poems of Thomas Little*: "But I swear I can't love for antiquity's sake,/Such a poor virtuoso am I."

to do with it—except getting him out of arrest—and trying to get him altogether out of the scrape.—This I mention—because I know in England—someone or other will probably transfer his adventures to me—after what has been said already—I have a right to suspect every thing and every body—so I state all this for your satisfaction—and that you may be able to contradict any such report.—Mr. Hobhouse & Trevannion—and indeed everybody—Italians & English—then at Milan—can corroborate this if necessary.—It occurred several days before Mr. H[obhouse] & myself left it.——So much for this.——
When we reach Venice I shall write to you again—I had received your acknowledgement of the journal &c. & the trinkets by Scrope—of which I delight to hear the reception.——In health I am pretty well—except that the confounded Lombardy rains of this season (the autumn) have given me a flying rheumatism—which is troublesome at times—and makes me feel ancient.—I am also growing grey & *giddy*—and cannot help thinking my head will decay;—I wish my memory would—at least my remembrance—except a parenthesis for *ou*-my dearest Augusta.—Ada—by the way Ada's name (which I found in our pedigree under King John's reign) is the same with that of the Sister of Charlemagne—as I read the other day in a book treating of the Rhine.

ever my own—thy own

P.S.—I forgot to tell you that my dog (Mutz by name & Swiss by nation) shuts a door when he is told—there—that's more than Tip can do.—Remember me to the child*er*—and to Georgiana—who I suppose is grown a prodigious penwoman.—I hope she likes her seals and all her share of Mont Blanc.—I have had so much of mountains that I am not yet reconciled to the plains—but they improve. Verona seems a fine city.

P.S. Novr. 7th.—I have been over Verona.—The Amphitheatre is superb—& in high preservation. Of the *truth* of the story of Juliet they seem very tenacious giving the date (1303) and shewing a tomb.—It is an open granite sarcophagus in a most desolate convent garden—which looks quite wild & withered—and once was a Cimetery since ruined—I brought away four small pieces of it for you & the babes (at least the female part of them) and for Ada & her mother if she will accept it from you. I thought the situation more appropriate to the history than if it had been less blighted.—This struck me more than all the antiquities—more even that the Amphitheatre.—

[TO AUGUSTA LEIGH] *Venice. Novr. 11th. 1816*

My dearest Augusta—Your letter with ⟨Miss Milbanke's⟩ Lady B[yron]'s answer through you has reached me here—where I arrived yesterday. I wrote to you from Verona—and once or twice from Milan.——The answer is little to the purpose—what I desire & request is—that in any case *my daughter* do not leave England—I require this to be *repeated* & *understood*—I trust I shall not be obliged to take *legal measures* to prevent such an occurrence—I repeat that I have no wish nor thought of troubling the mother more than can be avoided—but I will not suffer my child to quit her country—if I have power to prevent it—& whether I have or not—surely a more atrocious additional cruelty could hardly be devised than the attempting this contrary to my express wish and opinion.——Say this in what words you please.—I wrote to Lady B[yron] (enclosed to *you*) from Milan;—the information of her possible intention came *through* Lady Mel[bourn]e but *not to* me.——I am wretched enough as it is— whatever I may have done—I have suffered in proportion—and I hope that this woman will be at last satisfied—& not torture me through my child as in herself.

[Manuscript ends without signature]

[TO JOHN HANSON] *Venice. Novr. 11th. 1816*

My dear Sir—Information having reached me of an intention of Lady Byron to go upon the Continent—I wrote to my Sister to object to the *Child's* leaving England.—To this the answer has been that "Lady B. did not mean to quit England this winter" but not a word of reply on the subject of the *Child*.——*My daughter* shall *not* leave England with my consent—I protest against it for every reason—& in every possible form—and I beg & desire that you will immediately take the proper steps (*legal* if necessary) to prevent the possibility of such an occurrence.—If Lady B—thinks proper now—or hereafter—to travel— that is no business of mine—but my daughter and only legitimate child must not be of the party—I do not wish to take her from the family— let her in such a case remain with Lady Noel—or my sister (or *I* will return immediately if necessary to receive her—) but let it be *immediately settled & understood that in no case is my daughter to leave the country.*—Pray let me have an answer as soon as you conveniently can on this anxious subject—and do not delay ascertaining & arranging this point a moment—as it is to me of much consequence;—in the present state of the Continent—I would not have my child rambling over it for millions.——Address me here—viz. *Venise*—Italy—*Poste-Restante*

yrs. ever truly
Byron

P.S.—If necessary I could come to England *now*—but wish to defer my return till *Spring*—unless absolutely necessary—Pray write—& do not neglect or delay on this point—I suppose as having my power of Attorney you can act for me—if not—let me know at all events immediately.——

[RECOMMENDING ANGELO SPRINGHETTI]   [*Venice, Nov. 12, 1816*]

Angelo Springhetti—Vetturino—conducted me from Geneva to Milan—and subsequently from Milan to Venice. His Honesty, attention—and civility will strongly recommend him to other travellers . . .

[TO THOMAS MOORE]   *Venice, November 17th, 1816*

I wrote to you from Verona the other day in my progress hither, which letter I hope you will receive. Some three years ago, or it may be more, I recollect your telling me that you had received a letter from our friend Sam, dated "On board his gondola". *My* gondola is, at this present, waiting for me on the canal; but I prefer writing to you in the house, it being autumn—and rather an English autumn than otherwise. It is my intention to remain at Venice during the winter, probably, as it has always been (next to the East) the greenest island of my imagination. It has not disappointed me; though its evident decay would, perhaps, have that effect upon others. But I have been familiar with ruins too long to dislike desolation. Besides, I have fallen in love, which, next to falling into the canal, (which would be of no use, as I can swim.) is the best or the worst thing I could do. I have got some extremely good apartments in the house of a "Merchant of Venice," who is a good deal occupied with business, and has a wife in her twenty-second year. Marianna (that is her name)[1] is in her appearance altogether like an antelope. She has the large, black,

---

[1] Marianna Segati who with her husband, a draper, lived in the Frezzeria, a narrow street just off the Piazza San Marco.

oriental eyes, with that peculiar expression in them which is seen rarely among *Europeans*—even the Italians—and which many of the Turkish women give themselves by tinging the eyelid,—an art not known out of that country, I believe. This expression she has *naturally*,—and something more than this. In short, I cannot describe the effect of this kind of eye,—at least upon me. Her features are regular, and rather aquiline—mouth small—skin clear and soft, with a kind of hectic colour—forehead remarkably good: her hair is of the dark gloss, curl, and colour of Lady J * * 's [Jersey's]: her figure is light and pretty, and she is a famous songstress—scientifically so; her natural voice (in conversation, I mean) is very sweet; and the naiveté of the Venetian dialect is always pleasing in the mouth of a woman.

November 23.

You will perceive that my description, which was proceeding with the minuteness of a passport, has been interrupted for several days. In the meantime *

December 5

Since my former dates, I do not know that I have much to add on the subject, and, luckily, nothing to take away; for I am more pleased than ever with my Venetian, and begin to feel very serious on that point—so much so, that I shall be silent. * * * * * * * * * * * * *
By way of divertisement, I am studying daily, at an Armenian monastery,[2] the Armenian language. I found that my mind wanted something craggy to break upon; and this—as the most difficult thing I could discover here for an amusement—I have chosen, to torture me into attention. It is a rich language, however, and would amply repay any one the trouble of learning it. I try, and shall go on;—but I answer for nothing, least of all for my intentions or my success. There are some very curious MSS. in the monastery, as well as books; translations also from Greek originals, now lost, and from Persian and Syriac, &c.; besides works of their own people. Four years ago the French instituted an Armenian professorship. Twenty pupils presented themselves on Monday morning, full of noble ardour, ingenuous youth, and impregnable industry. They persevered, with a courage worthy of the nation and of universal conquest, till Thursday; when *fifteen* of the *twenty* succumbed to the six-and-twentieth letter of the

[2] The Armenian Mekhitarist Convent was founded by Peter Mekhitar in 1717. It was on the Island of San Lazzaro near the Lido about two miles from Venice.

alphabet. It is, to be sure, a Waterloo of an Alphabet[3]—that must be said for them. But it is so like these fellows, to do by it as they did by their sovereigns—abandon both; to parody the old rhymes, "Take a thing and give a thing"—"Take a King and give a King". They are the worst of animals, except their conquerors.

I hear that H[odgso]n is your neighbour, having a living in Derbyshire.[4] You will find him an excellent-hearted fellow, as well as one of the cleverest; a little, perhaps, too much japanned by preferment in the church and the tuition of youth, as well as inoculated with the disease of domestic felicity, besides being over-run with fine feelings about women and *constancy* (that small change of Love, which people exact so rigidly, receive in such counterfeit coin, and repay in baser metal); but, otherwise, a very worthy man, who has lately got a pretty wife, and (I suppose) a child by this time. Pray remember me to him, and say that I know not which to envy most—his neighbourhood, him, or you.

Of Venice I shall say little. You must have seen many descriptions; and they are most of them like. It is a poetical place; and classical, to us, from Shakespeare and Otway. I have not yet sinned against it in verse, nor do I know that I shall do so, having been tuneless since I crossed the Alps, and feeling, as yet, no renewal of the "estro".[5] By the way, I suppose you have seen "Glenarvon". Madame de Stael lent it me to read from Copet last autumn. It seems to me that, if the authoress had written the *truth*, and nothing but the truth—the whole truth—the romance would not only have been more *romantic*, but more entertaining. As for the likeness, the picture can't be good—I did not sit long enough. When you have leisure, let me hear from and of you, believing me,

Ever and truly yours most affectionately,

B

P.S.—Oh! *your Poem*—is it out? I hope Longman has paid his thousands: but don't you do as H[orace] T[wiss]'s father did,[6] who, having made money by a quarto tour, became a vinegar merchant; when, lo! his vinegar turned sweet (and be damned to it) and ruined him. My last letter to you (from Verona) was enclosed to Murray—

3 The Armenian alphabet has 38 characters.
4 Francis Hodgson, one of Byron's closest friends in England, was appointed on July 18, 1816, to the living at Bakewell in Derbyshire.
5 Inspiration, ardour, whim.
6 Horace Twiss's uncle, Richard Twiss (1741–1821), published *Travels through Portugal and Spain* (1775) which Dr. Johnson read and praised. He was ruined later, not by vinegar but by a speculation in making paper from straw.

have you got it? Direct to me *here, poste restante.* There are no English here at present. There were several in Switzerland—some women; but, except Lady Dalrymple Hamilton,[7] most of them as ugly as virtue—at least, those I saw.

[TO JOHN CAM HOBHOUSE]   *Novr. 20th. 1816*

My dear H.—I have made a bargain of about *three* francs or rather more a day—for *both* my horses—to be kept *here*—& recommend this to your notice.—Enclosed are some rhymes on the Helen[1]—

ever yrs. most truly
Bn

[TO JOHN MURRAY]   *Venice Novr. 25th. 1816*

Dear Sir—It is some months since I have heard from or of you—I think—*not* since I left Diodati.—From Milan I wrote once or twice;—but have been here some little time—and intend to pass the winter without removing.—I was much pleased with the Lago di Garda & with Verona—particularly the amphitheatre—and a sarcophagus in a Convent garden—which they show as Juliet's—they insist on the *truth* of her history.—Since my arrival at Venice—the Lady of the Austrian Governor[1] told me that between Verona & Vicenza there are still ruins of the Castle of the *Montecchi*—and a chapel once appertaining to the Capulets—Romeo seems to have been of *Vicenza* by the tradition—but I was a good deal surprized to find so firm a faith in Bandello's novel[2]—which seems really to have been founded on a fact.———Venice pleases me as much as I expected—and I expected much—it is one of those places which I know before I see them—and has always haunted me the most—after the East.———I like the gloomy gaiety of their gondolas—and the silence of their canals—I do not even dislike the evident decay of the city—though I regret the singularity of it's vanished costume—however there is much left still;

[7] Lady Hamilton was the eldest daughter of Adam, 1st Viscount Duncan. She married in 1800 Sir Hew Dalrymple Hamilton.
[1] These were Byron's lines "On the Bust of Helen by Canova". The bust had been given by Canova to the Countess Albrizzi, at whose home Byron saw it.
[1] Countess Goetz.
[2] Matteo Bandello (1450–1562) borrowed the story from Luigi da Porto in whose hands the old story first took on the Shakespearean form.

—the Carnival too is coming.——St. Mark's—and indeed Venice—is most alive at night—the theatres are not open till *nine*—and the society is proportionably late—all this is to my taste—but most of your countrymen miss & regret the rattle of hackney coaches—without which they can't sleep.——I have got remarkably good apartments in a private house—I see something of the inhabitants (having had a good many letters to some of them) I have got my gondola—I read a little—& luckily could speak Italian (more fluently though than accurately) long ago;—I am studying out of curiosity the *Venetian* dialect—which is very naive — soft & peculiar—though not at all classical—I go out frequently—and am in very good contentment.—— The *Helen* of Canova—(a bust which is in the house of M[adam]e the Countess d'Albrizzi³ whom I know) is without exception to my mind the most perfectly beautiful of human conceptions—and far beyond my ideas of human execution.—

———

In this beloved marble view
    Above the works & thoughts of Man—
What Nature *could*—but *would not* do—
    And Beauty and Canova *can*!
Beyond Imagination's power—
    Beyond the Bard's defeated art,
With immortality her dower—
    Behold the *Helen* of the *heart*!

———

Talking of the "heart" reminds me that I have fallen in love—which except falling into the Canal—(and that would be useless as I swim) is the best (or worst) thing I could do.——I am therefore in love— fathomless love—but lest you should make some splendid mistake—& envy me the possession of some of those Princesses or Countesses with whose affections your English voyagers are apt to invest them- selves—I beg leave to tell you—that my Goddess is only the wife of a "Merchant of Venice"—but then she is pretty as an Antelope,—is but two & twenty years old—has the large black Oriental eyes—with the Italian countenance—and dark glossy hair of the curl & colour of Lady Jersey's—then she has the voice of a lute—and the song of a Seraph (though not quite so sacred) besides a long postscript of graces—virtues and accomplishments—enough to furnish out a new Chapter for Solomon's song.—But her great merit is finding out

³ See Appendix IV.

mine—there is nothing so amiable as discernment.—Our little arrangement is completed—the usual oaths having been taken—and everything fulfilled according to the "understood relations" of such liaisons. The general race of women appear to be handsome—but in Italy as on almost all the Continent—the highest orders are by no means a well looking generation—and indeed reckoned by their countrymen very much otherwise.—Some are exceptions but most of them as ugly as Virtue herself.—If you write—address to me *here Poste Restante*—as I shall probably stay the winter over.—I never see a newspaper & know nothing of England—except in a letter now & then from my Sister.—Of the M.S. sent you I know nothing except that you have received it—& are to publish it &c. &c. but when—where—& how—you leave me to guess—. But it don't much matter.— —I suppose you have a world of works passing through your process for next year—when does Moore's poem appear?—I sent a letter for him addressed to your care the other day.—So—Mr. *Frere* is married —and you tell me in a former letter that he had "nearly forgotten that he was so—"[4]—he is fortunate.— —

> yrs ever & very truly
> B

My dear Kinnaird—Before I left Switzerland I answered your last letter & feel a little anxious to know that you have received it—as it was partly on business—that is to say on the disposition of Murray's proposed payment.—I fear there seems little chance of an immediate Sale of Newstead, which is to be wished for many reasons.— H[ob-house] & I have been some time in the North of Italy—& reached Venice about a fortnight ago—where I shall remain probably during the winter.— —It is a place which I like—and which I long anticipated that I should like—besides—I have fallen in love—and with a very pretty woman—so much so—as to obtain the approbation of the not easily approving H[obhouse]—who is in general rather tardy in his applause of the fairer part of the creation.— —She is married—so our arrangement was formed according to the incontinent continental

---

[4] Murray had written that Frere "came to see me while at breakfast this morning, and between some stanzas which he was repeating to me of a truly original poem of his own, he said carelessly, 'By the way, about *half-and-hour ago* I was so silly (taking an immense pinch of snuff and priming his nostrils with it) as to get *married*!'" (Smiles, I, *366.*)

system—which need not be described to you an experienced voyager—
and gifted withal with a modest self-confidence—which my bashful
nature is not endowed with—but nonetheless I have got the woman—
I do not very well know how—but we do exceedingly well together.—
She is not two and twenty—with great black Eastern eyes—and a
variety of subsidiary charms &c. &c. and amongst her other accomplishments—is a mighty & admirable singer—as most of the Italians
are—(though not a public one)—luckily I can speak the language
fluently—& luckily (if I did not) we could employ ourselves a little
without talking.———I meant to have given up gallivanting altogether
—on leaving your country—where I had been totally sickened of that
& every thing else—but I know not how it is—my health growing
better—& my spirits not worse—the "besoin d'aimer" came back
upon my heart again—after all there is nothing like it.———So much
for that matter.———I hear you are in a room with Dibdin & Fanny
Kelly[1]—& the Devil knows whom—Humph!———I hear also that at
the meeting or in the committee—you said that I was coming back in
spring—it is probable—& if you have said so I *will* come—for sundry
reasons—to see my daughter—my sister—and my friends—(and not
least nor last—yourself) to renew my proxy (if Parliament be
dissolved) for the Whigs—to see Mr. Waite & Mr. Blake[2]—and the
newest play—and the S[ub] committee—and to sell Newstead (if I
can) but not to reside in England again—it neither suits me—nor I
it—my greatest error was remaining there—that is to say—my
greatest error but *one*—my ambition—if ever I had merits—is over—
or at least limited—if I could but remain as I now am—I should not
merely be happy—but *contented* which in my mind is the strongest &
most difficult attainment of the two—for any one who will hazard
enough may have moments of happiness.———I have books—a decent
establishment—a fine country—a language which I prefer—most of
the amusements & conveniences of life—as much of society as I
choose to take—and a handsome woman—who is not a bore—and
does not annoy me with looking like a fool & ⟨pretending⟩ setting
up for a sage.—Life has little left for my curiosity—there are few

---

[1] Thomas John Dibdin (1771–1841) was a prolific writer of dramatic productions and songs. His musical plays were immensely popular. Byron as a boy
admired his song "The Maid of Lodi", and was later associated with him at Drury
Lane, where he was a member of the sub-committee of management. After the
death of Whitbread, Dibdin and Alexander Rae were appointed joint managers of
the theatre. Frances Maria (Fanny) Kelly was a popular actress and singer long
associated with Drury Lane.
[2] Waite was a dentist and Blake a fashionable hair-dresser or barber.

things in it of which I have not had a sight and a share—it would be silly to quarrel with my luck because it did not last—& even that was partly my own fault.——If the present does—I should not fall out with the past:—and if I could but manage to arrange my pecuniary concerns in England—so as to pay my debts—& leave me what would be here a very fair income—(though nothing remarkable at home) you might consider me as posthumous—for I would never willingly dwell in the "tight little Island".[3]——Pray write to me a line or two addressed to Venice—*Poste Restante*—I hope to remain here the winter—remember me to Maria—and believe me yrs. ever & truly & affectly.

B

P.S.—Colonel Finch[4] an English acquaintance of H[obhouse]'s & mine has I believe written to you to complain of his banker (who is also mine) and has with our permission mentioned our names to you as knowing him.—I must however say that *I* have no complaint whatever against (Mr. Siri) the banker—who has on the contrary been remarkably civil & attentive to both H & myself.——Of Col. Finch's row with him I understand nothing—but that he had one.——Pray let me hear from you—& tell me what Murray has done—& if you have received my letter from Geneva in answer to your former one.——

P.S.—If you write to me—pray—do not refer to any *persons* or *events*—except our own *theatrical—political—personal—attorneycal—poetical—& diabolical*—concerns. You see I give a pretty wide range still—but what I wish to put under Quarantine are (*my*) *family events*—& all allusion thereto past—present—or to come.—It is what I have laid an embargo on with all my other friends.—It will be better that the *Author* of these lines[5] (if spoken) be *not* avowed—pray—make it a secret & keep it so.——

[3] Byron was fond of this phrase from a song by Dibdin, "The Snug Little Island", in a musical play called *The British Raft* (1797).
[4] An Englishman living in Italy whom Byron had first met in Milan. Robert Finch, M.A. Balliol College, Oxford, was a parson, traveller, scholar, and antiquary, who assumed the title of Colonel. The Shelleys later met him in Rome and considered him ridiculous and a great bore.
[5] Byron's "Monody" on the death of Sheridan was spoken at Drury Lane without Byron's name as the author and later published thus by Murray.

Dear Sir—I have written to you so frequently of late—that you will think me a bore—as I think you a very impolite person for not answering my letters—from Switzerland—Milan—Verona—& Venice.—There are some things I wanted & want to know—viz whether Mr. Davies of inaccurate memory had or had *not* delivered the M.S. as delivered *to* him—because if he has not—you will find that he will bountifully bestow extracts & transcriptions to all the curious of his acquaintance—in which case you may possibly find your publication anticipated by the "Cambridge" or other Chronicles:[1]—in the next place—I forget what was next—but in the 3d. place—I want to hear whether you have yet published—or when you mean to do so—or why you have not done so—because in your last (Septr. 20th. you may be ashamed of the date) you talked of this being done immediately.— From England I hear nothing—& know nothing of any thing or any body—I have but one correspondent (except Mr. Kinnaird on business now & then) & that one is a female—& her letters are so full of mysteries & miseries—such a quantity of the trivial & conjectural—& such a dearth of any useful or even amusing information—that I know no more of your island—or city—than the Italian version of the French papers chooses to tell me,—or the advertisements of Mr. Colburn tagged to the end of your Quarterly review for the year *ago*.—I wrote to you at some length last week—so that I have little to add—except that I had begun & am proceeding in a study of the Armenian language—which I acquire as well as I can—at the Armenian convent where I go every day to take lessons of a learned Friar—and have gained some singular and not useless information with regard to the literature & customs of that Oriental people.——They have an establishment here—a church & convent of seventy monks—very learned & accomplished men—some of them—they have also a press— & make great efforts for the enlightening of their nation.—I find the language (which is *twin*, the *literal* and the *vulgar*) difficult but not invincible (at least I hope not)—I shall go on.——I found it necessary to twist my mind round some severer study—and this—as being the hardest I could devise here—will be a file for the serpent.——I mean to remain here till the Spring—so address to me *directly* to *Venice Poste restante.*———Mr. Hobhouse for the present is gone to Rome with his brother—brother's wife—& Sister—who overtook him here

---

[1] *The Cambridge Chronicle*, started in 1762, was a newspaper that gave more attention than most papers to literature. It published many poems.

—he returns in two months—I should have gone too—but I fell in love—& must stay that over—I shall think that—and the Armenian Alphabet—will last the winter—the lady has luckily for me been less obdurate than the language—or between the two I should have lost my remains of sanity. By the way—*she* is not Armenian but a Venetian —as I believe I told you in my last.—As for Italian I am fluent enough, even in it's Venetian modification—which is something like the Somersetshire version of English—and as for the more classical dialects—I had not forgot my former practice in it during my voyaging.— —

yrs. ever & truly
B

P.S.—Remember me to Mr. Gifford—and do not forget me to— but I don't think I have any other friends of your acquaintance.

[TO JOHN MURRAY]   *Venice. Decr. 9th. 1816*

Dear Sir—In a letter from England I am informed that a man named Johnson has taken upon himself to publish some poems called "a Pilgrimage to Jerusalem—a tempest—and an address to my daughter["] &c. and to attribute them to me—adding that he had paid five hundred guineas for them.—The answer to this is short.—*I never wrote such poems—never received the sum he mentions—nor any other in the same quarter—nor* (as far as moral or mortal certainty can be sure) *ever had directly or indirectly the slightest communication with Johnson in my life*;[1]—not being aware that the person existed till this intelligence—gave me to understand, that there were such people.— Nothing surprises me—or this perhaps *would*—& most things amuse me—or this probably would *not*.— —With regard to myself—the man has merely *lied*—that's natural—his betters have set him the example. —But with regard to you—his assertion may perhaps injure you in your publications—and I desire that it may receive the most public and

---

[1] The *Morning Chronicle* of Nov. 30, 1816, reported: "Court of Chancery, Westminster, Nov. 28th, Lord Byron's Poems.

"Lord Byron v. James Johnston

"Sir Samuel Romilly moved for an Injunction on the part of the Noble Plaintiff, to restrain the Defendant from publishing a spurious edition of his Works, entitled, 'Lord Byron's Pilgrimage to the Holy Land'—'The Tempest'—'Farewell to England'—'Ode to St. Helena'—'To my Daughter on the Morning of her Birth'— and 'To the Lily of France;' which the defendant advertised in the Newspapers. . . ." The injunction was granted.

unqualified contradiction.——I do not know that there is any punishment for a thing of this kind—& if there were —I should not feel disposed to pursue this ingenious mountebank further than was necessary for his confutation—but thus far it may be necessary to proceed.—You will make what use you please of this letter—and Mr. Kinnaird—who has power to act for me during my absence—will I am sure readily join you in any steps which it may be proper to take—with regard to the absurd falsehood of this poor creature. As you will have recently received several letters from me in my way to Venice—as well as two written since my arrival—I will not at present trouble you further.—

ever very truly yrs.
BYRON

P.S.—Pray let me know that you have received *this* letter—address to Venice—Poste *Restante*. To prevent the recurrence of similar falsifications you may state—that I consider myself responsible for no publication from the year 1812 up to the present date which is not from your press—I speak of course from that period—because previously Cawthorn—& Ridge had both printed compositions of mine.—"A Pilgrimage to *Jerusalem*"! how the devil should I write about *Jerusalem*—never having yet been there?—as for "a tempest" it was *not* a *tempest* when I left England—but a very fresh breeze—and as to an address to little Ada (who by the way is a year old tomorrow) I never wrote a line about her except in "Farewell" & the 3d. Canto of Childe H[arol]d.——

[TO DOUGLAS KINNAIRD]   *Venice. Decr. 17th. 1816*

My dear Kinnaird—I have written to you lately from this place.—Perceiving by yr. letter of the 19th. Septr. that Murray was to pay portions of his agreement at two—three—& four months—and it being now upon the verge of the 3d. moon—I will thank you to receive the same into yr. bank—& transmit to me *here* (addressed to the care of *Messrs. Siri* & *Willhalm Bankers Venice*) credit for the amount of such sums as M[urray] has paid already.——I should prefer *circular notes*—but if not—*letters* of credit—only making them as *general* as you can.——Pray answer me sans delay—for I have heard little—or nothing—lately from your island.——If M[urray] has not yet disbursed—give him a hint—& exact performance.——I suppose any sale of Newstead or Rochdale is hopeless for the present—but I wish to God—it could be accomplished—I have it so much at heart—to divorce myself as much as possible—from all connection with the country called England—feeling so much more tranquil & contented in my present situation—that one of my horrors is—the necessity of returning for business.——I wish you would give Hanson a fillip and try the sale of one or both N[ewstea]d or R[ochdal]e—my expectations are very moderate—my great object is to pay my debts—and whatever my income may be that [it] at least may be *clear*.—I wrote to you the other day—I have little to add concerning Venice—or myself—except that I am studying the Armenian language.—A few nights ago—I saw at the theatre a translation of Holcroft's "Tale of Mystery"[1] and a farce—the *same* by the way of which Dibdin translated one act & you another—it turns upon a Usurer personating a father—and did not succeed at D[rury] L[ane]. I think it was better acted here than there. ——What were the odds at that time—against my seeing the same farce at Venice?—Hobhouse is gone to Rome—with his brother—but returns to Venice in February.—I remain here—probably till Spring. —I believe I told you in my last that I had fallen in love—so that the last month has been one of the pleasantest—& withal the quietest—in my recollection.—Let me hear from you

ever yrs. very truly & affectly.
BYRON

P.S.—Remember me to Maria.—

Venice. Decr. 18th. 1816

My dearest Augusta—I have received one letter dated 19th. Novr. I think (or rather earlier by a week or two perhaps) since my arrival in Venice—where it is my intention to remain probably till the Spring. —The place pleases me—I have found some pleasing society—& the romance of the situation—& it's extraordinary appearance—together with all the associations we are accustomed to connect with Venice— have always had a charm for me—even before I arrived here— and I have not been disappointed in what I have seen.——I go every morning to the Armenian Convent (of *friars not nuns*—my child) to study the language—I mean the *Armenian* language—(for as you perhaps know—I am versed in the Italian which I speak with fluency

---

[1] Thomas Holcroft (1745–1809) wrote a number of sentimental melodramas, the best known of which, *The Road to Ruin* (1792), an exposé of the disasters of gambling, was long popular in England.

rather than accuracy—) and if you ask me my reason for studying this out of the way language—I can only answer that it is Oriental & difficult—& employs me—which are—as you know my Eastern & difficult way of thinking—reasons sufficient. Then I have fallen in love with a very pretty Venetian of two and twenty—with great black eyes —she is married—and so am I—which is very much to the purpose— we have found & sworn an eternal attachment—which has already lasted a lunar month—& I am more in love than ever—& so is the lady—at least she says so—& seems so,—she does not plague me (which is a wonder—) and I verily believe we are one of the happiest —unlawful couples on this side of the Alps.——She is very handsome —very Italian or rather Venetian—with something more of the Oriental cast of countenance;—accomplished & musical after the manner of her nation—her spouse is a very good kind of man who occupies himself elsewhere—and thus the world goes on here as elsewhere.——This adventure came very opportunely to console me— for I was beginning to be "like Sam Jennings very *unappy*" but at present—at least for a month past—I have been very tranquil—very loving—& have not so much embarrassed myself with the tortures of the last two years—and that virtuous monster Miss Milbanke, who had nearly driven me out of my senses.——Hobhouse has gone to Rome with his brother & sister—but returns here in February:—you will easily suppose that I was not disposed to stir from my present position. I have not heard recently from England & wonder if Murray has published the po's sent to him—& I want to know if you don't think them very fine & all that—Goosey my love—don't they make you "put finger in eye?"—You can have no idea of my thorough wretchedness from the day of my parting from you till nearly a month ago—though I struggled against it with some strength—at present I am better—thank Heaven above—& woman beneath—and will be a very good boy.——Pray remember me to the babes—& tell me of little *Da*—who by the way—is a year old—and a few days over.—— My love to you all—& to Aunt *Sophy*—pray tell *her* in particular that I have consoled myself;——and tell Hodgson that his prophecy is accomplished—he said—you remember—I should be in love with an Italian—so I am.—

ever dearest yrs.

B

P.S.—I forgot to tell you—that the *Demoiselle*—who returned to England from Geneva—went there to produce a new baby B.—who is now about to make his appearance—you wanted to hear some adventures—these are enough I think for one epistle.———Pray address direct to Venice. Poste Restante.

[TO JOHN CAM HOBHOUSE]   *Venice. Decr. 19th. 1816*

My dear Hobhouse—Your Bologna missive is arrived.—Thanks.— —Your horse then is dead—"Is the sable warrior fled? thy *steed* is gone, he rests among the dead"[1]—and so do—you best know—how many *francs*—expended in that precious purchase.—I presume that your surviving carrion will be promoted into a saddle-horse—unless you harness your Giuseppe in lieu of the defunct—and make him help to draw his injured master.———In return for the information new & various in your letter—I can send you but a poor requital—the varieties of Venice being no longer various to you—and my daily course of life being much the same—studious in the day & dissolute in the evening. My Armenian lectures still continue—I have about mastered thirty of the thirty eight cursed scratches of Mesrob the Maker of Alphabets and some words of one syllable;—my lessons are in the Psalms—& Father Pasqual[2] is a very attentive precep-tor.———By way of requital for his instructions (as I could not offer sordid money to these friars) I have taken upon me the expenses of his Armenian & English grammar—which is now printing—it costs but a thousand francs to print five hundred copies—and being the first published in these joint languages—I think "I do the state some service"[3] almost as much as Mr. Valpy of Tooke's court[4]—who is Polidori's printer——Madame Albrizzi I have seen some times, she desires her compliments;—the Countess G[oetz] through her—or else Countess Albrizzi of her own accord—has desired me to go again to the *Mansion-house* Conversazione—which I hardly expected after that pretty piece of omission you & I made in the dinner department— I shall go.—The Fenice[5] (or fire-office insurance) theatre opens in a

[1] Adapted from the lines in Gray's "The Bard" referring to the Black Prince: "Is the sable Warriour fled?/Thy son is gone. He rests among the Dead."

[2] Father Pasquale Aucher tutored Byron in the Armenian language and Byron later collaborated with him in an Armenian–English grammar and paid for its publication.

[3] *Othello*, Act V, scene 2.

[4] Abraham John Valpy (1787–1854) was a printer and part editor of various classical texts.

[5] The Fenice was the most popular theatre for opera and drama in Venice, and also served as a social gathering place. Byron frequently attended its performances.

week—I have taken a good box for the Carnival—there is to be a ballet & balls & I know not what—if the mumming of the maskers is good I will tell you all about it.—The other evening at the Benedetto[6]—I was regaled with two dramas—one—Holcroft's "tale of Mystery"—the other a farce damned last year at Drury Lane—of which Kinnaird & Dibdin translated an act apiece from the French.—There was also a row in the theatre as follows:—a Signor Cambon (I think) who is separated from his wife for mutual felicity—was in one box—and his extracted Rib in another.—Signor Cambon had become the Cavaliero servente of another lady not separated—& the separated Lady had provided herself with a substitute for Signor Cambon.—But Signor Cambon upon seeing his moiety went into choler—and then into the box—reprobating his wife—and bestemmiando nobilmente her Cavaliero.—The Cavaliero (who was once an officer in Eugene's army) replied in military phrase—& upon receiving a maledetto scopalotto—returned it with such interest—that much swearing & scuffling ensued—& both parties rolled skirmishing out into the passage;—but shewed no science—all rowly-powly—the vulgarest roundabout hitting you ever saw;—"constables came up for to take them into—custody" & the police settled the business.—Every body cried out against Signor Cambon—by which you may judge how morals are in these parts—they *said* it was a scandal to disturb amatory people at that rate.———My own amours go on very tranquilly—she plagues me less than any woman I ever met with—and I am indebted to her for the pleasantest month I can reckon this many a day.—I know you hate that sort of thing—so I will say no more about love & the like—except that in a letter from S[helle]y I hear that C[laire] is about to produce a young "it and I".—By the way—what think ye?—a bookseller—a villain—an imposter—in Cheapside— publishes a set of damned things calling them mine—Murray says & very truly they are not mine—when what does this fellow—why— publishes a counter-advertisement saying that they *are* mine and "that he paid to me *500 guineas* for the copyright!!" There's a story for you "Beck!"—does not this beat the annals of the trade from Curll & Osborne down to Tegg[7] & Johnson—the names of these ragamuffins.—I never set eyes upon the verses or the vendors of them in

[6] The Benedetto was a Venetian theatre which Byron frequented almost as much as the Fenice.

[7] Thomas Tegg (1776–1845) was a bookseller who made a fortune with cheap reprints and abridgements of popular works, and who was not too scrupulous about copyrights.

my days.——I believe Murray has by this time published the new Canto & Chillon &c. but I know nothing for certain.——The man of learning is still a prosperous gentleman—Berger[8] amuses himself with making love to some Harlotry on the other side of the street—out of the hall window—at least this is the household scandal—Stevens slumbers—and Mutz is learning to obey the word of command with a piece of bread upon his nose until permission is accorded to eat it—he has stolen some more legs of mutton—and I detected him myself in the street the other day investigating a barrel of tripe—whereupon I cuffed him soundly.——I have (to use young A's phrase) "done" some more "acquaintance" since you went but have mostly lived pleasant & sulky. I like Venice and it's marine melancholy—and rather—wish to *have seen* Rome than to *see* it—though to be sure having "done" Constantinople I must also do 't'other place.—I commend you to the Gods and am

ever very truly & affecty
B

P.S.—My respects to your family.—'Gin you see Baillie,[9] make my reverences.–

[TO AUGUSTA LEIGH]   *Venice. Decr. 19th. 1816*

My dearest Augusta—I wrote to you a few days ago.—Your letter of the 1st. is arrived—and you have "a *hope*" for me—it seems—what "hope"—child?—my dearest Sis. I remember a methodist preacher who on perceiving a profane grin on the faces of part of his congregation—exclaimed "no *hopes* for *them* as *laughs*"[1] and thus it is —with us—we laugh too much for hopes—and so even let them go—I am sick of sorrow—& must even content myself as well as I can—so here goes—I won't be woeful again if I can help it.—My letter to my moral Clytemnestra required no answer—& I would rather have none —I was wretched enough when I wrote it—& had been so for many a long day & month—at present I am less so—for reasons explained in my late letter (a few days ago) and as I never pretend to *be* what I am not you may tell her if you please that I am recovering—and the reason also if you like it.— I do not agree with you about Ada—there was *equivocation* in the answer—and it shall be settled one way or the

---

[8] Byron's Swiss guide who accompanied him to Venice.

[9] This was Hobhouse's friend nicknamed "Long" Baillie because of his height.

[1] In a note to *Hints from Horace* (line 382) Byron gave the name of the preacher as John Stickles.

other—I wrote to Hanson to take proper steps to prevent such a removal of my daughter—and even the probability of it—you do not know the woman so well as I do—or you would perceive in her *very negative answer*—that she *does intend* to take Ada with her—if she should go abroad.——I have heard of Murray's squabble with one of his brethren—who is an impudent impostor—and should be trounced. ——You do not say whether the *true po's* are out—I hope you like them.—You are right in saying that I like Venice—it is very much what you would imagine it—but I have no time just now for description;—the Carnival is to begin in a week—and with it the mummery of masking.——I have not been out a great deal—but quite as much as I like—I am going out this evening—in my *cloak* & *Gondola*—there are two nice Mrs. Radcliffe words for you—and then there is the place of St Mark—and conversaziones—and various fooleries—besides many *nau*[ghty]. indeed every body is *nau.* so much so that a lady with only *one lover* is not reckoned to have overstepped the modesty of marriage—that being a regular thing;—some have two—three—and so on to twenty beyond which they don't account—but they generally begin by one.——The husbands of course belong to any body's wives—but their own.——My present beloved—is aged two & twenty—with remarkably fine black eyes—and very regular & pretty features—figure light & pretty—hair dark—a mighty good singer—as they all are—she is married (of course) & has one child—a girl.— Her temper very good—(as you know it had need to be) and lively— she is a Venetian by birth—& was never further from Venice than Milan in her days—her lord is about five years older than me—an exceeding good kind of a man.—That amatory appendage called by us a lover—is here denominated variously—sometimes an "Amoroso" (which is the same thing) and sometimes a Cavaliero servente— which I need not tell you—is a serving Cavalier.——I told my fair one—at setting out—that as to the love and the Cavaliership—I was quite of accord—*but as to the servitude*—it would not suit me at all—so I begged to hear no more about it.—You may easily suppose I should not at all shine in the ceremonious department—so little so—that instead of handing the Lady as in duty bound into the Gondola—I as nearly as possible conveyed her into the Canal—and this at midnight— to be sure it was as dark as pitch—but if you could have seen the gravity with which I was committing her to the waves—thinking all the time of something or other not to the purpose;—I always forget that the streets are canals—and was going to walk her over the water —if the servants & the Gondoliers had not awakened me.——So much for love & all that.——The music here is famous—and there will be a whole tribe of singers & dancers during the Carnival—besides the usual theatres.—The Society here is something like our own—except that the women sit in a semicircle at one end of the room—& the men stand at the other.—I pass my mornings at the Armenian convent studying Armenian. My evenings here & there—tonight I am going to the Countess Albrizzi's—one of the noblesse—I have also been at the Governor's—who is an Austrian—& whose wife the Countess Goetz appeared to me in the little I have seen of her a very amiable & pleasing woman—with remarkably good manners—as many of the German women have.——There are no English here—except birds of passage—who stay a day & then go on to Florence—or Rome.—I mean to remain here till Spring.—When you write address *directly* here—as in your present letter.—

ever dearest yrs.

B

[TO THOMAS MOORE]   *Venice, December 24th, 1816*

I have taken a fit of writing to you, which portends postage—once from Verona—once from Venice, and again from Venice—*thrice* that is. For this you may thank yourself, for I heard that you complained of my silence—so, here goes for garrulity.

I trust that you received my other twain of letters. My "way of life"[1] (or "May of life," which is it, according to the commentators?) —my "way of life" is fallen into great regularity. In the mornings I go over in my gondola to babble Armenian with the friars of the convent of St. Lazarus, and to help one of them in correcting the English of an English and Armenian grammar which he is publishing. In the evenings I do one of many nothings—either at the theatres, or some of the conversaziones, which are like our routs, or rather worse, for the women sit in a semicircle by the lady of the mansion, and the men stand about the room. To be sure, there is one improvement upon ours—instead of lemonade with their ices, they hand about stiff *rum-punch—punch*, by my palate; and this they think *English*. I would not disabuse them of so agreeable an error,—"no, not for Venice".[2]

Last night I was at the Count Governor's, which, of course, comprises the best society, and is very much like other gregarious meetings

---

[1] *Macbeth*, Act V, scene 3.
[2] *Merchant of Venice*, Act IV, scene 1.

in every country,—as in ours,—except that, instead of the Bishop of Winchester, you have the Patriarch of Venice, and a motley crew of Austrians, Germans, noble Venetians, foreigners and, if you see a quiz, you may be sure he is a Consul. Oh, by the way, I forgot, when I wrote from Verona, to tell you that at Milan I met with a countryman of yours—a Colonel [Fitzgerald],[3] a very excellent, good-natured fellow, who knows and shows all about Milan, and is, as it were, a native there. He is particularly civil to strangers, and this is his history,—at least, an episode of it.

Six-and-twenty years ago, Col. [Fitzgerald], than an ensign, being in Italy, fell in love with the Marchesa [Castiglione],[4] and she with him. The lady must be, at least, twenty years his senior. The war broke out; he returned to England, to serve—not his country, for that's Ireland—but England, which is a different thing; and *she*— heaven knows what she did. In the year 1814, the first annunciation of the Definitive Treaty of Peace (and tyranny) was developed to the astonished Milanese by the arrival of Col. [Fitzgerald], who, flinging himself full length at the feet of Mad. [Castiglione], murmured forth, in half-forgotten Irish Italian, eternal vows of indelible constancy. The lady screamed, and exclaimed, "Who are you?" The Colonel cried, "What! don't you know me? I am so and so," &c., &c., &c.; till, at length, the Marchesa, mounting from reminiscence to reminiscence through the lovers of the intermediate twenty-five years, arrived at last at the recollection of her *povero* sub-lieutenant. She then said, "Was there ever such virtue?" (that was her very word) and, being now a widow, gave him apartments in her palace, reinstated him in all the rights of wrong, and held him up to the admiring world as a miracle of incontinent fidelity, and the unshaken Abdiel of absence.

Methinks this is as pretty a moral tale as any of Marmontel's. Here is another. The same lady, several years ago, made an escapade with a Swede, Count Fersen[5] (the same whom the Stockholm mob quartered and lapidated not very long since), and they arrived at an Osteria on the road to Rome or thereabouts. It was a summer evening, and, while they were at supper, they were suddenly regaled by a symphony of fiddles in an adjacent apartment, so prettily played, that, wishing to hear them more distinctly, the Count rose, and going into the musical

[3] The name, omitted by Moore, is supplied by Prothero from MS. notes of Rawdon Brown.

[4] The name again supplied by Prothero as indicated in note 3.

[5] Axel, Count Fersen (1750–1810) commander of the regiment called Suédois-Royal in France. In an attempt to save Louis XVI and Marie Antoinette, he drove the royal carriage in the flight to Varennes in June, 1791.

society, said, "Gentlemen, I am sure that, as a company of gallant cavaliers, you will be delighted to show your skill to a lady, who feels anxious," &c., &c. The men of harmony were all acquiescence—every instrument was tuned and toned, and, striking up one of their most ambrosial airs, the whole band followed the Count to the lady's apartment. At their head was the first fiddler, who, bowing and fiddling at the same moment, headed his troop and advanced up the room. Death and discord!—it was the Marquis himself, who was on a serenading party in the country, while his spouse had run away from town. The rest may be imagined—but, first of all, the lady tried to persuade him that she was there on purpose to meet him, and had chosen this method for an harmonic surprise. So much for this gossip, which amused me when I heard it, and I send it to you in the hope it may have the like effect. Now we'll return to Venice.

The day after to-morrow (to-morrow being Christmas-day) the Carnival begins. I dine with the Countess Albrizzi and a party, and go to the opera. On that day the Phenix, (not the Insurance Office, but) the theatre of that name, opens: I have got me a box there for the season, for two reasons, one of which is, that the music is remarkably good. The Contessa Albrizzi, of whom I have made mention, is the De Stael of Venice; not young, but a very learned, unaffected, good-natured woman; very polite to strangers, and, I believe not at all dissolute, as most of the women are. She has written very well on the works of Canova, and also a volume of Characters, besides other printed matter. She is of Corfu, but married a dead Venetian—that is, dead since he married.

My flame (my "Donna" whom I spoke of in my former epistle, my Marianna) is still my Marianna, and I her—what she pleases. She is by far the prettiest woman I have seen here, and the most loveable I have met with any where—as well as one of the most singular. I believe I told you the rise and progress of our *liaison* in my former letter. Lest that should not have reached you, I will merely repeat, that she is a Venetian, two-and-twenty years old, married to a merchant well to do in the world, and that she has great black oriental eyes, and all the qualities which her eyes promise. Whether being in love with her has steeled me or not, I do not know; but I have not seen many other women who seem pretty. The nobility, in particular, are a sad-looking race—the gentry rather better. And now, what art *thou* doing?

> What are you doing now,
> Oh Thomas Moore?

148

What are you doing now,
    Oh Thomas Moore?
Sighing or suing now,
Rhyming or wooing now,
Billing or cooing now,
    Which, Thomas Moore?

Are you not near the Luddites? By the Lord! if there's a row, but I'll
be among ye! How go on the weavers—the breakers of frames—the
Lutherans of politics—the reformers?

As the Liberty lads o'er the sea
Bought their freedom, and cheaply, with blood,
        So we, boys, we
Will *die* fighting, or *live* free,
And down with all kings but King Ludd!

When the web that we weave is complete,
And the shuttle exchanged for the sword,
        We will fling the winding-sheet
        O'er the despot at our feet,
And dye it deep in the gore he has pour'd.

Though black as his heart its hue,
Since his veins are corrupted to mud,
        Yet this is the dew
        Which the tree shall renew
Of Liberty, planted by Ludd!

There's an amiable *chanson* for you—all impromptu. I have written
it principally to shock your neighbour * * [Hodgson?], who is all
clergy and loyalty—mirth and innocence—milk and water.

But the Carnival's coming,
    Oh Thomas Moore,
The Carnival's coming,
    Oh Thomas Moore,

Masking and humming,
Fifing and drumming,
Guitarring and strumming,
    Oh Thomas Moore.

The other night I saw a new play,—and the author. The subject was
the sacrifice of Isaac. The play succeeded, and they called for the

149

author—according to continental custom—and he presented himself, a noble Venetian, Mali—or Malapiero, by name. Mala was his name, and *pessima* his production,—at least, I thought so; and I ought to know, having read more or less of five hundred Drury Lane offerings, during my coadjutorship with the sub-and-super Committee.

When does your Poem of Poems come out? I hear that the E[*dinburgh*] R[*eview*] has cut up Coleridge's Christabel, and declared against me for praising it.[6] I praised it, firstly, because I thought well of it; secondly, because Coleridge was in great distress, and after doing what little I could for him in essentials, I thought that the public avowal of my good opinion might help him further, at least with the booksellers. I am very sorry that J[effrey] has attacked him, because, poor fellow, it will hurt him in mind and pocket. As for me, he's welcome—I shall never think less of J[effrey] for any thing he may say against me or mine in future.

I suppose Murray has sent you, or will send (for I do not know whether they are out or no) the poem, or poesies, of mine, of last summer. By the mass! they're sublime—"Ganion Coheriza"[7]—gainsay who dares! Pray, let me hear from you, and of you, and, at least, let me know that you have received these three letters. Direct right *here*, *poste restante*.

Ever and ever, &c.

P.S.—I heard the other day of a pretty trick of a bookseller, who has published some d[amne]d nonsense, swearing the bastards to me, and saying he gave me five hundred guineas for them. He lies—I never wrote such stuff, never saw the poems, nor the publisher of them, in my life, nor had any communication, directly or indirectly, with the fellow. Pray say as much for me, if need be. I have written to Murray, to make him contradict the imposter.

[TO JOHN HANSON]   *Venice Decr. 26th. 1816*

My dear Sir—The Baronet's letter is equivocal—"at present"— I require an explicit answer with regard to the child—and am more inclined to credit what they prove than what they say.—It is nothing to me what Lady Byron's intentions are with regard to herself—but I

---

[6] Byron praised *Christabel* in a note to *The Siege of Corinth* (line 522).

[7] The motto of the Macdonalds, chiefs of Clanranald, properly written *Dhandeon co heirogha*. Byron probably was following the spelling given in Scott's *Waverley* (chapter 44).

desire a declaration & an assurance that my daughter shall not be taken out of the country—if that is refused—pray take all proper & legal measures without delay to prevent such a step—why the intention is manifest in his very answer—in case of the mother's leaving England they *would* try to take the Child.—At all events the question must be settled one way or the other—he gives no answer whatsoever with regard to the child—which I again require & demand —or I once more desire that you will take the legal steps in my behalf proper to put the point at rest.——I shall have no comfort till I know this.—it would be too late to wait for her being in readiness to set off— the infant might be over the Channel before you could prevent it.— I am glad to hear that Claughton has got H[afod?]—but I wish something would be done about Newstead—I approve very much of poor Joe being put in good plight.——Pray make my regards to your family—of whose welfare I rejoice to hear—& Believe me

ever & truly yrs.
BYRON

P.S.—Address as before—Venice—Poste restante.—

[TO JOHN MURRAY]   *Venice Decr. 27th. 1816*

Dear Sir—As the Demon of Silence seems to have possessed you— I am determined to have my revenge in postage.—This is my sixth or seventh letter since summer and Switzerland.—My last was an injunction to contradict & consign to confusion that Cheapside imposter—who (I heard by a letter from your island) had thought proper to append my name to his spurious poesy—of which I know nothing—nor of his pretended purchase or copyright.——I hope you have at least received *that* letter. As the news of Venice must be very interesting to you I will regale you with it.——Yesterday being the feast of St. Stephen—every mouth was put in motion—there was nothing but fiddling and playing on the virginals—and all kinds of conceits and divertisements on every canal of this aquatic city.——I dined with the Countess Albrizzi and a Paduan and Venetian party— and afterwards went to the Opera—at the Fenice theatre (which opens for the Carnival on that day) the finest by the way I have ever seen— it beats *our* theatres hollow in beauty & scenery—and those of Milan & Brescia bow before it.——The Opera and its Syrens were much like all other operas & women—but the subject of the said Opera was something edifying—it turned—the plot & conduct thereof—upon a fact narrated by Livy[1]—of a hundred & fifty married ladies having *poisoned* a hundred & fifty husbands in the good old times—the bachelors of Rome believed this extraordinary mortality to be merely the common effect of matrimony or a pestilence—but the surviving Benedicts being all seized with the cholic examined into the matter—and found that "their possets had been drugged"[2] the consequence of which was much scandal and several suits at law.—This is really & truly the subject of the Musical piece at the Fenice—& you can't conceive what pretty things are sung & recitativoed about the "horrenda strage"[;] the conclusion was a Lady's head about to be chopped off by a lictor—but (I am sorry to say) he left it on—and she got up & sung a trio with the two Consuls—the Senate in the background being chorus.—The ballet was distinguished by nothing remarkable—except that the principal she-dancer went into convulsions because she was applauded at her first appearance—and the manager came forward to ask if there was "ever a physician in the theatre"—there was a Greek one in my Box whom I wished very much to volunteer his services—being sure that in this case these would have been the last convulsions which would have troubled the Ballerina —but he would not.———The crowd was enormous—and in coming out—having a lady under my arm—I was obliged in making way to "beat a Venetian & traduce the state"[3] being compelled to regale a person with an English punch in the guts—which sent him as far back as the squeeze and the passage would admit—he did not ask for another—but with great signs of disapprobation & dismay appealed to his compatriots—who laughed at him.———I am going on with my Armenian studies in a morning—and assisting & stimulating in the English portion of an English & Armenian grammar now publishing at the Convent of St. Lazarus.———The Superior of the Friars is a Bishop and a fine old fellow—with the beard of a meteor.—My spiritual preceptor—pastor—and master—Father Paschal—is also a learned & pious soul—he was two years in England———I am still dreadfully in love with the Adriatic lady I spoke of in a former letter (and *not* in *this*—I add for fear of mistakes—for the only one mentioned in the first part of this epistle is elderly and bookish—two things which I have ceased to admire) and love in this part of the world is no sinecure.—This is also the season when every body make up their intrigues for the ensuing year—and cut for partners for the next deal.

[1] The story is in Livy, Book VIII, c. 18.
[2] *Macbeth*, Act II, scene 2.
[3] *Othello*, Act V, scene 2.

————And now if you don't write—I don't know what I won't say or do—nor what I will.—send me some news—good news—

yrs. very truly &c. &c. &c.

B

P.S.—Remember me to Mr. G[ifford] with all duty.—I hear that the E[dinburgh] R[eview] has cut up Coleridge's Christabel & me for praising it—which omen I think bodes no great good to your forth-come—or coming Canto and Castle (of Chillon)—my run of luck within the last year seems to have taken a turn every way but never mind—I will bring myself through in the end—if not—I can but be where I began—in the mean time I am not displeased to be where I am —I mean—at Venice.—My Adriatic nymph is this moment here— and I must therefore repose from this letter "rocked by the beating of her heart."

[*To?*]   [*1817?*]

[Fragment] . . . tail of the Comet,—and these persons were the tail of an old Gown cut into a waistcoat for Jackey[1]—but being both *tails*— I have compared one with the other—though very unlike like all Similies.—I write in a passion—and a Sirocco—and I was up till six this morning at the Carnival.—But I *protest*—as I did in my former letter.——

[TO AUGUSTA LEIGH]   *Venice, January 2d. 1817*

My dearest Augusta—On this day the anniversary of my marriage —I receive your letter dated the 10th Decr. (the birth-day of my daughter Ada[)]. Is not this an odd coincidence?—And on this day the anniversary also of the publication of the "Corsair"[1] I receive a letter from Murray announcing the publication of the poems which I sent to England in the Autumn.—and is not that odd?—You will tell Lady B[yron] from me—that I require an explicit answer that Ada shall not be taken out of the country on any pretext whatever—if not—let her look to the consequences—I have ordered Mr. Hanson to proceed *legally*—immediately—if this is not answered—recollect—that *I* have

[1] Unidentified.

[1] Byron had forgotten that the *Corsair* was published on February 2, 1814, not January 2, which was, however, the date of his prefatory letter to Moore.

not sought this—& inform Lady B[yron]—of my determination—& my regret that she *will* compel me to measures—which whatever be their result—can only produce more bitterness between her & me.—I repeat that I have no desire to take the child from her—while she remains in England—but I demand that the infant shall not be removed —& a promise to this effect.—Say this from me—from yourself what you please.—I wrote again last week to Mr. Hanson—Sir R[alph]'s answer was insolent & equivocal.—They had better let me alone— They are not quite aware of what I can & will do if thoroughly roused —& my reasonable requests treated with a heedless contempt.— Enough.—Of Venice I sent you some account a few days ago—at present I am a little pressed for time—but will write again in a week —pray did you receive a letter from me from Milan containing some of the hand-writing of Monti the poet?—I gave it you to give to any of your acquaintance—to Lady B[yron] if you like—as she is fond of collecting such things—I bear her no animosity & she might receive these at least from you.—I have little to add about Venice—to what I said before—in my former letter—

ever yrs. in haste & most affectly.

B

P.S.—You do not say a word of the *po's*—published some time— how odd—have you not had them sent to you?

[TO JOHN MURRAY]   *Venice.—January 2d. 1817*

My dear Sir.—Your letter has arrived.—Pray—in publishing the 3d. Canto—have you *omitted* any passage or passages?—I hope *not*— and indeed wrote to you on my way over the Alps to prevent such an accident—say in your next whether or not the *whole* of the Canto (as sent to you) has been published.————I wrote to you again the other day (*twice* I think—) and shall be glad to hear of the reception of these letters.—To day is the 2d. January—on this day *3* years ago the Corsair's publication is dated I think in my letter to Moore—on this day *two* years I married—"Whom the Lord loveth he chasteneth— blessed be *the* name of the Lord!"—I shan't forget the day in a hurry— & will take care to keep the anniversary before the Evening is over. ——It is odd enough that I this day received a letter from you announcing the publication of C[hil]d H[arol]d on the day of the date of "the Corsair—and that I also received one from my Sister written on the *10th.* of Decr. my daughter's birth-day (and relative chiefly to my daughter) & arriving on the day of the date of my marriage—this present 2d. [of] January the month of my birth and various other Astrologous matters which I have no time to enumerate.—By the way —you might as well write to Hentsch my Genevese Banker—and enquire whether the *two packets* consigned to his care—were or were not delivered to Mr. St. Aubyn[1]—or if they are still in his keeping.— One contains papers, letters & all the original M.S. of your 3d Canto —as first conceived—& the other—some bones from the field of Morat.——Many thanks for your news—& the good Spirits in which your letter is written.——Venice & I agree very well—but I do not know that I have any thing new to say—except of the last new Opera —which I sent in my last letter.—The Carnival is commencing—and there is a good deal of fun here & there—besides business—for all the world are making up their intrigues for the season—changing—or going on upon a renewed lease.—I am very well off with Marianna who is not at all a person to tire me—firstly because I do not tire of a woman *personally*—but because they are generally bores in their disposition—& secondly—because she is amiable & has a tact which is not always the portion of the fair creation—& 3dly she is very pretty—& 4thly—but there is no occasion for further specification.— I have passed a great deal of my time with her since my arrival at Venice—and never a twenty-four hours—without giving and receiving from one to three (and occasionally an extra or so) pretty unequivocal proofs of mutual good contentment.—So far we have gone on very well—as to the future I never anticipate—"Carpe diem" the past at least is one's own—which is one reason for making sure of the present. ——So much for my proper liaison.—The general state of morals here is much the same as in the Doge's time—a woman is virtuous (according to the code) who limits herself to her husband and one lover—those who have two three or more are a little *wild*;—but it is only those who are indiscriminately diffuse—and form a low connection —such as the Princess of Wales with her Courier (who by the way is made a Knight of Malta) who are considered as overstepping the modesty of marriage.—In Venice—the Nobility have a trick of marrying with dancers or singers—& truth to say—the women of their own order are by no means handsome—but the general race—the women of the 2d & other orders—the wives of the Advocates—merchants & proprietors—& untitled gentry are mostly "bel' sangue" and it is with these that the more amatory connections are usually formed

[1] See Oct. 5, 1816, to Murray (*a*), and Jan. 24, 1817, to Murray.

—there are also instances of stupendous constancy—I know a woman of fifty who never had but one lover who dying early—she became devout—renouncing all but her husband—she piques herself as may be presumed upon this miraculous fidelity—talking of it occasionally with a species of misplaced morality—which is rather amusing.—There is no convincing a woman here—that she is in the smallest degree deviating from the rule of right or the fitness of things—in having an "Amoroso". The great sin seems to lie in concealing it—or in having more than one—that is—unless such an extension of the prerogative is understood & approved of by the prior claimant.—In my case—I do not know that I had any predecessor—& am pretty sure that there is no participator—& am inclined to think from the youth of the party—& from the frank undisguised way in which every body avows everything in this part of the world—when there is any thing to avow—as well as from some other circumstances—such as the marriage being recent &c &c—that this is the "premier pas"—it does not much signify.———In another sheet I send you some sheets of a grammar English & Armenian for the use of the Armenians—of which I promoted & indeed induced the publication; (it cost me but a thousand francs of French livres) I still pursue my lessons in the language—without any rapid progress—but advancing a little daily— Padre Paschal—with some little help from me as a translator of his Italian into English—is also proceeding in an M.S. grammar for the *English* acquisition of Armenian—which will be printed also when finished.—We want to know if there are any *Armenian types* or letter-press in England—at Oxford—Cambridge or elsewhere?—You know I suppose that many years ago the two Whistons[2] published in England an original text of a history of Armenia with their own Latin trans-lation.—Do these types still exist? & where.—Pray enquire among your learned acquaintance.—When this grammar—(I mean the one now printing) is done will you have any objection to take 40 or fifty copies which will not cost in all above five or ten guineas—& try the curiosity of the learned with the sale of them.—Say yes or no as you like.—I can assure you that they have some very curious books & M.S. chiefly translations from Greek originals now lost.—They are besides a much respected and learned community & the study of their language was taken up with great ardour by some literary Frenchmen in

[2] John Whiston (d. 1780), son of William Whiston (1667–1752), a divine whose unorthodox Newtonian views caused the loss of his Cambridge professor-ship. The younger Whiston was a bookseller in Fleet Street.

Buonaparte's time.[3]—I have not done a stitch of poetry since I left Switzerland—& have not at present the *"estro"* upon me—the truth is that you are *afraid* of having a *4th.* Canto *before* September—& of another copyright—but I have at present no thoughts of resuming that poem nor of beginning any other.—If I write—I think of trying prose —but I dread introducing living people or applications which might be made to living people—perhaps one day or other—I may attempt some work of fancy in prose—descriptive of Italian manners & of human passions—but at present I am preoccupied.—As for poesy—mine is the *dream* of my sleeping Passions—when they are awake—I cannot speak their language—only in their Somnambulism.—& Just now they are dormant.———If Mr. G[ifford] wants Carte blanche as to the

[3] What appears to have been intended as a preface to the Armenian Grammar was, according to Prothero, found among Byron's papers. It was not used because Father Pasquale Aucher objected to the attack on the Turks in it, according to Mackay (*Lord Byron at the Armenian Convent*, p. 79). The preface follows.

"The English reader will probably be surprised to find my name associated with a work of the present description, and inclined to give me more credit for my attainments as a linguist than they deserve.

"As I would not willingly be guilty of a deception, I will state, as shortly as I can, my own share in the compilation, with the motives which led to it. On my arrival at Venice, in the year 1816, I found my mind in a state which required study, and study of a nature which should leave little scope for the imagination, and furnish some difficulty in the pursuit.

"At this period I was much struck—in common, I believe, with every other traveller—with the society of the Convent of St. Lazarus, which appears to unite all the advantages of the monastic institution, without any of its vices.

"The neatness, the comfort, the gentleness, the unaffected devotion, the accomplishments, and the virtues of the brethren of the order, are well fitted to strike the man of the world with the conviction that 'there is another and a better' even in this life.

"These men are the priesthood of an oppressed and a noble nation, which has partaken of the proscription and bondage of the Jews and of the Greeks, without the sullenness of the former or the servility of the latter. This people has attained riches without usury, and all the honours that can be awarded to slavery without intrigue. But they have long occupied, nevertheless, a part of the House of Bondage, who has lately multiplied her many mansions. It would be difficult, perhaps, to find the annals of a nation less stained with crimes than those of the Armenians, whose virtues have been those of peace, and their vices those of compulsion. But whatever may have been their destiny—and it has been bitter—whatever it may be in future, their country must ever be one of the most interesting on the globe; and perhaps their language only requires to be more studied to become more attractive. If the Scriptures are rightly understood, it was in Armenia that Paradise was placed —Armenia, which has paid as dearly as the descendants of Adam for that fleeting participation of its soil in the happiness of him who was created from its dust. It was in Armenia that the flood first abated, and the dove alighted. But with the disappearance of Paradise itself may be dated almost the unhappiness of the country; for though long a powerful kingdom, it was scarcely ever an independent one, and the satraps of Persia and the pachas of Turkey have alike desolated the region where God created man in his own image." (*LJ*, IV, 44–45.)

"Siege of Corinth"—he has it—& may do as he likes with it.—I sent you a letter contradictory of the Cheapside man—(who invented the story you speak of) the other day.—My best respects to Mr. Gifford —& such of my friends as you may see at your house.—I wish you all prosperity & new years gratulation & I am

Yrs ever & truly

B

[TO DOUGLAS KINNAIRD] *Venice January 12th. 1817*

My dear Kinnaird/—Since my arrival in Venice I have written to you *twice*—to request that you would have the goodness to transmit as soon as convenient letters for the credit of such sum or sums as Murray may have paid "according to the tenor" concluded on Septr. last.— Address to me here—either Post restante—or to the care of Messers. Siri & Wilhalm bankers of this city—it is my intention to remain here probably till Spring.—Hobhouse is gone to Rome with his brother & Sister but will return in March or so.—I hope that you have received at least one of my letters.—in these I told you all the gossip I could think of—& shall be glad to have a letter in return.—to my surprize Murray in a recent letter tells me that you are out of the committee— an event which it requires no great sagacity to attribute to the illus- trious Frances Kelly[1] of comic memory.—if you recollect—(for I am a wonderful judge in all concerns but my own) I foreboded long ago disasters to some of you—or us—or one or more—from the inter- vention of that worthy young woman—and you may also recollect— that for my own part—among the very few pieces of prudence which grace my graceless history—one was to steer very clear of any colloquy or communion with that fair favourite of elderly gentlemen— I don't mean in an immodest way—for she is a Vestel as is well known —but in the chaster attentions which my coadjutors including yourself were accustomed to pay her.—I kept to distant politeness—& verily I have my reward—as you it seems have for being her friend first—& her manager afterwards.—Seriously—if this vexes you I am very sorry for it—but I know nothing of the matter—though I can't help thinking that if I had been at your elbow—& had not lost my temper at the pretty speeches you would have made me in the course of our dialogues —I could have prevented this—at least I should have tried.—I say no

[1] Frances Maria Kelly (1790–1882) was a leading actress at Drury Lane from its reopening in 1812.

more—where the Devil are the other Committed?—Essex——George
—& Mr. Peter Moore?[2] & my locum tenens who ever he be?—You
will tell me these matters in your next.—Murray tells me the poems
are out—with what success I know not except from his letter—which
is written in good spirits.—I wonder if he published them *as sent*—if
he has made alterations or omissions—I shall not pardon him—I
suspect him as a *Tory*—of softening my M.S.—if he *has*—by the Ass
by Balaam! He shall endure my indignation.—He tells me of a row
with an Impostor—a book-seller who has been *injunctioned*—by the aid
of an *oath* from Scrope Davies—I would give a trifle to see Scrope's
affidavit—& to have heard half the good things he has said upon the
subject.—"Hath he laid perjury upon his Soul?"—no doubt he will say
so—as he always adds his sins to the other obligations he has conferred
upon me—when he left Switzerland he was determined to see a "Boa-
Constrictor"—God knows why—but what ever he saw—he always
wished for the addition of that amiable reptile.——I hope that Fortune
has had the good taste to stick to him—turf or table—doth he drink as
of old?—we were sadly sober all the autumn—but I hope some day or
other to revive & quench our antient thirst in the way of our youth.—
He promised to write—I trust that his affidavit was of a different
complexion from his promise.——

[TO AUGUSTA LEIGH]   *Venice, Jan 13th 1817*

My dearest Augusta.—I wrote to you *twice* within the last and
present months. Your letter of the 24th arrived to-day. So you have
got the po's. Pray tell me if Murray has omitted any stanzas in the
publication; if he has I shall be very seriously displeased with him.
The number sent was *118* to the 3d Canto. You do not mention the
concluding *4* to my daughter Ada which I hoped would give *you*
pleasure at least. I care not much about opinions at this time of day,
and I am certain in my mind that this Canto is the *best* which I have ever
written; there is depth of thought in it throughout and a strength of
repressed passion which you must feel before you find; but it requires
reading more than once, because it is in part *metaphysical*, and of a
kind of metaphysics which every body will not understand. I never
thought that it would be *popular* & should not think well of it if it were,

---

[2] George, 5th Earl of Essex, George Lamb, Douglas Kinnaird and Peter Moore
were associated with Byron as members of the Sub-committee of Management of
Drury Lane in 1815.

but those for whom it is intended will like it. Pray remember to tell me if any have been omitted in the publication. The lines on Drachenfels originally addressed to *you*, ought to be (& I suppose *are*) in the centre of the Canto—and the number of Stanzas in the whole *118*—besides *4* of ten lines beginning with "Drachenfels" the lines which I sent to *ou* (sic) at the time from Coblentz—with the violets dearest +.

Have you also got *Chillon* & the *Dream* & do you understand the latter?

If Murray has mutilated the MS. with his *Toryism*, or his notions about *family* considerations I shall not pardon him & am sure to know it sooner or later & to let him know it also.

I wrote to you the other day about Ada, if the *answer* is still refused I shall take *legal measures* to enforce it, and have ordered H[anson] to do so. *Remember I* do not seek this, I wish it not, I regret it, but I require an explicit promise that Ada shall on no consideration quit the country, whether the mother does or no, and by all that is most sacred, there is no measure which I will not take to prevent it, failing in a reply to my just demand. So say—and so I will do. They will end by driving me mad, I wonder they have not already.

Of Venice I gave you some account in one of my letters. I have not much to add to it. I told you that I had fallen in love and that I shall probably remain here till the Spring, and that I am studying the Armenian language.

Marianna is not very well to-day, and I shall stay with her to nurse her this Evening. It is the Carnival, but the height of the Masquing is not yet begun. Catalani comes here on the 20th, but we have famous Music already, and a better opera than in London and a finer theatre, the Fenice by name, where I have a box, which costs me about *14* pounds sterling for the season instead of *four hundred* as in London, and a better box and a better opera, besides the music the Scenery is most superb. There is also a ballet inferior to the singing. The Society is like all foreign Society. There is also a Ridotto. My paper's out.

Ever yrs.

B

[TO DOUGLAS KINNAIRD]   *Venice—January 20th. 1817*

My dear Kinnaird—Your letter and its contents (viz. the circulars & indication for £500) are safely arrived—thanks——I have been up all night at the Opera—& at the Ridotto & it's Masquerade—and the

devil knows what—so that my head aches a little—but to business.—
—My affairs ought to be in a small compass—if Newstead were sold
they would be settled without difficulty—and if Newstead & Rochdale
both were sold—I should think with ease—but till one or both of
these are disposed of—they are in a very unpleasant situation.—It is
for this reason I so much urge a sale—even at almost any price.—
With regard to Hanson—I know not how to act—& I know not what
to think—except that I think he wishes me well—it is certainly not
his fault that Claughton could not fulfil the conditions of sale.——
Mr. Riley[1] has reason—but he must really wait till something can be
done about the property—if he likes he may proceed against *it*,—but
as to the produce of my *brain*—my M. S.—my Night mare is my own
personalty—& by the Lord as I have earned the sum—so will I
expend it upon my own proper pleasances—voyagings & what not—
so that I request that you will *not* disburse a ducat save to *me* the
owner.—You do not say a word about the publication itself—from
which I infer that it has failed—if so—you may tell me at once—on
Murray's account rather than on mine—for I am not to be perturbed
by such matters at this time of day—as the fall of the thermometer of a
poetical reputation—but I should be sorry for M[urray] who is a very
good fellow.——However—as with one thing or another—he—
Murray must have cleared on the whole account—dating from the
commencement—I feel less anxious for him than I otherwise should.
—Your quotation from Shakespeare—humph—I believe that it is
applied by Othello to his *wife*—who by the way was *innocent*—the
Moor made a mistake—& so have you.——My desire that Murray
should pay in the agreement will not appear singular—when you
recollect that the time has elapsed within a few days when three
quarters of the whole were to have been disbursed by him.——
Since my departure from England I have not spent (in nine months)
within some hundreds of two thousand pounds so that neither my
pleasures nor my perils—when you consider the ground I have gone
over & that I had a physician (now gone thank heaven) to fee & feed
out of it—a very extravagant silly gentleman he was into the bargain.
——By the way—I should wish to know if Hanson has been able to
collect *any rent* at all (but little it can be in these times) from
N[ewstead]—if he has & there be any balance—it may also come to me
in the shape of circulars—the time is also approaching when—there
will be something due from that magnificent father *at* law of mine—

1 Unidentified. It is apparent that he was one of Byron's creditors.

Sir R[alph] N[oel]—from whom I expect punctuality—& am not disposed to remit him any of his remaining duties—let him keep to his time—even in trifles.———You tell me Shelley's wife has drowned herself—the devil she has—do you mean his *wife*—or his Mistress?—Mary Godwin?—I hope not the last—I am very sorry to hear of anything which can plague poor Shelley—besides I feel uneasy about another of his *menage*.—You know—& I believe saw once that oddheaded girl—who introduced herself to me shortly before I left England—but you do not know—that I found her with Shelley & her sister at Geneva—I never loved nor pretended to love her—but a man is a man—& if a girl of eighteen comes prancing to you at all hours—there is but one way—the suite of all this is that she was with *child*—& returned to England to assist in peopling that desolate island.—Whether this impregnation took place before I left England or since—I do not know—the (carnal) connection had commenced previously to my setting out—but by or about this time she has—or is about to produce.—The next question is is the brat *mine*?—I have reason to think so—for I know as much as one can know such a thing—that she had *not lived* with S[helley] during the time of our acquaintance—& that she had a good deal of that same with me.—This comes of "putting it about" (as Jackson calls it) & be damned to it—and thus people come into the world.———So you wish me to come to England—why? for what?—my affairs—I wish they could be settled without—I repeat that your country is no country for me.—I have neither ambition nor taste for your politics—and there is nothing else among you which may not be had better elsewhere.—Besides—Caroline Lamb—& Lady B[yron]—my "Lucy" & my "Polly" have destroyed my *moral* existence amongst you—& I am rather sick of being the theme of their mutual inventions—in ten years I could unteach myself even to your language—& am very sure that—but I have no time nor space for futher tirade at present—

ever yrs. very truly
B

P.S.—Pray write soon.——

Venice[2] & I agree very well—in the mornings I study Armenian—& in the evenings I go out sometimes—& indulge in coition always.——I mentioned my liaison to you in a former letter—it still continues—& probably will—It has however kept me here instead of

---

[2] This detached sheet may or may not belong with this letter. but the context indicates that its date must be near that of the preceding letter.

gadabouting the country.—The Carnival is begun—but the zenith of the masking will not arrive for some weeks.—There is a famous Opera—& several theatres—Catalani is to be here on the 20th—Society is like other foreign society—I see as much of it as I wish—& might see more if I liked it.—

ever yrs. most truly

B

P.S.—My respects to *Madame*—pray answer my letters—& mention anything or everything except my—*family*—I will say—for the other word makes me unwell.——

[TO JOHN MURRAY]   *Venice—January 24th. 1817*

Dear Sir—By the enclosed you will perceive that Mr. Hentsch consigned to Mr. St. Aubyn the packages long ago—I will therefore thank you to enquire after the said Mr. St. Aubyn of the university of Oxford, Son of Sir John St. Aubyn & lately travelling in Switzerland[1] —he had them before the 17th Novr.—& as it was at his own offer & desire that he took this trouble—I hope he has—or will fulfill it—the parcel for Mrs. Leigh contained papers—& the one addressed to you some relics of Morat.—I have been requested by the Countess Albrizzi here to present her with "the works"[.] I wish you therefore to send me a copy that I may comply with her requisition—you may include the last published of which I have seen & know nothing but from your letter of the 13th of December.—Mrs. Leigh tells me that most of her friends prefer the 2 first cantos—I do not know whether this be the general opinion or not (it is *not hers*) but it is natural it should be so—I however think differently—which is natural also—but who is right or who is wrong is of very little consequence.——Dr. Polidori as I hear from him by letter from Pisa is about to return to England—to go to the Brazils on a medical Speculation with the Danish Consul—as you are in the favour of the powers that be—could you not get him some letters of recommendation from some of your Government friends—to some of the Portuguese settlers—he understands his profession well—& has no want of general talents—his faults are the faults of a pardonable vanity & youth—his remaining with me was out of the question—I have enough to do to manage my own scrapes—& as precepts without example are not the most gracious homilies—I thought it better to give him his congé—but I

1 See Oct. 5, 1816, to Murray (*a*)

163

know no great harm of him—& some good—he is clever—& accomplished—knows his profession by all accounts well—and is honourable in his dealings—& not at all malevolent.—I think with luck he will turn out a useful member of society (from which he will lop the diseased members) & the college of Physicians.—If you can be of any use to him—or know any one who can—pray be so—as he has his fortune to make.—He has kept a *medical journal* under the eye of *Vacca*[2] (the first Surgeon on the Continent) at Pisa—Vacca has corrected it—& it must contain some valuable hints or information on the practice of this Country.—If you can aid him in publishing this also—by your influence with your brethren—do—I do not ask you to publish it yourself—because that sort of request is too personal & embarrassing.—He has also a tragedy—of which having seen nothing I say nothing—but the very circumstance of his having made these efforts (if they are only efforts) at one & twenty—is in his favour & proves him to have good dispositions for his own improvement.——So if in the way of commendation or recommendation you can aid his objects with your government friends—I wish you would—I should think some of your Admiralty board might be likely to have it in their power.——

yrs very truly
B

[TO THOMAS MOORE]   *Venice, January 28th, 1817*

Your letter of the 8th is before me. The remedy for your plethora is simple—abstinence. I was obliged to have recourse to the like some years ago, I mean in point of *diet*, and, with the exception of some convivial weeks and days, (it might be months, now and then), have kept to Pythagoras ever since. For all this, let me hear that you are better. You must not *indulge* in "filty beer," nor in porter, nor eat *suppers*—the last are the devil to those who swallow dinner. * * * * * *
* *
I am truly sorry to hear of your father's misfortune[1]—cruel at any time, but doubly cruel in advanced life. However, you will, at least, have the satisfaction of doing your part by him, and, depend upon it, it will not be in vain. Fortune, to be sure, is a female, but not such a b * * as the rest (always excepting your wife and my sister from such

___

[2] See March 3, 1817 to Murray, note 2.
[1] John Moore, Thomas Moore's father, was dismissed from his post as barrack-master at Dublin.

164

sweeping terms); for she generally has some justice in the long run. I have no spite against her, though between her and Nemesis I have had some sore gauntlets to run—but then I have done my best to deserve no better. But to *you*, she is a good deal in arrear, and she will come round—mind if she don't: you have the vigour of life, of independence, of talent, spirit, and character all with you. What you can do for yourself, you have done and will do; and surely there are some others in the world who would not be sorry to be of use, if you would allow them to be useful, or at least attempt it.

I think of being in England in the spring. If there is a row, by the sceptre of King Ludd, but I'll be one; and if there is none, and only a continuance of "this meek, piping time of peace,"[2] I will take a cottage a hundred yards to the south of your abode, and become your neighbour; and we will compose such canticles, and hold such dialogues, as shall be the terror of the *Times* (including the newspaper of that name), and the wonder, and honour, and praise, of the Morning Chronicle and posterity.

I rejoice to hear of your forthcoming in February[3]—though I tremble for the "magnificence," which you attribute to the new Childe Harold. I am glad you like it; it is a fine indistinct piece of poetical desolation, and my favourite. I was half mad during the time of its composition, between metaphysics, mountains, lakes, love unextinguishable, thoughts unutterable, and the nightmare of my own delinquencies. I should, many a good day, have blown my brains out, but for the recollection that it would have given pleasure to my mother-in-law; and, even *then*, if I could have been certain to haunt her—but I won't dwell upon these trifling family matters.

Venice is in the *estro* of her carnival, and I have been up these last two nights at the ridotto and the opera, and all that kind of thing. Now for an adventure. A few days ago a gondolier brought me a billet without a subscription, intimating a wish on the part of the writer to meet me either in gondola or at the island of San Lazaro, or at a third rendezvous, indicated in the note. "I know the country's disposition well"—in Venice "they do let Heaven see those tricks they dare not show,"[4] &c. &c.; so, for all response, I said that neither of the three

2 *Richard III*, Act I, scene 1: "Why, I, in this weak piping time of peace,/ Have no delight to pass away the time."
3 Moore's *Lalla Rookh* was published by Longman in 1817.
4 *Othello*, Act III, scene 3:

"I know our country disposition well;
In Venice they do let Heaven see the pranks
They dare not show their husbands."

places suited me; but that I would either be at home at ten at night *alone*, or at the ridotto at midnight, where the writer might meet me masked. At ten o'clock I was at home and alone (Marianna was gone with her husband to a conversazione), when the door of my apartment opened, and in walked a well-looking and (for an Italian) *bionda* girl of about nineteen, who informed me that she was married to the brother of my *amorosa*, and wished to have some conversation with me. I made a decent reply, and we had some talk in Italian and Romaic (her mother being a Greek of Corfu), when lo! in a very few minutes, in marches, to my very great astonishment, Marianna S[egati], *in propria persona*, and after making polite courtesy to her sister-in-law and to me, without a single word seizes her said sister-in-law by the hair, and bestows upon her some sixteen slaps, which would have made your ear ache only to hear their echo. I need not describe the screaming which ensued. The luckless visitor took flight. I seized Marianna, who, after several vain efforts to get away in pursuit of the enemy, fairly went into fits in my arms; and, in spite of reasoning, eau de Cologne, vinegar, half a pint of water, and God knows what other waters beside, continued so till past midnight.

After damning my servants for letting people in without apprizing me, I found that Marianna in the morning had seen her sister-in-law's gondolier on the stairs, and, suspecting that his apparition boded her no good, had either returned of her own accord, or been followed by her maids or some other spy of her people to the conversazione, from whence she returned to perpetrate this piece of pugilism. I had seen fits before, and also some small scenery of the same genus in and out of our island: but this was not all. After about an hour, in comes—who? why, Signor S[egati], her lord and husband, and finds me with his wife fainting upon the sofa, and all the apparatus of confusion, dishevelled hair, hats, handkerchiefs, salts, smelling-bottles—and the lady as pale as ashes without sense or motion. His first question was, "What is all this?" The lady could not reply—so I did. I told him the explanation was the easiest thing in the world; but in the mean time it would be as well to recover his wife—at least, her senses. This came about in due time of suspiration and respiration.

You need not be alarmed—jealousy is not the order of the day in Venice, and daggers are out of fashion; while duels, on love matters, are unknown—at least, with the husbands. But, for all this, it was an awkward affair; and though he must have known that I made love to Marianna, yet I believe he was not, till that evening, aware of the extent to which it had gone. It is very well known that almost all the married women have a lover; but it is usual to keep up the forms, as in other nations. I did not, therefore, know what the devil to say. I could not out with the truth, out of regard to her, and I did not choose to lie for my sake;—besides, the thing told itself. I thought the best way would be to let her explain it as she chose (a woman being never at a loss—the devil always sticks by them)—only determining to protect and carry her off, in case of any ferocity on the part of the Signor. I saw that he was quite calm. She went to bed, and next day—how they settled it, I know not, but settle it they did. Well—then I had to explain to Marianna about this never to be sufficiently confounded sister-in-law; which I did by swearing innocence, eternal constancy, &c. &c. * * * But the sister-in-law, very much discomposed with being treated in such wise, has (not having her own shame before her eyes) told the affair to half Venice, and the servants (who were summoned by the fight and the fainting) to the other half. But, here, nobody minds such trifles, except to be amused by them. I don't know whether you will be so, but I have scrawled a long letter out of these follies.

Believe me ever. &c.

[TO DOUGLAS KINNAIRD]   *Venice—February 3d. 1817*

My dear Kinnaird—I have acknowledged your letter of the 3d. January & it's contents duly—but as in that epistle you intimated the possibility of it's being followed by a *second* with the like enclosure—I write again—in case you should have sent the same—to apprize you that up to this date *it* (the *second*) has *not* arrived—my reason for this —being that your letter might miscarry (as well as mine) & it might be of consequence to you as well as to me—that you should be aware of such an event—as any ragamuffin might otherwise use my name & your credit in any part of Europe to the detriment of both—without this precaution—supposing the letter to have fallen in other hands than the person to whom it is addressed.——The moment it arrives I shall acknowledge the receipt as of the former—viz—yours dated the 3d. January.—in my answer I added a few observations on other points. —I was a little surprized to find Murray before his day—or rather *days*—for *three quarters* by the agreement were to be paid in before the 20th. January—and from your last it should seem that he had not—or but just—paid in the first.—I hate boring you about such matters—

but what can I do?—I have hardly any other correspondent—& no other of any use—or in whom I have much faith—to say any.—Hobhouse is at Rome—& wants me to join him there—I am undecided—(as usual)—at any rate I shall outstay the Carnival at Venice.—all I know of your deposition or resignation is from yourself—of England I know nothing—hear nothing (never looking into a paper foreign or Italian) and desire to hear nothing—beyond some good (if it were possible of my own damned concerns) or of my friends—I suppose & fear that your row plagued you sufficiently—but what could be expected from the Green-room?—Sooner or later you will have your revenge—& so shall I (in other matters) you on the stage & I off—& by Nemesis—you shall build a new Drury—which shall pay *one* per Cent to the Subscribers—& I will write you a tragedy which shall reduce your pounds to shillings—besides for my own particular injuries—(while this play is representing with much applause) ordaining a proscription to which that of Sylla shall be a comic opera—& that of Collot d' Herbois at Lyons[1]—a symphony.—In the meantime—as Candide says & Cincinnatus might have said "il faut cultiver notre jardin".—I expect by the way that you will write to me a letter now & then—with as much or as little as you choose to say.—I wish you well in your senatorial debut[2]—but you have not hypocrisy enough for a politician—as to Oratory (having made so many prior speeches) your Maiden speech will be a "Spinning-house Maidenhead" if you recollect that *Cant*—or rather *Cunt* term of our Alma Mater.———of Venice I say nothing—there is little going on but fiddling—masquing—singing—& t'other thing—Catalani is just arrived to add to the buffooneries of the day.—Direct here as before.—Tell me of Scrope—is he as full of "fierce embraces" as when I last saw him?—he had made then innumerable conquests—according to his own account—I wish he would marry & beget some Scrooples[3]—it is a pity the dynasty should not be prolonged—I do not know anyone who will leave such "a gap in Nature".—I hope also that he wins the specie still left among you.—

Yrs. ever & very truly
B

P.S.—My respects to Mrs. K.—

---

[1] Collot d'Herbois (1750–1796) a member of the Convention, and on the Committee of Public Safety, was deported to Cayenne.

[2] Kinnaird had been elected to Parliament for Bishop's Castle.

[3] The pun is not as forced as it may seem, since it is probable that Scrope's name was pronounced Scroop. (Moore in his diary spelled it "Scroope".)

168

Dear Sir—I have received your two letters—but not the parcel you mention.—As the Waterloo spoils are arrived—I will make you a present of them—if you choose to accept them—pray do.—I do not exactly understand from your letter what has been omitted—or what not—in the publication—but I shall see probably some day or other—I could not attribute any but a *good* motive to Mr. G[ifford] or yourself in such omission—but as our politics are so very opposite—we should differ as to the passages—however if it is only a *note* or notes—and a line or so—it cannot signify.[1]—You say "a *poem*" *what poem?*—you can tell me in your next.—Of Mr. H[obhouse]'s quarrel with the Quarterly R[eview]—I know very little—except Barrow's article[2] itself—which was certainly harsh enough—but I quite agree that it would have been better not to answer—particularly after Mr. W. W. who never more will trouble you—trouble you.[3]——I have been uneasy—because Mr. H[obhouse] told me that his letter or preface was to be addressed to *me*—now he & I are friends of many years—I have many obligations to him—& he none to me—which have not been cancelled & more than repaid—but Mr. G[ifford] & I are friends also and he has moreover been literarily so—through thick & thin—in despite of difference of years—morals—habits—& even *politics* (which last would I believe if they were in heaven divide the Trinity—& put the Holy Ghost out of place) and therefore I feel in a very awkward situation between the two Mr. G. & my friend H.—& can only wish that they had no differences—or that such as they have were accomodated.—The answer I have not seen—for it is odd enough—for people so intimate—but Mr. H. & I are very sparing of our literary confidences—for example—the other day he wished to have an M.S. of the 3d Canto to read over to his brother &c. which was refused;—and I have never seen his journals—nor he mine—(I only kept the short

---

[1] The omissions, on Gifford's advice, were of a political nature. One in the *Prisoner of Chillon*, following line 378, was a gratuitous slur on the character of kings: "Nor slew of my subjects one;/What sovereign hath so little done." The poem was in fact improved by the omission. Another was the omission of a note, in Murray's words some "personal allusion to poor Louis XVIII."

[2] Hobhouse's *Letters written by an Englishman resident at Paris during the reign of Napoleon* was criticized with personal invective by John Wilson Croker in the *Quarterly Review* for January, 1816, Vol. XIV, pp. 443–452. Hobhouse protested to Murray in a letter of May 22, 1816, saying that he hoped the review was not by Gifford.

[3] Wedderburn Webster's reply to the review of his *Waterloo and Other Poems* in the *Quarterly Review* of January, 1816, was published in the *Morning Chronicle*, December 19, 1816. It was severely critical of Gifford, editor of the *Quarterly*.

one of the mountains for my sister) nor do I think that hardly ever he or I saw any of our own productions previous to publication.—The article in the E[dinburgh] R]eview] on Coleridge[4] I have not seen— but whether I am attacked in it or not—or in any other of the same journal—I shall never think ill of Mr. Jeffrey on that account—nor forget that his conduct toward me has been certainly most handsome during the last four or more years.—I forgot to mention to you—that a kind of poem in dialogue (in blank verse) or drama—from which "the Incantation" is an extract[5]—begun last summer in Switzerland is finished—it is in three acts—but of a very wild—metaphysical—and inexplicable kind.—Almost all the persons—but two or three—are Spirits of the earth & air—or the waters—the scene is in the Alps—the hero a kind of magician who is tormented by a species of remorse— the cause of which is left half unexplained—he wanders about invoking these spirits—which appear to him—& are of no use—he at last goes to the very abode of the Evil principle in propria persona—to evocate a ghost—which appears—& gives him an ambiguous & disagreeable answer—& in the 3d. act he is found by his attendants dying in a tower —where he studied his art.—You may perceive by this outline that I have no great opinion of this piece of phantasy—but I have at least rendered it *quite impossible* for the stage—for which my intercourse with D[rury] Lane had given me the greatest contempt.——I have not even copied it off—& feel too lazy at present to attempt the whole —but when I have I will send it you—& you may either throw it into the fire or not—I would send you the [the end of the manuscript is missing]

[TO AUGUSTA LEIGH]   *Venice. February [19?] 1817*

My dearest Augusta—Fletcher has requested me to remind you that *one* of his *boys* was to be a candidate for the Blue coat School—& as you

---

[4] In the *Edinburgh Review* of December 1816 (Vol XXVII, pp. 444–459) there was a review of Coleridge's *The Statesman's Manual . . . A Lay Sermon*, in which there was no mention of Byron. But in the same number (Article No. 1) there was a laudatory review of *Childe Harold's Pilgrimage, Canto the Third* and *The Prisoner of Chillon*. Byron may have expected some reference to his praise of Coleridge, for in the previous number (Sept. 1816, Vol. XXVII, pp. 58–67) the reviewer of *Christabel* and *Kubla Khan* quoted Byron's note in *The Siege of Corinth*, where he called *Christabel* "a wild and singularly beautiful poem" and added that "some of his [Byron's] latest *publications* dispose us to distrust his authority."

[5] The drama was of course *Manfred*, which was not finished until May 5. It was published on June 17, 1817. The "Incantation" was first published with the *Prisoner of Chillon*, Dec. 5, 1816.

know the Bentincks[1] (who are governors) he begs by me that you will use your interest to obtain theirs.—he has spoken to you (he says) on the subject already—& *Easter* is the *time*—so that you will not forget his request he hopes.———The Carnival closed last night—and I have been up all night at the masked ball of the Fenice—and am rather tired or so—it was a fine sight—the theatre illuminated—and all the world buffooning.—I had my box full of visitors—masks of all kinds —and afterwards (as is the custom) went down to promenade the pit—which was boarded over level with the stage.—All the Virtue & Vice in Venice was there—there has been the same sort of thing every night these six weeks—besides Operas—Ridottos—parties—& the Devil knows what—I went out *now* & *then*—but was less dissipated than you would expect.———I have hardly time for a word now but will write again soon—

Yrs. ever
B

P.S.—I am *not* "P.P."[2] I assure you upon my honour—& do not understand to what book you allude—so that all your compliments are quite thrown away.—

[TO DOUGLAS KINNAIRD]   *Venice. February 24th. 1816* [*1817*]

My dear K—I have in all received from you two letters since my arrival in Venice—the one with the £500 in circulars—& the second enclosed to Messrs. Siri & Wilhalm—announcing the order of your partners to my credit for a similar sum.———I have no wish to press Murray—nor any one else when I can help it—but I do not like to anticipate and begin drawing upon you—till you have the needful— nor shall I—for I have eleven hundred in eleven of Hammersley's notes still in hand—but this does not prevent me from expecting the said John Murray Esqre. "to come up to time" because then I know the precise extent of my floating funds—and in these hard times—this is desirable—for the sake of all parties.———The Carnival is over—on

[1] Lord William Cavendish Bentinck (1774–1839) had been a general in the Napoleonic wars and was later the first Governor-General of India.

[2] The book which Mrs. Leigh believed was by Byron was a pseudonymous work, actually by Walter Scott, *The Black Dwarf* and *Old Mortality*, the first of the series of *Tales of My Landlord*. In the preface the author was said to be Peter, or Patrick Pattieson. What made Mrs. Leigh suspect Byron's authorship was the character of David Ritchie in *The Black Dwarf* who resided in solitude and was "haunted by a consciousness of his own deformity, and a suspicion of being generally subjected to the scorn of his fellowmen."

Tuesday last—I am glad of it—for though I am subsided into a moderate dissipation—the last three or four up all nights—did me no good & my constitution is a little in arrear—however Lent will bring me round again with early hours—& temperance.———Your "one or two letters" announcing "the complete success" of the poesies—reached me not—but those with the cash (which is much better) did.———As you had not even alluded to the publications—I had begun to think—what was probable enough—that "the learned world had said nothing at all to my paradoxes"[1]—"nothing at all Sir"—and to console myself with the usual consolation of authors—with posterity—and the discernment of the "happy few".———I however rejoice in the good taste of the age—& will requite it accordingly. ———Hobhouse's epistle to the Quarterly—I have not seen—but I suppose it to be a wrathful composition.—He will not be pleased to hear that Wedderburne Webster was his precursor in reply to the Quarterly—Murray tells me that W. W. answered in the M[ornin]g Chronicle—in a new style of controversy.—I saw in Switzerland in the autumn—the poems of Webster and I suspect that he made more by the prose of the St. James's Ledger—than he will by his own poetry.— —Amongst the ingredients of his volume I was not a little astonished to find an epitaph upon *myself*—the desert of which I would postpone for a few years at least—just to see out the row which is beginning amongst you.—If I can be of any use—I will come over—but it would be as well to have something else to do than "speak & write"—you may tell B[urdet]t[2] so—with my best remembrances.———I quite agree with you that you are as well out of D[rury] Lane but I suppose you have still a penchant for the scene—I did not mention Kean— because to say the truth—I had a little forgotten the Green room—but I am glad to hear of his successes.—You do not tell me if Scrope has won himself home from last Summer—or whether he has yet seen a "Boa Constrictor".—You do not mention Mrs. K[innair]d either—to whom I waft my humble duty.———Of myself I have little to relate out of the routine—except that about a month ago—there was a battle in my room between two damsels—which ended in the flight of one & the fits of the other—after about sixteen slaps given & received—with one or two which I incurred in the act of separating them—the little one won.—They were sisters in law—& all passed so rapidly that I had hardly time to interfere—but there was a deal of eau de Cologne—

[1] *Vicar of Wakefield*, Chapter 20.
[2] Sir Francis Burdett was a leader of Radical Reform in Parliament, a cause which Hobhouse and Kinnaird supported.

& burnt feathers—and all the apparatus of evanition—before things could be placed upon a right footing.———The cause was one finding the other in a place and position which was supposed not to belong to her—and the assailant had watched her time & made her appearance when nobody expected or indeed desired it.———Hobhouse is still at Rome—I mean to remain here at least until the Spring—unless any thing unexpected occurs.—I should like to stay out another year or more—if I could—but I presume we must all come back—and put our "musty morrions on"[3] (as Beaumont & Fletcher have it) so "now Gregory remember thy swashing blow".[4]

ever yrs very truly
B

[TO JOHN MURRAY (*a*)]   *Venice. February 25th. 1817*

Dear Sir—I wrote to you the other day in answer to your letter—at present I would trouble you with a commission if you will be kind enough to undertake it.———You perhaps know Mr. Love the Jeweller of old Bond Street.—In 1813—when in the intention of returning to Turkey—I purchased of him—and paid (argent comptant) about a dozen snuff boxes of more or less value—as presents for some of my Mussulman acquaintances.—These I have now with me.—The other day—having occasion to make an alteration in the lid of one (to place a portrait in it) it has turned out to be *silver-gilt* instead of *Gold*—for which last it was sold & paid for.—This was discovered by the workman in trying it before taking off the hinges—& working upon the lid.—I have of course recalled & preserved the box in statu quo.— what I wish you to do is to see the said Mr. Love and inform him of this circumstance adding from me that I will take care he shall not have done this with impunity.———if there is no remedy in law—there is at least the equitable one of making known his guilt—that is—his silver-*gilt*—and be damned to him.———I shall carefully preserve all the purchases I made of him on that occasion—for my return—as the Plague in Turkey is a barrier to traveling there—at present—or rather the endless Quarantine which would be the consequence—before one could land in coming back.———Pray state the matter to him with due ferocity.———I sent you the other day some extracts from a kind of

---

[3] Beaumont and Fletcher, *Philaster*, Act V, scene iv, 104. A morrion (various spellings) was a kind of helmet without beaver or visor, worn during the 16th and 17th centuries.

[4] *Romeo and Juliet*, Act I, scene i, 62.

drama—which I had begun in Switzerland—& finished here, you will
tell me if they are received—they were only in a letter.——I have not
yet had energy to copy it out—or I would send you the whole in
different covers.——The Carnival closed this day last week.——Mr.
Hobhouse is still at Rome.—I believe.—I am at present a little unwell
—sitting up too late—& some subsidiary dissipations have lowered
my blood a good deal—but I have at present the quiet & temperance
of Lent before me

> Believe me very truly yrs. &c.
>
> B

P.S.—Remember me to Mr. G[iffor]d.—I have not received your
parcel—or parcels.—Look into "Moore's (Dr. Moore's) view of
Italy"[1] for me—in one of the volumes you will find an account of the
Doge Valiere (it ought to be Falieri) and his conspiracy—or the
motives of it—get it transcribed for me & send it in a letter to me
soon—I want it—& can not find so good an account of that business
here—though the veiled portrait—& the place where he was once
crowned—and afterward decapitated still exists—& are shown.—I
have searched all the libraries—but the policy of the old Aristocracy
made their writers silent on his motives which were a private grievance
against one of the Patricians.—I mean to write a tragedy upon the
subject which appears to me very dramatic—an old man—jealous—
and conspiring against the state of which he was the actual reigning
Chief—the last circumstance makes it the most remarkable — &
only fact of the kind in all history of all nations.—

[TO JOHN MURRAY (*b*)]   [*February 25, 1817?*][1]

If you publish this—publish the original Spanish also[2]—which [I]
enclose—as I wish to show that I have kept near the text.——Mr.
Frere will be the best *corrector*—if he would have the goodness to take
the trouble.——

---

[1] John Moore, M.D. (1729–1802), author of the novel *Zeluco,* which Byron
admired, published in 1781 *View of Society and Manners in Italy; with anecdotes
relating to some eminent characters.* In the preface to Byron's poetic drama *Marino
Faliero* he spoke disparagingly of Moore's account of the Doge as "false and
flippant."

[1] The date is written in a hand not Byron's at the top of the page.

[2] This apparently refers to "A Very Mournful Ballad on the Siege and Conquest
of Alhama", which was first published with the fourth Canto of *Childe Harold* in
1818. See *Poetry*, IV, 529–534. See also letter of March 31, 1817, to Kinnaird.

Dearest Augusta—I believe you have received all my letters—for I sent you no description of Venice—beyond a slight sketch in a letter which I perceive has arrived—because you mention the "*Canal* &c"— that was the longest letter I have written to you from this city of the seventy islands.—Instead of a description of the lady whom Aunt Sophy wants to have described—I will show you her picture which is just finished for me[1]—some of these days or other.—The Carnival is over—but I am not in a descriptive mood—and will reserve all my wonders for word of mouth, when I see you again.—I know nothing which would make you laugh much—except a battle some weeks ago—in my apartment—between two of the fair "*sect*" (sisters in law) which ended in the flight of one & the fits of the other—and a great deal of confusion and eau de Cologne—and asterisks—& all that.—The cause was—one paying me an evening visit.——The other one gone out to a Conversazione—as was supposed for the evening ——but lo & behold—in about half an hour—she returned & entering my room—without a word—administered (before I could prevent her) about sixteen such slaps to her relation—as would have made your ear ache only to hear them.—The assaulted lady screamed & ran away—the assailant attempted pursuit—but being prevented by me—fairly went into asterisks—which cost a world of water of all sorts—besides fine speeches—to appease—& even then she declared herself a very ill used person—although victorious over a much taller woman than herself.—Besides she wronged my innocence—for nothing could be more innocent than my colloquy with the other.——You may tell this to Sophy if she wants amusement.—I repeat (as in my former letter) that I really & truly know nothing of P.P.——I have published nothing but what you know already.—I am glad to hear of Ada's progress in her mother tongue—I hope you will see her again soon.—What you "hope" may be—I do not know—if you mean a reunion between Lady B. & me—it is too late.—it is now a year—and I have repeatedly offered to make it up, with what success you know. —At present if she would rejoin me tomorrow—*I* would not accept the proposition.—I have no spirit of hatred against her—however.— I am too sensitive not to feel injuries—but far too proud to be vindic- tive.—She's a fool—& when you have said that—it is the most that can be said for her.——

Ever very truly yrs.

B

---

[1] This portrait of Marianna Segati has not survived, or at least is not known.

You will, perhaps, complain as much of the frequency of my letters now, as you were wont to do of their rarity. I think this is the fourth within as many moons. I feel anxious to hear from you, even more than usual, because your last indicated that you were unwell. At present, I am on the invalid regimen myself. The Carnival—that is, the latter part of it—and sitting up late o'nights, had knocked me up a little. But it is over,—and it is now Lent, with all its abstinence and Sacred Music.

The mumming closed with a masked ball at the Fenice, where I went, as also to most of the ridottos, etc., etc.; and, though I did not dissipate much upon the whole, yet I find "the sword wearing out the scabbard," though I have but just turned the corner of twenty-nine.

> So we'll go no more a roving
>   So late into the night,
> Though the heart be still as loving,
>   And the moon be still as bright.
>
> For the sword outwears its sheath,
>   And the soul wears out the breast,
> And the heart must pause to breathe,
>   And Love itself have rest.
>
> Though the night was made for loving,
>   And the day returns too soon,
> Yet we'll go no more a roving
>   By the light of the moon.

I have lately had some news of litter*atoor*, as I heard the editor of the Monthly[1] pronounce it once upon a time. I hear that W. W. has been publishing and responding to the attacks of the Quarterly, in the learned Perry's Chronicle. I read his poesies last autumn, and amongst them found an epitaph on his bull-dog, and another on *myself*. But I beg to assure him (like the astrologer Partridge) that I am not only alive now but was alive also at the time he wrote it. ∗ ∗ ∗ ∗ Hobhouse has (I hear, also) expectorated a letter against the Quarterly, addressed to me. I feel awkwardly situated between him and Gifford, both being my friends.

And this is your month of going to press—by the body of Diana! (a

---

[1] George Edward Griffiths was the editor of the *Monthly Review* for which Byron's friend Hodgson wrote frequently.

Venetian oath,) I feel as anxious—but not fearful for you—as if it were myself coming out in a work of humour, which would, you know, be the antipodes of all my previous publications. I don't think you have any thing to dread but your own reputation. You must keep up to that. As you never showed me a line of your work, I do not even know your measure; but you must send me a copy by Murray forthwith, and then you shall hear what I think. I dare say you are in a pucker. Of all authors, you are the only really *modest* one I ever met with,—which would sound oddly enough to those who recollect your morals when you were young—that is, when you were *extremely* young— I don't mean to stigmatise you either with years or morality.

I believe I told you that the E[dinburgh] R[eview] had attacked me, in an article on Coleridge (I have not seen it)—*"Et tu,* Jeffrey?"— "there is nothing but roguery in villanous man." [2] But I absolve him of all attacks, present and future; for I think he had already pushed his clemency in my behoof to the utmost, and I shall always think well of him. I only wonder he did not begin before, as my domestic destruction was a fine opening for all the world, of which all, who could, did well to avail themselves.

If I live ten years longer, you will see, however, that it is not over with me—I don't mean in literature, for that is nothing; and it may seem odd enough to say, I do not think it my vocation. But you will see that I will do something or other—the times and fortune permitting —that, "like the cosmogony, or creation of the world, will puzzle the philosophers of all ages." [3] But I doubt whether my constitution will hold out. I have, at intervals, exorcised it most devilishly.

I have not yet fixed a time of return, but I think of the spring. I shall have been away a year in April next. You never mention Rogers, nor Hodgson, your clerical neighbour, who has lately got a living near you. Has he also got a child yet?—his desideratum, when I saw him last.
* * * * * * * *
Pray let me hear from you, at your time and leisure, believing me ever and truly and affectionately, &c.

[TO JOHN MURRAY]   *Venice—Feby. 28th. 1817*

Dear Sir—Enclosed in this & another cover is the first act of the

[2] *Henry IV, Part I,* Act II, scene 4.
[3] *Vicar of Wakefield,* Chapter XIV.

kind of dramatic poem[1]—from which I sent you some extracts in a recent letter [.] I will copy out the rest at leisure & send it you piecemeal by the post.

yrs. ever
B

[TO JOHN MURRAY]   *Venice—March 3d. 1817*

My dear Sir—In acknowledging the arrival of the article from the "Quarterly" [1] which I received two days ago—I cannot express myself better than in the words of my sister Augusta—who (speaking of it) says that it is written in a spirit "of the most feeling & kind nature".— It is however something more—it seems to me—(as far as the subject of it may be permitted to judge) to be *very well* written as a composition—& I think will do the journal no discredit—because—even those who may condemn its partiality, must praise it's generosity.——— The temptations to take another & less favourable view of the question have been so great & numerous—that what with public opinion— politics—&c.—he must be a gallant as well as a good man—who has ventured in that place—and at this time—to write such an article even anonymously.—Such things however are their own reward—& I even flatter myself that the writer whosoever he may be (and I have no guess) will not regret that the perusal of this has given me as much gratification—as any composition of that nature could give—& more than any other ever has given—and I have had a good many in my time—of one kind or the other.—It is not the mere praise, but there is a *tact* & a *delicacy* throughout not only with regard to me—but to *others*—which as it had not been observed *elsewhere*—I had till now doubted—whether it could be preserved *any where*.———Perhaps some day or other you will know or tell me the writer's name—be assured— had the article been a harsh one—I should not have asked it.———I have lately written to you frequently—with *extracts* &c. which I hope you have received—or will receive with—or before this letter.—Ever since the conclusion of the Carnival—I have been unwell—(do not mention this on any account to Augusta for if I grow worse—she will

---

1 *Manfred.*
1 In the *Quarterly Review* for October, 1816 (vol. XVI, pp. 172–208) appeared a very favourable review of *Childe Harold, Canto III*, and *The Prisoner of Chillon, a Dream, and other Poems.* The review, as Murray told Byron later, was by Walter Scott.

know it too soon—& if I get better there is no occasion that she should know it at all) & have hardly stirred out of the house—however I don't want a Physician & if I did—very luckily those of Italy are the worst in the world—so that I should still have a chance.—They have I believe one famous Surgeon—Vacca[2]—who lives at Pisa—who might be useful in case of dissection.—But he is some hundred miles off.— My malady is a sort of lowish fever—originating from what my pugilistic "pastor & master" Jackson[3] would call—"taking too much out of oneself" however I am better within this day or two.——I missed seeing the new Patriarch's procession to St. Mark's the other day (owing to my indisposition) with six hundred and fifty priests in his rear—a "goodly army".—The admirable government of Vienna in its edict from thence—authorizing his installation—prescribed as part of the pageant—a "*Coach* & four horses" to show how very very "*German* to the matter" this was—you have only to suppose our Parliament commanding the Archbishop of Canterbury to proceed from Hyde park Corner to St. Paul's Cathedral in the Lord Mayor's Barge—or the Margate Hoy.—There is but St. Marc's place in all Venice—broad enough for a carriage to move—& it is paved with large smooth flagstones—so that the Chariot & horses of Elijah himself would be puzzled to manoeuvre upon it—those of Pharaoh might do better—for the Canals & particularly the Grand Canal are sufficiently capacious & extensive for his whole host.—of course no coach could be attempted—but the Venetians who are very naive as well as arch—were much amused with the ordinance.——The Armenian Grammar is published—but my Armenian studies are suspended for the present—till my head aches a little less.—I sent you the other day in two covers—the first act of "Manfred" a drama as mad as Nat. Lee's Bedlam tragedy—which was in 25 acts & some odd scenes[4]—mine is but in three acts.——I find I have begun this letter at the wrong end—never mind—I must end it at the right

Yrs. ever very truly & obligedly
BYRON

P.S.—Marianna is very well—she has been sitting for her picture for me—a miniature which is very like.—

2 Andrea Vacca Berlinghieri (1772–1826) studied in London under Bell and Hunter. Byron used his services later in Pisa.

3 John ("Gentleman") Jackson, the pugilist.

4 While in Bethlehem Hospital (Bedlam), Nathaniel Lee reputedly wrote a tragedy in 25 acts. (Tom Brown, *Works*, ed. 1730, Vol. II, pp. 187, 188)

A letter from Mr. Hanson apprizes me of the result of his correspondence with Sir Ralph Noel—(of which he has transmitted the copy)
and of his interviews with Dr. Lushington on the subject of ⟨my⟩ our
daughter.—I am also informed of a bill in Chancery filed against me
last Spring by Sir Ralph Noel—of which this is the first intimation—&
of the subject of which I am ignorant.—Whatever may be the result
of these discussions—& the measures which have led to them—& to
which they may lead—remember that I have not been the first to
begin—but being begun—neither shall I be the first to recede.——I
feel at length convinced that the feeling which I had cherished through
all—& in despite of all—namely—the hope of a reconciliation &
reunion—however remote—is indu[bitably?] useless—& although, all
things considered, it could not be very sanguine—still it was sincere—
& I cherished it as a sickly in[fatuation?] & now I part with it with a
regret perhaps bitterer of [than?] that which I felt in parting with
yourself. It was generally understood—if not expressed—that all legal
proceedings were to terminate in the act of our separation—to what
then I am to attribute the bill of which I am apprized—I am at a loss
to conjecture.—The object is evident—it is to deprive me of my
paternal right over my child—which I have the less merited as I
neither abused nor intended to abuse it. You & yours might have
been satisfied with the outrages I have already suffered—if not by
your design—at least by your means—I know your defence & your
apology—duty & Justice ⟨were the words⟩—but "Qui n'est que juste
—est dur" or if the French aphorism should seem light in the balance—
I could refer you to an older language & a higher authority—for the
condemnation of conduct—which you may yet live to condemn in
your own heart.—Throughout the whole of this unhappy business— I
have done my best to avoid the bitterness which however is yet
amongst us—⟨though I did wrong—& admitted it—⟩ & it would be
as well if even you at times recollected—that the man who has been
sacrificed in fame—in feelings—in every thing ⟨which [even ye?] have
endeavoured to render bitterness & of which nothing but the want of
power⟩ to the convenience of your family—was he whom you once
loved—& who—whatever you may imagine to the contrary—loved
you.——If you conceive that I could be actuated by revenge against
you—you are mistaken.—I am not humble enough to be [vindictive?]
—Irritated I may have been—& may be—is it a wonder?—but upon
such irritation beyond it's momentary expression—I have not acted—

from the hour that you quitted me—to that in which I am made aware
that our daughter is to be the entail of our disunion—the inheritor
of our bitterness. If you think to reconcile yourself to yourself—by
accumulating harshness against me—you are again mistaken—you
are not happy nor even tranquil—nor will you ever be so—even to
the very moderate degree this is permitted to ge[neral?] humanity.—
For myself I have a confidence in my Fortune which will yet bear me
through—ταὐτόματον ἡμῶν καλλων Βουλευεται[1]—the reverses which
have occurred—were what I should have expected—and in considering
you & yours merely as the instruments of my more recent adversity—
it would be difficult for me to blame you—did not every thing appear
to intimate a deliberate intention of as wilful malice on your parts as
could well be digested into a system.—However ⟨I shall live to have
to pity you all one day or the other—if I live—& if not I die⟩ time &
Nemesis will do that which I would not—even were it in my power
remote or immediate.—You will smile at this piece of prophecy—do
so—but recollect it.——it is justified by all human experience—no one
was ever even the involuntary cause of great evils to others—without
a requital—I have paid and am paying for mine—so will you.—⟨The
bitterness is not any novelty to me—but I have a [preview?] of its
truth—as for you [you are?] more a philosopher.⟩[2]

[TO JOHN CAM HOBHOUSE]   *Venice—March 7th. 1817*

My dear Hobhouse—I received both your letters and answered the
first—the second was from Rome—to which my indecision has prevented a reply.—I thought of joining you but have procrastinated till it
is too late—as the influx of strangers previous to Holy week—and the
coming Spring (which is the Malaria season I understand) would
render my stay too short for any useful purpose—besides crowding
me while I remained.——The Carnival here was gay and foolish
enough to be very amusing—two Englishmen were here—one of
whom introduced himself (& friend) as the friend of Capt. G[eorg]e
Byron;—his name was Capt. Stuart of the Navy—an agreeable person
—I helped them to Made. Albrizzi's Helen—& went with them to the
Ridotto—to the Fenice (where I had a box) & such other mummeries
as were diverting—and gave them a letter to Col. Fitz[geral]d of
Milan—& a message for Breme. I am sorry to say that I do not see any

---

[1] "Chance is more just than we are." The Greek is hard to read and may be
inaccurate.
[2] From a manuscript draft in the Murray MSS.

chance of our meeting at Rome which is entirely my own fault—& I
regret it extremely—firstly—because I would rather have seen it with
you than any other person—& 2dly because I must see it if possible—
before I return to democratize England.—Dr. Skinas[1] lately sent
a proposition through Mustoxithi[2] to Made. Albrizzi to accompany me
to Greece—which I have declined because of Pestilence there—and
undefined Quarantine on one's return.———I have lately had news of
course from England.—Scrope flourishing by the account—Kinnaird
in good health and great hurry as usual—Burdett & politics advancing.
—Walter Scott's brother—(who was Isle of Man-ned for malversation
of Ld. Sommerville's concerns—or not being able to give an account of
his accounts—& is lately gone to Canada) is *positively* (Murray says)
the Author of Waverley &c.[3] he also published another—"Tales of
my Landlord" which is generally deemed even greatly *superior* to all
the former.—Murray sent it to me but I have not received it—and I
fear that it's arrival—is problematical.—Wedderburne Webster
having been quizzed in a former Quarterly—has replied to the Editor
in a letter to the learned Perry—which he concludes by leaving *him*
(the Editor of the Quarterly) "with *feelings* of contempt and *oblivion*"
———I am afraid it will not please you—that this same evil genius
W.W. should be also a respondent to the Critics—as I recollect in
Switzerland you gave him & his preface to the devil for having taken
in vain with his awkward compliments the name of a friend of yours—
not so much for the sake of the friend—as of a projected preface—in
which you were pleased to be gracious.—The Patriarch of Venice was
installed the other Sunday—the court of Vienna—decreed in an edict—
that he should proceed to St. Mark's in a "Coach & four"—but (as
Incledon says in "the Son & heir of Sir William Meadows") "thauts
impossible"[4] the Venetians grinned, as you may suppose, at the
knowledge of topography displayed in this Cesarean decree—which
was truly "German to the matter".———Catalani sung here in three
or four Academias—given by her at San Benedetto—and carried off a
quantity of Lira Venete—her voice seemed to me the same as ever—

[1] Unidentified.

[2] Mustoxithi (or Mustoxidi?) was a learned Greek living in Venice, who
introduced Byron to the custodian of the Marciana Library, the Abbé Morelli.

[3] The author of *Waverley* was still kept a secret. Scott himself fostered the
rumour that his brother Thomas was the author.

[4] Charles Incledon (1763–1826), a celebrated tenor, sang in operas including
The Beggar's Opera at Covent Garden. According to Leigh Hunt, Byron in his
cups was fond of imitating him. (Hunt, *Autobiography*, ed. J. E. Morpurgo, 1949,
p. 354.) Sir William Meadows is a character in Bickerstaff's *Love in a Village*, a
comic opera performed at Drury Lane Theatre.

and her figure & face not much older.—Her "Signor Procolo" Mounseer. (I forget the fellow's name) made himself not less ridiculous by the accounts given of his demeanour—here than in London—where he was a prodigious mountebank.——I have heard twice from the Dr. Polidori—who was been visiting the sick at Pisa— he has written a tragedy called the Duke of Athens—& is by this time on his way to England—& from England he means to go to the Brazils with the Danish Consul (whom he found at Pisa—) to teach the Portuguese medicine—which they are fond of to distraction.—— I saw your correspondent of Sir R. Wn.—the Countess Mustani[5] with M[adam]e. Albrizzi & she enquired after you with great politeness— & regretted that she was not at Verona during your transits.—She is a fair—full—& rather handsome personage of some seven and thirty summers date.—I have not the least idea where I am going—nor what I am to do—and am

Yrs ever very truly

B

P.S.—My reverence to Bailey[6] if he is still at Rome.—

[TO JOHN MURRAY] *Venice. March 9th. 1817*

My dear Sir—In remitting the third act of the sort of dramatic poem of which you will by this time have received the two first—(at least I hope so) which were sent within the last three weeks—I have little to observe except that you must *not* publish it (if it ever is published) without giving me previous notice.—I have really & truly no notion whether it is good or bad—& as this was not the case with the principal of my former publications—I am therefore inclined to rank it but humbly.—You will submit it to Mr. G[iffor]d & to whomsoever you please besides.—With regard to question of copyright (if it ever comes to publication—) I do not know whether you would think *three hundred* guineas[1]—an over estimate—if you do you may diminish it— I do not think it worth more—so you may see I make some difference between it and the others.———I have received your two reviews[2]—

[5] Unidentified.
[6] Hobhouse's friend "Long" Baillie.
[1] This was the sum Murray eventually, paid for *Manfred.*
[2] The two reviews were of the third canto of *Childe Harold,* by Jeffrey in the *Edinburgh Review* (for December, 1816, published February 14, 1817), and by Walter Scott in the *Quarterly Review* (for October, 1816, published February 11, 1817).

(but not the "Tales of my Landlord") the Quarterly I acknowledged particularly in a letter to you on it's arrival, ten days ago.—what you tell me of Perry petrifies me—it is a rank imposition.[3]—In or about February or March 1816—I was given to understand that Mr. Croker was not only a coadjutor in the attacks of the Courier in 1814—but the author of some lines tolerably ferocious then recently published in a Morning paper.[4]—Upon this I wrote a reprisal—the whole of the lines I have forgotten & even the purport of them I scarcely remember —for on *your* assuring me that he was not &c. &c. I put them into the *fire before your face*—& there *never was* but that *one rough* copy.—Mr. Davies the only person who ever heard them read—wanted a copy— which I refused.—If however by some *impossibility*—which I cannot divine—the ghost of those rhymes should walk into the world—I never will deny what I have really written but hold myself personally responsible for satisfaction—though I reserve to myself the right of disavowing all or any *fabrications*.—To the previous facts you were a witness—& best know how far my recapitulation is correct—& I request that you will inform Mr. Perry from me that I wonder he should permit such an abuse of my name & his paper—I say an *abuse*— because my absence at least demands some respect—& my presence & positive sanction could alone justify him in such a proceeding—even were the lines mine—& if false—there are no words for him.—I repeat to you that the original was burnt before you on your *assurance* —& there *never* was a *copy* nor even a verbal repetition—very much to the discomfort of some zealous whigs—who bored me for them (having heard it bruited by Mr. D. that there were such matters) to no purpose—for having written them solely with the notion that Mr. C[roker] was the aggressor—& for my *own* & not party reprisals—I would not lend me to the zeal of any sect—when I was made aware that he was not the writer of the offensive passages.—*You know* if there was such a thing I would not deny it—I mentioned it openly at the time to you—& you will remember why and where I destroyed it— & no power nor wheedling on earth should have made or could make me (if I recollected them) give a copy after that—unless I was well assured that Mr. C[roker] was really the author of that which you assured me he was not.———I intend for England this spring where I

[3] Murray had written to Byron (Feb. 18, 1817): "A paragraph was inserted in the *Morning Chronicle* of last week, headed, 'Mr. Croker and Lord B——'. and saying you had written his character, which they would give in a few days."

[4] Murray suggested to Byron that the attacks were by Henry Brougham. This increased Byron's undying hatred of Brougham, whom he intended to challenge to a duel as a first order of business when and if he returned to England.

have some affairs to adjust;—but the post hurries me. For this month past I have been unwell—but am getting better—and thinking of moving homewards towards May,—without going to Rome as the unhealthy season comes on soon—& I can return when I have settled the business I go upon which need not be long.—You say that "Margaret of Anjou" & "Ilderim"[5] do not keep pace with your other saleables—I should have thought the Assyrian tale very succeedable.— I saw in Mr. Wedderburne Webster's poetry that he had written my epitaph—I would rather have written his.—The thing I have sent you you will see at a glimpse—could never be attempted or thought of for the stage—I much doubt it for publication even.—It is too much in my old style—but I composed it actually with a *horror* of the stage—& with a view to render even the thought of it impracticable, knowing the zeal of my friends, that I should try that for which I have an invincible repugnance—viz—a representation.——I certainly am a devil of a mannerist—& must leave off—but what could I do? without exertion of some kind—I should have sunk under my imagination and reality.—My best respects to Mr. Gifford—to Walter Scott & to all friends.—

yrs. ever
BYRON

[TO THOMAS MOORE]   *Venice, March 10th, 1817*

I wrote again to you lately, but I hope you won't be sorry to have another epistle. I have been unwell this month, with a kind of slow and low fever, which fixes upon me at night, and goes off in the morning; but, however, I am now better. In spring it is probable we may meet; at least I intend for England, where I have business, and hope to meet you in *your* restored health and additional laurels.

Murray has sent me the Quarterly and the Edinburgh. When I tell you that Walter Scott is the author of the article in the former, you will agree with me that such an article is still more honourable to him than to myself. I am perfectly pleased with Jeffrey's also, which I wish you to tell him, with my remembrances—not that I suppose it is of any consequence to him or ever could have been, whether I am pleased or not,—but simply in my private relation to him, as his well-wisher, and it may be one day as his acquaintance. I wish you would also add, what

5 *Margaret of Anjou, a Poem*, by Margaret Holford, 1816; *Ilderim, a Syrian Tale*, by H. Gally Knight, 1816.

you know—that I was not, and, indeed, am not even *now*, the misanthropical and gloomy gentleman he takes me for, but a facetious companion, well to do with those with whom I am intimate, and as loquacious and laughing as if I were a much cleverer fellow.

I suppose now I shall never be able to shake off my sables in public imagination, more particularly since my moral * * [Clytemnestra?] clove down my fame. However, nor that, nor more than that, has yet extinguished my spirit, which always rises with the rebound.

At Venice we are in Lent, and I have not lately moved out of doors, —my feverishness requiring quiet, and—by way of being more quiet —here is the Signora Marianna just come in and seated at my elbow.

Have you seen * * *'s book of poesy? and, if you have seen it, are you not delighted with it? And have you—I really cannot go on. There is a pair of great black eyes looking over my shoulder, like the angel leaning over St. Matthew's, in the old frontispieces to the Evangelists, —so that I must turn and answer them instead of you.

Ever, &c.

[TO THOMAS MOORE]   *Venice, March 25th, 1817*

I have at last learned, in default of your own writing (or *not* writing—which should it be? for I am not very clear as to the application of the word *default*), from Murray, two particulars of (or belonging to) you; one, that you are removing to Hornsey,[1] which is, I presume, to be nearer London; and the other, that your Poem is announced by the name of Lalla Rookh. I am glad of it,—first that we are to have it at last, and next, I like a tough title myself—witness The Giaour and Childe Harold, which choked half the Blues at starting. Besides, it is the tail of Alcibiades's dog,[2]—not that I suppose you want either dog or tail. Talking of tail, I wish you had not called it a *"Persian Tale."*[3] I am very sorry that I called some of my own things "Tales," because I think that they are something better. Besides, we have had Arabian, and Hindoo, and Turkish, and Assyrian Tales. But, after all, this is frivolous in me; you won't, however, mind my nonsense.

---

[1] Moore moved to Hornsey in the spring of 1817, but remained there only until November.

[2] Plutarch related the incident of Alcibiades cutting off the tail of his dog, and when his friends blamed him for it, he said: "I would have the Athenians rather prate upon that, than they should say worse of me."

[3] Byron was misinformed. Moore's subtitle was "an Oriental Romance".

Really and truly, I want you to make a great hit, if only out of self-love, because we happen to be old cronies; and I have no doubt you will—I am sure you *can*. But you are, I'll be sworn, in a devil of a pucker; and *I* am *not* at your elbow, and Rogers *is*. I envy him; which is not fair, because he does not envy any body. Mind you send to me—that is, make Murray send—the moment you are forth.

I have been very ill with a slow fever, which at last took to flying, and became as quick as need be. But, at length, after a week of half-delirium, burning skin, thirst, hot headache, horrible pulsation, and no sleep, by the blessing of barley water, and refusing to see any physician, I recovered. It is an epidemic of the place, which is annual, and visits strangers. Here follow some versicles, which I made one sleepless night.

I read the "Christabel,"
  Very well:
I read the "Missionary";[4]
  Pretty—very:
I tired at "Ilderim";
  Ahem!
I read a sheet of "Marg'ret of *Anjou*";
  Can you?
I turn'd a page of W[ebster]'s "Waterloo";
  Pooh! pooh!
I look'd at Wordsworth's milk-white "Rylstone Doe":
  Hillo!
I read "Glenarvon," too, by Caro. Lamb—
  God damn!

* *
* *

I have not the least idea where I am going, nor what I am to do. I wished to have gone to Rome; but at present it is pestilent with English,—a parcel of staring boobies, who go about gaping and wishing to be at once cheap and magnificent. A man is a fool who travels now in France or Italy, till this tribe of wretches is swept home again. In two or three years the first rush will be over, and the Continent will be roomy and agreeable.

I stayed at Venice chiefly because it is not one of their "dens of thieves;" and here they but pause and pass. In Switzerland it was really noxious. Luckily, I was early, and had got the prettiest place on

---

[4] *The Missionary of the Andes, a Poem*, by W. L. Bowles, 1815.

all the Lake before they were quickened into motion with the rest of [the] reptiles. But they crossed me every where. I met a family of children and old women half-way up the Wengen Alp (by the Jungfrau) upon mules, some of them too old and others too young to be the least aware of what they saw.

By the way, I think the Jungfrau, and all that region of Alps, which I traversed in September—going to the very top of the Wengen, which is not the highest (the Jungfrau itself is inaccessible) but the best point of view—much finer than Mont-Blanc and Chamouni, or the Simplon. I kept a journal of the whole for my sister Augusta, part of which she copied and let Murray see.

I wrote a sort of mad Drama, for the sake of introducing the Alpine scenery in description: and this I sent lately to Murray. Almost all the *dram. pers.* are spirits, ghosts, or magicians, and the scene is in the Alps and the other world, so you may suppose what a Bedlam tragedy it must be: make him show it you. I sent him all three acts piecemeal, by the post, and suppose they have arrived.

I have now written to you at least six letters, or letter*ets*, and all I have received in return is a note about the length you used to write from Bury Street to St. James's-street, when we used to dine with Rogers, and talk laxly, and go to parties, and hear poor Sheridan now and then. Do you remember one night he was so tipsy, that I was forced to put his cocked hat on for him—for he could not,—and I let him down at Brookes's, much as he must since have been let down into his grave. Heigh ho! I wish I was drunk—but I have nothing but this d—d barley-water before me.

I am still in love,—which is a dreadful drawback in quitting a place, and I can't stay at Venice much longer. What I shall do on this point I don't know. The girl means to go with me, but I do not like this for her own sake. I have had so many conflicts in my own mind on this subject, that I am not at all sure they did not help me to the fever I mentioned above. I am certainly very much attached to her, and I have cause to be so, if you knew all. But she has a child; and though, like all the "children of the sun,"[5] she consults nothing but passion, it is necessary I should think for both; and it is only the virtuous, like ∗ ∗ ∗, [Lady Byron] who can afford to give up husband and child, and live happy ever after.

[5] From Young's *Revenge*, Act V, scene 2, a play for which Byron had an early fondness. He recited a passage from *The Revenge* for his first speech-day performance at Harrow, and he credited Young's phrase as having suggested lines 16 and 17 of *The Bride of Abydos*: "'Tis the clime of the East—'tis the land of the Sun—/Can he smile on such deeds as his children have done?"

The Italian ethics are the most singular ever met with. The perversion, not only of action, but of reasoning, is singular in the women. It is not that they do not consider the thing itself as wrong, and very wrong, but *love* (the *sentiment* of love) is not merely an excuse for it, but makes it an *actual virtue*, provided it is disinterested, and not a *caprice*, and is confined to one object. They have awful notions of constancy; for I have seen some ancient figures of eighty pointed out as Amorosi of forty, fifty, and sixty years' standing. I can't say I have ever seen a husband and wife so coupled.

Ever, &c.

P.S.—Marianna, to whom I have just translated what I have written on our subject to you, says—"If you loved me thoroughly, you would not make so many fine reflections, which are only good *forbirsi i scarpi*,"—that is, "to clean shoes withal,"—a Venetian proverb of appreciation, which is applicable to reasoning of all kinds.

[TO JOHN HANSON]   *Venice—March 25th. 1817*

Dear Sir/—I have been ill of a fever which prevented me from answering your letter.—Tell Charles I have got his paper—& will sign it—but I cannot find a witness at present there being no English of my acquaintance here.———The answer of Lady B. & Co—is no answer—whatever be the event I will try the *question* to the *last*—& I request you to get me the best advice how to proceed in Chancery—because I am determined to *reclaim* the child to myself—as the natural guardian;—in consequence of their recent conduct—the last piece of treachery I little thought of—but the view is obvious—but this shall not deter me from asserting my right—get *this* Chancery *Bill*—answer it—& proceed upon it—I shall apply to have the child—in short as they have begun—I will go on—come of it what will.—I have done what I could to avoid extremities—but the die is cast—& I authorize —& desire you to take the proper steps—& obtain for me the best advice—how & in what manner to assume the care & personal charge of my daughter.—I will return directly if necessary.———Mrs. B[yro]n of Nottingham[1] writes for her interest—if there is any residue from the rents—let her have what you can—her—& Joe Murray—poor old man,—Sir R. Noel's year being due—let him pay it.———I hope you are well—& doing well—I quite approve of your diligence—&

[1] The Hon. Mrs George Byron, great-aunt of the poet.

what you have already done on my daughter's account—but *I* must proceed—

ever yrs. very truly & affectly.

BYRON

P.S.—As it was understood & assented that all legal proceedings on the part of Lady B. & the Noels—were to terminate with our separation,—Noel's Chancery Bill—is an infraction of the understood relations between us—& you may tell him from *me* he is *guilty* of a breach of his word.—However *on with* it—as they began—they shall have enough.———

[TO AUGUSTA LEIGH]   *Venice—March 25th. 1817*

My dearest Augusta—I have had a fever which prevented me from writing.—it was first slow—& then quick—& then it went away.—I got well without a Physician—you will think it odd for me who am so fond of *quacking*—but on this occasion—though bad enough—I would see none—& refused to see one who was sent for by Madame Segati on purpose—& so I got well.—I had the *slow* one upon me sometime ago—but I thought it better to say nothing to you till I recovered altogether.———Lady Byron & her family have behaved as *ill* as *possible* about Ada—& it is not over yet—they instituted a Chancery bill against me on purpose to deprive me of all authority over my daughter—but I will try the question to the very last.—I have been too ill to write to Lady Byron myself—but I desire you to repeat what I have said & say.—I have forgiven everything up to this—but this I never will forgive—& no consideration on earth shall now prevail on me to look upon her as otherwise than my worst enemy.—I curse her from the bottom of my heart—& in the bitterness of my soul—& I only hope she may one day feel what she made me suffer;—they will break my heart or drive me mad one day or the other—but she is a wretch & will end ill—she was born to be my destruction—& has been so—ten thousand curses be upon her and her father and mother's family now & forever.—I must speak of something else.—So you have seen Holmes[1] —by the way—some foolery of Scrope's—he had cut my hair in his picture—(not quite so well as Blake) I desired him to restore it— pray make him do so—or see that he has done so—he may send his print in a letter if he likes—unless you see it—& don't like it.—I have

---

[1] James Holmes, the painter, who made a number of miniatures of Byron before he left England.

been sitting for *two* miniatures for *you*—one the view of the face—
which you like—& the other different—but *both* in my *usual* dress—&
as they are the only ones so done—I hope you will like them.—The
Painter is an Italian named Prepiani[2]—reckoned very good—he made
some fine ones of the Viceroy Eugene.—I will send or bring them.———
You amuse me with Le Mann's Marquis's message[3]—a pretty compliment!—to set a sick man *asleep*—however—I am glad to have done the
old gentleman any good.—Believe me (in total ignorance of P.P.[4] of
which I really know nothing)—

yrs. ever very truly & affectly
B

[TO JOHN MURRAY]   *Venice. March 25th. 1817*

Dear Sir—Your letter & enclosure are safe—but "English gentlemen" are very rare—at least in Venice—I doubt whether there are at
present any—save the Consul & vice-Consul—with neither of whom
I have the slightest acquaintance.—The moment I can pounce upon a
witness—I will send the deed properly signed—but must he necessarily
be genteel? would not a servant or a merchant do?—Venice is not a
place where the English are gregarious—their pigeon-houses are
Florence—Naples—Rome &c.—& to tell you the truth this was one
reason why I staid here—till the season of the purgation of Rome from
these people—which is infected with them at this time—should arrive
—besides I abhor the nation—& the nation me;—it is impossible for
me to describe my *own* sensation on that point—but it may suffice to
say—that if I met with any of the race in the beautiful parts of
Switzerland—the most distant glimpse or aspect of them poisoned the
whole scene—& I do not choose to have the Pantheon & St Peter's &
the Capitol spoiled for me too.—this feeling may be probably owing to
recent events—& the destruction with which my moral Clytemnestra
hewed me down—but it does not exist the less—& while it exists I
shall conceal it as little as any other.—I have been seriously ill with
a fever—but it is gone.—I had no physician.—I believe or suppose it

---

[2] Prepiani was a Venetian miniature painter who achieved no fame, for his name
is not in any dictionary of painters. The Countess Guiccioli prized one of the
Prepiani portraits of Byron and thought it the best likeness. She allowed Joseph
Fagnani to make a copy in Paris in 1860. Fagnani's portrait is reproduced opposite
page 45 in Emma Fagnani's *The Art Life of a XIXth Century Portrait Painter,
Joseph Fagnani.*

[3] Unidentified.

[4] See Feb. [19?], 1817, to Augusta, note 2.

was the indigenous fever of the place which comes every year at this time, & of which the Physicians change the name annually to dispatch the people sooner—it is a kind of Typhus—& kills occasionally;—it was pretty smart—but nothing particular—& has left me some debility & a great appetite.—there are a good many ill at present I suppose of the same.—I feel sorry for Horner[1]—if there was any thing in the world to make him like it—and still more sorry for his friends— as there was much to make them regret him.—I had not heard of his death till by your letter.—Some weeks ago I wrote to you my acknowledgements of W[alter] S[cott]'s article—now I know it to be his—it cannot add to my good opinion of him—but it adds to that of myself.—*He* & Gifford & Moore are the only *regulars* I ever knew who had nothing of the *Garrison* about their manner—no nonsense—nor affectations look you!—as for the rest whom I have known—there was always more or less of the author about them—the pen peeping from behind the ear—& the thumbs a little inky or so.—"Lalla Rookh"— you must recollect that in the way of title—the "*Giaour*" has never been pronounced to this day—& both it & Childe Harold sounded very formidible & facetious to the blue-bottles of wit & honour about town —till they were taught & startled into a proper deportment—& there- fore Lalla Rookh which is very orthodox & oriental—is as good a title as need be—if not better.—I could wish rather that he had not called it "a *Persian tale*" firstly because we have had "Turkish tales" and Hindoo tales—& Assyrian tales—already—& *tale* is a word of which it repents me to have nick-named poesy—fable would be better; —and secondly—"Persian tale" reminds one of the lines of Pope—on Ambrose Phillips—though no one can say to be sure that this tale has been "turned for half a crown"[2] still it is as well to avoid such clashings. —"Persian *story*" why not?—or romance?—I feel as anxious for Moore as I could do for myself for the soul of me—& I would not have him succeed otherwise than splendidly—which I trust he will do.—— With regard to the "witch drama" I sent all the three acts—by post— week after week—within this last month.—I repeat that I have not an idea if it is good or bad—if bad it must on no account be risked in publication—if good—it is at your service—I value it at *three hundred* guineas—or less if you like it—perhaps if published the best way will

[1] Francis Horner (1778–1817), lawyer and politician, was one of the founders of the *Edinburgh Review*, for which he wrote frequently. As a member of Parliament he took an active part in the debates and was an impressive speaker.

[2] Pope attacked Ambrose Philips for his translation of *Contes Persans* of Petit de la Croix (1709) in the *Epistle to Dr. Arbuthnot* (line 179 ff): "Who turns a Persian tale for half-a-crown."

be to add it to your winter volume—& not publish separately.—The price will shew you I don't pique myself upon it—so speak out—you may put it in the fire if you like—& Gifford *don't* like.—The Armenian grammar is published—that is *one*—the other is still in M.S.—My illness has prevented me from moving this month past—& I have done nothing more with the Armenian.—Of Italian or rather Lombard Manners—I could tell you little or nothing.—I went two or three times to the Governor's Conversazione, (& if you go once you are free to go always) at which as I only saw very plain women—a formal circle—in short a *worse sort* of rout—I did not go again.—I went to some Academie & to Madame Albrizzi's—where I saw pretty much the same thing—with the addition of some literati—who are the same—*blue* by God!—all the world over.—I fell in love the first week with Madame Segati & I have continued so ever since—because she is very pretty & pleasing—& talks Venetian—which amuses me—& is naive & I can besides see her & make love with her at all or any hours—which is convenient, with my temperament.—I have seen all their spectacles & sights—but I do not know anything very worthy of observation—except that the women *kiss* better than those of any other nation—which is notorious—and is attributed to the worship of images and the early habit of osculation induced thereby.—

very truly yrs. &c.
B

P.S.—Pray send the red toothpowder by a *safe hand* & Speedily.—

I read the "Christabel"
  Very well.—
I read the "Missionary"
  Pretty—very.—
I tried at "Ilderim"
  Ahem!
I read a sheet of "Margaret of *Anjou*"
  Can—You?
I turned a page of "Webster's Waterloo"
  Pooh! Pooh!
I looked at Wordsworth's "milk-white Rylstone Doe,"
  Hillo!
I read "Glenarvon" too by Caro. Lamb,
  God damn!

To hook the Reader—you—John Murray—
  Have published "Anjou's Margaret,"
Which won't be sold off in a hurry,
  (At least, it has not been as yet)
And then still further to bewilder him
Without remorse you set up "Ilderim,"
  So mind you don't get into debt,—
Because—as how—if you should fail—
These books would be but baddish bail.—
And mind—you do *not* let escape
  These rhymes to Morning Post, or Perry,—
  Which would be very treacherous—*very*—
And get me into such a scrape.—
For firstly I should have to sally
All in my little boat against a *Galley*—
And should I chance to slay the Assyrian wight
Have next to combat with the female knight—
And pricked to death expire upon her needle,
A sort of end which I should take indeed ill!—

You may show these matters to Moore and the *select*—but not to the *prophane*.—And tell Moore—that I wonder he don't write to me now & then.—

[TO DOUGLAS KINNAIRD]   *Venice—March 25th. 1817*

My dear Kinnaird—I have been unwell with a fever—which has delayed my response to your letter—for which I am obliged to you—as well as for all your kindness & promptitude.—I wrote to Scrope some time ago—directed to Brookes's I suppose it will find him.—I am at present undecided—& think to return—but I do not like returning without having first gone to Rome—but yet—I doubt that my health—& the quantity of English there will prevent me from proceeding thither for some time—if I go even at all.—I have hardly been out of the house the last month—but am now quite well again —but not over strong.—I have heard from Murray with all the fine things of the Edinburgh and Quarterly—what you may suppose are sufficiently agreeable to my selflove—I have no tragedy nor tragedies —but a sort of metaphysical drama which I sent to Murray the other day—which is the very Antipodes of the stage and is meant to be so— it is all in the Alps & the other world—and as mad as Bedlam—I do

194

not know that it is even fit for publication—the persons are all magicians—ghosts—& the evil principle—with a mixed mythology of my own—which you may suppose is somewhat of the strangest.— — It has no pretense to being called a drama—except that it is in dialogue & acts.—Moray has announced Moore's poem—Lallah Rookh. I am very desirous that he should make a hit & I have no doubt that he will.—I shall be glad to hear your anticipation of Maturin's success confirmed[1]—for his sake as well as that of Drury Lane.— — I shall also be happy to hear how the same Passions succeed in the Oratorio—Do not set out till you know either that I am coming home —or that I have found some place to lie to for you—I should be very much vexed to arrive while you & Scrope are away—and very glad to meet you both on this side of the Alps—but perhaps I could return & set out again—for I have some business in England it may be of more kinds than one.— —

ever &c. very truly & affectly yrs.

B

[TO DOUGLAS KINNAIRD]   *Venice March 29th. 1817*

My dear Kinnaird/—I wrote to you the other day—you will think me a great bore to trouble you again.—Siri & Wilhalm have received the *order* of your house in my favour—but they say that *I* should also have a letter of *credit* for the sum specified as more regular—and the same for the sum lodged at Rome (with Tortolia [Torlonia]) which your letter announced to me.—As I think it better according to your advice to reserve the *circulars*—you will perhaps send me what they require—or tell me what to do;—they are very civil, & have honoured my draft the same.—Yours in haste

ever & very truly

BYRON

P.S.—I suppose you had not sent me *any letter* except *the usual one* with the *circulars*—because if so—it had *not arrived*.—The circulars &c. came very safely.

[TO DOUGLAS KINNAIRD]   *Venice. March 31st. 1817*

My dear Kinnaird/—I wrote to you a day or two ago to mention that Siri & Wilhalm had demurred a little because *I* should have had

---

[1] Maturin's second tragedy, *Manuel*, was produced at Drury Lane on March 8, 1817, with Kean in the title role, but it failed and was withdrawn after five nights.

a letter of credit as well as the order of Messrs. M[orland] & R[ansom] on them the last of which they had received.—Perhaps you had better send me one for the £500—as well as the like for Torlonia at Rome—where you have sent the same order.—I will have marked down upon Siri's letter whatever sums may have been drawn for before I leave Venice.—I shall follow your advice & retain the circulars till the orders are drawn upon.———Your letter of ye 14th. is before me.—I have no poem nor thought of a poem called the *Gondola*—nor any similar subject.—I have written nothing but a sort of metaphysical poem which was sent to M[urray] the other day—not for publication—but to show to Mr. Gifford.—Tell him to show it to you,—I would not have it published unless G[iffor]d thought it good for anything—for myself I have really & truly no notion what it is good for. I have nothing else—except a translation from a Spanish & Moorish ballad[1] & an Italian translation or two—As to tragedy, I may try one day—but *never* for the *stage*—don't you see I have no luck there?—my two addresses were not liked—& my Committee-ship did but get me into scrapes—no—no—I shall not tempt the Fates that way—besides I should risk more than I could gain—I have no right to encroach on other men's ground—even if I could maintain my own.—You tell me that Maturin's second tragedy has failed—is not this an additional warning to everybody as well as to me—however if the whim seized me I should not consider that nor anything else—but the fact is that success on the stage is not to me an object of ambition—& I am not sure that it would please me to triumph—although it would doubtless vex me to fail.—For these reasons I never will put it to the test.—Unless I could beat them all—it would be nothing—& who could do that? nor I nor any man—the Drama is complete already—there can be nothing like what has been.—You will say this applies to other poetry also—true—but the range is wider—& I look upon the path I struck out in C[hilde] Harold as a new one—& therefore there can be no comparisons as yet good or bad—I have done—not much—but enough for me—& having just turned nine & twenty I seriously think of giving up altogether—unless Rome should madden me into a fourth Canto—which it may or may not.—I am sorry for Maturin—but as he had made himself considerable enough to have enemies—this was to be expected—he must not however be discouraged.—Make my remembrances acceptable to L[eigh] Hunt—& tell him I shall be very glad to hear from him.—I have had a fever.—Remember me to Scrope to

[1] See [Feb. 25?] 1817, to Murray.

Moore & everybody—your account of Mrs. K's success is very agreeable

ever & truly yrs. most affect.

B

P.S.—The *Morning Chronicle* has been taken out of your letter I
suppose in France—it is useless to send newspapers—they hardly ever
arrive—at least the opposition ones.

[TO JOHN CAM HOBHOUSE]   *Venice, March 31st. 1817*

My Dear Hobhouse—In verity the *Malaria* was a pretext as I
knew it was a Summer and not a Spring production—but the English
crowd of the Holy week was as sincere an excuse as need to be.—
Since I wrote to you I have had a fever—like one I had from the
Marshes of Elis—which nearly finished me at Patras—but this was
milder, and of shorter duration—it however left me weakly.—It had
been approaching by slow degrees ever since the Carnival & at last
came on rather sharply—it was not however the low vulgar Typhus
which is at present decimating Venice—& has half unpeopled Milan—
but a sharp gentlemanly fever that went away in a few days. —I saw no
Physician—they sent for one without telling me—& when I heard he
was below—I had him sent out of the house.—And so I recovered.—It
was not Aglietti I believe—but you may be sure if it had—that prig
should never have had a fee of mine.—At present I am very well with
a monstrous appetite.—I think of coming on to Rome this ensuing
month—in case you should be gone—will you delegate some friend to
get me in without custom-house research—& will you tell me what
hostel or inn I am to lay down my wallet in & how about lodgement?
truly wroth am I to hear the rumours you wot of—particularly the
first—but one is as false as the other.—The origin of the latter I take
to be a lie which was rife here about the *Fabre* or *Fabri* (which is it?),
the singer from Milan—the girl we saw there—she sang here at the
Fenice—during the Carnival—& was in high & magnificent mainten-
ance by a Sigr. Papadopoli a Venetian of great wealth & concupiscence.
—But a man in a Cloak was seen coming out of her abode one very
early morning—& this man they would have to be me (I never saw
her in my life but on the stage), & not content with this—it was added
that I had decamped with her for Naples—& I had as much difficulty in
proving my presence here—as Partridge in re-establishing his

197

existence.—The origin of these unseemly reports I take to be a translation in some Venetian Gazette of the Jena review of C. L.'s
Glenarvon[1]—& another of the last canto of C[hilde] H[arol]d the one
stating the scratching attempt at *can*icide of that "two-handed whore"
at Lady Heathcote's and the other representing me as the most decided
panegyrist of Buonaparte.—I have you may be sure noticed neither
one nor the other of these matters.—The Quarterly I have read (which
is written by Walter Scott—so M[urray] says) both it & the Edinburgh
are as favourable as the author could wish—& more so than could be
wished by anybody else—the Edinburgh by Jeffrey himself.—I am
very glad that anybody likes the Canto—but particularly glad that
Baillie does—because he is a very superior if not a *supreme* man;—as
for you & I we are such old friends—that "we have travelled over one
another's minds long ago" don't you remember what a pet that
sentence used to put you into? But never mind, it is not true [is it not
true?]—In case you should not have heard from England I will tell
you some news of Litera*toor*.—K[innair]d writes to me that Mrs. K.
under the colours of Keppel[2], has become "*a* PUBLIC *character*" at Drury
Lane as well as at Covent Garden with great success—I suppose he
means of course as a Singer—but it is as well to be distinct.—Maturin's
second tragedy (he says) has not succeeded—& he gives some very
good reasons why it should not—which sound remarkably well—
particularly as his very last letter save this anticipated its "complete
success." For my part I say nothing—but this I will say—*Did* I *ever*—
No, I *never*—&c. &c. &c. &c. &c. &c. Do you understand me? no one
else can.—I have heard of my daughter who is very fine—they say—
but there is a dispute about her suscitated between me & my moral
Clytemnestra—some day or other—Ada will become my Orestes &
Electra too, both in one.—This dispute will probably end in a lawsuit
—having heard that they thought of voyaging—I refused to allow the
child to leave the country—& demanded an explicit declaration that
on no account should the attempt be made—this was evaded—& at
last a sort of half reluctant kind of paper signed—which I have refused
to accept—& so we are all at or about law.—That old fool Noel last
year—I hear for the first time—had filed a bill in Chancery against me
—upon some remote question of property—purely to make my
daughter a ward of the court & circumscribe my right over her—or

[1] See [April?] 1817, to the editor of a Venice newspaper, and April 2, 1817, to
Murray.
[2] Kinnaird's wife was a singer, who went back on the stage under her maiden
name.

rather my authority;—I can tell you however that Hanson has behaved very well & briskly in this business—for I have copies of the correspondence.—*They* have begun—& by the Lord—I must go on—pretty separation!—we are as fast as ever only pulling the chain different ways—till one of us tumbles.—My Star is sure to win in the long run.—You do not say a word of your "paradoxes" or of the Pope—only think of Dr. Polidori coming too!—well, I'm sure! Is he any sager? I suppose you mean that despicable lisping old Ox & Charlatan Frederic North by the successor to Ld. Guilford.[3]—Of all the perambulating humbuggerers that aged nondescript is the principal. —I send you a catalogue of some books "of poeshie of the king my master" as Freytag said to Voltaire.—

> I read the "Christabel."
> > Very well.
> I read the "Missionary,"
> > Somewhat visionary.
> I tried at "Iderim,"
> > Ahem!
> I read a sheet of "Margaret of *Anjou*,"
> > Can *you*?
> I skimmed a page of Webster's Waterloo,
> > Pooh!—Pooh!—
> I looked at Wordsworth's milkwhite "Rylstone Doe,"
> > Hillo!!
> I read "Glenarvon," too, by Caro. Lamb,
> > God damn.

I have bought several books which must be left for my bankers to forward to England—amongst others a complete Voltaire in 92 volumes[4]—whom I have been reading—he is delightful but dreadfully inaccurate frequently.—One of his paragraphs (in a letter—) begins "*Jean Jacques* is a *Jean foutre*" which he seems to say with all his heart and soul.—This is one of the things which make me laugh—being a

---

[3] Frederick North (1766–1827) succeeded his brother as the 5th Earl of Guilford in 1817. Byron had taken a particular dislike to him, perhaps because of his pretensions as a Philhellene. He wore a Greek costume and entered the Greek church. He later promoted the Ionian University at Corfu and became its first chancellor.

[4] This was the 12mo edition published at Kehl, 1785–1789: *Oeuvres Complètes de Voltaire. De l'Imprimerie de la Société Littérarie Typographique.*

"clever Tom Clinch"[5] & perhaps will have the like effect on you.—

yrs ever & very truly & affectly

B

My best respects to your brother—I congratulate him.———

[TO THOMAS MOORE]   *Venice, March 31st, 1817*

You will begin to think my epistolary offerings (to whatever altar you please to devote them) rather prodigal. But until you answer, I shall not abate, because you deserve no better. I know you are well, because I hear of your voyaging to London and the environs, which I rejoice to learn, because your note alarmed me by the purgation and phlebotomy therein prognosticated. I also hear of your being in the press; all which, methinks, might have furnished you with subject-matter for a middle-sized letter, considering that I am in foreign parts, and that the last month's advertisements and obituary would be absolute news to me from your Tramontane country.

I told you, in my last, I have had a smart fever. There is an epidemic in the place; but I suspect, from the symptoms, that mine was a fever of my own, and had nothing in common with the low, vulgar typhus, which is at this moment decimating Venice, and which has half unpeopled Milan, if the accounts be true. This malady has sorely dis-comfited my serving men, who want sadly to be gone away, and get me to remove. But, besides my natural perversity, I was seasoned in Turkey, by the continual whispers of the plague, against apprehensions of contagion. Besides which, apprehension would not prevent it; and then I am still in love, and "forty thousand" fevers should not make me stir before my minute, while under the influence of that paramount delirium. Seriously speaking, there is a malady rife in the city—a dangerous one, they say. However, mine did not appear so, though it was not pleasant.

This is passion-week—and twilight—and all the world are at vespers. They have an eternal churching, as in all Catholic countries, but are not so bigoted as they seem to be in Spain.

I don't know whether to be glad or sorry that you are leaving Mayfield.[1] Had I ever been at Newstead during your stay there,

[5] "Clever Tom Clinch Going to Be Hanged" was the title of a poem by Swift (1726?).

[1] Moore gave up Mayfield Cottage in Derbyshire where he had lived since June, 1813, and settled in a cottage in Hornsey (March, 1817), six miles from London, where he remained until November when he moved again to Sloperton Cottage near Lord Lansdowne's estate of Bowood in Wiltshire.

(except during the winter of 1813-14, when the roads were impracticable,) we should have been within hail, and I should like to have made a giro of the Peak with you. I know that country well, having been all over it when a boy. Was you ever in Dovedale? I can assure you there are things in Derbyshire as noble as Greece or Switzerland. But you had always a lingering after London, and I don't wonder at it. I liked it as well as any body, myself, now and then.

Will you remember me to Rogers? whom I presume to be flourishing, and whom I regard as our poetical papa. You are his lawful son, and I the illegitimate. Has he begun yet upon Sheridan?[2] If you see our republican friend, Leigh Hunt, pray present my remembrances. I saw about nine months ago that he was in a row (like my friend Hobhouse) with the Quarterly Reviewers. For my part, I never could understand these quarrels of authors with critics and with one another. "For God's sake, gentlemen, what do they mean?"

What think you of your countryman, Maturin? I take some credit to myself for having done my best to bring out Bertram; but I must say my colleagues were quite as ready and willing. Walter Scott, however, was the *first* who mentioned him, which he did to me, with great commendation, in 1815; and it is to this casualty, and two or three other accidents, that this very clever fellow owed his first and well-merited public success. What a chance is fame!

Did I tell you that I have translated two Epistles?—a correspondence between St. Paul and the Corinthians, not to be found in our version, but the Armenian—but which seems to me very orthodox, and I have done it into scriptural prose English.[3]

Ever, &c.

[TO THE EDITOR OF A VENICE NEWSPAPER]   [*April* ? *1817*]

Sir,—In your Journal of 27th. March I perceive an article purporting to be translated from the literary Gazette of Jena, and referring to a recent publication of mine in England.—In this there are misstatements which I must be permitted to correct.——It is there asserted that Buonaparte is the protagonist of the poem under a fictitious name.——

---

[2] Moore finally wrote the *Life of Sheridan*, assisted by Rogers. It was published in 1825.

[3] Byron's translations (with the assistance of Pasquale Aucher, the Armenian Friar) are given in an Appendix by Prothero (*LJ*, IV, 429-436).

Buonaparte is not the protagonist of the poem under any name—& where he is mentioned it is openly, & by his own,—the canto is a continuation of a work begun several years ago, & on a very different subject.—It is true that he is treated of—in a part of the poem referring to the battle of Waterloo—as an historical personage;—& I have spoken of him in the language of my country—& with the freedom of my nation;—as a man of great qualities & considerable defects;—but with the respect due to misfortune—I have no hesitation in saying that I see neither crime nor merit in having alluded to an English prisoner without bitterness—had he been still Emperor of France & the enemy of my country—I should have either spoken of him differently or not at all.—I did not flatter him then—& that is probably a reason (if we may judge from example) why I do not abuse him now.——It is added that I show myself in this work extremely angry that peace order & repose are reestablished in Europe—this is another mistake—I trouble myself as little about Europe—as Europe can possibly trouble herself about me—but I can hardly be out of humour with a peace which has enabled [me] to see so beautiful a country as Italy.—It is asserted also that I do not love my country—excuse me—I love it well enough to smile at such an imputation—& to look back to my every vote which I have given in her Parliament as a refutation of the charge.——It is said in this article—that Buonaparte is my Idol—& that I have written nothing on Lord Wellington;—the first is false—and the latter true, & neither of these circumstances is of any consequence.——The conclusion that I "surpass all the *other admirers* of Buonaparte" appears to me to be a "non sequitur" of the literary Gazette of Jena—are there none surviving of all who once were so? what is become of France & Italy—to say nothing of other nations of Europe? to conclude I beg leave to assure you that I am neither admirer nor vituperator of Buonaparte—were I either one or the other I should not conceal it— the admiration of him has also ceased to be dangerous—but if it were so I should not conceal it the more on that account.—With regard to the observations in general which have drawn from me this reply—I must be permitted to add—that as a Stranger who is not conscious of having either obtruded his opinions political or otherwise upon your countrymen—and who has during the residence here lived as retired & without pretension of any kind as an Individual could well do—I should have looked for more courtesy than the insertion of such remarks upon an untranslated foreign work—which it would be as well to understand before it is criticised—or at any rate that the remarks should be more on the work & less on the author.—

202

Dear Sir,—I sent you the whole of the drama—at *three several* times —act by act, in separate covers—I hope that you have or will receive some—or the whole of it.——So Love has a conscience—by Diana! —I shall make him take back the box though it were Pandora's;—the discovery of its intrinsic silver occurred on sending it to have the lid adapted to admit Marianna's portrait[1]—of course I had the box remitted in Statu quo—& had the picture set in another—which suits it (the picture) very well.—The defaulting box is not touched hardly —it was not in the man's hands above an hour.—I am aware of what you say of Otway—and am a very great admirer of his—all except of that maudlin bitch of chaste lewdness & blubbering curiosity Belvidera[2] —whom I utterly despise, abhor, & detest—but the story of Marino Falieri—is different & I think so much finer—that I wish Otway had taken it instead;—the head conspiring against the body—for refusal of redress for a real injury;—jealousy, treason—with the more fixed and inveterate passions (mixed with policy) of an old or elderly man— the Devil himself could not have a finer subject—& he is your only tragic dramatist.———When Voltaire was asked why no woman has ever written even a tolerable tragedy? "Ah (said the Patriarch) the composition of a tragedy requires *testicles*".—If this be true Lord knows what Joanna Baillie does—I suppose she borrows them. There is still, in the Doge's palace the black veil painted over Falieri's picture & the staircase whereon he was first crowned Doge, & subsequently decapitated.—This was the thing that most struck my imagination in Venice—more than the Rialto, which I visited for the sake of Shylock—and more too than Schiller's *"Armenian"*[3]—a novel which took a great hold of me when a boy—it is also called the "Ghost Seer"—& I never walked down St. Mark's by moonlight without thinking of it &—"at nine o'clock he died!"—But I hate things *all fiction* & therefore the *Merchant* & *Othello*—have no great associations to me—but *Pierre* has—there should always be some foundation of fact for the most airy fabric—and pure invention is but the talent of a liar.——Maturin's tragedy.[4]—By your account of him last year to me he seemed a bit of a coxcomb personally;—poor fellow—to be sure he had a long seasoning of adversity—which is not so hard to bear as

---

[1] See Feb. 25, 1817, to Augusta, note 1, and Feb. 25, 1817, to Murray (*a*).
[2] Belvidera was a favourite part of Mrs. Siddons in Otway's *Venice Preserved*.
[3] Schiller's novel *Geisterseher* was translated as *The Armenian, or the Ghost-seer* by W. Bender (1800).
[4] *Manuel.*

t'other thing—I hope that this won't throw him back into the "Slough of Despond"—let him take heart—"whom the Lord loveth he chasteneth [;] blessed be the name of the Lord!" This sentence by the way is a contrast to the other one of "Quem Deus vult perdere prius dementat" which may be thus done into English—

> God maddens him whom 'tis his will to lose,
> And gives the choice of death or phrenzy—Choose!

You talk of "marriage"—ever since my own funeral—the word makes me giddy—& throws me into a cold sweat—pray don't repeat it.— Tell me that Walter Scott is better—I would not have him ill for the world—I suppose it was by sympathy that I had my fever at the same time.—I joy in the success of your Quarterly—but I must still stick by the *Edinburgh*—Jeffrey has done so by me I must say through everything—& this is more than I deserved from him.—I have more than once acknowledged to you by letter the "Article" (& Articles) say that you have received the said letters—as I do not otherwise know what letters arrive.—Both reviews came—but nothing more. M[aturin]'s play & the extract not yet come.——There have been two Articles in the Venice papers one a review of C. Lamb's "Glenarvon" (whom may it please the beneficent Giver of all Good to damn in the next world! as she has damned herself in this) with the account of her scratching attempt at *Canicide* (at Lady Heathcote's) —and the other a review of C[hilde] Har[ol]d in which it proclaims me the most rebellious & contumacious Admirer of Buonaparte—now surviving in Europe;—both these articles are translations from the literary Gazette of German Jena.—I forgot to mention them at the time—they are some weeks old.—They actually mentioned Caro Lamb—& her *mother's* name at full length—I have conserved these papers as curiosities.——Write to say whether or no my Magician has arrived with all his scenes spells &c.[5]

Yours ever
B

P.S.—Will you tell Mr. Kinnaird—that the two recent letters I wrote to him were owing to a mistake of a booby of a Partner of Siri and Wilhalm (the Bankers here) & that one of them called this morning to say all was right—& that there was no occasion for a further letter—however heaven knows whether they are right or not— I hope I shall not have the same bother at Rome.——You should

[5] *Manfred.*

close with Madame de Stael—this will be her best work[6]—& permanently historical—it is on her father—the revolution—& Buonaparte, &c. Bonstetten told me in Switzerland it was *very great*. I have not seen it myself—but the author often—she was very kind to me at Coppet.—I like your delicacy—*you* who print *Margaret*—& *Ilderim* and then Demur at Corinne.—The failure of poor M[aturin]'s play will be a cordial to the aged heart of *Saul*[7]—who has been "kicking against the pricks" of the managers so long and so vainly—they ought to act his "Ivan"—as for Kean he is an *"infidus Scurra"* and his conduct on this occasion is of a piece with all one ever heard of him.—Pray look after *Mr. St. Aubin*—He is an Oxonian—it is very odd & something more than negligent that he has not consigned the letters &c. it was his own offer.—It is useless to send to the *Foreign Office* nothing arrives to me by that conveyance—I suppose some zealous Clerk thinks it a Tory duty to prevent it.——

[TO SAMUEL ROGERS] *Venice. April 4th. 1817*

My dear Rogers—It is a considerable time since I wrote to you last —& I hardly know why I should trouble you now—except that I think you will not be sorry to hear from me now and then.—You and I were never correspondents—but always something better—which is —very good friends.—I saw your friend Sharpe[1] in Switzerland—or rather in Genevan territory—(which is & is not Switzerland) & he gave Hobhouse & me a very good route for the Bernese Alps—however we took another from a German—& went by Clarens over the Dent de Jamant to Montbovon & through the Simmenthal to Thoun— & so on to Lauterbrunen—except that from thence to the Grindelwald instead of round about we went right over the Wengen Alp's very summit, & being close under the Jungfrau saw it—it's Glaciers—& heard the avalanches in all their Glory—having famous weather there*for*.—We of course went from the Grindelwald over the Shadack [*sic*] to Brientz & it's lake—past the Reichenbach & all that mountain road—which reminded me of Albania & Ætolia—& Greece—except

---

[6] Madame de Staël's *Considérations sur la Révolution Française* was offered to Murray for £4000, but before an agreement was reached she died (July 14, 1817). The book was published by Baldwin and Cradock.

[7] William Sotheby's *Saul: a Poem in Two Parts* was published in 1807. In 1815 Byron recommended Sotheby's play *Ivan* for production at Drury Lane. It was accepted but because of objections by Kean it was not put on the stage.

[1] Richard ("Conversation") Sharp.

that the people here were more civilized & rascally.—I did not think
so very much of *Chamouni*—except the source of the Avveyron [sic] to
which we went up to the teeth of the ice so as to look into & touch the
cavity against the warning of the guides only one of whom would go
with us so close—as of the Jungfrau & the Pissevache & Simplon.—
which are quite out of all mortal computation.—I was at Milan about
a moon—& saw Monti—& some other living curiosities—& thence on
to Verona—where I did not forget your story of the assassination—
during your sojourn there—& brought away with me some fragments
of Juliet's tomb—& a lively recollection of the Amphitheatre. The
Countess Goetz (the Governor's wife here) told me that there is still
a ruined castle of the Montecchi between Verona and Vicenza—I have
been at Venice since November—but shall proceed to Rome shortly—
for my deeds here—are they not written in my letters to the unreplying
Thomas Moore? to him I refer you—he has received them all & not
answered me.——Will you remember me to Ld. & Lady Holland—I
have to thank the former for a book which I have not yet received—
but expect to reperuse with great pleasure on my return[2]—viz—the
2d. Edition of Lope de Vega.———I have heard of Moore's forthcoming poem—he cannot wish himself more success than I wish &
augur for him.———I have also heard great things of "Tales of my
Landlord" but I have not yet received them—by all accounts they
beat even Waverley &c.—& are by the same author.[3] Maturin's 2d.
tragedy has it seems failed—for which I should think every body will
be sorry—except perhaps Sotheby—who—I must say—was
capriciously & evilly entreated by the Sub-committee—about poor
dear "Ivan" whose lot can only be parallelled by that of his original—
I don't mean the *author*—who is anything but original—but the deposed
imperial infant who gave his name & some narrative to the drama
thereby entitled.—My health was very victorious—till within the last
month—when I had a fever.——There is a Typhus in these parts, but
I don't think it was that.—However I got well without a Physician or
drugs.——I forgot to tell you that last Autumn—I furnished Lewis
with "bread & salt" for some days at Diodati—in reward for which
(besides his conversation) he translated "Goethe's Faust" to me by
word of mouth;—& I set him by the ears with Madame de Stael about
the Slave trade.——I am indebted for many & kind courtesies to our

[2] Lord Holland's *Some Account of the Life and Writings of Lope Felix de Vega
Carpio* appeared anonymously in 1807, and was republished with the author's name
in 1817.

[3] Byron was apparently not aware that Scott was the author of *Waverley*.

Lady of Coppet—& I now love her—as much as I always did her
works—of which I was and am a great admirer.——When are you
to begin with Sheridan? what are you doing? & How do you do?

ever & very truly & affectionately yrs.

B

[TO PROFESSOR PICTET[1]]   *Venice. April 7, 1817*

Sir—When I arrived at Geneva last year I presented a letter of
recommendation to you—of which—if I did not avail myself sufficiently
—the loss was *mine*—and *not yours*.——That letter however is nearly
my sole pretension to trouble you with this—and to say the truth I
should hardly dare to write it—if I did not think that the Bearer would
sufficiently recommend herself without it.——The Countess Albrizzi
—a lady well known in Italian Literature—& more particularly
distinguished as the Illustrator of the works of Canova—hearing that
I had passed through Geneva—*requested* me to give her a letter to you
—will this be my Apology?—I do not know—but her acquaintance
(if it is made by you) will—for you will find her a well informed—and
very agreeable woman.——You will have the goodness not to
examine too narrowly into my *right* to address letters of recommendation to you—but be assured that I would not solicit your notice to any
one whom I did not believe to be worthy of it.—On this occasion I have
ventured—because I was asked to do so—and I will take care not to
trespass again in the same manner.———I have the honour to be with
great respect

yr. obliged & obedient very faithful Servt.

BYRON

[TO JOHN MURRAY]   *Venice—April—9th. 1817*

Dear Sir,—Your letters of the 18th. & 20th, are arrived—In my
own I have given you the rise, progress—decline—and fall—of my
recent malady—it is *gone* to the Devil—I won't pay him so bad a compliment as to say it *came* from him—*he* is too much of a Gentleman.—
It was nothing but a slow fever—which quickened it's pace towards

[1] Marc-Auguste Pictet was a prominent literary and political figure in Geneva.
Byron may have been apologetic in addressing him because when Pictet and
Bonstetten came to dinner at Diodati, he absented himself, according to his own
account, because Dr. Polidori had taken it upon himself to invite them without
consulting with him.

the end of it's journey—I had been bored with it some weeks—with nocturnal burnings—& morning perspirations—but I am quite well again—which I attribute to having had neither medicine nor Doctor thereof.— —In a few days I set off for Rome—such is my purpose—I shall change it very often before Monday next—but do you continue to direct & address to *Venice* as heretofore;—If I go—letters will be forwarded—I say *"if,"* because I never know what I shall do—till it is done—and as I mean most firmly to set out for Rome—it is not unlikely I may find myself at St. Petersburg.— —You tell me to "take care of myself—" faith and I will—I won't be posthumous yet if I can help it—notwithstanding—only think—what a "Life & adventures"— while I am in full scandal—would be worth—together with the "membra" of my writing-desk—the *sixteen* beginnings of poems never to be finished—Do you think I would not have shot myself last year —had I not luckily recollected that Mrs. Clermont & Lady Noel & all the old women in England would have been delighted—besides the agreeable "Lunacy" of the "Crowner's Quest"—and the regrets of two or three or half a dozen? Be assured—that I *would live* for two reasons—or more—there are one or two people whom I have to put out of the world—& as many into it—before I can "depart in peace" if I do so before—I have not fulfilled my mission—Besides, when I turn thirty—I will turn devout—I feel a great vocation that way in Catholic churches—& when I hear the Organ.—So—Webster is writing again—is there no Bedlam in Scotland?—nor thumb-screw?— nor Gag?—nor handcuff?—I went upon my knees to him almost some years ago to prevent him from publishing a political pamphlet which would have given him a livelier idea of "Habeas Corpus" than the world will derive from his present production upon that suspended subject—which will doubtless be followed by the suspension of other (his Majesty's) subjects.—I condole with Drury Lane—and rejoice with Sotheby—that is in a modest way,—on the tragical end of the new tragedy.— —You & L[eig]h Hunt have quarrelled then it seems;[1] I introduce him & his poem to you—in the hope that (malgré politics) the union would be beneficial to both—and the end is eternal enmity— & yet I did this with the best intentions—I introduce Coleridge & Christabel & Coleridge runs away with your money.—My friend Hobhouse quarrels too with the Quarterly: and (except the last) I am the innocent Istmhus (damn the word I can't spell it—though I have crossed that of Corinth a dozen times) of these enmities.— —I will

---

[1] Murray had published Hunt's *The Story of Rimini* in 1816, but Hunt complained of the sum Murray offered for it. See *LJ*, IV, 99.

tell you something about Chillon.—A Mr. *De Luc* ninety years old—a Swiss—had *it* read to him & is pleased with it—so my Sister writes.[2]— He said that he was *with Rousseau* at *Chillon*—& that the description is perfectly correct—but this is not all—I recollected something of the name & find the following passage in "The Confessions"—vol. 3. page 247. Liv. 8th—

"De tous ces amusemens celui qui me plut davantage—fut une promenade autour du Lac—que je fis en bateau avec *De Luc* pere—sa bru—ses *deux fils*—et ma Thérèse.—Nous mimes sept jours a cette tournée par le plus beau temps du monde. J'en gardai le vif souvenir des sites qui m'avoient frappé a l'autre extremité du lac, et dont je fis la description quelques années apres, dans la Nouvelle Heloise."

This nonagenarian De Luc must be one of the "deux fils". He is in England—infirm but still in faculty.———It is odd that he should have lived so long—& not wanting in oddness that he should have made this voyage with Jean Jacques—& afterwards at such an interval read a poem by an Englishman (who had made precisely the same circumnavigation) upon the same scenery.—As for "Manfred"—it is of no use sending *"proofs"* nothing of that kind comes.—I sent the whole at different times—The 2 first acts are the best—the third so so—but I was blown with the first and second heats.—You must call it "a poem," for it is *no drama* (& I do not choose it to be called by so Sothebyish a name)—a "poem in dialogue" or—pantomine if you will —anything—but a Green room Synonime.—And this is your Motto

"There are more things in heaven & earth, Horatio,
Than are dreamt of in your philosophy."—

Yours ever,
B

My love and thanks to Mr. G[iffor]d.—

Don't forget my *tooth powder*—it's of no use to send it by the damned and double-damned conveyances—but by some private hand— by Mr. Kinnaird,—or Mr. Davies if they come out—or any body— let it be left at my bankers here "Siri & Wilhalm."—I mean to be in Venice again in July.——*Nothing yet* whatever from the foreign office—why do you send anything to such a "den of thieves" as that?

[2] John André de Luc (1727–1817) had been a reader to Queen Charlotte, wife of George III. He was born in Geneva but spent most of his life in England.

I shall continue to write to you while the fit is on me, by way of penance upon you for your former complaints of long silence. I dare say you would blush, if you could, for not answering. Next week I set out for Rome. Having seen Constantinople, I should like to look at t'other fellow. Besides, I want to see the Pope, and shall take care to tell him that I vote for the Catholics and no Veto.

I sha'n't go to Naples. It is but the second best sea-view, and I have seen the first and third, viz. Constantinople and Lisbon (by the way, the last is but a river-view; however, they reckon it after Stamboul and Naples, and before Genoa), and Vesuvius is silent, and I have passed by Ætna. So I shall e'en return to Venice in July; and if you write, I pray you to address to Venice, which is my head, or rather my *heart-*quarters.

My late physician, Dr. Polidori, is here on his way to England, with the present Lord G[uilford] and the widow of the late earl.[1] Dr. Polidori has, just now, no more patients, because his patients are no more. He had lately three, who are now all dead—one embalmed. Horner and a child of Thomas Hope's are interred at Pisa and Rome. Lord G[uilford] died of an inflammation of the bowels: so they took them out, and sent them (on account of their discrepancies), separately from the carcass, to England. Conceive a man going one way, and his intestines another, and his immortal soul a third!—was there ever such a distribution? One certainly has a soul; but how it came to allow itself to be enclosed in a body is more than I can imagine. I only know if once mine gets out, I'll have a bit of a tussle before I let it get in again to that or any other.

And so poor dear Mr. Maturin's second tragedy has been neglected by the discerning public! [Sotheby] will be d—d glad of this, and d—d without being glad, if ever his own plays come upon "any stage."

I wrote to Rogers the other day, with a message for you. I hope that he flourishes. He is the Tithonus of poetry—immortal already.—You and I must wait for it.

I hear nothing—know nothing. You may easily suppose that the English don't seek me, and I avoid them. To be sure, there are but few or none here, save passengers. Florence and Naples are their Margate and Ramsgate, and much the same sort of company too, by all accounts,—which hurts us among the Italians.

[1] Francis North, second son of Lord North, George III's Prime Minister succeeded his elder brother as the 4th Earl of Guilford in 1802. He died in Pisa in 1817, and was succeeded by his younger brother Frederick.

I want to hear of Lalla Rookh—are you out? Death and fiends! why don't you tell me where you are, what you are, and how you are? I shall go to Bologna by Ferrara, instead of Mantua: because I would rather see the cell where they caged Tasso, and where he became mad and * *, than his own MSS. at Modena, or the Mantuan birthplace of that harmonious plagiary and miserable flatterer,[2] whose cursed hexameters were drilled into me at Harrow. I saw Verona and Vicenza on my way here—Padua too.

I go *alone*,—but *alone*, because I mean to return here. I only want to see Rome. I have not the least curiosity about Florence, though I must see it for the sake of the Venus, &c., &c.; and I wish also to see the Fall of Terni, I think to return to Venice by Ravenna and Rimini, of both of which I mean to take notes for Leigh Hunt, who will be glad to hear of the scenery of his Poem. There was a devil of a review of him in the Quarterly, a year ago[3], which he answered. All answers are imprudent: but to be sure, poetical flesh and blood must have the last word—that's certain. I thought, and think, very highly of his Poem; but I warned him of the row his favourite antique phraseology would bring him into.

You have taken a house at Hornsey[4]: I had much rather you had taken one in the Apennines. If you think of coming out for a summer, or so, tell me, that I may be upon the hover for you.

Ever, &c.

[TO JOHN MURRAY (*a*)]   *Venice, April 14th. 1817*

Dear Sir,—The present proofs (of the whole) begin only at the *17th* page—but as I had corrected—& sent back the 1st act, it does not signify.——The third act is certainly d—d bad[1]—& like the Archbishop of Grenada's homily (which savoured of the palsy) has the dregs of my fever—during which it was written.—It must on *no account* be published in its present state;—I will try & reform it—or re-write it altogether—but the impulse is gone—& I have no chance of making anything out of it. I would not have it published as it is on any account.—The speech of Manfred to the Sun is the only part of

---

[2] Virgil was born near Mantua.
[3] See *Quarterly Review*, Vol. XIV, p. 473.
[4] Moore had moved from Derbyshire to what was later known as Lalla Rookh Cottage, Muswell Hill, Hornsey, to be nearer London.
[1] Byron rewrote the third act of *Manfred* during his trip to Rome and sent it to Murray on May 5, 1817.

this act I thought good myself—the rest is certainly as bad as bad can be—& I wonder what the devil possessed me—I am very glad indeed that you sent me Mr. Gifford's opinion without *deduction*—do you suppose me such a Sotheby as not to be very much obliged to him?— or that in fact I was not, & am not, convinced & convicted in my conscience of the absurdity of this same overt act of nonsense?—I shall try at it again—in the mean time lay it upon the Shelf (the whole drama, I mean) but pray correct your copies of the 1st. & 2d. acts by the original MS.——I am not coming to England—but going to Rome in a few days—I return to Venice in *June*—so—pray—address all letters &c. to me *here* as usual—that is to—*Venice*.—Dr. Polidori this day left this city with Ld. Guilford for England—he is charged with some books—to your care (from me), and two miniatures also to the same address—*both*—for my sister.—Recollect—*not* to publish upon pain of I know not what—until I have tried again at the third act. —I am not sure that I *shall* try—and still less that I shall succeed if I do —but I am very sure—that (as it is) it is unfit for publication or perusal—& unless I can make it out to my own satisfaction—I won't have any part published.——I write in haste—& having lately written very often.

Yours ever truly,
Bn

P.S.—Enclosed are the 2 letters.——

[TO JOHN MURRAY (*b*)]   *Venice—April 14th. 1817*

Dear Sir,—By the favour of Dr. Polidori—who is here on his way to England with the present Lord Guilford—(the late Earl having gone to England by another road—accompanied by his bowels in a separate coffer) I remit to you to deliver to Mrs. Leigh *two Miniatures*—but previously you will have the goodness to desire Mr. Love (as a peace offering between him & me) to set them in plain gold—with my arms complete—and "Painted by Prepiani—Venice—1817"—on the back. —I wish also that you would desire Holmes to make a copy of *each* that is both for myself—and that you will retain the said copies till my return. One was done while I was very unwell—the other in my health —which may account for their dissimilitude.—I trust that they will reach their destination in safety.—I recommend the Doctor to your good offices with your Government friends—& if you can be of any use to him in a literary point of view—pray—be so.——To-day or rather yesterday—for it is past midnight—I have been up to the battlements of the highest tower in Venice, & seen it & it's view in all the glory of a clear Italian sky.—I also went over the Manfrini palace —famous for it's pictures—amongst them there is a Portrait of *Ariosto* by *Titian* surpassing all my anticipation of the power of painting —or human expression—it is the poetry of portrait—& the portrait of poetry.—There was also one of some learned lady—centuries old whose name I forget—& it is forgotten—but whose features must always be remembered—I never saw greater beauty—or sweetness or wisdom—it is the kind of face to go mad for—because it cannot walk out of its frame.—There is also a famous dead Christ & live apostles— for which Buonaparte offered in vain five thousand Louis—& of which though it is a capo d'opera of Titian—as I am no connoisseur I say little—& thought less except of one figure in it.—There are ten thousand others—& some very fine Giorgiones amongst them, &c. &c. —There is an Original Laura & Petrarch—very hideous both— Petrarch has not only the dress—but the features & air of an old woman —& Laura looks by no means like a young one,—or a pretty one.— What struck me most in the general collection was the extreme resemblance of the style of the female faces in the mass of pictures—so many centuries or generations old—to those you see & meet every day amongst the existing Italians.—The queen of Cyprus & Giorgione's wife[1]—particularly the latter—are Venetians as it were of yesterday— the same eyes and expression—& to my mind there is none finer.— You must recollect however—that I know nothing of painting—& that I detest it—unless it reminds me of something I have seen or think it possible to see—for which [reason] I spit upon & abhor all the saints & subjects of one half the impostures I see in the churches & palaces—& when in Flanders, I never was so disgusted in my life as with Rubens & his eternal wives & infernal glare of colours[2]—as they appeared to me,—& in Spain I did not think much of Murillo & Velasquez.—Depend upon it of all the arts it is the most artificial & unnatural—& that by which the nonsense of mankind is the most imposed upon.—I never yet saw the picture—or the statue—which came within a league of my conception or expectation—but I have seen

---

[1] Byron most admired in the Manfrini palace the portrait by Giorgione which he supposed to be that of the artist's wife. But, according to Vasari, Giorgione was never married. The picture was in a group known as the *Famiglia di Giorgione* representing "an almost nude woman, probably a gipsy, seated with a child in her lap, and a standing warrior gazing upon her, a storm breaking over the landscape". (*Poetry*, IV, 163) See *Beppo*, stanzas 11–13.

[2] See May 1, 1816, to Hobhouse, and May 1, 1816, to Augusta.

many mountains & Seas—& Rivers and views—& two or three women —who went as far beyond it—besides some horses; and a Lion (at Veli Pasha's) in the Morea & a tiger at supper in Exeter 'change.—— When you write continue to address to me at *Venice*—where do you suppose—the books you sent to me are?—At *Turin*—this comes of *"the foreign office"*—which is foreign enough God knows for any good it can be of to me, or any one else—& be damned to it—to it's last Clerk—& first Charlatan Castlereagh.——This makes my hundredth letter at least.

Yours ever and truly,

B

[TO JOHN MURRAY (*c*)]   *April 14th. 1817*

[written on last page of proof of Act II of *Manfred*]
Recollect to correct this by the original M. S.—There are many errors—& I have not had time to look over it carefully

B~N~

I do not return the third act for reasons mentioned in my letter under another cover.—

[TO JOHN CAM HOBHOUSE]   *Venice April 14th. 1817*

My Dear Hobhouse—On next Thursday (the 17th, I guess) it is my indelible purpose to be upon my way to Rome—*by Ferrara*—& it is not less my intention to lose as little time as the expenditure of it upon sights will admit of.—I "prendo la posta"—& think of taking your hint of Rimini instead of Florence—first for brevity & next that I may give Leigh Hunt some Nimini pimini for his "Rimini" in the way of information about the Malatestas & Francesca—such as can be picked up from story or tradition on the spot.—Of course I can hardly name my precise day of arrival—but I shall delay as little as need be— and go by post—according to your advice.——I wish you would lay hands on the letters for me—& secure them against my arrival—I have no notion from whom such can be—as all my correspondents know that I am at Venice—as I know too by the postage they make me pay for their damned nonsense.——How could you suppose that I should bring any (carnal) baggage with me? do you suppose me quite out of my senses?—I had enough of that in Switzerland—though G—d knows I was innocent of "the water going to the man—& not the man going to the water—Argal &"—I assure you I have no such intention—but the contrary. So be *aisy.*——I shall write to you more than once on the road—to report progress—it would delight me to make our Consular entry together—as we did into the city of the Archons.—— There is a long manifesto in the papers of Napoleon against that b[ugge]r Hudson Lowe[1]—who treats him more like an officer (Sheriff's) than a Gentleman—in which I am pretty sure there is a direct complaint (amongst fifty others) of your book not being delivered to the Emperor[2]—I shall save the paper for you to see if you do not agree with me that it is to you he alludes.—Dr. Polidori has this day departed with all the Guilfords he has left alive, for England— a successful young person that in the drug line—he has attended Lord Guilford whom he succeeds in embalming—he attends Mr. Horner, who is dead—& Mr. Hope's Son who is buried—in short, he seems to have had no luck unless he has had any with Lady W[estmorland]'s Clitoris—which is supposed to be of the longest.—I have advised him to marry if only to fill up the gap which he has already made in the population.—He called on me every day—& I think he is improved in manner, but he is a little too full of "high lived company"— Shakespeare & the ["]musical glasses."[3] He travelled to Florence with the Sapphic Westmoreland—and that black sheep—Mrs. George Lamb—& thence with the as yet unembowelled Lord G., Lady G., & a Miss Somebody;—Frederic North called yesterday but I missed him by seeing sights—the Manfrini palace of pictures—which is stupendous—it is impossible not to be struck with it.—Scrope has won back £3,000—which is something & augurs well for the rest. Maturin's tragedy has failed—but I believe I told you that,—The Coterie Nolbachique[4] I have heard no more of since I wrote to you— but I shall give the "lengthening chain" a tug or two that will make it snap before I have done—however—that is all their own fault—& that of their "complot." I wish with all my heart they were in the hands of Jean Jacques—what work he would have made of them.—I have read a good deal of Voltaire lately—I wish you were with me— for every now and then there is something to kill me with laughing— what I dislike is his extreme inaccuracy—if his citations were correct

[1] Sir Hudson Lowe (1769–1844), Lieutenant-General and Governor of St. Helena, where he had custody of Napoleon.
[2] Hobhouse's *Letters written by an Englishman resident at Paris during the last reign of Napoleon* was perhaps too favourable to the Emperor to be welcomed by the Tory English governor.
[3] *The Vicar af Wakefield*, Chap. 9.
[4] Unidentified.

he might have upset a hundred ——s—upon that point I do not know
what to believe—or what to disbelieve—which is the devil—to have
no religion at all—all sense & senses are against it—but all belief &
much evidence is for it—it is walking in the dark over a rabbit warren
—or a garden with steel traps and spring guns.—for my part I have
such a detestation of *some* of the articles of faith—that I would not
subscribe to them—if I were as sure as St. Peter *after* the Cock crew.
——The most consistent infidel was the Prussian Frederic—because
during all the disasters of the 7 years' war—he was as full of his
materialism as when in quiet at Potsdam—& like his friend La Metrie
who died "denying G—d & the physicians."[5]——Let me find you at
Rome & there we will project.——Murray begs to have the refusal of
your next quarto—& presents his compliments—though he is very
much displeased with your preface.——I commend you to the Gods
of Rome ancient and modern—

yrs. ever & truly and affectly.

B

[TO JOHN CAM HOBHOUSE]   *Firenze—April 22d. 1817*

My Dear Hobhouse—I am arrived thus far on my way to you &
Rome.—The "man of learning"[1] forgot some chattels which detained
me a day at Bologna—which I employed in seeing bottled children &
"parts of shame" in waxwork at the institute—where I must needs
say that there is as pretty a system of Materialism as could well be
desired.—What a superb face there is in Guido's innocents in the
Gallery! not the *shrieking* mother—but the *kneeling* one—it is the
image of Lady Ponsonby—who is as beautiful as Thought.——I
proceed by way of Perugia—as being the longest, and most
picturesque-e-e-e-e.——My efforts have been prodigious—up at 4—
"but *thauts* impossible"[2]—however it is as true as the Miracles—and
off at 5, six, & so forth—I hope (barring accidents) to be with you at
the usual average of time—(allowing a day for *Terni*—and one—
to-morrow for the Venus of Canova & de Medicis—and the tombs of
Machiavel—Michael Angelo—& Alfieri—which is & are all I care

[5] Julien Offray de la Mettrie, French physician and philosopher (1709–1751)
had a penchant for revolting against accepted opinions. His studies led him to
materialist conclusions, and he was rejected by both Catholics and Jansenists.
Frederick the Great called him to his court at Berlin. He corresponded with
Voltaire.
[1] Fletcher.
[2] See March 7, 1817, to Hobhouse, note 4.

to see here—were I to stay seasons[)].—I can't say that I am very much struck with much since a piece of bread (literally *grass bread*) which I brought from the Appennines as a curiosity (pray have Appennines one *p* or two?) this morning—I took it out of the mouth of a crying child to whom I gave a Paulo in exchange—you never saw anything like the distress of these poor creatures.——I came by Ferrara—& have crossed the "winding Po," as well as the "lazy Scheldt" (by Anvers) Tasso's cell—& Ariosto's tomb—as well as the old Castle are I think—very well worth your seeing—& I advise you whether you return with me or no to take them—all the Gerusalemme—all Guarini's original Pastor Fido—&c. &c.—letters of Titian to Ariosto—& Tasso's correspondence about his dirty shirts —are all duly displayed.—From Padova I diverged to Arqua to Petrarch's present & former habitation—the present is in the best repair—but both are rather ragged & somewhat poetical.———The old Castle of Ferrara has the actual court as heretofore where Parisina and Hugo lost their heads—according to Gibbon—I wonder where he got his authority?—Mutz is here—he was promoted into a *Bear* in the natural History of the Bolognese (who might have learned better at the Institute) a character which he has by no means sustained in point of valour—he having been defeated with loss of honour—hair—& almost the small remains of tail which the Docker had left him—by a moderate-sized Pig on the top of the Pennine Alps—the Pig was first thrown into confusion & compelled to retire with great disorder over a steep stone wall but somehow he faced about in a damned hollow way or defile & drove Mutz from all his positions—with such slaughter that nothing but night prevented a total defeat.—— Recollect—I shall do my best to be up with you soon—I am called to a *warm bath*—& to bed—having been up since 4—I set off Thursday— in great haste—

ever yrs. very truly

B

[TO JOHN MURRAY]   *Foligno—April 26th. 1817*

Dear Sir—I wrote to you the other day from Florence—inclosing an M.S.S. entitled the "Lament of Tasso"—it was written in consequence of my having been lately at Ferrara.—In the last section of this M.S. *but one* (that is the penultimate)—I think that I have omitted a line in the copy sent to you from Florence—viz—after the line

> "And woo compassion to a blighted name ["]
> Insert
> "Sealing the sentence which my foes proclaim."

The *context* will show you *the sense*—which is not clear in this quotation —*remember*—*I write this in the supposition that you have received my Florentine packet.*—At Florence I remained but a day—having a hurry for Rome to which I am thus far advanced.—However—I went to the two galleries—from which one returns drunk with beauty—the Venus is more for admiration than love—but there are sculpture and painting—which for the first time at all gave me an idea of what people mean by their *cant* & (what Mr. Braham[1] calls) "entusimusy" (i.e. enthusiasm) about those two most artificial of the arts.—What struck me most were the Mistress of Raphael a portrait—the mistress of Titian a portrait—a Venus of Titian in the Medici gallery—*the* Venus—Canova's Venus also in the other gallery—Titian's mistress is also in the other gallery (that is, in the Pitti Palace gallery—) the Parcae of Michel Angelo, a picture—and the Antinous—the Alexander —& one or two not very decent groupes in marble—the Genius of Death—a sleeping figure &c. &c.———I also went to the Medici Chapel—fine frippery in great slabs of various expensive stones—to commemorate fifty rotten & forgotten carcases—it is unfinished & will remain so. The church of "Santa Croce" contains much illustrious nothing—the tombs of Machiavelli—Michel Angelo—Galileo Galilei and Alfieri—make it the Westminster abbey of Italy.—I did not admire *any* of these tombs—beyond their contents.—That of Alfieri is heavy —and all of them seem to me overloaded—what is necessary but a bust & a name?—and perhaps a date?—the last for the unchronological —of whom I am one.—But all your Allegory & eulogy is infernal— & worse than the long wigs of English numskulls upon Roman bodies in the statuary of [the] reign[s] of Charles—William—and Anne.— When you write—write to *Venice* as usual—I mean to return there in a fortnight.—I shall not be in England for a long time.—This after-noon I met Lord and Lady Jersey—& saw them for some time—all well—children grown & healthy—she very pretty but sunburnt—he very sick of travelling—bound for Paris.—There are not many English on the move—& those who are are mostly homewards—I shall not return till business makes me—being much better where I am

[1] See Vol. 3, p. 209, note 5.

in health &c. &c.———For the sake of my personal comfort—I pray send me immediately *to Venice—mind—Venice*—viz—*Waite's tooth powder—red* a quantity—*Calcined Magnesia* of the best quality—a quantity—and all this by safe sure & speedy means—& by the Lord! do it.—I have done nothing at *Manfred's* third act—you must wait—I'll have at it—in a week or two—or so.—

Yours ever,
B

[TO JOHN MURRAY]   *Rome, May 5th. 1817*

Dear Sir,—By this post (or next at farthest) I send you in two *other* covers—the new third act of 'Manfred."—I have rewritten the greater part—& returned what is not altered in the *proof* you sent me.—The Abbot is become a good man—& the Spirits are brought in at the death—you will find I think some good poetry in this new act here & there—& if so print it—without sending me further proofs—*under Mr. G[iffor]d's correction*—if he will have the goodness to overlook it.—Address all answers to *Venice* as usual—I mean to return there in ten days.—*"The Lament of Tasso"* which I sent from Florence has I trust arrived—I look upon it as a "these be good rhymes"—as Pope's papa said to him—when he was a boy—For the *two—it* & the drama—you will disburse to me (via Kinnaird) *Six* hundred guineas—you will perhaps be surprized that I set the same price upon this—as upon the drama—but, besides that I look upon it as *good*—I won't take less than three hundred g[uinea]s for anything.—The two together will make *you* a larger publication than the "Siege & Parisina"—so you may think yourself let off very easy—that is to say—if these poems are good for anything, which I hope and believe.—I have been some days in Rome—the wonderful—I am seeing sights—& have done nothing else—except the new third act for you—I have this morning seen a live Pope & a dead Cardinal—Pius 7th has been burying Cardinal Bracchi—whose body I saw in State at the Chiesa nuova——Rome has delighted me beyond everything since Athens—& Constantinople—but I shall not remain long this visit—Address to Venice.

Ever yours,
Bn

P.S.—I have got my saddle-horses here & have ridden & am riding all about the country.——

219

My Dear Sir/—Address all answers to Venice for there I shall return in fifteen days—God willing.——I sent you from Florence the "Lament of Tasso"—& from Rome the reformed third act of Manfred —both of which I trust will duly arrive.—The terms of these two—I mentioned in my last—& will repeat in this—it is three hundred for each—or six hundred guineas for the two—that is—if you like—& they are good for any thing.——At last one of the parcels is arrived— in the notes to C[hilde] H[arol]d there is a blunder of yours or mine— you talk of arrival at *St. Gingo* and immediately after add—"on the height is the Chateau of Clarens"—This is sad work—Clarens is on the *other* side of the lake—& it is quite impossible that I should have so bungled—look at the MS., and at any rate rectify this.—The "Tales of my Landlord" I have read with great pleasure—& perfectly under- stand now why my Sister & aunt are so very positive in the very erroneous persuasion that they must have been written by me[1]—if you knew me as well as they do—you would have fallen perhaps into the same mistake;—some day or other I will explain to you *why* when I have time—at present it does not matter—but you must have thought this blunder of theirs very odd—& so did I—till I had read the book.—Croker's letter to you is a very great compliment—I shall return it to you in my next.——Southey's Wat Tyler is rather awkward[2]—but the Goddess Nemesis has done well—he is—I will not say what—but I wish he was something else—I hate all intolerance— but most the intolerance of Apostacy—& the wretched vehemence with which a miserable creature who has contradicted himself—lies to his own heart—& endeavours to establish his sincerity by proving him- self a rascal—*not* for changing his opinions—but for persecuting those who are of less malleable matter—it is no disgrace to Mr. Southey to have written Wat Tyler—& afterwards to have written his birthday or Victory Odes (I speak only of their *politics*) but it is something for which I have no words for this man to have endeavoured to bring to the stake (for such would he do) men who think as he thought—& for no reason but because they think so still, when he has found it con-

---

[1] See Feb [19?]. 1817, to Augusta, note 2.

[2] Southey's *Wat Tyler* was a poetic drama written in 1794, when the author was enthusiastic about the French Revolution. It was surreptitiously printed by a pirating bookseller in 1817, to the embarrassment of Southey, who had become Poet Laureate in 1813, and who advocated strong Tory measures against those who published similar revolutionary works. The Lord Chancellor refused to stop the piracy on the ground that the poem was seditious and could not have the protection of copyright.

venient to think otherwise.—Opinions are made to be changed—or how is truth to be got at? we don't arrive at it by standing on one leg? or on the first day of our setting out—but though we may jostle one another on the way that is no reason why we should strike or trample —*elbowing's* enough.—I am all for moderation which profession of faith I beg leave to conclude by wishing Mr. Southey damned—not as a poet—but as a politician. There is a place in Michael Angelo's last judgment in the Sistine Chapel which would just suit him—and may the like await him in that of our Lord and (*not his*) Saviour Jesus Christ—Amen! I perceive you are publishing a *Life* of Raffael d'Urbino[3]—it may perhaps interest you to hear that a set of German artists here allow their *hair* to grow & trim it into *his fashion*—thereby drinking the cummin of the disciples of the old philosopher[4],—if they would cut their hair & convert it into brushes & paint like him it would be more "German to the matter."———I'll tell you a story.— The other day a man here—an English—mistaking the statues of Charlemagne and Constantine—which are *Equestrian* for those of Peter and Paul—asked another—*which* was Paul of these same horse-men?—to which the reply was, "I thought Sir that St. Paul had never got on horseback since his *accident?*"—I'll tell you another. Henry Fox[5] writing to some one from Naples the other day after an illness— adds "and I am so changed that my *oldest creditors* would hardly know me."———I am delighted with Rome—as I would be with a bandbox— that is it is a fine thing to see—finer than Greece—but I have not been here long enough to affect it as a residence—& I must go back to Lom-bardy—because I am wretched at being away from M[ariann]a.—— I have been riding my saddle horses every day—and been to Albano—it's lakes—& to the top of the Alban mount—& to Frascati—Aricia—&c. &c.—with an &c. &c. &c. about the city & in the city—for all which— vide Guide-book.—As a *whole*—*ancient* & *modern*—it beats Greece— Constantinople—every thing—at least that I have ever seen.—But I can't describe because my first impressions are always strong and confused—& my Memory *selects* & reduces them to order—like distance in the landscape—& blends them better—although they may be less distinct—there must be a sense or two more than we have as mortals—which I suppose the Devil has—(or t'other) for where there

---

[3] Richard Duppa was the author of a *Life of Raffaele* published by Murray in 1816.
[4] Pliny (*Natural History*, lib. XX, cap. XIV) says that cummin (a carrot-like plant) was used by the followers of Porcius Latro, the rhetorician, to produce a studious complexion.
[5] Henry Stephen Fox (1791–1846) was a nephew of Charles James Fox.

is much to be grasped we are always at a loss—and yet feel that we ought to have a higher and more extended comprehension.——I have had a letter from Moore—who is in some alarm about his poem —I don't see why.——I have had another from my poor dear Augusta who is in a sad fuss about my late illness—do, pray, tell her—(the truth) that I am better than ever—& in importunate health—growing (if not grown) large & ruddy—& congratulated by impertinent persons on my robustious appearance—when I ought to be pale and interesting.——You tell me that George B[yron] has got a son—and Augusta says—a daughter—which is it?—it is no great matter—the father is a good man—an excellent officer—& has married a very nice little woman[6]—who will bring him more babes than income—howbeit she had a handsome dowry—& is a very charming girl—but he may as well get a ship.——I have no thoughts of coming amongst you yet a while—so that I can fight off business—if I could but make a tolerable sale of Newstead—there would be no occasion for my return & I can assure you very sincerely—that I am much happier—(or at least have been so) out of your island than in it.——

Yours ever truly,
B

P.S.—There are few English here—but several of my acquaintance —amongst others, the Marquis of Lansdowne with whom I dine tomorrow—I met the Jerseys on the road at Foligno—all well—Oh— I forgot—the Italians have printed Chillon &c. a *piracy* a pretty little edition prettier than yours and published as I found to my great astonishment on arriving here & what is odd is, that the English is quite correctly printed—why they did it or who did it I know not— but so it is—I suppose for the English people.—I will send you a copy.

[TO JOHN MURRAY]   [*Rome*], *May 10th. 1817*

Dear Sir—Will you forward the enclosed letter to it's address.— The person to whom it is addressed will probably have a parcel for me in a fortnight after the receipt of this letter—which I have desired him to consign to *you*—& I request you will have the goodness if possible to get it forwarded to me *at Venice* by some safe & sure conveyance— which may surely be done—though I have not been lucky with my parcels hitherto.——If Mr. Kinnaird or Mr Davies come out—they

[6] See March, 1, 1816, to Lady Byron, note 2.

would convey it—but I want it to be sent sooner—so perhaps some other way would be better.—I also would thank you to send me some *calcined Magnesia*—& toothpowder.

Yours very truly,
B

I have written to you often lately.

My dearest Augusta—I have taken a flight down here (see the Map) but shall return to Venice in fifteen days from this date, so address all answers to my usual head—(or rather *heart-*) quarters—that is—to Venice.—I am very well, quite recovered—& as is always the case after all illness—particularly fever—got large—ruddy—& robustous to a degree which would please you—& shock me.—I have been on horse-back several hours a day for this last ten days—besides now & then on my journey—proof positive of high health—& curiosity, & exercise.—Love me—& don't be afraid—I mean of my sicknesses. I got well—& shall always get so—& have luck enough still to beat most things—& whether I win or not—depend upon it— I will fight to the last.——Will you tell my wife "mine excellent wife" that she is brewing a Cataract for herself & me in these foolish equivocations about *Ada*,—a job for lawyers—& more hatred for every body, for which—(God knows), there is no occasion.—She is surrounded by people who detest me—Brougham the lawyer—who never forgave me for saying that Mrs. G[eorg]e Lambe was a damned fool (by the way I did not then know he was in love with her) in 1814— & for a former savage note in my foolish satire—all which is good reason for *him*—but not for *Lady B[yro]n* besides her mother—&c. &c. &c.—so that what I may say or you may say is of no great use— however—*say it.*—If she supposes that I want to hate or plague her (however wroth circumstances at times may make me in words & in temporary gusts or disgusts of feeling), she is quite out—I have no such wish—& never had—& if she imagines that I now wish to become united to her again she is still more out—*I never will.*—I *would* to the end of the *year* succeeding our separation—(expired nearly a month ago, *legal reckoning*), according to a resolution I had taken thereupon— but the day & the hour is gone by—and it is irrevocable.—But all this is no reason for further misery & quarrel;—Give me but a *fair share* of my daughter—the half—my natural right & authority—& I

am content;—otherwise I come to England & "law & claw before they get it," all which will vex & out live Sir. R. & Ly. N. besides making Mrs. Clermount bilious—& plaguing Bell herself—which I really by the great God! wish to avoid—now—pray see her—& say so —it may do good—& if not—she & I are but what we are—& God knows that is wretched enough—at least to me.——Of Rome I say nothing—you can read the Guide-book—which is very accurate.——
I found here an old letter of yours dated November 1816—to which the best answer I can make—is none—you are sadly ⟨coward⟩ timid my child—but so you all shewed yourselves when you could have been useful—particularly—but never mind.—I shall not forget *him*,[1] though I do not rejoice in any ill which befalls him,—is the fool's spawn a *son* or a *daughter*? you say one—& others another: so Sykes works him—*let him*—I shall live to see him & W.[2] destroyed—& more than them—& then—but let all that pass for the present.——

yrs. ever

B

P.S.—Hobhouse is here. I travelled from V—*quite alone* so do not fuss about women &c.—I am not so rash as I have been.——

[TO AUGUSTA LEIGH]   [*May 11, 1817*]

[first sheet missing] . . . I met the Jerseys on the road at Foligno— all well—but Lady J. sunburnt a good deal.—I dined yesterday (10th.) with Lord Lansdowne who returns towards England in a few days. ——I have seen a live Pope & a dead Cardinal (lying in state) they both looked very well.—I have been on horseback several hours daily ever since my arrival—which may satisfy you of my recovery—do not forget to state to Lady B[yron] what I say in this letter because she is not aware of the mischief which will ensue in case of more disputes about Ada—I do not say this out of menace—but it is so.—All I require is *an assurance that on no account Ada shall leave England without my consent*—I am aware that they have made her a Chancery ward— & have filed a bill against me—but there is *law* & *right* for me also— and situated as I am—alone & unsupported—I have no fear—but will try the last—& it may be as well not to drive me too far—but *surely*

---

[1] George Anson Byron, who sided with Lady Byron during the separation proceedings.

[2] Possibly Wilmot Horton who was also on Lady Byron's side during the separation, though he acted as a supposed impartial mediator.

previously to those steps which they will make me take—there can be no harm in suggesting to them that I shall adopt them with reluctance.—If not—I shall return & apply to the Chancellor for my *daughter* to be delivered to me her natural Guardian;—& whatever the event of such a contest may be—recollect—that I sought it not—& that with whomever the miserable triumph of a decision against the other may rest—I regret—& deprecate—but am compelled to bring it to an issue.——Say this——I have one word more to say *of* Mr. Brougham—(& a great many *to* him whenever he & I meet which we shall if I live) at the time of the separation—he suggested to Mr. Kinnaird—whether it would not be better if a *Scotch divorce* could be obtained—this may show the Spirit in which he took up the business—I was not till lately aware of all *the things* he B[rougha]m has *said* & *done*—but being now aware of them depend upon it—he shall answer it—not as Lady B[yron]'s advocate—for to all such she has a right—but for his conduct & assertions since—in which I know from good authority—that he has gone out of his character as an advocate—& been guilty of very improper language the more so as I was too far distant to be told in time.—However—that which is deferred is *not* lost.—I live to think on't.—However I forgive her the injuries she has done me—but it is as well she should know that she has done me injury—because—apparently—she acts as if I had sustained none—& could feel nothing.—Good day—

yrs ever

B

[TO DOUGLAS KINNAIRD]   *Rome—May 11th. 1817*

My Dear Kinnaird—I have betaken myself to Rome instead of England—for a season—but address your answer to Venice—where I shall return in a few days—at least such is my intention.—Hobhouse is here but will leave it about the same time—though for a different quarter—at least for the present.—I shall perhaps take another year of it abroad or several months—but shall not stir from Venice or it's vicinity during that period.—Your letter I have—Siri and Wilhalm did as they were bid—and the Torlonias[1] are as civil as need be.——I have sent Murray two recent things—one a sort of drama—the other a poem called "the Lament of Tasso" for which he must pay to my

[1] Torlonia was Byron's banker in Rome to whom his letters from Venice were forwarded. A letter sent by him to 66 Piazza di Spagna furnishes a clue to Byron's residence in Rome.

account *six hundred guineas*—the which you will perhaps have the kindness to arrange for me with him—as heretofore.—I wish you would also desire Hanson to pay in any superflux however trifling of Newstead rents—& of another trifle due from Sir R[alph] N[oe]l these probably amount to very little—but still I choose to have that whatever it is—added to the rest;—& something there must be—because it is now a considerable time since the N[ewstead] tenants have paid at all & something they must have paid lately if ever.—And even these trifles which look but scant in pounds sterling—seem respectable & go a good way in francs—& even scudi.——I would also press upon you the necessity of selling at all risks—& at any loss—that property of N[ewstea]d this *summer*—I do not care for what—but sold it must be—for by God—I will procrastinate no longer—so—do pray—make Hanson act upon this & *make* it be put up for sale—& sold if possible. —You say you have been there lately—with Miss Rawdon of the party.—apropos of the Rawdons—*you* know them all well don't you? —I don't—but there is a foolish story circulated that Mrs. R[awdo]n *refused* to see me at Geneva—& this is said to be on *her authority*— now—the fact is that I *did see* her to request her to take a letter for Hobhouse[2]—which she did—at the same time showing me Miss R.'s veil—which had received a bullet through it in some adventure with robbers—and is it possible that she can have sanctioned such a story? I can hardly believe it and it is perhaps scarce worth ascertaining— except that as I have always had a very harmless but sincere admiration of *Bessy*—& her beauty and accomplishments—& have wished her and wish her so well—that what would have only made me laugh if asserted of another quarter—has made me feel a little hurt from this.——These are pretty things to plague you with—but never mind. —Pray—press the *sale* of Newstead & do not answer me that "the times," &c.—damn the times—they won't mend in my time—& sold it must be—I would take eighty thousand *entre nous*—more or less— or anything—but by the Pope's toe! it must be sold—& this summer— or I shall go mad.——A word from you in your *Committee* manner would drive Hanson who will do nothing of himself for some d—d reason or other—this sale would enable me to clear or nearly—& also empower me to live abroad comfortably—which I have lately done —and to which my ambition is limited—I hate your country—& everything in it—except as an occasional stranger.——

ever yours most truly
BYRON

2 See May 27, 1816, to Mrs. Rawdon.

I have received your letter here, where I have taken a cruise lately; but I shall return back to Venice in a few days, so that if you write again, address there, as usual. I am not for returning to England so soon as you imagine; and by no means at all as a residence. If you cross the Alps in your projected expedition, you will find me somewhere in Lombardy, and very glad to see you. Only give me a word or two beforehand, for I would readily diverge some leagues to meet you.

Of Rome I say nothing; it is quite indescribable, and the Guidebook is as good as any other. I dined yesterday with Lord Lansdowne, who is on his return. But there are few English here at present; the winter is *their* time. I have been on horseback most of the day, all days since my arrival, and have taken it as I did Constantinople. But Rome is the elder sister, and the finer. I went some days ago to the top of the Alban Mount, which is superb. As for the Coliseum, Pantheon, St. Peter's, the Vatican, Palatine, &c. &c.—as I said, vide Guidebook. They are quite inconceivable, and must *be seen*. The Apollo Belvidere is the image of Lady Adelaide Forbes[1]—I think I never saw such a likeness.

I have seen the Pope alive, and a cardinal dead,—both of whom looked very well indeed. The latter was in state in the Chiesa Nuova, previous to his interment.

Your poetical alarms are groundless; go on and prosper. Here is Hobhouse just come in, and my horses at the door; so that I must mount and take the field in the Campus Martius, which, by the way, is all built over by modern Rome.

Yours very and ever, &c.

P.S.—Hobhouse presents his remembrances, and is eager, with all the world, for your new Poem.

My dearest Augusta—I am thus far on my return from Rome to Venice. From Rome I wrote to you at some length.—Hobhouse is gone to Naples for a short time.—I received a letter or two from you during my stay—one old—& one new,—my health is reestablished— & has continued so through some very warm weather—& a good deal of horse & mountain exercise—& scrambling—for I lived out of doors

---

[1] Moore had once tried to promote a match between Byron and Lady Adelaide Forbes. See May 28, 1814, to Lady Melbourne, note 1 (vol. 4, p. 119).

ever since my arrival.———I shall be glad to hear from or of you—&
of your children—& mine—by the way—it seems that I have got
another—a *daughter*—by that same lady whom you will recognize by
what I said of her in former letters—I mean *her* who returned to
England to become a Mamma incog.—& whom I pray the Gods to
keep there.[1]———I am a little puzzled how to dispose of this new
production (which is two or three months old though I did not receive
the accounts till at Rome), but shall probably send for & place it in a
Venetian convent—to become a good Catholic—& (it may be) a
Nun—being a character somewhat wanted in our family.—They tell
me it is very pretty—with blue eyes & dark hair—& although I never
was attached nor pretended attachment to the mother—still in case
of the eternal war & alienation which I foresee about my legitimate
daughter—Ada—it may be well to have something to repose a hope
upon—I must love something in my old age—& probably circumstances will render this poor little creature a greater (& perhaps my
only) comfort than any offspring from that misguided & artificial
woman—who bears & disgraces my name.—I look to nothing from
the Noel quarter—but all that can harass & torture——however—I
have made up my mind—& have borne enough to bear anything;—
but neither they—nor you—can have any idea of the extent—& depth
of the consequences of their conduct (or mine if you like it) in the
separation—it has literally made me as much an object of proscription
—as any political plot could have done—& exactly the same as if I had
been condemned for some capital offence—you would hardly believe
this—but a little enquiry would shew you that it is not exaggerated.—
To suppose that this has no effect upon a character like mine—would
be absurd; but I bear it—although it is unabated—& may be unabating.
———I forgive Lady B[yron]—too—who would probably say—that it
is her *duty*—& that she has done me no *intentional* injury.———May be
so—& people sometimes lose a limb by accident—with a friend who is
an awkward sportsman—& he is very sorry for it—which to be sure
mends the matter amazingly—but neither extracts shot—nor repairs
members nor optics.[2]———However I forgive her the injuries she has
done me—but it is as well she should know that she has done me
injury—because apparently she acts as if I had sustained none, &
could feel nothing.

[1] Byron's daughter (Allegra) by Claire Clairmont was born January 12, 1817,
at Bath, where Claire was living with Shelley and Mary.
[2] The manuscript ends here; the remainder is in a copy with the manuscript letter
in the Lovelace Papers.

Dear Sir—I returned from Rome two days ago—& have received your letter but no sign nor tidings of the parcel sent through Sir—— Stuart[1] which you mention;—after an interval of months a packet of "Tales," &c. found me at Rome—but this is all—& may be all that ever will find me—the post seems to be the only sane conveyance—& *that only for letters.*—From Florence I sent you a poem on Tasso— and from Rome the new third act of "Manfred," & by Dr. Polidori two pictures for my sister. I left Rome & made a rapid journey home. —You will continue to direct here as usual.—Mr. Hobhouse is gone to Naples—I should have run down there too for a week—but for the quantity of English whom I heard of there—I prefer hating them at a distance—unless an Earthquake or a good real eruption of Vesuvius were insured to reconcile me to their vicinity.—I know no other situation except Hell which I should feel inclined to participate with them—as a race—always excepting several individuals.—There were few of them in Rome—& I believe none whom you know—except that old Blue-*bore* Sotheby—who will give a fine account of Italy in which he will be greatly assisted by his total ignorance of Italian—& yet this is the translator of Tasso.—The day before I left Rome I saw three robbers guillotined—the ceremony—including the *masqued* priests— the half-naked executioners—the bandaged criminals—the black Christ & his banner—the scaffold—the soldiery—the slow procession —& the quick rattle and heavy fall of the axe—the splash of the blood —& the ghastliness of the exposed heads—is altogether more impressive than the vulgar and ungentlemanly dirty "new drop" & dog-like agony of infliction upon the sufferers of the English sentence. Two of these men—behaved calmly enough—but the first of the three—died with great terror and reluctance—which was very horrible—he would not lie down—then his neck was too large for the aperture—and the priest was obliged to drown his exclamations by still louder exhortations—the head was off before the eye could trace the blow—but from an attempt to draw back the head—notwithstanding it was held forward by the hair—the first head was cut off close to the ears—the other two were taken off more cleanly;—it is better than the Oriental way—& (I should think) than the axe of our ancestors.—The pain seems little —& yet the effect to the spectator—& the preparation to the criminal —is very striking & chilling.—The first turned me quite hot and

---

[1] Sir Charles Stuart (1779–1845) held various diplomatic posts. He was later (1828) created Baron Stuart de Rothesay.

thirsty—& made me shake so that I could hardly hold the opera-glass (I was close—but was determined to see—as one should see every thing once—with attention) the second and third (which shows how dreadfully soon things grow indifferent) I am ashamed to say had no effect on me—as a horror—though I would have saved them if I could.———It is some time since I heard from you—the *12th April* I believe.—

yrs. ever truly,
B

[TO DOUGLAS KINNAIRD]   *Venice May 30th. 1817*

My Dear Kinnaird—I wrote to you from Rome before my departure. —Two days ago I returned to Venice—where you can address to me as usual, as I feel very great reluctance to return to England without absolute and imperious necessity.—Hobhouse I left well & on the eve of setting out for Naples.—He will be up again in Lombardy before he returns to electioneer amongst you—and I shall probably see him here in no very long time.—I wrote to you to impress upon you as strongly as I could the indispensable obligation I feel of disposing of Newstead without further delay in the course of the present summer at *any price* which it will bring—no present loss can possibly be so great as the ruinous delay which has already occurred & which every year & month renders worse.—Two years ago a Mr. Wilson offered eighty thousand pounds for it which (*by advice*) was then declined—I do not know that he or anybody else would give so much now—though it is in fact worth a good deal more—or would be in decent times—but I shall never feel a moment's tranquillity till the property is sold;—& I therefore do most urgently press upon you—my request—& beg of you to use a little of your *most peremptory* manner with Mr. Hanson to have it once more put in the market (& Rochdale Manor also) & whatever be the result—my obligation to you will be the same.—I apply to you in preference to addressing myself to Hanson—firstly, because you are acting for me equally—& secondly, I know your promptitude & ability in the dispatch of business—when you choose to set about it—& I know that unless urged strongly—Mr. H. (from notions which I do not understand) will do nothing to advance the disposal of that property—unless for a price—which in these times—cannot be obtained.———With regard to other points—I have no design or desire to return *wittingly* to England—unless for an occasional—& by no means—a speedy visit—to form decisive resolutions is idle—but I tell you very sincerely—that if I could or can expatriate myself altogether I would and will—all my wishes with regard to my property there are bounded to seeing my affairs in some train for settlement—which would be the case in any sale—but in any case do not let me be obliged to return to England—if it can be helped—you can have no idea of my disgust & abhorrence to the thought of living there even for a short time.—I am serious. My health is very good again—& during my stay at Rome I was hardly off my horse's back the whole time—except in poring over churches & antiquities. You will perceive that my anxiety about these sales is not from any immediate pressure—as I am in very good present cash—but really & truly from a full sense of the importance of cutting short all delay—because every year adds to the embarrassment & a few more such years would render all extrication impracticable—and I should not like to shoot myself—during the lifetime of that bitch my mother in law & her housekeeper [Mrs. Clermont]—because they would be but too happy. ——Now do not write to me some of your "exquisite reasons" for a further postponement—but *spur* Hanson—who will do if you drive him—let me hear that something is to be done—and above all excuse the trouble to which you are so frequently put by

yrs. ever & truly & affectionately,
BYRON

P.S.—My remembrances to the Songstress[1]—I hope she succeeds.

[TO AUGUSTA LEIGH]   *Venice.—June 3d.–4th. 1817*

Dearest Augusta—I returned home a few days ago from Rome—but wrote to you on the road—at Florence I believe—or Bologna—the last city you know—or do not know—is celebrated for the production of Popes—Cardinals—painters—& sausages—besides a female professor of anatomy—who has left there many models of the art in waxwork—some of them not the most decent.—I have received all your letters—I believe—which are full of woes—as usual—megrims & mysteries—but my sympathies remain in suspense—for—for the life of me I can't make out whether your disorder is a broken heart or the ear-ache—or whether it is *you* that have been ill or the children—or what your melancholy—& mysterious apprehensions tend to—

[1] Kinnaird's wife, who was a singer, had gone back on the stage.

or refer to—whether to Caroline Lamb's novels—Mrs Clermont's evidence—Lady Byron's magnanimity—or any other piece of imposture;—I know nothing of what you are in the doldrums about at present—I should think—all that could affect *you*—must have been over long ago—& as for me—leave me to take care of myself—I may be ill or well—in high or low spirits—in quick or obtuse state of feelings—like every body else—but I can battle my way through— better than your exquisite piece of helplessness G[eorge] L[eigh] or that other poor creature George Byron—who will be finely helped up in a year or two with his new state of life—I should like to know what they would do in my situation—or in any situation—I wish well to your George—who is the best of the two a devilish deal—but as for the other I shan't forget him in a hurry—& if ever I forgive or allow an opportunity to escape of evincing my sense of his conduct (& of more than his) on a certain occasion—write me down—what you will —but do not suppose me asleep—"let them look to their bond"— sooner or later time & Nemesis will give me the ascendant—& then "let them look to their bond." I do not of course allude only to that poor wretch—but to all—to the 3d. & 4th. generations of these accursed Amalekites—& the woman who has been the stumbling block of my—

June 4th. 1817

I left off yesterday at the stumbling block of my Midianite marriage— but having received your letter of the 20th. May—I will be in good humour for the rest of this letter.—I had hoped you would like the miniatures at least one of them—which is in pretty good health—the other is thin enough to be sure—& so was I—& in the ebb of a fever when I sate for it.—By the "man of fashion" I suppose you mean that poor piece of affectation and imitation Wilmot—another disgrace to me & mine—that fellow. I regret not having shot him—which the persuasions of others—& circumstances which at that time would have rendered combats presumptions against my cause—prevented.— I wish you well of your indispositions which I hope are slight—or I should lose my senses—

yours ever & very truly

B

[TO JOHN MURRAY] *Venice—June 4th. 1817*

Dear Sir—I have received the proofs of ye "Lament of Tasso" which makes me hope that you have also received the reformed third act of Manfred—from Rome—which I sent soon after my arrival there. —My date will apprize you of my return home within these few days. —For me I have received *none* of your packets—except—after long delay—the "Tales of my Landlord" which I before acknowledged.—I do not at all understand the *why nots*—but so it is—no Manuel[1]—no letters—no tooth powder, no *extract* from Moore's Italy concerning Marino Falieri—no *nothing*—as a man hallooed out at one of Burdett's elections—after a long ululatus of No Bastille! No Governor Aris![2] no —God knows who or what—but his ne plus ultra was no nothing!— & my receipts of your packages amount to about his meaning.—I want the extract from *Moore's* Italy very much—& the tooth powder —& the magnesia—I don't care so much about the poetry—or the letters—or Mr. Maturin's by-Jasus tragedy.—Most of the things sent by the post have come—I mean proofs & letters—therefore send me Marino Falieri by the post, in a letter.—I was delighted with Rome— & was on horseback all round it many hours daily besides in it the rest of my time—bothering over its marvels.—I excursed and skirred the country round to Alba—Tivoli—Frascati—Licenza—&c. &c. besides I visited twice the fall of Terni—which beats every thing.—On my way back, close to the temple by its banks—I got some famous trout out of the river Clitumnus—the prettiest little stream in all poesy—near the first post from Foligno—& Spoletto.—I did not stay at Florence, being anxious to get home to Venice—& having already seen the galleries—& other sights—I left my commendatory letters the evening before I went so I saw nobody.—To-day, Pindemonte[3] the celebrated poet of Verona—called on me—he is a little thin man— with acute and pleasing features—his address good & gentle—his appearance altogether very philosophical—his age about sixty—or more—he is one of their best going.—I gave him *Forsyth*[4] as he speaks or reads rather a little English—& will find there a favourable account of himself.—He enquired after his old Cruscan friends Parsons— Greathead—Mrs. Piozzi—and Merry[5]—all of whom he had known in his youth.—I gave him as bad an account of them as I could— answering as the false "Solomon Lob" does to "Totterton" in the

[1] Maturin's play.
[2] Keeper of the Coldbath Fields Prison, reputed to be rigorous and hard-hearted.
[3] Ippolito Pindemonte (1753–1828), born at Verona, was known as a translator of the *Odyssey* and the *Georgics* and other classics, and was the author of several volumes of poetry.
[4] Joseph Forsyth in his *Remarks on Antiquities, Arts*, &c. praised Pindemonte.
[5] Byron had attacked the Della Cruscan poets in *English Bards and Scotch Reviewers* (lines 759–764).

farce[6]—that they were "all gone dead,"—& damned by a satire more than twenty years ago—that the name of their extinguisher was Gifford[7]—that they were but a sad set of scribes after all—& no great things in any other way.—He seemed—as was natural—very much pleased with this account of his old acquaintances—and went away greatly gratified with that & Mr. Forsyth's sententious paragraph of applause in his own (Pindemonte's) favour.—After having been a little libertine in his youth—he is grown devout—& takes prayers—& talks to himself—to keep off the Devil—but for all that he is a very nice little old gentleman.—I forgot to tell you that at Bologna—(which is celebrated for producing Popes—Painters—and Sausages) I saw an Anatomical gallery—where there is a deal of waxwork—in which the parts of shame of both sexes are exhibited to the life—all made & moulded by a *female* Professor whose picture & merits are preserved & described to you—I thought the male part of her performance not very favourable to her imagination—or at least to the Italian Originals—being considerably under our Northern notions of things—& standard of dimensions in such matters—more particularly as the feminine display was a little in the other extreme—which however is envy also as far at least as my own experience & observation goes on this side of the Alps—& both sides of the Appennines.—I am sorry to hear of your row with Hunt—but suppose him to be exasperated by the Quarterly—& your refusal to *deal*—& when one is angry—& edites a paper I should think the temptation too strong for literary nature—which is not always human. I can't conceive in what—& for what he abuses you—what have you done? you are not an author—nor a politician—nor a public character—I know no scrape you have tumbled into.—I am the more sorry for this because I introduced you to Hunt—& because I believe him to be a very good man—but till I know the particulars I can give no opinion.—Let me know about *Lallah Rookh*—which must be out by this time.—I restore the proofs—but the *punctuation* should be corrected—I feel too lazy to have at it myself—so beg & pray Mr. Gifford for me.—Address to Venice—in a few days I go to my *Villeggiatura* in a Casino near the Brenta—a few miles only on the main land—I have determined on another year & *many years* of residence if I can compass them.—Marianna is with me—hardly recovered of the fever—which has been

---

[6] *Love Laughs at Locksmiths* by George Colman the Younger, Act II, scene 1.
[7] Gifford ridiculed the Della Cruscan school in his satires *The Baviad* and *The Maeviad*. See *Poetry*, I, 358n.

attacking all Italy last winter—I am afraid she is a little hectic—but I hope the best.—

ever yours truly,
B

P.S.—Torwaltzen has done a bust of me at Rome for Mr. Hobhouse[8] —which is reckoned very good—he is their best after Canova—& by some preferred to him.—I have had a letter from Mr. Hodgson— maudlin & fine-feeling—he is very happy—has got a living—but not a child—if he had stuck to a Curacy—babes would have come of course because he could not have maintained them.——Remember me to all your friends, &c. &c. An Austrian officer the other day, being in love with a Venetian—was ordered with his regiment into Hungary— distracted between love & duty he purchased a deadly drug which dividing with his mistress both swallowed—The ensuing pains were terrific but the pills were purgative—& not poisonous—by the contrivance of the unsentimental apothecary—so that so much suicide was all thrown away—you may conceive the previous confusion & the final laughter—but the intention was good on all sides.——

[TO JOHN MURRAY]   *Venice—June 8th. 1817*

Dear Sir/—The present letter will be delivered to you by two Armenian Friars—on their way by England to Madras—they will also convey some copies of the Grammar, which I think you agreed to take. If you can be of any use to them either amongst your naval or East-Indian acquaintances—I hope you will so far oblige me—as they & their Order have been remarkably attentive & friendly towards me since my arrival at Venice.—Their names are Father Sukias Somalian and Father Sarkis Theodorosian—they speak Italian—& probably French or a little English. Repeating earnestly my recommendatory request—believe me

very truly yrs.
BYRON

Perhaps you can help them to their passage or give or get them letters for India.—

[8] Bertel Thorwaldsen, the Danish sculptor, had made the bust while Byron was in Rome. It now stands in the publishing house of John Murray.

[TO JOHN HANSON]   *Venice—June 14th. 1817*

Dear Sir/—Since my return from Rome I have twice written to Mr. Kinnaird & to Mr. Scrope Davies—to request them to transmit to you my particular & earnest desire that Newstead (& if possible Rochdale also) may be brought once more to the hammer without delay this present summer.—I regret now very much not having accepted Mr. Wilson's proposition (of eighty thousand guineas) & it seems to be in vain to expect more or to wait longer. Every year is an additional loss & a greater embarrassment—and beyond the present summer it were idle to wait.——Mr. Kinnaird & yourself have full powers to act for me during my absence—my instructions are very simple—let the estate be put up & sold to the highest responsible bidder.—It is useless to speak to me of the "times &c."—"the times" will not improve—& I must take the market price—both in justice to my creditors and to myself.—I wish the same to be done by Rochdale. These requests are *definitive*—& I beg that you will have the goodness to attend to them without fail.—Pray send me an early answer.—If Sir R[alph] N[oel] has paid the last year's account—or if there is any balance from Newstead rents—have the goodness to transmit the same to Mr. Kinnaird & through his partner Mr. Morland's bank to my credit by their means.—I received your Son Charles's (to whom and to all yours—I beg my remembrances may be made acceptable) paper—which I shall transmit to England by a private hand on the first safe opportunity—as from the delay & omission of many things addressed to me from England—I should rather not send it by post.—Above all I recommend you my above requests—as I have no immediate intentions whatever of returning to England—and still less of settling there as a resident.—

                              ever yours very truly,
                                             BYRON

P.S.—I presume that Sir R. N. has of course paid the £200—if not he will please to pay it in.—From Newstead there should surely be some balance[;] it is now more than a year since I quitted England (a year & two months) & the tenants were in great arrear before[;] at all events let me hear.——Address to Venice as usual.——

[TO AUGUSTA LEIGH]   *Venice June 14th. 1817*

Dearest Augusta/—I write to you a few lines merely to request you to urge to Mr. Kinnaird & Mr. Hanson from me my request that

236

Newstead be put up for sale & *definitively sold* to the highest bidder—
this summer—as every year would become an additional loss &
embarrassment—by the delay—I am sick of objections—& will hear
none—as there is but this alternative for my creditors or myself—*any
price* were better than the ruin occasioned by protracted delay—
because no price in that case could liquidate the accumulation.——
It is amongst my regrets that I did not accept Mr. Wilson's proposition
in 1815—as it seems useless to wait longer or expect more.—Pray do
not forget to press my desire & order strongly on Hanson.—

yrs. very truly
B

P.S.—I wrote to you lately.——You will not see me in England—
unless in case of absolute business.——

[TO JOHN MURRAY]   *La Mira.—Venice—June 14th. 1817*

Dear Sir/—I write to you from the banks of the Brenta[1]—a few
miles from Venice—where I have colonized for six months to come.—
Address as usual to Venice.—Three months after date (*17th* March)
like the unnegociable bill despondingly received by the reluctant
tailor—your dispatch has arrived containing the extract from Moore's
Italy—& Mr. Maturin's bankrupt tragedy. It is the absurd work of a
clever man.—I think it might have done upon the stage, if he had
made Manuel (by some trickery—in a masque or vizor) fight his own
battle instead of employing Molineux as his champion—& after
defeating Torrismond have made him spare the son of his enemy by
some revulsion of feeling not incompatible with a character of extravagant and distempered emotions—but as it is—what with the Justiza
—& the ridiculous conduct of the whole dram. Pers. (for they are all
as mad as Manuel—who surely must have had greater interest
with a corrupt bench—than a distant relation & heir presumptive
somewhat suspect of homicide) I do not wonder at its failure—as a
play it is impracticable—as a poem—no great things.—Who was the
"Greek that grappled with Glory naked?" the Olympic wrestler? or
Alexander the great when he ran stark round the tomb of t'other

[1] Byron had leased the Villa Foscarini on the left bank of the Brenta River at
La Mira, a village about seven miles inland from the river's mouth at Fusina on the
Venetian lagoon. He removed there soon after his return from Rome. At this
"*Villegiatura*" he wrote the fourth canto of *Childe Harold* and *Beppo*, and the
following summer he began *Don Juan* there.

fellow?[2] or the Spartan who was fined by the Ephori for fighting without his armour?[3] or who?—& as to "flinging off life like a garment," Helas! that's in Tom Thumb—see King Arthur's soliloquy—

> "Life's a mere rag, not worth a prince's wearing;
> I'll cast it off."[4]

and the stage-directions—"staggers among the bodies"—the slain are too numerous—as well as the blackamoor Knight-penitent being one too many—and De Zelos is such a shabby Monmouth-street villain—without any redeeming quality—Stap my vitals!—Maturin seems to be declining into Nat. Lee,[5] but let him try again—he has talent—but not much taste—I 'gin to fear—or to hope that Sotheby after all is to be the Æschylus of the age—unless Mr. Shiel[6]—be really worthy his success.—The more I see of the stage—the less I would wish to have anything to do with it—as a proof of which I hope you have received the 3d of M[anfre]d—which will at least prove that I wish to steer very clear of the possibility of being put into scenery.— I sent it from Rome.—I returned the proof of Tasso—by the way have you never received a translation of St. Paul?[7] which I sent you *not* for publication—before I went to Rome? I am at present on the Brenta— opposite is a Spanish Marquis—ninety years old—next his Casino is a Frenchman's besides the natives—so that as Somebody said the other day—we are exactly one of Goldoni's comedies (La Vedova Scaltra) where a Spaniard—English—& Frenchman are introduced;—but we are all very good neighbours, Venetians, &c. &c. &c.——I am just getting on horseback for my evening ride—& a visit to a Physician who has an agreeable family of a wife & four unmarried daughters—all under eighteen—who are friends of Signora Segati—and enemies to nobody;—there are and are to be besides Conversaziones & I know

---

[2] Byron was probably relying on Plutarch's account: "Achilles, whose grave he (Alexander) anointed with oile, and ranne naked about it with his familiars, according to the ancient custome of funerals." (North's Plutarch's *Lives*, ed. 1631, p. 680)

[3] This is also probably from Plutarch. The Spartan was Isadas, who was crowned for his valour but fined 1000 drachmas for going into battle before the legal age and without the appropriate armour.

[4] In Fielding's *Tom Thumb*, Act II, scene 8, King Arthur says: "My life is worn as ragged as a coat / A beggar wears; a prince should put it off."

[5] Nathaniel Lee (1653?–1692) a dramatist who drew most of his tragic plots from classical history. He was for a time confined in Bethlehem (Bedlam), having lost his reason from intemperance.

[6] Richard Lalor Sheil (1791–1851), whose tragedy *The Apostate* was produced at Covent Garden, May 3, 1817.

[7] See March 31, 1817, to Moore, note 3.

not what at a Countess Labbia's & I know not whom. The weather is mild—the thermometer *110* in the *Sun* this day & eighty odd in the shade.

Yours,
B

[TO JOHN MURRAY] *La Mira—nr. Venice.—June 17th. 1817*

Dear Sir/—It gives me great pleasure to hear of Moore's success—& the more so that I never doubted that it would be complete—whatever good you can tell me of him & his poem will be most acceptable; —I feel very anxious indeed to receive it; I hope that he is as happy in his fame & reward as I wish him to be—for I know no one who deserves both more—if any so much.—Now to business—our own.— For the drama I required three hundred guineas—& desire no more—& for the other—three hundred guineas & will take no less.—When you say that the Drama is of the same length & will form the same-sized publication as most of the preceding—it is probable that you will charge the same price to the purchaser—& in that case (unless the publication fails altogether) will probably be not less a gainer than upon the former—at least it seems that you can hardly be a loser—when the author's demand has not been a *third* of what you have already paid for productions of the like calibre. Do you mean to say that it is dearer or shorter than Mr. R[ogers]'s *Jaqueline?* or than my Lara? or than the Giaour? or the Bride? Or do you mean to say that it is inferior to these as Poetry? or that its dramatic form renders it less susceptible of profit? I will tell you that to you from its being the first poem of mine in that form—it must to a certain degree be more advantageous—as far as an object of curiosity—& although it is not a drama properly—but a dialogue—still it contains poetry and passion —although I by no means look on it as the best—or conceive that it will be the most fortunate of compositions by the same writer.—— When therefore you talk to me as of its being a dear purchase—I answer you in so many words—that if I had not named the prior price (with which by the way I was satisfied & had no wish to enlarge) *you* would yourself have offered me a greater—& if you would not—I could find those who would.———As to the other poem—I look upon that as good of its kind—& the price not at all out of proportion to what writers require and obtain.—You are to print in what form you please—that is your concern;—as far as your connection with myself

239

has gone—you are the best judge—how far you have lost or gained—
probably sometimes one and sometimes the other—but when you
come to me with your *"can"* and talk to me about the copy of Manfred
as if "the force of purchase would no further go—to *make* a book he
separates the *two"*—I say unto you, verily it is not so—or as the
Foreigner said to the Waiter after asking him to bring a glass of
water—to which the man answered "I will—Sir,"—"You *will!*—
God d[—]n—I say—you *mush!*"—And I will submit this to the
decision of any person or persons to be appointed by both on a fair
examination of the circumstances of this as compared with the preceding publications—so—there's for you;—there is always some row
or other previously to all our publications—it should seem that on
approximating we can never quite get over the natural antipathy of
author & bookseller—& that more particularly the ferine nature of the
latter must break forth.———You are out about the third [*sic*] Canto—
I have not done—nor designed a line of continuation to that poem—I
was too short a time at Rome for it—& have no thoughts of recom-
mencing—but if ever I do—I will put it to market to the best bidder—
or will desert at once to the *"Row"*—if you come over me with your
pitiful-hearted speeches—about "can" & *"not"* of which if you are not
ashamed—you deserve to be the publisher of *Saul*[1]—on your sole
account—(paying the author five pounds copyright) with all expenses
for ever—now & to posterity.———I cannot well explain to you by
letter what I conceive to be the origin of Mrs. Leigh's notion about
"tales of my L[andlor]d"[2]—but it is some points of the characters of
Sir E. Manley—& Burley—as well as one or two of the jocular
portions—on which it is founded probably.———If you have received
Dr. Polidori—as well as a parcel of books—& you can be of use to
him be so.—I never was much more disgusted with any human production—than with the eternal nonsense—& tracasseries—& emptiness
—& ill-humour—& vanity of that young person—but he has some
talent—& is a man of honour—and has dispositions of amendment—in
which he has been aided by a little subsequent experience—& may
turn out well—therefore, use your government interest for him—for
he is improved and improvable.—

Yours ever truly,
B<small>N</small>

P.S.—Bowles's Story of the interview at the *"common* friend's["]

---

[1] *Saul: a Poem in Two Parts* by William Sotheby was published in 1807.
[2] See Feb. [19?] to Augusta, note 2.

("common" enough the Gods know) is not correct.—It did not occur "*soon* after the publication" &c. but in 1812—three good years after— I recollect nothing of "seriousness" now as the company were going into another room—he said to me that all his friends had bothered him crying out "Eh Bowles how come you to make the *woods* of Madeira tremble to a kiss" whereas it was not the woods but the lovers who trembled[3]—though I see no great reason why they should either.— — I have had no opportunity of restoring the "trembling" to it's right owners—as I had previously suppressed the Satire at Rogers's particular suggestion "that it would gratify Ld. Holland" and I beg leave to observe that this was some time after I was acquainted with Ld. Holland and *a consequence not a cause* of that connection.—Bowles was courteous and civilized enough & so was I too I hope.—

[TO JOHN MURRAY]   *Venice.—La Mira—June 18th. 1817*

Dear Sir/—Enclosed is a letter to *Dr.* Holland[1] from Pindemonte— not knowing the Doctor's address I am desired to enquire & perhaps being a literary man—you will know or discover his haunt near some populous churchyard.—I have written to you a scolding letter—I believe upon a misapprehended passage in your letter—but never mind—it will do for next time—& you will surely deserve it.— Talking of Doctors reminds me once more to recommend to you one who will not recommend himself—the Doctor Polidori.—If you can help him to a publisher do—or, if you have any sick relation—I would advise his advice—all the patients he had in Italy are dead—Mr. Hope's son—Mr. Horner—& Ld. Guilford—whom he embowelled with great success at Pisa.——The present Ld. Guilford—who was the Charlatan Frederic North & the Lady Westmoreland—will I hope do something for him—it is a pity the last don't keep him—I think he would suit her—he is a very well looking man—& it would not be for her discredit.——Remember me to Moore—whom I congratulate.— How is Rogers? How does he look? eh!—and what is become of

[3] Byron had ridiculed some lines in Bowles's *Spirit of Discovery* in his *English Bards and Scotch Reviewers* (line 360). He later wrote a note in his copy of the fifth edition (never published): "Mis-quoted and misunderstood by me; but not intentionally. It was not the 'woods', but the people in them who trembled. . . ." (*Poetry*, I, 325)
[1] Dr. Henry (later Sir Henry) Holland (1788–1873) had been a medical attendant to Caroline, Princess of Wales, on the continent. He had also travelled extensively. He published in 1815 his *Travels in the Ionian Isles, Albania, Thessaly, and Greece in 1812–13.*

241

Campbell & all t'other fellows of the Druid order?—I got Maturin's Bedlam at last—but no other parcel—I am in fits for the tooth powder —& the Magnesia.—I want some of Burkitt's *Soda* powders.—Will you tell Mr. Kinnaird that I have written him two letters on pressing business (about Newstead, &c.) to which I humbly solicit his attendance.—I am just returned from a gallop along the banks of the Brenta—time—Sunset.

Yours,
B

[TO AUGUSTA LEIGH] *Venice.—June 19th. 1817*

Dearest Augusta—Since the pictures are so bad—they need not be copied—the poor painter seems to have been ignorant of the art of flattery.—It is to be recollected that I was ill at the time—& had been so for months—that one of them was done in the climax of a slow fever—and that the other is an attempt to supply the health which I had not recovered.—Send me Holmes's print—one or two copies— they can come by the common post—not being heavy.—The last (the Venice) need not be copied.—I fear that not any good can be done by your speaking to Ly. Biron—but I think it my duty to give fair warning—because *they* have *broken* their *word*;—they are not aware that if I please I can dissolve the separation—which is not a legal act— nor further binding than the will of the parties; I shall therefore not only take all proper & legal steps—but the former correspondence shall be published—& the whole business from the beginning investigated in all the points of which it is susceptible;—unless the reasonable assurance which I have required with regard to my daughter be accorded—& now—come what may—as I have said—so will I do—& have already given the proper instruction to the proper persons—to prepare for the steps above mentioned.——Recollect only that I have done all in my power to avoid this extremity.——I am not at Venice but a few miles on the mainland—on the road to Padua—address as usual to Venice. I ride daily.—

yrs. truly
B

P.S.—I repeat to you again and again—that it would be much better at once to explain your mysteries—than to go on with this absurd obscure hinting mode of writing.—What do you mean?—what is there known? or can be known? which *you* & *I* do not know much better? &

what concealment can you have from me? *I* never shrank—& it was on your account principally that I gave way at all—for I thought they would endeavour to drag you into it—although they had no business with anything previous to my marriage with that infernal fiend—whose destruction I shall yet see.—Do you suppose that I will rest—while any of their branch is unwithered? do you suppose that I will turn aside till they are trodden under foot?—do you suppose that I can breathe till they are uprooted?—Do you believe that time will alter them or me?—that I have suffered in vain—that I have been disgraced in vain—that I am reconciled to the sting of the scorpion—& the venom of the serpent? which stung me in my slumber?——If I did not believe—that Time & Nemesis—& circumstances would requite me for the delay—I would ere this have righted myself.—But "let them look to their bond"——

[TO JOHN CAM HOBHOUSE]　　　　　　*[La Mira] June 20th. 1817*

My Dear Hobhouse—I rejoice in your approximation—& pity your disasters—you will find me near Venice in a Cassino at La Mira (whence I write), whence I will accompany you to Venice.—My abode is not like Diodati—but it is well enough—with more space than splendour—& not much of that—& like all the Venetian ex-marine habitations too near the road—they seem to think they never can have dust enough to compensate for their long immersion.——If you write beforehand—I will meet you at Padua on a given day.—Fix it —& depend upon my being there.—I protest against & prohibit the *"laurels"*[1]—which would be a most awkward assumption and anticipation of that which may never come to pass.—Besides they belong to the butchers & not to the ballad-singers.—*You* would like them naturally because the verses won't do without them—but I won't have my head garnished like a Xmas pie with Holly—or a Cod's head and Fennel—or whatever the damned weed is they strew round it.—I wonder you should want me to be such a mountebank.——Talking of *"bank"* (not mounte*bank*) puts me in mind of Kinnaird who threatens to come out directly—& to drag the Boa Constrictor[2] with him an it be

[1] Hobhouse wanted to have a laurel wreath placed on the poet's brow on the bust for which Byron had sat to Thorwaldsen in Rome and which Hobhouse had commissioned.

[2] Scrope Davies, when he was in Switzerland with Byron, had insisted that he wanted to see a boa constrictor. See Jan. 12, 1817, to Kinnaird.

possible. I write to you in great haste to catch you at Florence if possible.

ever yrs. most truly
B

P.S.—Health & respects to all.

[TO JOHN MURRAY]   *La Mira—nr. Venice—July 1st. 1817*

Dear Sir—Since my former letter—I have been working up my impressions into a *4th.* Canto of C[hild]e H[arold] of which I have roughened off about rather better than thirty stanzas—& mean to go on—& probably to make this "Fytte" the concluding one of the poem so that you may propose against the Autumn to draw out the Conscription for 1818.—You must provide monies as this new resumption bodes you certain disbursements;—somewhere about the end of September or October—I propose to be under way (i.e. in the press); but I have no idea yet of the probable length or calibre of ye. canto—or what it will be good for—but I mean to be as mercenary as possible —an example (I do not mean of any individual in particular & least of all any person or persons of our mutual acquaintance) which I should have followed in my youth—& I might still have been a prosperous Gentleman.——No tooth powder—no packet of letters—no recent tidings of you.—Mr. Lewis[1] is at Venice & I am going up to stay a week with him there—as it is one of his enthusiasms also to like the City.—

> I stood in Venice, on the "Bridge of Sighs"
>> A palace and a prison on each hand
> I saw from out the wave her structures rise
>
>> As from the stroke of the/an enchanter's wand:
> A thousand Years their cloudy wings expand
>> Above me, and a dying Glory smiles
> O'er the far times when many a subject land
>> Looked to the winged Lion's marble piles
> Where Venice sate in state—throned on her Seventy Isles.

The "Bridge of Sighs" (i.e. Ponte dei sospiri) is that which divides or rather joins the palace of the doge to the prison of the state—it has two passages—the criminal went by the one to judgement—& returned by the other to death—being strangled in a chamber adjoining

---

[1] Matthew Gregory ("Monk") Lewis.

—where there was a mechanical process for the purpose.—This is the
first stanza—of the new canto & now for a line of the second—

> In Venice Tasso's echo is no more
> And silent rows the songless gondolier
> Her palaces &c. &c.

You know that formerly the Gondoliers sang always—& Tasso's
Gerusalemme was their ballad—Venice is built on Seventy two islands.
——There—there is a brick of your new Babel! & now, Sirrah!—
what say you to the sample?

yrs. most truly

B

P.S.—I shall write again by & bye.——

[TO DOUGLAS KINNAIRD]

Venice—that is La Mira[1] a few miles between it & Padua.— July 3d.
1817

My dear Kinnaird—I have received your letter of the 17th. this
day—& have to thank you for your kind endeavours—& businesslike
Map of my affairs—which you have laid before me.—I am fully disposed to sell either or both N[ewstead] & R[ochdale] for whatever they
may bring—at the market—public auction—or private contract—a
Mr. Wilson offered 80–000 for the former, perhaps he might treat
again—he is a responsible man.——I should prefer this to the
raising more money—there is a sum of six thousand pounds to a Mr.
Sawbridge an annuity—(six thousand *principal* that is) & a bond for
three thousand more to Mr. Claughton[2]—this is all (I believe) except
the Israelites.—As for Rochdale—it has too long been the stumbling
block of all arrangements—exaggerated statements of it's intrinsic
value—& remonstrances there*for* having prevented me from selling
it—but weariness & experience have converted me to so humble an
opinion of it & myself—that I will take *whatever it may bring*—the sum
you mention—or more—or less.—You see there will be no obstruction
on my part—to whatever you may decide upon—& so that the
business passes under *your eyes*—I shall be satisfied that the best has

1 See June 14, 1817, to Murray.
2 When Thomas Claughton finally gave up his contract to purchase Newstead
Abbey in 1814, he forfeited £25,000 of the £28,000 he had paid on account.
Having spent the whole to settle debts and for other purposes, Byron was apparently
forced to give Claughton a bond for the £3,000 due him.

been done—& circumstanced as I am—almost any decisive arrangement must be for the better.——These are my sentiments—& wishes—particularly to avoid delays if possible—I know the times are not favourable—yet they are no worse than in 1815—when the last sale was attempted—& when I might—(had I not been a fool) have taken Wilson's offer—& another (rather better than the sum you name) for Rochdale—though now I will accept even *that*.——I should be obliged if you will see to Mr. Murray—who will have to pay in the coming Autumn the remainder (600) of the last Canto copyright—& 600 guineas more for "Manfred" & the "Lament of Tasso"—Perhaps he may have already paid the former—but it is not due till October.— You see that I have turned my brains to some account—but as that is of all tenures the frailest—I do not consider them amongst my goods & chattels.—At present I am in the country—a few miles from Venice—where I am quiet & healthy.—A few days ago I had a small row in the road—I was on horseback & a man in the Diligence was impudent & tried to frighten my horse—in a fit of facetious impertinence;—I stopt his vehicle—& gave him a slap in the face—this sent him with a woeful countenance to the Police—which rejected his complaint—& said that he was rightly served—& that if I had not boxed his ears—they would have sent him into durance.—I feel so much obliged to you for all yr. toils in my behalf—that I don't know how to thank you.——And so—"father in law Sir Jacob"[3] has been baffled by the Jews—"How say you—Tubal—? are you sure on't? my good *Tubal*!—an Argosie cast away—"[4]—if I can but live to tear down the columns of that house of Dagon & its Philistine family—I shall not have lived in vain—& if Time & Nemesis but do their usual part—& reverse the present tide of human fortunes—see whether I leave one stone of their hearths upon another—or a fibre of their hearts unscorched by fire.——Excuse the length of this epistle & believe me

ever & truly yrs.

B

[TO DOUGLAS KINNAIRD]   *Venice—July 8th. 1817*

My dear Kinnaird/—On reconsidering your transcription of Mr. Hanson's statement—I perceive—or imagine that he states the

---

[3] Byron's nickname for Sir Ralph Noel. See Jan. 19, 1815, to Moore, note 5.

[4] *Merchant of Venice*, Act III, scene I. As usual, Byron makes a rather free use of Shakespeare's phrases.

principal of the Jewish annuities at £9000.—This is wrong—because altogether they did not amount to much more originally—& six thousand pounds have been paid off which were originally guaranteed by Scrope Davies to whom I reimbursed the money which he had himself discharged a few years ago.—Since I came of age I raised only one sum between two & three thousand pounds principal—and subsequently another of six or seven *hundred pounds*—& of these I paid off just before leaving England most of the interest & *one principal* sum of *600* pds. redeeming the annuity thereof of which Mr. H[anson] has the restored papers.——The sum therefore to the Jews cannot by any means be so much—unless he includes *Sawbridge's* annuity which is not a Jewish transaction.—There were some others for which a Mrs. Massingberd (since dead) was security—but for these time can be taken because they cannot come upon the legality of the transaction being during minority—& though I shall give them their *principal* & *legal* interest—yet I am not so far prepossessed by the treatment I have had from these gentry as to liquidate that claim—until *all* the others—contract debts & all—are discharged & liquidated.——I can only repeat what I have said in my former letters—& leave you *Carte blanche* as to my affairs—sell—sell—sell—any sale is better than suspense & increasing difficulties—& all for the precarious hope of a better bargain—God knows when.—I think it necessary to add that Hanson's notions as to the value of Rochdale must be tempered down —or not attended to—I want to get rid of that manor if only to shake off the anxiety & litigation it has given me the last seventeen years— sell it for anything—& N[ewstea]d the same—

yrs. ever & truly

B

P.S.—I wrote in answer to yr. last a few days ago.—Many thanks.—

[TO JOHN MURRAY] *La Mira—nr. Venice—July 8th. 1817*

Dear Sir—If you can convey the enclosed letter to its address—or discover the person to whom it is directed you will confer a favour upon the Venetian Creditor of a deceased Englishman.—This epistle is a dun to his Executor for house rent—the name of the insolvent defunct is or was *Porter Valter* according to the account of the plaintiff which I rather suspect ought to be *Walter Porter* according to our mode of

Collocation—if you are acquainted with any dead man of the like name a good deal in debt—pray dig him up—& tell him that "a pound of his fair flesh" or the ducats are required—& that "if you deny them, fie upon your law"[1]—I hear nothing more from you about Moore's poem —Roger[s]'s looks—or other literary phenomena—but tomorrow being post-day will bring perhaps some tidings.—I write to you with people talking Venetian all about—so that you must not expect this letter to be all English.——The other day I had a squabble on the highway as follows.—I was riding pretty quickly from Dolo home about 8 in the Evening—when I passed a party of people in a hired carriage—one of whom poking his head out of the window began bawling to me in an inarticulate but insolent manner—I wheeled my horse round & over-taking, stopped the coach & said "Signor have you any commands for me?" He replied impudently as to manner *"No"*—I then asked him what he meant by that unseemly noise to the dis-comfiture of the passers by—he replied by some piece of impertinence —to which I answered by giving him a violent slap in the face.—I then dismounted (for this passed at the window—I being on horseback still) & opening the door desired him to walk out—or I would give him another.—But the first had settled him—except as to words—of which he poured forth a profusion in blasphemies swearing that he would go to the police & avouch a battery sans provocation—I said he lied and was a b—& if he did not hold his tongue should be dragged out & beaten anew—he then held his tongue.—I of course told him my name & residence & defied him to the death if he were a gentleman —or not a gentleman & had the inclination to be genteel in the way of combat.—He went to the police—but there having been bystanders in the road—particularly a soldier—who had seen the business—as well as my servant—notwithstanding the oaths of the Coachman & five insides besides the plaintiff—and a good deal of perjury on all sides —his complaint was dismissed—he having been the aggressor—and I was subsequently informed that had I not given him a blow he might have been had into durance. So set down this "that in Aleppo once—" I "beat a Venetian"[2] but I assure you that he deserved it—for I am a quiet man like Candide—though with somewhat of his fortune in being forced to forego my natural meekness every now & then.—

yrs.

B

---

[1] *Merchant of Venice*, Act IV, scene 1.
[2] *Othello*, Act V, scene 2.

Dear Sir—I have got the sketch & extracts from Lallah Rookh—which I humbly suspect will knock up "Ilderim"[1] & shew young Gentlemen that something more than having been across a Camel's hump is necessary to write a good Oriental tale.—The plan as well as the extract I have seen please me very much indeed & I feel impatient for the whole——With regard to the critique on "Manfred"[2]—you have been in such a devil of a hurry that you have only sent me the half—it breaks off at page 294—send me the rest—& also page 270—where there is "an account of the supposed origin of this dreadful story,"—in which by the way whatever it may be—the Conjecturer is out—& knows nothing of the matter—I had a better origin than he can devise or divine for the soul of him.——You say nothing of Manfred's luck in the world—& I care not—he is one of the best of my misbegotten—say what they will.—I got at last an extract—but *no parcels*—They will come I suppose some time or other.—I am come up to Venice for a day or two to bathe—& am just going to take a swim in the Adriatic—so—Good evening—the Post waits.

yrs. [very truly?]

B

P.S.—Pray was Manfred's speech to *the Sun* still retained in Act 3d? —I hope so—it was one of the best in the thing—& better than the Colosseum.—I have done *56* stanzas of Canto 4th. Childe Harold—so down with your ducats.

[TO THOMAS MOORE] *La Mira, Venice, July 10th, 1817*

Murray, the Mokanna[1] of booksellers, has contrived to send me extracts from Lalla Rookh by the post. They are taken from some magazine, and contain a short outline and quotations from the two first Poems. I am very much delighted with what is before me, and very thirsty for the rest. You have caught the colours as if you had been

---

[1] *Ilderim, a Syrian Tale* by H. Gally Knight.

[2] *Blackwood's Edinburgh Monthly Magazine* for June, 1817, contained (pages 270–273) a "Sketch of a Tradition related by a Monk in Switzerland", wherein it was suggested that there was a striking resemblance between that sketch and parts of *Manfred*. In the same number (pp. 289–295) was a review of *Manfred*. The missing page contained some critical remarks on the imperfections of the versification of the poem.

[1] Byron was referring to the Veiled Mokanna in *Lalla Rookh*, who said: "That Prophet ill sustains his holy call,/Who finds not Heavens to suit the tastes of all."

in the rainbow, and the tone of the East is perfectly preserved; so that [Ilderim?] and its author must be somewhat in the back-ground, and learn that it required something more than to have been upon the hunch of a dromedary to compose a good oriental story. I am glad you have changed the title from "Persian Tale." * * * * * * *

I suspect you have written a devilish fine composition, and I rejoice in it from my heart; because "the Douglas and the Percy both together are confident against a world in arms."[2] I hope you won't be affronted at my looking on us as "birds of a feather;" though, on whatever subject you had written, I should have been very happy in your success.

There is a simile of an orange-tree's "flowers and fruits," which I should have liked better, if I did not believe it to be a reflection on * *
* * * * * *

Do you remember Thurlow's poem to Sam—"*When* Rogers[3];" and that d—d supper at Rancliffe's that ought to have been a *dinner?* "Ah, Master Shallow, we have heard the chimes at midnight."[4] But,

> My boat is on the shore,
> And my bark is on the sea;
> But, before I go, Tom Moore,
> Here's a double health to thee!
>
> Here's a sigh to those who love me,
> And a smile to those who hate;
> And, whatever sky's above me,
> Here's a heart for every fate.
>
> Though the ocean roar around me,
> Yet it still shall bear me on;
> Though a desert should surround me,
> It hath springs that may be won.
>
> Were't the last drop in the well,
> As I gasp'd upon the brink,
> Ere my fainting spirit fell,
> 'Tis to thee that I would drink.
>
> With that water, as this wine,
> The libation I would pour
> Should be—peace with thine and mine,
> And a health to thee, Tom Moore.

[2] *Henry IV*, Part I, Act V, scene 1.
[3] See Vol. 3, p. 54, note 1.
[4] *Henry IV*, Part II, Act III, scene 2.

This should have been written fifteen moons ago—the first stanza was. I am just come out from an hour's swim in the Adriatic; and I write to you with a black-eyed Venetian girl before me, reading Boccac[c]io. * * * *

Last week I had a row on the road (I came up to Venice from my casino, a few miles on the Paduan road, this blessed day, to bathe) with a fellow in a carriage, who was impudent to my horse. I gave him a swinging box on the ear, which sent him to the police, who dismissed his complaint. Witnesses had seen the transaction. He first shouted, in an unseemly way, to frighten my palfry. I wheeled round, rode up to the window, and asked him what he meant. He grinned, and said some foolery, which produced him an immediate slap in the face, to his utter discomfiture. Much blasphemy ensued, and some menace, which I stopped by dismounting and opening the carriage door, and intimating an intention of mending the road with his immediate remains, if he did not hold his tongue. He held it.

Monk Lewis is here—"how pleasant!" He is a very good fellow, and very much yours. So is Sam—so is every body—and amongst the number,

Yours ever,
B

P.S.—What think you of Manfred? * * * *

[TO JOHN MURRAY]   *La Mira, nr. Venice, July 15th, 1817*

Dear Sir—I have finished (that is written—the file comes afterwards) ninety & eight stanzas of the 4th. Canto which I mean to be the concluding one;—it will probably be about the same length as the *third*—being already of the dimensions of the first or second cantos. I look upon parts of it as very good—that is if the three former are good —but this we shall see—and at any rate good or not—it is rather a different style from the last—less metaphysical—which at any rate will be a variety. I sent you the shaft of the column as a specimen the other day—i.e. the first stanza. So you may be thinking of its arrival towards Autumn—those winds will not be the only ones to be raised if *so be as how that* it is ready by that time.—I lent Lewis who is at Venice (in or on the Canalaccio the Grand Canal) your extracts from Lalla Rookh— & Manuel[1]—& out of contradiction it may be—he likes the last—& is

---

1 Moore's *Lalla Rookh* was published by Longman; Maturin's *Manuel*, his second and unsuccessful play, was published by Murray.

not much taken with the first of these performances.—Of Manuel I think with the exception of a few capers, it is as heavy a Nightmare as was ever bestrode by Indigestion.———Of the extracts I can but judge as extracts & I prefer the "Peri" to the "Silver Veil"—he seems not so much at home in his versification of the "Silver Veil" & a little embarrassed with his horrors—but the Conception of the Character of the Impostor is fine—& the plan of great scope for his Genius—& I doubt not that as a whole it will be very Arabesque and beautiful.——
Your late epistle is not the most abundant in information—& has not yet been succeeded by any other—so that I know nothing of your own concerns—or of any concerns—and as I never see or hear from anybody but yourself—who does not tell me something as disagreeable as possible—I should not be sorry to hear from you—And as it is not very probable—if I can by any device or possible arrangement with regard to my personal affairs so manage it—that I shall return soon—or reside ever in England—all that you tell me will be all I shall know or enquire after as to our beloved realm of Grub-street—& the black brethren and blue Sisterhood of that extensive Suburb of Babylon.— Have you had no new Babe of Literature sprung up to replace the dead —the distant—the tired & the re-tired? no prose—no verse—no *nothing*?

> No infant Sotheby whose dauntless head
>   Translates misunderstood a deal of German;[2]
> No city Wordsworth more admired than read—
>   No drunken Coleridge with a new "Lay Sermon."[3]

Talking of Sotheby—you will perceive that I more than once make dishonorable mention of that venerable Mokanna.—Hear then why— besides my previous & impartial opinion of his being a tiresome man. —Some time ago—I received the Italian Edition of some poems of mine—with an *anonymous* note containing some gratuitously impertinent remarks—which might or might not be well founded—but should not have been sent in that manner. This is no great matter—because I suppose in my life I have received at least two hundred anonymous letters—aye—three hundred—of love—literature—advice—abuse— menace—or—consolation—upon all topics & in every shape.—But I happen to know the hand of that man of age—& the style—(I would swear to the word *"effulgence"* & two or three other blue technicals)

[2] Sotheby's translation of Wieland's *Oberon* appeared in 1798.
[3] Coleridge first "Lay Sermon", *The Statesman's Manual,* was published in 1816; the second, *On the Existing Distresses and Discontents* appeared in 1817.

252

because I was once in doleful correspondence about his un-damned tragedy "Ivan" when I was a Committer of D[rury] L[ane] Theatre.— I say—says I—I know the hand—& I think it a piece of impertinence —in him to write *to* me at all unless on business—& it is at any rate usual for well-conditioned persons to put their names.—So—let him look to it—he had better have written to the Devil a criticism upon Hell-fire—I will raise him such a Samuel for his "Saul"[4] as will astonish him without the Witch of Endor.—An old tiresome blockhead —blundering through Italy without a word of the language—or of any language except the wretched affectations of our own which he called English—to come upon poor dear quiet me with his nonsense—but never mind—we shall see.——If he had attacked me in print—that's all fair—*"foul* is fair" at least among authors—but to come upon me with his petty—mincing—paltry—dirty—notes—& nameless as he will be himself years hence—Sunburn me! if I don't stick a pin through this old Blue-bottle.—'Gin you doubt—ask him—& if he don't own it —why I will read his next or last work through—that's all.——Since this epistle [was] begun—the stanzas of Canto 4th. have jumped to *104.*—& *Such stanzas!* by St. Anthony! (who has a church at my elbow and I like to be neighbourly) some of them are the right thing.——

yours,
B

[TO JOHN MURRAY] *Venice, July 20th. 1817*

Dear Sir—I write to give you notice that I have completed the *4th.* and *ultimate* Canto of Childe Harold—it consists of *126* stanzas & is consequently the longest of the four.—It is yet to be copied and polished—& the notes are to come—of which it will require more than the *third* Canto—as it necessarily treats more of works of art than of Nature.—It shall be sent towards Autumn—& now for our barter— what do you bid? eh? you shall have samples an it so please you—but I wish to know what I am to expect (as the saying is) in these hard times—when poetry does not let for half it's value.—If you are disposed to do what Mrs. Winifred Jenkins calls "the handsome thing" I may perhaps throw you some odd matters to the lot—translations— or slight originals—there is no saying what may be on the anvil between this & the booking Season.—Recollect that it is the *last* Canto—& completes the work—whether as good as the others—I

---

4 See June 17, 1817, to Murray, note 1.

cannot judge in course—least of all as yet—but it shall be as little worse as I can help,—I may perhaps give some little gossip in the notes as to the present state of Italian literati & literature; being acquainted with some of their *Capi*—men as well as books—but this depends upon my humour at the time;—so now—pronounce—I say nothing.——When you have got the whole 4 cantos—I think you might venture on an edition of the whole poem in quarto—with spare copies of the two last for the purchasers of the old edition of the first two.—There is a hint for you worthy of the Row—& now—perpend—pronounce.—I have not received a word from you of the fate of "Manfred" or "Tasso" which seems to me odd—whether they have failed or succeeded. As this is a scrawl of business—& I have lately written at length & often on other subjects I can only add that I am,

Yrs. [ever truly?]

B

[TO JOHN MURRAY]   *La Mira, nr. Venice—August 7th. 1817*

Dear Sir/—Your letter of the 18th, & what will please you as it did me the parcel sent by the good-natured aid & abetment of Mr. Croker are arrived.——Messrs. Lewis & Hobhouse are here—the former in the same house—the latter—a few hundred yards distant. You say nothing of Manfred, from which its failure may be inferred—but I think it odd you should not say so at once—I know nothing—and hear absolutely nothing of anybody or any thing in England—& there are no English papers—so that all you say will be news—of any person or thing—or things—I am at present very anxious about Newstead—& sorry that Kinnaird is leaving England at this minute—though I do not tell him so—& would rather he should have *his* pleasure—though it may not in this instance tend to my profit.———If I understand rightly —you have paid into Morland's[1] 1500 *pounds*—as the agreement in the paper is two thousand *Guineas*—there will remain therefore *six* hundred *pounds* & not five hundred—the odd hundred being the extra to make up the specie.—Six hundred and thirty pounds will bring it to the like for Manfred and Tasso—making a total of twelve hundred & thirty—I believe—for I am not a good calculator.—I do not wish to press you—but I tell you fairly—that it will be a convenience to me to have it paid as soon as it can be made convenient to yourself.——The new & last Canto is 130 Stanzas in length—& may be made more or

---

[1] Ransom and Morland's Bank, in which Douglas Kinnaird was a partner.

less.—I have fixed no price even in idea—& have no notion—of what it may be good for—there are *no* metaphysics in it—at least I think not.—Mr. H[obhous]e has promised me a copy of Tasso's will for the notes—& I have some curious things to say about Ferrara—& Parisina's story—& perhaps a farthing candle's worth of light upon the present state of Italian literature.—I shall hardly be ready by October—but that don't matter.—I have all to copy and correct—and the notes to write.—I do not know whether Scott will like it—but I have called him the "Ariosto of the North," in my *text*. If he *should not*—say so in time.—Lewis[,] Hobhouse & I went the other day to the circumcision of a sucking Shylock—I have seen three men's heads & a child's foreskin cut off in Italy.—The ceremonies are very moving—but too long for detail in this weather.—An Italian translation of "Glenarvon" came lately to be printed at Venice—the Censor (Sr. Petrotini) refused to sanction the publication till he had seen me upon the subject;—I told him that I did not recognise the slightest relation between that book and myself—but that whatever opinions might be upon that subject—*I* would never prevent or oppose the publication of *any* book in *any* language—on my own private account;—& desired him (against his inclination) to permit the poor translator to publish his labours.—It is going forwards in consequence.—You may say this with my compliments to the Author.

Yours [ever sincerely?]
B

P.S.—Mrs. Leigh has written me an uncomfortable letter—from which I suppose George Leigh's affairs are in disorder—is it so? or what is the matter? I can make out nothing from her letter—it is very foolish to torment me with ambiguities at this distance.—Do tell me that Gifford is better—& well.——There are some sad errors in your 5th. volume—*not* for "*nor* Cypress nor [yew?] let us see"[2] in one of the songs?—& in the Monody—a whole passage made absolute nonsense. —Do pray [join]

"Ye Orators when still our councils yield" to the preceding lines— it does *not* begin a separate paragraph.——

[STATEMENT ON SEPARATION]

La Mira, near Venice, August 9, 1817

It has been intimated to me, that the persons understood to be the legal advisers of Lady Byron, have declared "their lips to be sealed up"

2 A line in the early poem (written 1808; published 1815) beginning: "Bright be the place of thy soul!".

on the cause of the separation between her and myself. If their lips are sealed up, they are not sealed up by me, and the greatest favour *they* can confer upon me will be to open them. From the first hour in which I was apprized of the intentions of the Noel family to the last communication between Lady Byron and myself in the character of wife and husband (a period of some months), I called repeatedly and in vain for a statement of their or her charges, and it was chiefly in consequence of Lady Byron's claiming (in a letter still existing) a promise on my part to consent to a separation if such was *really* her wish, that I consented at all; this claim and the exasperating and inexplicable manner in which their object was pursued, which rendered it next to an impossibility that two persons so divided could ever be re-united, induced me reluctantly then, and repentantly still, to sign the deed, which I shall be happy—most happy—to cancel, and go before any tribunal which may discuss the business in the most public manner.

Mr. Hobhouse made this proposition on my part, viz., to abrogate all prior intentions—and go into Court—the very day before the separation was signed, and it was declined by the other party, as also the publication of the correspondence during the previous discussion. Those propositions I beg here to repeat, and to call upon her and hers to say their worst, pledging myself to meet their allegations—whatever they may be—and only too happy to be informed at last of their real nature.

BYRON

P.S.—I have been, and am now, utterly ignorant of what description her allegations, charges, or whatever name they may have assumed, are; and am as little aware for what purpose they have been kept back—unless it was to sanction the most infamous calumnies by silence.

BYRON

[TO JOHN MURRAY]   *Venice, August 12th 1817*

Dear Sir—I have been very sorry to hear of the death of M[adam]e. de Stael—not only because she had been very kind to me at Coppet—but because now I can never requite her.—In a general point of view she will leave a great gap in society & literature.——With regard to death—I doubt that we have any right to pity the dead for their own sakes.——The copies of Manfred & Tasso are arrived—thanks to Mr.

Croker's cover.—You have destroyed the whole effect & moral of the poem by omitting the last line of Manfred's speaking[1]—& why this was done I know not.—Why you persist in saying nothing of the thing itself I am equally at a loss to conjecture—if it is for fear of telling me something disagreeable—you are wrong—because sooner or later I must know it—& I am not so new nor so raw nor so inexperienced—as not to be able to bear—not the mere paltry petty disappointments of authorship—but things more serious—at least I hope so—& that what you may think irritability is merely mechanical—& only acts like Galvanism on a dead body,—or the muscular motion which survives sensation.——If it is that you are out of humour because I wrote to you a sharp letter—recollect that it was partly from a misconception of your letter—& partly because you did a thing you had no right to do without consulting me—I have, however, heard good of Man[fre]d from two other quarters—& from men—who would not be scrupulous in saying what they thought—or what was said—& "So Good Morrow to you—Good Master Lieutenant."[2]—I wrote to you twice about the 3d [*sic* in MS.] Canto—which you will answer at your pleasure.—Mr. Hobhouse & I have come up for a day to the city—Mr. Lewis is gone to England—& I am

yrs. ever
B

[TO JOHN MURRAY]
La Mira—Near Venice—August 21st. 1817

Dear Sir—I take you at your word about Mr. Hanson—& will feel obliged if you will *go* to him—& request Mr. Davies also to visit him by my desire—& repeat that I trust that neither Mr. Kinnaird's absence nor mine will prevent his taking all proper steps to accelerate and promote the sales of Newstead and Rochdale—upon which the whole of my future personal comfort depends—it is impossible for me to express how much any delays upon these points would inconvenience me—& I do not know a greater obligation that can be conferred upon me than the pressing these things upon Hanson—& making him act according to my wishes.—I wish you would *speak out* at least to *me* &

---

[1] The last line of *Manfred*, which Murray had omitted in the first printing was "Old man! 'tis not so difficult to die." On Byron's insistence it was replaced in subsequent editions.

[2] *Othello*, Act III, scene 1: "Good morrow, good lieutenant."

tell me what you allude to by your odd way of mentioning him—all mysteries at such a distance are not merely tormenting—but mischievous—& may be prejudicial to my interests—so pray—expound—that I may consult with Mr. Kinnaird when he arrives—& remember that I prefer the most disagreeable certainties to hints & inuendoes—the devil take every body—I never can get any person to be explicit about any thing—or any body—& my whole life is past in conjectures of what people mean—you all talk in the style of Caroline Lamb's novels.———It is not Mr. St. John—but *Mr. St. Aubyn,*[1] Son of Sir John St. Aubyn.—*Polidori* knows him—& introduced him to me—he is of Oxford—& has got my parcel—the Doctor will ferret him out or ought.—The Parcel contains many letters—some of Madame de Stael's and other people's—besides M.S.S., &c.—By G—d—if I find the gentleman & he don't find the parcel—I will say something he won't like to hear.—You want a "civil and delicate declension"[2] for the medical tragedy? Take it—

> Dear Doctor—I have read your play
> Which is a good one in it's way
> Purges the eyes & moves the bowels
> And drenches handkerchiefs like towels
> With tears that in a flux of Grief
> Afford hysterical relief
> To shatter'd nerves & quickened pulses
> Which your catastrophe convulses.
> I like your moral & machinery
> Your plot too has such scope for Scenery!
> Your dialogue is apt & smart
> The play's concoction full of art—
> Your hero raves—your heroine cries
> All stab—& every body dies;
> In short your tragedy would be
> The very thing to hear & see—
> And for a piece of publication
> If I decline on this occasion
> It is not that I am not sensible
> To merits in themselves ostensible

[1] See Oct. 5, 1816, to Murray (*a*).

[2] Murray had written to Byron, Aug. 5, 1817 (Smiles, I, 386): "Polidori has sent me his tragedy! Do me the kindness to send by return of post a *delicate* declension of it, which I engage faithfully to copy."

But—and I grieve to speak it—plays
Are drugs—mere drugs, Sir, nowadays—
I had a heavy loss by "Manuel"—[3]
Too lucky if it prove not annual—
And Sotheby with his damned "Orestes"
(Which by the way the old Bore's best is,)
Has lain so very long on hand
That I despair of all demand—
I've advertized—but see my books—
Or only watch my Shopman's looks—
Still Ivan—Ina[4] & such lumber
My back shop glut—my shelves encumber.—
There's Byron—too—who once did better
Has sent me—folded in a letter—
A sort of—it's no more a drama[5]
Than Darnley—Ivan—or Kehama[6]—
So altered since last year his pen is—
I think he's lost his wits at Venice—
Or drained his brains away as Stallion
To some dark-eyed & warm Italian;[7]
In short—Sir—what with one & t'other
I dare not venture on another—
I write in haste, excuse each blunder
The Coaches through the Street so thunder.
My Room's so full—we've Gifford here
Reading M.S.S.—with Hookham Frere
Pronouncing on the nouns & particles
Of some of our forthcoming articles,
The Quarterly—Ah Sir! if you
Had but the Genius to review—
A smart Critique upon St. Helena
Or if you only would but tell in a
Short compass what—but, to resume
As I was saying—Sir—the Room—

[3] Maturin's tragedy was produced at Drury Lane March 8, 1817, with Kean in
the title role, but it failed. Murray published it as he had Maturin's successful play
Bertram.

[4] Mrs. Wilmot's tragedy. See April 23, 1815, to Moore.

[5] *Manfred*.

[6] *Darnley* and *Ivan* by Sotheby; *Kehama* by Southey.

[7] This line and the preceding one were omitted in E. H. Coleridge's edition of
the *Poetry*.

The Room's so full of wits & bards—
Crabbes—Campbells—Crokers—Freres—& Wards,
And others neither bards nor wits;
My humble tenement admits
All persons in the dress of Gent.
From Mr. Hammond[8] to Dog Dent.[9]
A party dines with me today
All clever men who make their way,[10]
They're at this moment in discussion
On poor De Stael's late dissolution—
"Her book they say was in advance—
Pray Heaven! she tell the truth of France,[11]
'Tis said she certainly was married
To Rocca—& had twice miscarried,
No—not miscarried—I opine—
But brought to bed at forty-nine,
Some say she died a Papist—Some
Are of opinion *that's* a Hum—
I don't know that—the fellow Schlegel[12]
Was very likely to inveigle
A dying person in compunction
To try the extremity of Unction.—
But peace be with her—for a woman
Her talents surely were uncommon.
Her Publisher (& Public too)
The hour of her demise may rue—
For never more within his shop he—
Pray—was not she interred at Coppet?["]
Thus run our time and tongues away—
But to return Sir—to your play—

---

8 George Hammond (1763–1853), a diplomatist and one time Under Secretary
of State for Foreign Affairs, was an intimate friend of Canning and was associated
with the foundation of the *Anti-Jacobin* and the *Quarterly Review*. It was as a
frequenter of Murray's drawing room that Byron met him.

9 John Dent, M.P., banker, was nicknamed "Dog Dent" because of his concern
for the Dog-tax Bill in 1796.

10 Byron subsequently added two lines here: "Crabbe, Malcolm, Hamilton and
Chantrye,/Are all partakers of my pantry."

11 See April 2, 1817, to John Murray, note 6.

12 August Wilhelm von Schlegel (1767—1845) was a frequenter of Madame de
Staël's salon at Coppet. He and Byron did not like each other. Byron attributed
Schlegal's dislike to the fact that he would not flatter him.

Sorry—Sir—but I can not deal—
Unless 'twere acted by O'Neill[13]—
My hands are full—my head so busy—
I'm almost dead—& always dizzy—
And so with endless truth & hurry—
Dear Doctor—I am yours
                                    John Murray.

P.S.—I've done the 4th & last Canto—which mounts 133 Stanzas.—
I desire you to name a price—if you don't—*I* will—so I advise you in
time.
                                                                    yrs.
    there will be a good many notes.

[TO JOHN HANSON]   *Venice. August 26th. 1817*

    Dear Sir/—Although I wrote to you some time ago on the same
subject—my anxiety induces me to repeat that I hope that neither
Mr. Kinnaird's temporary absence nor mine will make any difference
in your endeavours to get Newstead sold to the best bidder.—My
determination on the *sale* is decisive—& it is with great regret that I
hear of some delays about that of Rochdale also—which I wish also to
have sold for whatever it may bring;—I have been too long fed with
vain hopes of profit or advantage from it's long lawsuit—to trust to
the decisions of courts—or the speculations of remote contingencies.—
Any sale of both or either of these properties must be far more advantageous to me if immediate—than any possible future profit or increase
of price from delay—since every year till they are sold—can but
increase my difficulties & add to my debts.—If the product of the sales
—should not do much more than cover the settlement of Sixty
thousand pounds—after the surplus has been applied to the liquidation
of my debts—a part of the income can be set aside for a series of years
—to the adjustment of the remaining claims.——I trust that neither
you nor *I* are now so insane—as to expect any thing like the price for
Newstead which Claughton proposed & could not make good—a *safe
sure* & *moderate* purchaser such as Wilson is all we want—and such I
trust may still be found.——Pray favour me with a line—remember
me to yr. family, & believe me
                                                    yrs. ever truly
                                                            B

    [13] Miss Eliza O'Neil was a leading actress at Drury Lane, taking the place of
Mrs. Siddons in tragic parts.

P.S.—If there is any little balance from the rents (which by the way there should be) let it be sent to my credit through *Messrs. Morlands, bankers—Pall Mall.*—I suppose of course Sir R. Noel has paid the year due last March—if not—*let him* be *made* to pay instantly—I desire nothing but short accounts with that family.——

[TO JOHN MURRAY]   *Septr. 4th. 1817*

Dear Sir—Your letter of the 15th has conveyed with it's contents the impression of a Seal to which the "Saracen's head" is a Seraph— and the "Bull and Mouth" a delicate device.—I knew that Calumny had sufficiently *blackened* me of later days—but not that it had given the features as well as complexion of a Negro.—Poor Augusta is not less —but rather more shocked than myself—and says, "people seem to have lost their recollection strangely" when they engraved such a "blackamoor."—Pray don't seal (at least to me) with such a Caricature of the human numskull altogether—& if you don't break the Seal-cutter's head—at least crack his libel (or likeness, if it should be a likeness) of mine.—Mr. Kinnaird is not yet arrived—but expected— he has lost by the way all the tooth powder—as a letter from Spa informs me.——By Mr. Rose[1]—I received safely though tardily— Magnesia—and Tooth-powder—"Phrosine" and "Alashtar"[2]—I shall clean my teeth with one—and wipe my——not shoes with the other. —Why do you send me such trash—worse than trash—the Sublime of Mediocrity?—Thanks for Lallah however which is good—& thanks for the Edin[burg]h and Quarterly—both very amusing and well-written.—Paris in 1815[3] &c. good.—Modern Greece[4] Good for nothing—written by some one who has never been there—and not being able to manage the Spenser Stanza has invented a thing of it's own—consisting of two elegiac stanzas a heroic line and an Alexand-rine twisted on a string—besides why *"modern"*?—you may say

[1] William Stewart Rose (1775–1843) was early fascinated with romances and legendary lays. He had translated from the French the first three books of Amadis de Gaule and published a ballad, "The Red King", much admired by Walter Scott. After the peace he travelled to Italy, married a Venetian (1818), and immersed himself in Italian literature. His *Letters from the North of Italy to Henry Hallam, Esq.* (1819), his version of Casti's *Animali Parlanti* (1819), and other translations were greatly admired by Byron.

[2] *Phrosyne, a Grecian Tale, and Alashtar, an Arabian Tale,* both by Henry Gally Knight, were published in 1817.

[3] A poem by the Rev. George Croly (1780–1860), in imitation of *Childe Harold,* published in 1817.

[4] *Modern Greece, A Poem* (anonymous, by Felicia D. Hemens).

modern Greeks but surely *Greece* itself is rather more ancient than ever it was.—Now for business.—You offer 1500 guineas for the new Canto—I won't take it.—I ask two thousand five hundred guineas for it—which you will either give or not as you think proper. It concludes the poem—and consists of 144 Stanzas—the Notes are numerous and chiefly written by Mr. Hobhouse—whose researches have been indefatigable—and who I will venture to say has more real knowledge of Rome & its environs than any Englishman—who has been there since Gibbon.—By the way—to prevent any mistakes—I think it necessary to state the fact that *he*, Mr. H[obhouse] has no interest whatever in the price or profit to be derived from the copyright of either poem or notes, directly or indirectly—so that you are not to suppose that it is by—for—or through him—that I require more for this Canto than the preceding.—No—but if Mr. Eustace[5] was to have had two thousand for a poem on education—if Mr. Moore is to have three thousand for Lallah &c.—if Mr. Campbell is to have three thousand for his prose on poetry—I don't mean to disparage these gentlemen or their labours—but I ask the aforesaid price for mine.— You will tell me that their productions are considerably *longer*—very true—& when they shòrten them—I will lengthen mine, and ask less. —You shall submit the M.S. to Mr. Gifford—and any other two gentlemen to be named by you (Mr. Frere—or Mr. Croker or whomever you please except such fellows as your Galley Knights & Sothebys) and if they pronounce this Canto to be inferior as a *whole* to the preceding—I will not appeal from their award—but burn the manuscript and leave things as they are.

yrs. very truly

BYRON

P.S.—In answer to your former letter, I sent you a short statement of what I thought the state of our present copyright account—viz— six hundred *pounds* still (or lately) due on Childe Harold—& six hundred *guineas* [on] Manfred and Tasso—making a total of twelve hundred and thirty pounds—If we agree about the new poem I shall take the liberty to reserve the choice of the manner in which it should be published—viz—a Quarto certes.—If we do not agree—recollect that you have had the refusal.—

5 The Rev. John Chetwode Eustace, author of *A Classical Tour through Italy*, died at Naples in 1815. Hobhouse spoke slightingly of him in *Historical Illustrations of the Fourth Canto of Childe Harold* (1818, page 240n).

I set out yesterday morning with the intention of paying my respects, and availing myself of your permission to walk over the premises.[1] On arriving at Padua, I found that the march of the Austrian troops had engrossed so many horses, that those I could procure were hardly able to crawl; and their weakness, together with the prospect of finding none at all at the post-house of Monselice, and consequently either not arriving that day at Este, or so late as to be unable to return home here the same evening, induced me to turn aside in a second visit to Arqua, instead of proceeding onwards; and even thus I hardly got back in time.

Next week I shall be obliged to be in Venice to meet Lord Kinnaird and his brother, who are expected in a few days. And this interruption, together with that occasioned by the continued march of the Austrians for the next few days, will not allow me to fix any precise period for availing myself of your kindness, though I should wish to take the earliest opportunity. Perhaps, if absent, you will have the goodness to permit one of your servants to show me the grounds and house, or as much of either as may be convenient; at any rate, I shall take the first occasion possible to go over, and regret very much that I was yesterday prevented.

I have the honour to be your obliged, &c.

Dear Sir—I enclose a sheet for correction if ever you get to another edition—you will observe that the blunder in printing makes it appear as if the Chateau was *over* St. Gingo—instead of being on the opposite shore of the lake over Clarens—so—separate the paragraphs otherwise my *top*ography will seems as inaccurate as your *typ*ography on this occasion.[1]——The other day I wrote to convey my proposition with regard to the 4th & concluding Canto—I have gone over—& extended it to one hundred and fifty stanzas which is almost as long as the two first were originally—& longer by itself—than any of the

[1] R. B. Hoppner, British Consul in Venice, had occupied a country house or "villegiatura" called "I Cappucini" in the Euganean Hills near Este. Byron later sublet it from Hoppner, but never lived there. He loaned it to Shelley in the summer of 1818, and sent Allegra there to be with her mother, Claire Clairmont, for a few weeks. For an account of Hoppner and Byron's relations with him, see Appendix IV.

[1] Byron here refers to the third canto of *Childe Harold*.

smaller poems except the "Corsair"—Mr. Hobhouse has made some very valuable & accurate notes of considerable length—& you may be sure I will do for the text all that I can to finish with decency.—I look upon C[hild]e Harold as my best—and as I begun—I think of concluding with it—but I make no resolutions on that head—as I broke my former intention with regard to "the Corsair"—however—I fear that I shall never do better—& yet—not being thirty years of age for some moons to come—one ought to be progressive as far as Intellect goes for many a good year—but I have had a devilish deal of wear & tear of mind and body—in my time—besides having published too often & much already. God grant me some judgement! to do what may be most fitting in that & every thing else—for I doubt my own exceedingly.——I have read "Lallah Rookh"—but not with sufficient attention yet—for I ride about—& lounge—& ponder &—two or three other things—so that my reading is very desultory & not so attentive as it used to be.—I am very glad to hear of its popularity—for Moore is a very noble fellow in all respects—& will enjoy it without any of the bad feelings which Success—good or evil—sometimes engenders in the men of rhyme.—Of the poem itself I will tell you my opinion when I have mastered it—I say of the *poem*—for I don't like the *prose* at all—at all—and in the mean time the "Fire-worshippers" is the best and the "Veiled Prophet" the worst, of the volume.——With regard to poetry in general[2] I am convinced the more I think of it—that he and *all* of us—Scott—Southey—Wordsworth—Moore—Campbell—I—are all in the wrong—one as much as another—that we are upon a wrong revolutionary poetical system—or systems—not worth a damn in itself—& from which none but Rogers and Crabbe are free—and that the present & next generations will finally be of this opinion.—I am the more confirmed in this—by having lately gone over some of our Classics—particularly *Pope*—whom I tried in this way— I took Moore's poems & my own & some others—& went over them side by side with Pope's—and I was really astonished (I ought not to have been so) and mortified—at the ineffable distance in point of sense—harmony—effect—and even *Imagination* Passion—& *Invention* —between the little Queen Anne's Man—& us of the lower Empire— depend upon it [it] is all Horace then, and Claudian now among us —and if I had to begin again—I would model myself accordingly—

[2] Murray showed this letter to Gifford who wrote the following note with respect to Byron's critique of modern poets and his judgment of Pope: "There is more good sense, and feeling and judgment in this passage, than in any other I ever read, or Lord Byron wrote." (*LJ*, IV, 169n.)

Crabbe's the man—but he has got a coarse and impracticable subject—
& Rogers the Grandfather of living Poetry—is retired upon half-pay,
(I don't mean as a Banker)—

> Since pretty Miss Jaqueline
> With her nose aquiline

and has done enough—unless he were to do as he did formerly.—

[TO JOHN MURRAY]   *Venice. Septr. 17th. 1817*

  Dear Sir—I shall send the assignment by Mr. Kinnaird—who is not
yet arrived here—but your rectification of guineas does not bring you
quite right yet—you said a thousand pounds—it is however—twelve
hundred & thirty pounds—*viz*—a balance of £ six hundred—on the
3d C[ant]o & three hundred g[uinea]s Manfred—& three hundred
Tasso—making six hundred & thirty pounds on the latter—according
to my Cocker.———As to the time of payment—I repeat that I don't
wish to press you—but that when it suits your convenience—it will
not be incompatible with mine;—By Messrs. Morland's last account
I perceive that a sum which I imagined to have been from your quarter
came instead from Mr. Hanson—so that it should seem you are more
in my books than I thought—for which reason I am thus precise as to
items.—Mr. Hobhouse purposes being in England in November—he
will bring the 4th Canto with him notes and all—the text contains one
hundred and fifty stanzas—which is long for that measure.—With
regard to the "Ariosto of the North" surely their themes Chivalry—
war—& love were as like as can be—and as to the compliment—if you
knew what the Italians think of Ariosto—you would not hesitate about
that.—But as to their "measures," you forget that Ariosto's is an
octave stanza—and Scott's anything but a Stanza.—If you think Scot[t]
will dislike it—say so—& I expunge.—I do not call him the "*Scotch*
Ariosto" which would be sad *provincial* eulogy—but the "Ariosto of
the *North*"—meaning of *all countries* that are *not* the *South*.—I have
received your enclosed letter from Lady Caroline Lamb—& am truly
sorry (as she will one day be) that she is capable of writing such a
letter—poor thing—it is a great pity.—As I have recently troubled
you rather frequently—I will conclude repeating that I am

                              yrs ever very truly,
                                                    B

Dear Sir—Mr. Kinnaird & his brother Lord K. have been here—and are now gone again; all your missives came except the tooth-powder —of which I request further supplies at all convenient opportunities— as also of Magnesia & Soda-powders—both great luxuries here—& neither to be had good—or indeed hardly at all of the natives.—In Coleridge's life[1] I perceive an attack upon the then Committee of D[rury] L[ane] Theatre—for acting Bertram—and an attack upon Mathurin's Bertram for being acted—considering all things—this is not very grateful nor graceful on the part of the worthy auto-biographer —and I would answer—if I had *not* obligated him.—Putting my own pains to forward the views of Coleridge out of the question—I know that there was every disposition on the part of the S[ub] C[ommitte]e to bring forward any production of his were it feasible—the play he offered—though poetical—did not appear at all practicable—and Bertram did—and hence this long tirade—which is the last Chapter of his vagabond life.—As for Bertram, Mathurin may defend his own begotten—if he likes it well enough—I leave the Irish Clergyman and the new Orator Henley[2] to battle it out between them—satisfied to have done the best I could for *both*—I may say this to *you*—who know it.—Mr. Coleridge may console himself with the "fervour—the almost religious fervour" of his and Wordsworth's disciples as he calls it—if he means that as any proof of their merits—I will find him as much "fervour" in behalf of Richard Brothers[3] and Joanna Southcote[4]—as ever gathered over his pages—or round his fireside. He is a shabby fellow—and I wash my hands of, and after him.———My answer to your proposition—about the 4th Canto you will have received—and I await yours—perhaps we may not agree. I have since written a poem (of 84 octave Stanzas) humourous, in or after the excellent manner of Mr. Whistlecraft (whom I take to be Frere), on a Venetian anecdote —which amused me[5]—but till I have your answer—I can say nothing

---

[1] Coleridge reviewed Maturin's *Bertram* in Chapter 23 of his *Biographia Literaria* published in 1817.

[2] Byron compared Coleridge to John Henley whom Pope had ridiculed as "Zany of thy age". (*Dunciad*, Book III, line 206.)

[3] Richard Brothers (1757–1824) believed that, in 1795, he was to be revealed to be Prince of the Hebrews and ruler of the world. He was arrested and confined as a lunatic.

[4] See Sept. 2, 1814, to Murray, note 6. (vol. 4, p. 164).

[5] For the anecdote which was the foundation of the story of *Beppo*, see Marchand, *Byron: A Biography*, II, 708. The verse form, the ottava rima as used by John Hookham Frere in his mock heroic poem, supposedly by William and Robert Whistlecraft, had recently come to Byron's attention.

more about it.—Mr. Hobhouse does not return to England in Novr. as he intended, but will perhaps winter here—and as he is to convey the poem or poems—for there may perhaps be more than the two mentioned (which by the way I shall not perhaps include in the same publication or agreement) I shall not be able to publish so soon—as expected—but I suppose there is no harm in the delay.—I have *signed* and sent your former *copyrights* by Mr. Kinnaird—but *not the receipt*— because the money is not yet paid—Mr. K[innaird] has a power of Attorney to sign for me—and will when necessary.—Many thanks for the Edin[burgh] R[eview] which is very kind about Manfred—and defends it's originality⁶—which I did not know that any body had attacked.—I *never read*—& do not know that I ever saw—the "Faustus of Marlow" and had & have no Dramatic works by me in English— except the recent things you sent me;—but I heard Mr. Lewis trans- late verbally some scenes of *Goethe's Faust* (which were some good & some bad) last Summer—which is all I know of the history of that magical personage;—and as to the germs of Manfred—they may be found in the Journal which I sent to Mrs. Leigh (part of which you saw) when I went over first the Dent de Jamant & then the Wengeren [sic] or Wengeberg Alp & Sheideck and made the giro of the Jungfrau Schreckhorn &c. &c. shortly before I left Switzerland—I have the whole scene of Manfred before me as if it was but yesterday—& could point it out spot by spot, torrent and all.——Of the Prometheus of Æschylus I was passionately fond as a boy—(it was one of the Greek plays we read thrice a year at Harrow) indeed that and the "Medea"— were the only ones—except the "Seven before Thebes" which ever much pleased me.—As to the "Faustus of Marlow"—I never read— never saw—nor heard of it—at least thought of it—except that I think Mr. Gifford mentioned, in a note of his which you sent me— something about the catastrophe,—but not as having any thing to do with mine—which may or may not resemble it—for any thing I know. ——The Prometheus—if not exactly in my plan—has always been so much in my head—that I can easily conceive its influence over all or anything that I have written;—but I deny Marlow & his progeny— & beg that you will do the same.——If you can send me the paper in question—which the *E[dinburgh] R[eview]* mentions—*do*—The Review

⁶ In commenting on an article in Blackwood's *Edinburgh Magazine* for July, 1817 (pp. 388–395) which compared Marlow's *Faustus* and *Manfred*, the *Edinburgh Review* for August, 1817, (pp. 430, 431) defended *Manfred's* originality and "depth and force" as compared with the "weak and childish" performance of Faustus, the "vulgar sorcerer". The reviewer, probably Jeffrey, also commented on the resemblance of *Manfred* to the *Prometheus* of Æschylus.

in the Magazine you say was written by Mr. Wilson[7]—it had all the
air of being a poet's, & was a very good one.—The Edin. Review—I
take to be Jeffrey's own by it's friendliness.—I wonder they thought it
worth while to do so—so soon after the former;—but it was evidently
with a good motive.——I saw Hoppner the other day—whose
country-house at Este—I have taken for two years—if you come out
next Summer—let me know in time;—love to Gifford.

Yrs. ever truly

B

"Crabbe—Malcolm—Hamilton and Chantrey,
    Are all partakers of my pantry."—
these two lines were omitted in your letter to the Doctor—after
    "All clever men who make their way."

[TO JOHN MURRAY]   *Venice Octr. 23d. 1817*

Dear Sir—Your two letters are before me—and our bargain is so
far concluded.—How sorry I am to hear that Gifford is unwell—pray
tell me that he is better—I hope it is nothing—but *cold*—as you say his
illness originates in cold—I trust it will get no further.——Mr.
Whistlecraft has no greater admirer than myself—I have written a
story in 89 stanzas—in imitation of him—called *Beppo* (the short name
for Giuseppe—that is the *Joe* of the Italian Joseph) which I shall throw
you into the balance of the 4th Canto—to help you round to your
money—but you perhaps had better publish it anonymously—but this
we will see to by and bye.—In the notes to Canto 4, Mr. Ho[bhous]e
has pointed out *several errors* of Gibbon[1]—you may depend upon H.'s
research and accuracy.—As to the form you may print it in what shape
you please.—With regard to a future large Edition—you may print all
or any thing except "English Bards" to the republication of which at
no time will I consent—I would not reprint them on any consideration
—I don't think them good for much—even in point of poetry—and as
to the other things—you are to recollect that I gave up the publication
on account of the *Hollands*—and I do not consider that any time or
circumstances can neutralise my suppression;—add to which that after

    [7] John Wilson (1785–1854) who wrote in *Blackwood's* as "Christopher North"
reviewed *Manfred* in the *Edinburgh Magazine* of June, 1817 (pp. 289–295).
    [1] Hobhouse wrote a number of notes for the fourth canto of *Childe Harold*, but
they became so voluminous that he published most of them as a separate volume,
Historical Illustrations of the Fourth Canto of Childe Harold (1818). Rather reluctantly, at Byron's insistence, Murray undertook the publication.

being on terms with almost all the bards and Critics of the day—it would be savage at any time—but worst of all *now when* in *another country*—to revive this foolish lampoon.——I am glad that you and the Chancellor clapped an extinguisher on Master Cawthorn—I thought that person's impudence would get him into a scrape.——The Review of Manfred came very safely—and I am much pleased with it. It is odd that they should say—(that is somebody in a magazine whom the Edinburgh controverts) that it was taken from Marlow's Faustus which I never read—nor saw.—An American who came the other day from Germany—told Mr. Hobhouse that Manfred was taken from *Goethe's Faust.*—The devil may take both the Faustus's, German and English—I have taken neither.——Will you send to *Hanson* and say that he has not written since *9th* September—at least I have had no letter since to my great surprize.—Will you desire Messrs. Morland—to send out whatever additional sums have or may be paid in credit immediately & always—to their Venice correspondents.——It is two months ago—that they sent me out an additional credit for *one thousand pounds.* I was very glad of it—but I don't know how the devil it came—for I can only make out 500 of Hanson's payment—and I had thought the other 500 came from you—but it did not it seems—as by yours of the 7th. instant—you have only just paid the £1230 balance.—Mr. Kinnaird is on his way home with the assignments.—I can fix no time for the arrival of Canto 4th. which depends on the journey of Mr. Hobhouse home—and I do not think that this will be immediate.——

Yours in great haste and very truly,

B

P.S.—Morlands have not yet written to my Bankers apprising the payment of your balances—pray—desire them to do so.—Ask them about the *previous* thousand—of which I know 500 came from Hanson's —& make out the other 500—that is—whence it came.

[TO ELIZABETH, DUCHESS OF DEVONSHIRE.[1]]

Venice, November 3, 1817

Madam,—I was yesterday honoured by your Grace's letter of the 19th ult. The newspapers have, I fear, deceived your Grace in common

---

[1] Lady Elizabeth Hervey (1759–1824), daughter of the 4th Earl of Bristol, married in 1776 John Thomas Foster. After his death she was a much sought-after widow. Gibbon proposed to her but she refused him. In 1809 she married the 5th Duke of Devonshire, and after his death in 1811, she lived much abroad. Hobhouse had leased her house in Piccadilly for Byron in March, 1815, for £700 a year.

with many others, for, up to my last letters from England, Newstead Abbey had not been sold;—and should it be so at this moment I shall be agreeably surprized.

Amongst the many unpleasant consequences of my residence in Piccadilly, or, rather, of the cause of that residence, I can assure your Grace that I by no means look upon it as the least painful that my inconveniences should have contributed to your's.

Whatever measures Mr. Denen[2] might find it proper to take were probably what he deemed his duty, and, though I regret that they were necessary, I am still more sorry to find that they seem to have been inefficacious. Indeed, till very lately I was not aware that your Grace was so unlucky as to have me still amongst the number of your debtors. I shall write to the person who has the management of my affairs in England, and, although I have but little control over either at present, I will do the best I can to have the remaining balance liquidated.

I have the honour to be, with great respect, your Grace's

Most obedt. very humble Servt,

BYRON

[TO CHARLES HANSON]   *Venice November 14th. 1817*

Dear Charles—I did not answer your two letters of August & Septr. 9th. because they led me to expect a third—as the last of the two announced enquiries which might possibly induce a sale (or treaty for a sale) of Newstead—but since that period I have heard no further, and I infer from thence that no sale has taken place.—Upon this subject I can only repeat that nothing can or could be more detrimental to my comfort and my interests;—that any price ought to have been taken— rather than permit the estate to remain unsold—and that the delay must be far more prejudicial to me—than any price which covered the settlement;—as I should be prepared to resign a portion of the income in the event of the sale of the property—to liquidate the debts remaining unpaid in case the surplus money should be insufficient.—I hope that you will do what you can to induce a sale by private contract —as public auction seems unavailing;--above all do not hope for a *high* price—*that* has been the fatal error of the former auctions & the cause of the property remaining unsold;—sell it by *lots* in any shape or

2 Mr. Denen was the Duchess of Devonshire's agent. See Feb. 7, 1816, to [?], and April 24, 1816, to Hanson.

271

form—but let it be *sold.*——With regard to Rochdale—Mr. Kinnaird
—(who is I hope by this time returned) is in possession of my opinion.
—I hope that you & your father are well—as well as all your family.

believe me very truly & affectly yrs.

BYRON

P.S.—Whatever surplus remains from the Michaelmas rents—may
be transmitted through Messrs. Morlands' bank to this place.

[TO JOHN MURRAY] *Venice November 15th. 1817*

Dear Sir/—Mr. Kinnaird has probably returned to England by this
time—& will have conveyed to you any tidings you may wish to have
of us and ours.—I have come back to Venice for the Winter—Mr.
Hobhouse will probably set off in Decr. but what day or week I know
not—he is my opposite neighbour at present.——I wrote yesterday
in some perplexity and no very good humour to Mr. K[innair]d to
inform me about Newstead and the Hansons—of which & whom I
hear nothing since his departure from this place—except in a few
unintelligible words from an unintelligible woman.——I am as sorry
to hear of Dr. Polidori's accident as one can be for a person for whom
one has a dislike—and—something of contempt—when he gets well
tell me—and how he gets on in the sick line—poor fellow! how came he
to fix there?

I fear the Doctor's Skill at Norwich
Will hardly salt the Doctor's porridge.

Methought he was going to the Brazils to give the Portuguese physic
(of which they are fond to desperation) with the Danish Consul—and
the patronage of Frederic North (the most illustrious humbug of his
age and country) and the blessing of Lady Westmoreland—William
Ward's Madwoman.——Your new Canto has expanded to one
hundred & sixty seven stanzas—it will be long you see—and as for the
notes by H[obhouse]—I suspect they will be of the heroic size; you
must keep Mr. Hobhouse in good humour—for he is devilish touchy
yet about your review and all which it inherits—including the Editor—
the Admiralty—and it's bookseller;—I used to think that *I* was a good
deal of an author in amour propre and "noli me tangere"—but these
prose fellows are worst after all about their little comforts.——Do
you remember my mentioning some months ago the Marquis Moncada
—a Spaniard of distinction and fourscore years—my summer neighbour

at La Mira?—Well—about six weeks ago he fell in love with a Venetian girl of family & no fortune or character—took her into his mansion—quarrelled with all his former friends for giving him advice (except me who gave him none) and installed her present concubine and future wife & Mistress of himself and furniture;—at the end of a month in which she demeaned herself as ill as possible he found out a correspondence between her and some former keeper—and after nearly strangling—turned her out of the house—to the great scandal of the keeping part of the town—and with a prodigious eclât which has occupied all the Canals and Coffeehouses in Venice.—He said she wanted to poison him—& she says—God knows what—but between them they have made a great deal of noise.—I know a little of both the parties—Moncada seemed a very sensible old man—a character which he has not quite kept up on this occasion;—and the woman is rather showy than pretty—for the honour of religion she was bred in a convent—and for the credit of Great Britain taught by an Englishwoman.

yrs. [sincerely],
B

[TO DOUGLAS KINNAIRD]   *Venice, Novr. 19th. 1817*

Dear Douglas—Inferring that you are by this time in England again—I assail you on the old subject—to tell you that since your departure I have never heard from the Hansons—from which I augur that Newstead is not likely to be sold—& that I am one degree further in the latitude of hell.—Except a foolish & perplexing passage in a letter of Mrs. Leigh's I have heard not one word more upon the subject at all—and as her way of putting the most common things is more like a riddle than anything else—I can only say that I am farther than ever from understanding her—or it—or Hanson—or anything—or anybody—and unless you take compassion upon me & give me a little common sense—I shall remain in the ignorance and anxiety of the last two months upon the same topic.—If you see Augusta give my love to her and tell her—that I do not write because I really and truly do not understand one single word of her letters—to answer them is out of the question—I don't say it out of ill nature—but whatever be the subject—there is so much paraphrase—parenthesis—initials—dashes—hints—& what Lord Ogilby calls "Mr. Sterling's damned crinkum crankum"[1] that—Sunburn me! if I know what the meaning or no meaning is—and am obliged to study Armenian as a relief.——— Hobhouse is here—and very much yours—of Scrope we know no further—of you we have talk & regrets—Good bye—I am just going to a Comedy of Goldoni's.[2]

Yours ever & truly,

B

P.S.—Murray writes that he has paid the balance—but I have not yet been advised thereof from your house.—My respects to Mrs. K[innair]d. [In another hand]:

£50 per Londra ad R 4.40		R220.
mia Provige. ad 1%	R 2.20	
Idem conto delli Sig Siri e Wilhalm		
	2.20	4.40
		———————
		R215.60

[In Byron's handwriting]:

Mem.—The account is in *Scudi Romani*—the bills go right to London —& yet the dogs Siri & Wilhalm require a toll for a turnpike never passed through.———

My dear Doug.—You see!—will you back those b—g–rs?

[TO R. B. HOPPNER]   *Venice—Nov. 20, 1817*

Dear Sir—I shall endeavour to keep the conditions of the lease and I had already decided to retain in my service the man whom you left in care of the place.[1] I took the liberty of sending to request that you would accept cash for the draft immediately as I was making up some accounts, and also on account of the exchange as I wished to draw before it lowered still further which I understand will shortly be the case. I have sent you the publications you honoured me by requesting, and also the last poem of my friend Moore and one by Coleridge— which you have perhaps not seen—and of which I beg your acceptance

[1] In Garrick and George Colman the Elder's *The Clandestine Marriage*, Act IV, scene 2, Lord Ogleby says: ".... but there is such a deal of this damned crinkum crankum, as Sterling calls it, that one sees people for half an hour before one can get to them."

[2] Carlo Goldoni (1710–1793) was known as the "Italian Molière". He wrote 150 comedies, many of which were produced in Venice during Byron's sojourn.

[1] The Villa d'Este which Byron had sublet from Hoppner.

as I have other copies of the same works and these can be spared
without the least inconvenience to myself. If you have not read "Tales
of my Landlord" I have duplicates and a set is at your service—they
are well worth the perusal—and I will send them whenever you like.
I have the honour to be

Very truly your obedient & faithful svt.,
BYRON

[TO R. B. HOPPNER]   *Venice—Nov. 28th. 1817*

Dear Sir,—I seem fated to give you trouble. Certain persons (or
person) unknown this day walked into my hall and during the sleep or
neglect of the Servants carried off a blue great coat—a water proof
cloak—and a pair of Silver Candlesticks—of which larceny I have
given notice to the Police—but they tell me that my complaint will
come with greater weight—if the proofs be transmitted through your
office and backed by some forms of which I am incompetent or
ignorant.—If I am misinformed I hope you will excuse me and blame
the bearer (an Italian in my service who has brought me back this
information & whom I have instructed to apprize you of all particulars)
and if not may I beg your assistance or instruction—not to recover the
Chattels or the thief—for that is hopeless—but to make the degree of
objection to such conveyance—requisite to apprize the Venetian
public that I would rather not be robbed if I could avoid it.—I should
have done myself the honour of waiting on you instead of troubling
you with this note had I not been laid up with a Cold which has made
me deaf and inarticulate.—I have the honour to be

very truly your obliged & faith[ful] St.
BYRON

[TO JOHN MURRAY]   *Venice. Decr. 3d. 1817*

Dear Sir—A Venetian lady,[1] learned and somewhat stricken in
years, having in her intervals of love and devotion taken upon her to
translate the letters—& write the life of lady M[ar]y W[ortle]y
Montague,[2]—to which undertaking there are two obstacles—firstly

[1] Possibly the Countess Albrizzi.
[2] Lady Mary Wortley Montagu (1689–1762), noted as a letter writer and for
her association with Alexander Pope, spent much of her later life at Venice and
other places in Italy. Byron referred to her as "the charming Mary Montagu" in
Don Juan (Canto 5, stanza 3).

ignorance of English—and secondly—a total dearth of information on the subject of her projected biography—has applied to me for facts or falsities upon this promising project. Lady M[ary] lived the last twenty or more years of her life in or near Venice I believe, but here they know nothing—and remember nothing—for the story of today— is succeeded by the scandal of tomorrow—and the wit and beauty and gallantry which might render your countrywoman notorious in her own country—must have been here no great distinction —because the first is in no request—and the latter are common to all women—or at least the last of them.—If you can therefore tell me anything or get any thing told of Lady. W. M.—I shall take it as a favour—& will transfer & translate it to the "Dama" in question— and I pray you besides to send me by some quick and safe voyager the edition of her letters—and the stupid life by Dr. Dallaway[3]—published by her proud & foolish family.——The death of the Princess Charlotte[4] has been a shock even here—and must have been an earthquake at home—The Courier's list of some three hundred heirs to the Crown (including the house of Wirtemberg with that blackguard Paul of disreputable memory[5]—whom I remember seeing at various balls during the visit of the Muscovites &c. in 1814) must be very consolatory to all true lieges as well as foreigners except Signor Travis a rich Jew Merchant of this city—who complains grievously of the length of British Mourning—which has countermanded all the Silks which he was on the point of transmitting, for a year to come.—The death of this poor Girl is melancholy in every respect—dying at twenty or so—in childbed—of a *boy* too—a present princess and future queen—and just as she began to be happy—and to enjoy herself and the hopes which she inspired.—To be sure Providence is a fine fellow and does wonders—"the Gods take care of Cato."[6]——I think as far as I can recollect she is the first royal defunct in childbed upon record in *our* history.—I feel sorry in every respect;—for the loss of a female reign—and a woman hitherto harmless—and all the lost rejoicings, and addresses, and drunkenness, and disbursements, of

[3] James Dallaway (1763–1834), chaplain and physician to the British Embassy at Constantinople where Lady Mary had lived with her husband, Edward Wortley Montagu, the British Ambassador. He published in 1803 *Letters and other Works of Lady Mary Wortley Montagu, from her Original MSS., with Memoirs of her Life.*
[4] Princess Charlotte, only child of the Prince Regent, whom Byron had addressed in his "To a Lady Weeping", died on November 6, 1817.
[5] Prince Paul of Würtemberg, stepson of the Princess Royal of England, came to London with the allied sovereigns in the summer of 1814. He was referred to in the *Journal of Mary Frampton* (p. 220) as "a sad blackguard".
[6] Addison, *Cato*, Act II, scene 1.

John Bull on the occasion.—but not surprized—because "the Lord giveth and the Lord taketh away—blessed be the name of the Lord"—The Prince will marry again after divorcing his wife, and Mr. Southey will write an elegy now—and an ode then—the Quarterly will have an article against the Press—and the Edinburgh an article *half* and *half*, about Reform and right of divorce—[five lines crossed out] the British will give you Dr. Chalmers' funeral Sermon much commended —with a place in the Stars for deceased Royalty—and the Morning Post will have already yelled forth its "Syllables of dolour."—

Woe, woe, Nealliny!—the young Nealliny![7]

It is some time since I have heard from you—are you in bad humour? I suppose so.—I have been so myself—it is your turn now—and by & by mine will come round again.—

yrs truly
BYRON

P.S.—Countess Albrizzi come back from Paris has brought me a medal of himself [i.e. Denon]—a present from Denon[8] to me—and a likeness to the *death* of Mr. Rogers (belonging to her) by Denon also—I never saw so good a portrait—"And the trumpet shall sound and the dead shall be raised."

[TO JOHN HANSON]   *Venice. Decr. 11th. 1817*

Dear Sir—The Sale of Newstead has been equally unexpected and agreeable to me and the price much better than could be expected considering the times—with regard to the Purchaser Major Wildman[1] —I am unacquainted with his means or his property;—but I recollect him as my old schoolfellow and a man of honour—and would rather as far as my personal feelings are concerned that he should be the

---

7 Southey's *Curse of Kehama*, I, 11.

8 Dominique Vivant, Baron de Denon (1747–1825) had arranged Mme. de Pompadour's collection of gems. He became an attaché to the French embassy at St. Petersburg, visited and painted Voltaire at Ferney, and later gained the patronage of Napoleon. He had spent some time in Venice and was the subject of one of Countess Albrizzi's *Ritratti*.

1 Major (later Colonel) Thomas Wildman (1787–1859) eldest son of Thomas Wildman of Bacton Hall, Suffolk, had been at Harrow with Byron. He entered the 7th Hussars in 1807, served in the Peninsular War and was aide-de-camp to Lord Uxbridge at Waterloo. He paid £94,500 for Newstead Abbey, and in subsequent years spent almost as much in renovation and improvements, though he tried to keep the Abbey as it was in Byron's day.

purchaser than another; I need hardly say that I shall gladly concur in every proper measure to bring the treaty to a satisfactory conclusion, & that I am obliged by your exertions and rejoiced by their probable success.—The first step in the event of a satisfactory conclusion will be the liquidation of my debts;—the list of annuities sent by Mr. Kinnaird including Jews and Sawbridge amounts to twelve thousand eight hundred & odd pounds.—Of these I think you will find the sum stated by *Hicks Spring* and *Thorpe* as a *thousand* pounds— to amount (by the papers) to only *seven* hundred principal—you will also remember that I paid off one small annuity shortly before I left England—and I presume you have the papers and acquittance —as I recollect consulting you on the subject at the time & giving you the parchment.——The *Massingberd annuities—principal* stated at *three thousand three hundred* may *wait* as they are *Minority* debts—and must only have interest at five per cent—at any rate *they shall* wait for the present—till a *fair* arrangement can be made—as the treatment I have received from the Israelites has not been such as to make me very indulgent towards them—tho' I will be equitable.—The remainder—Thomas & Co. should be paid off by the first opportunity—also Sawbridge—and Claughton's bond (now held by your Son) which with Baxter's (Coachmaker's) bond—is I think all (except Mrs. Byron of Nottingham's) *not* simple contract debts—and for these also Arrangements should be made, and the accounts called in—I know of few or none of any amount, except my taylor and bookseller and house-rent to the Duchess of Devonshire.— I should also be very glad to have *your account*—and in short I wish to apply my means as far as in me lies, to the discharge of all fair & examined claims upon me—and I request you & Mr. Kinnaird to take the proper steps therefor—according to circumstances arising out of the sale, supposing it to proceed without difficulties.—I presume you have between you full power to act for me—I am quite contented & pleased with the terms of the sale—if acted upon and complied with. ——With regard to *Rochdale*, do your best for me—but you know that speedy arrangements would suit me best after such long delays.— Pray examine *closely* into all accounts—annuities, &c. that they may not take advantage of my absence.—I do not wish to return to England at present if it can be helped, and should think that a Clerk dispatched with the necessary papers might arrive here with less expence and trouble than would be produced either by your journey or mine.—The English Consul or other competent witnesses might be in readiness.—I write in haste—& will take up my pen again shortly—

in the mean time—with my best regards to Charles, all your family, and Self,

I am, ever yours truly and affectly.,
BYRON

P.S.—Before I left England I entrusted to Mr. Hobhouse's care several boxes of papers—some full of receipts which may be referred to or consulted in settling my affairs.—Mr. Hobhouse is now here—but intends to be in England in a couple of Months.

[TO RICHARD BELGRAVE HOPPNER]
Venice, December 15th, 1817

I should have thanked you before, for your favour a few days ago, had I not been in the intention of paying my respects, personally, this evening, from which I am deterred by the recollection that you will probably be at the Count Goess's[1] this evening, which has made me postpone my intrusion.

I think your Elegy a remarkably good one, not only as a composition, but both the politics and poetry contain a far greater proportion of truth and generosity than belongs to the times, or to the professors of these opposite pursuits, which usually agree only in one point, as extremes meet. I do not know whether you wished me to retain the copy, but I shall retain it till you tell me otherwise; and am very much obliged by the perusal.

My own sentiments on Venice, &c., such as they are, I had already thrown into verse last summer, in the Fourth Canto of Childe Harold, now in preparation for the press; and I think much more highly of them, for being in coincidence with yours.

Believe me yours, etc.

[1] Probably Moore's misreading of "Count Goetz", the Austrian governor of Venice.

Appendix I

LIST OF LETTERS AND SOURCES

VOLUME 5

Date	Recipient	Source of Text	Page

Date	Recipient	Source of Text	Page

Date	Recipient	Source of Text	Page

FORGERIES OF BYRON'S LETTERS

June 27, [1816]: To Mr. Bonstetten. MS. Pierpont Morgan Library.

Oct. 18, 1816: To Sir Godfrey Webster. Ehrsam, *Major Byron*, "cited by Lord Lovelace in a letter to John Murray".

Oct. 28, 1816: To M. de Bonstetten. Schultess-Young, X, 169–71.

Nov. 1, 1816: To W. Webster. Schultess-Young, IV, 162–64.

Nov. 18, 1816: To Capt. Hay. Maggs, Cat. 256, 1910.

Nov. 22, 1816: To M. de Bonstetten. MS. Berg Collection, New York Public Library (Text same as Nov. 28, 1818, to Hoppner.)

[1817?]: To D. Kinnaird. MS. Bodleian Library.

[Jan., 1817]: To[?]. Sotheby Cat., May 10, 1900.

Jan. [1817?]: To Kinnaird. Sotheby Cat., June 10, 1909 (Source, Disraeli, *Venetia*, Book IV, Chapter 4).

Feb. 13, 1817 To M. la Baronne de Staël. Schultess-Young, XI, 171–72.

March, 1817: To Kinnaird. Sotheby Cat., July 22, 1909.

[April] 1817: To Douglas Kinnaird. Schultess-Young, XII, 172–74.

June 17, 1817: To W. Webster. MS. Royal College of Surgeons Library.

Appendix III

BIBLIOGRAPHY FOR VOLUME 5

(*Principal short title or abbreviated references*)

Astarte—Lovelace, Ralph Milbanke, Earl of: *Astarte: A Fragment of Truth, Concerning George Gordon Byron, Sixth Lord Byron.* Recorded by his grandson. New Edition by Mary Countess of Lovelace, London, 1921.

Bixby—*Poems and Letters of Lord Byron . . . from . . . Manuscripts . . . of W. K. Bixby.* Society of Dofobs, Chicago, 1912.

Dictionary of National Biography.

Elwin, Malcolm: *Lord Byron's Wife*, London 1962; New York 1963.

LBC—*Lord Byron's Correspondence*, ed. John Murray, 2 vols., London 1922.

LJ—*The Works of Lord Byron. A New, Revised and Enlarged Edition. Letters and Journals*, ed. Rowland E. Prothero, 6 vols., London, 1898–1901.

Marchand, Leslie A.: *Byron: A Biography*, 3 vols., New York, 1957; London, 1958.

Mayne, Ethel Colburn: *The Life and Letters of Anne Isabella Lady Noel Byron*, London, 1929.

Moore, Doris Langley: *Lord Byron: Accounts Rendered*, London, 1974.

Moore, Thomas: *Letters and Journals of Lord Byron: with Notices of his Life*, 2 vols., London, 1830.

Nathan, Isaac: *Fugitive Pieces and Reminiscences of Lord Byron*, London, 1829.

Poetry—*The Works of Lord Byron. A New and Enlarged Edition. Poetry*, ed. Ernest Hartley Coleridge, 7 vols., London, 1898–1904.

Smiles, Samuel: *A Publisher and his Friends: Memoir and Correspondence of the Late John Murray*, 2 vols., London, 1891.

Appendix IV

BIOGRAPHICAL SKETCHES OF PRINCIPAL CORRESPONDENTS AND PERSONS FREQUENTLY MENTIONED

(See also Sketches in previous Volumes)

COUNTESS ISABELLA TEOTOCHI ALBRIZZI

The Countess Albrizzi (1761?–1836) was a widow when Byron first met her in Venice in the autumn of 1816. She was born in Corfu but claimed that her family was Athenian. Her father Antonio Teotochi was said to be head of an old Greek family. Isabella married a Venetian nobleman, Carlo Antonio, in 1776 and came to live in Venice. She was divorced in 1795 and the following year married Giuseppe Albrizzi. Their son, Giuseppino, born in 1800, Byron mentioned in a note to *Marino Faliero* as "the accomplished son of an accomplished mother." The Countess Albrizzi's second husband died in 1812. When Byron met her, she conducted the most celebrated salon, or *conversazione*, in Venice. A friend of Canova, Pindemonte, Morelli, Alfieri, Ugo Foscolo, and most of the literati and artists of the day, she was called the Madame de Staël of Italy (Hobhouse, perhaps reflecting Byron's view, noted in his diary that she was "a very poor copy, indeed, though she seems a very good natured woman"). Many Greeks came to her *conversazioni*. She had literary ambitions and published several editions of her *Ritratti* (line portraits with letterpress) or portraits of the famous men whom she had known. During his first years in Venice Byron frequented her *conversazioni*. Though he resisted her efforts to include him in her *Ritratti*, she added his portrait in the edition of 1826.

CLAIRE CLAIRMONT

Mary Jane Clairmont, who took the name of Clara or Clare (later Claire) to distinguish herself from her step-sister Mary Godwin, was not yet eighteen when she persistently insinuated herself into the embraces of Byron briefly before he went abroad in April, 1816. William Godwin had married her mother, Mrs. Clairmont, a widow, after the death of his first wife, Mary Wollstonecraft, author of the *Vindication of the*

293

Rights of Women. Mary Godwin, who eloped with and later married Shelley, was the daughter of Godwin and Mary Wollstonecraft. Claire and Mary had grown up in the ultra-liberal and free-thinking household of Godwin. Claire had accompanied Percy Shelley and Mary Godwin on their honeymoon elopement to France and Switzerland in 1814. Her too great fondness for Shelley was resented by Mary, and it was perhaps with the intent to show that she too could captivate a poet, and one more famous than Shelley though no less unorthodox, that she thrust herself on Byron. In spite of his increasing indifference, she planned to meet him in Geneva, where she accompanied Mary and Shelley in May, 1816. Byron's association with Shelley during the summer on the Lake of Geneva gave her a chance to come "prancing to [him] at all hours". As he told Augusta, he could "not exactly play the Stoic" with her. After she returned to England to bear his child, born January 12, 1817, and named Allegra by Byron, he would no longer communicate with her directly but only through Shelley. In 1818 he undertook the rearing of the child. But Claire's efforts to use the little girl as a sentimental link between them only reinforced Byron's determination to cut off the relationship entirely, except through Shelley, with whom he remained on the best of terms. Claire's love turned to hatred and bitterness through the years, and when he put Allegra into a convent for education, against her wishes, she concocted various abortive schemes to rescue her. Her conduct made Byron irrational and in the end cruel. Allegra's death in the convent in 1822 was a blow to both of them but estranged them further. Claire never married but supported herself as a governess or tutor in Vienna and then in Russia. In her last years in Florence, she became a Catholic but did not abate her bitterness toward Byron in her letters to Trelawny. As one who had known Shelley and Byron, she became a romantic figure whose legend inspired Henry James's fiction *The Aspern Papers.* She died in 1879 at the age of eighty-one.

RICHARD BELGRAVE HOPPNER

Hoppner (1786–1872), second son of John Hoppner, R.A., who rivalled Lawrence as a portrait painter, had also studied painting and had some literary ability and ambitions. He was appointed British Consul in Venice in 1814. His wife was Swiss. Since Byron made an effort to avoid the English during his first year in Venice, he did not meet Hoppner until the summer or autumn of 1817. Before long they were on easy terms. Hoppner was impressed with his distinguished countryman, and Byron found him agreeable and willing to serve him in practical matters. He catered to Hoppner's literary interests by lending him books. After Hobhouse left for England at the beginning of 1818, Hoppner accompanied Byron on his daily rides on the Lido sands. Byron later told Lady Blessington that Hoppner was "a good listener, and his remarks were acute and original; he is besides a thoroughly good man. . . ." Byron leased Hoppner's villa at Este and, though he never used it himself, he loaned it to the Shelleys on their visit in 1818. After Byron followed the Countess Guiccioli to Ravenna, he relied on Hoppner to attend to his affairs in Venice. The Hoppners kept Allegra for a time and arranged for her care when they left for a visit to Switzerland before Byron sent for her to join him in Bologna and later Ravenna. The Hoppners, however, disapproved of Byron's liaison with the Countess Guiccioli. Byron was annoyed but never broke his ties of friendship. Byron half believed Hoppner's gossip on Shelley and Claire, but he passed it on to Shelley.

DR. JOHN WILLIAM POLIDORI

Dr. Polidori, son of an Italian emigré, who had once been secretary to the dramatist Alfieri, was an uncle of Dante Gabriel, Christina, and William Michael Rossetti. He received his medical degree at Edinburgh at the age of 19 and was only 21 when Byron employed him as travelling physician just before he left England in April, 1816. Murray offered Polidori £500 for the right to publish a diary of his tour with Byron, which he kept from the time they left Dover. Hobhouse dissuaded Polidori from publishing the diary in 1820 and it did not appear until 1911, edited by his nephew, William Michael Rossetti. It is a valuable source, though perhaps not always accurate, of Byron's activities and movements on his tour to Switzerland and of his association with Shelley. Polidori had literary ambitions and was youthfully brash and conceited. In September, before leaving for Italy, Byron dismissed him from his service but continued to take an interest in him and befriend him. He wrote later that he had been disgusted with "the eternal nonsense, and *tracasseries*, and emptiness, and ill humour, and vanity of that young person . . .". But he wrote to Murray asking him to find a publisher for Polidori or get him a berth through his influence with the admiralty. The Doctor preceded him to Italy and Byron saw him again at Milan, where he tried unsuccessfully to extricate him from the consequences of a quarrel with some Austrian officers. Polidori, on returning to England, published Byron's unfinished ghost story, which he completed as *The Vampyre*. When Murray asked Byron to write a "delicate declension" for him of Polidori's tragedy, Byron sent him one of his cleverest *jeu d'esprits* in verse. Disappointed in his career and in his literary ambitions, Polidori took his own life with poison in 1821.

MARY (GODWIN) SHELLEY

Byron first met Mary Godwin in April, 1816, just before he went abroad. Claire Clairmont had brought her to see him, and by Claire's account she was agreeably surprised by his manners. "How mild he is! how gentle! So different from what I expected." She saw much of him during the summer at Geneva, and later recalled with great feeling the agreeable impression he made upon her during the boating excursions on the lake with Shelley, Byron and Claire. It was after a rainy night at Diodati when they all told ghost stories that Mary conceived the story of *Frankenstein*. After the Shelleys returned to England, it was Mary who wrote to Byron to announce the birth of Allegra, his daughter by Claire. When she saw him again in Venice in 1818, she had become Shelley's legal wife, but she was still fascinated by Byron. Only a few days after the death of their daughter Clara, she accompanied Shelley to the Palazzo Mocenigo, where she read with admiration the manuscript of the first canto of *Don Juan*, which he had just finished, and she agreed to copy the manuscripts of *Mazeppa* and the *Ode on Venice*. Both Mary and Shelley approved of Byron's placing Allegra in the convent school near Ravenna and defended him against Claire's outraged protestation. When Byron came to Pisa they were closely associated with him until Shelley's death in July, 1822. After that event, while she was in Pisa, she was grateful for Byron's kindness to her. When they all moved to Genoa in the autumn Byron continued his assistance, writing to his lawyer to try to get Sir Timothy Shelley to give her an allowance for her child, acting as her banker when she needed money, and giving her manuscripts to copy. He had offered her money to return to England, but, partly through the interference of Leigh Hunt, she quarrelled with Byron before he left for Greece. Yet she continued to cherish his memory, and she was shocked by news of his death, writing in her diary; "Albè—the dear, capricious, fascinating Albè—has left this desert world! God grant I may die young!" Mary, who had been unequal to viewing Shelley's remains at Via Reggio, went to see Byron's in London, and after watching the funeral procession, she wrote to Trelawny: ". . . connected with him in a thousand ways, admiring his talents & with all his faults feeling affection for him, it went to my heart when the other day the he[a]rse that contained his lifeless form, a form of beauty which in life I often delighted to behold, passed my window going up Highgate Hill on his last journey. . . ." (For an analysis of Mary Shelley's subconscious preoccupation with Byron, in her journals and novels, in several of which he seems to be the model for her heroes, see Ernest J. Lovell, Jr. "Byron and Mary Shelley", *Keats-Shelley Journal*, Vol. II (Jan. 1953) pp. 35–49.)

PERCY BYSSHE SHELLEY

Byron had probably never heard of Shelley before Claire Clairmont gave him glowing accounts of the wonder-boy in April, 1816. When they met in Geneva in the following month they established an intellectual *rapport* at once. They were closely associated during the summer in their boat on the lake and in free and wide ranging conversations at the Villa Diodati. The association was beneficial to both and mutually stimulating to their poetic output. Shelley influenced Byron to read Wordsworth more sympathetically as is evidenced in the third canto of *Childe Harold*. The Promethean theme, congenial to both, found eventual expression in their poems. Their free-thinking coincided on many subjects, though Byron was sometimes shocked by Shelley's "rage against religion," and Shelley was inclined at times to think Byron "no better than a Christian." But they shared iconoclasms with regard to politics and the conventions of society. Shelley understood Byron's relationship with Claire and protected him against her importunities and took care of his daughter by her until Byron took her to raise and educate. Byron would communicate with Claire only through Shelley, who remained the buffer between them. When the Shelleys visited Byron in Venice in 1818, he and Mary were both deeply impressed with the first canto of *Don Juan*, but Shelley was distressed by Bryon's dissipated life at the time. He was again exhilarated by their conversation as is reflected in his "Julian and Maddalo." When Shelley visited Byron in Ravenna in August, 1821, he found him in every way improved by his liaison with the Countess Guiccioli. He was again impressed with Byron's poetic powers, and depressed that he could not equal him. He thought every word of *Don Juan* "pregnant with immortality." They carried on their literary conversations far into the night and all night. Shelley visited Allegra in the convent and persuaded Byron to move with the Gambas and Teresa to Pisa, where he found the Casa Lanfranchi for him. There for several months they were almost daily together along with Shelley's English friends, Williams, Trelawny, Medwin and others. Toward the end of his life Shelley was somewhat disillusioned with Byron, partly because of his treatment of Claire, but he continued to admire Byron's poetry. He had written: "I despair of rivalling Lord Byron, and there is no other with whom it is worth contending." Byron had no great appreciation of Shelley's poetry but was unreserved in his praise of him as a man, calling him, "without exception, the *best* and least selfish man I ever knew. I never knew one who was not a beast in comparison."

INDEX OF PROPER NAMES

Page numbers in italics indicate main references and Biographical Sketches in the Appendix. Such main biographical references in earlier volumes are included in this index and are in square brackets.

Acerbi, Giuseppe, 124 and n
Addison, Joseph, *Cato*, 276 and n
Aeschylus, *Prometheus* compared with *Manfred*, 268n
Albrizzi, Countess Isabella Teotochi, (?) 275–6, 277, *293*; bust of Canova, 132n, 133; illustrator of his works, 207; friendship with B., 142, 146, 151, 163; B. on, 148; *Ritratti*, 277n, 293
Alexander VI, Pope, 114, 123
Alfieri, Count Vittorio, 218
Antwerp, 72, 73, 74
Ariosto, Ludovico, 218, *266*; Titian's portrait, 213, 217
Aris, Governor, of Coldbath Fields prison, 233 and n
Armstrong and Crooke, sale of B.'s books, 42n, 51
Arnold, Samuel James, 107 and n; *The Prior Claim*, 107n
Aubonne, 104
Aucher, Fr Pasquale, B.'s Armenian tutor, 137, 142 and n, 152, 157n; helps B translate two Epistles, 201 and n, 238; Armenian–English grammar, 146, 152, 156–7, 157n, 179, 235
Aventicum, 78

Baillie, Joanna, 203
Baillie, 'Long', 144 and n, 183 and n, 198
Baillie, Dr. Matthew, consulted by Lady B., 33 and n
Bainbridge, Mr., unidentified, 30 and n
Baldwin, Mr., libels Lady Frances Webster, 28 and n
Baldwin and Cradock, publishers, 205n
Bandello, Matteo, 132 and n
Barbieri, Giovanni Francesco (il Guercino), 116 and n
Barton, Bernard, [*Vol. 2, 178n*], 89–90

Baxter, coachmaker, 72 and n, 278
Bayman, footman to B. 75
Beaumont, F. and Fletcher, J., *Philaster*, 173 and n
Beccaria, Cesare Bonesana, Marchese di, 117 and n; *Dei Delitti e delle Pene*, 117n
Bembo, Cardinal, letters from Lucretia Borgia, 114, 116 and n, 123
Bender, W., *The Armenian* (trans.), 203n
Bentinck, Lord Frederick, 95 and n
Bentinck, Lord William Cavendish, 171 and n
Berger, B.'s Swiss guide, 60 and n, 71, 97, 144
Berlinghieri, Andrea Vacca, 164 and n, 179 and n
Bernese Alps, 104, 108
Bickerstaff, Isaac, *Love in a Village*, 182 and n
Blair, Hugh, sermons, 97
Blake, Mr., barber, 135 and n, 190
Blücher, Gerhard von, 76, 98 and n
Bologna, 231, 234
Bonn, 76
Bonstetten, Charles Victor de, 86 and n, 87, 205, 207n
Borgia, Cæsar, 114
Borgia, Lucretia, Duchess of Ferrara, letters to Cardinal Bembo, 114–15, 116, 118 and n, 123
Borromean Islands, 114, 115, 117, 125
Borromeo, Carlo, 125 and n
Bowles, William Lisle, 111n, 240–1; *The Missionary of the Andes*, 187 and n, 193, 199; *Spirit of Discovery*, 241n
Bracchi, Cardinal, 219, 224
Breme, Luigi (Ludovico) the Abbate, 124 and n
Breme, Marchese di, 121, 124, 181
Brientz, 102–3, 205
Broglie, Albertine, Duchesse de (née de Staël), 86 and n, 111

Lara, 29
'Lines to a Lady Weeping', 276n
Manfred, 170n, 177–8, 179, 185, 204 and n, 209, 239; Alpine inspiration, 99n, 188, 194–5, 268; B. rewrites Act III, 211 and n, 212, 214, 219, 220; supposed origin, 249 and n; B. receives copies, 256–7; omission of last line, 257 and n; reviewed by Blackwood's *Edinburgh Magazine*, 249 and n, 268 and n, 270
Marino Faliero, 174n, 203, 293
'Monody on the Death of the Right Hon. R. B. Sheridan', 82nn, 83–4, 106, 107, 110, 111–12, 136n, 139, 255
'My boat is on the shore', 250
Occasional poems: 'As the Liberty lads o'er the sea', 149; 'Dear Doctor—I have read your play', 258–61; 'I stood in Venice, on the Bridge of Sighs', 244; 'What are you doing now', 148–9
'Ode from the French', appears in *Morning Chronicle*, 33–4, 34nn
'On the Bust of Helen by Canova', 132 and n, 133
Parisina, published with *Siege of Corinth*, 13n, 22n, incest theme, 13n; resemblance to *Marmion*, 22 and n
Poetry IV, 174n, 213n
The Prisoner of Chillon, 83, 87, 90, 160, 209; inspiration, 80n; Gifford's suggested omissions, 169; laudatory review in *Edinburgh Review*, 170n; Italian piracy, 222; published with 'A Dream and Other Poems', 178 and n
'She walks in beauty like the night', 47n
The Siege of Corinth, 158, 170n; published with *Parisina*, 13n, 22n, 28n, 32 and n; payment for, 13n, 16, 17–18, 22n; metrical form, 29
'A Sketch' ('Born in the garret'), 58 and n, 60 and n
'So we'll go no more a-roving', 176
'Stanzas to Augusta', 68n, 89 and n, 106, 111; Augusta objects to their publication, 91n, 110
'There's not a joy the world can give', 45
'A Very Mournful Ballad on the Siege and Conquest of Alhama'

(trns. from the Spanish), 174 and n, 196
'When we two parted', 28n
Byron, Sir John, first Baron Byron of Rochdale, 19n
Byron, Admiral Hon. John, marriage to Sophia Trevanion, 117n
Bysshe, Edward, *The Art of English Poetry*, 29 and n

Cambon, Signor, 143
The Cambridge Chronicle, 137 and n
Campbell, Thomas, 242, 260, 265
Canning, Stratford (later Lord Stratford de Redcliffe), [*Vol. 1, 242n*], 260n
Canova, Antonio, 132n, 148, 207, 216, 218, 235, 293
Carlsruhe, 76–7
Caroline, Princess of Wales, 155, 241n
Casti, Giambattista, 'Animali Parlante', 80; *Novelle Amorose*, 80 and n
Castiglione, Marchesa, 147 and n
Castlereagh, Robert Stewart, Viscount, 86, 214
Catalani, Angelica, 160, 163, 168, 182–3
Catullus, 'Sirmio', 123 and n
Cawthorn, James, 91, 108–9, 139, 270
Cesto, 113, 116, 117
Chalmers, Dr. Thomas, 277
Chamouni, 89, 97, 106, 188, 206; Bossons glacier, 102
Charlotte, Princess, death, 276 and n
Charlotte, Queen, 209n
Chateau de Chillon, 82, 97, 98, 209
Chateaubriand, François René, Vicomte de, 34 and n
Cincinnatus, Lucius, 168
Clairmont, Claire, 264n, 293–4; besieges B., 59 and n, 293, 296; with child, 143, 162, 228n, 295; later years, 294; and the Shelleys, 296, 297
Clarens, Lake Geneva, 81, 82, 96–8, 108, 220, 264
Claudianus, 123, 265
Claughton, Thomas, one time bidder for Newstead, 89, 151, 161; debt to B., 245 and n, 278
Clermont, Mary Anne, maid to Lady Noel, 31 and n, 36, 56; B.'s satire on, 58n; accused by him, 62–4
Coblenz, 7, 76

246, 254; *Siege of Corinth*, 13n, 16
and n; *Parisina*, 18, 22n; *Tasso*,
225–6, 239, 246, 254
Mustani, Countess (unidentified), 183
Mustoxithi, learned Greek, 182 and n
Mutz, B.'s dog, 103–4, 127, 144, 217

Nathan, Isaac, 68–9
Newstead Abbey, 134, 139–40, 161;
acquisition, 19n; B.'s inheritance,
26n; 'earthquake', 52, 53; bought
by Wildman (1818), 70n, 277 and
n; urgency of its sale, 226, 230,
236–7, 245–6, 257–8, 271–2;
purchase price, 277n
Noel, Sir Ralph (formerly Milbanke),
154, 161–2, 189; proposes his
daughter should leave B., 20 and n,
31; files a Bill against him, 180,
190, 198–9; owes him money, 226,
236, 262; nicknamed Tubal by B.,
246 and n
Noel, Lady, and Ada, 36, 109
North, Christopher, *see* Wilson, John
North, Francis (later fourth Earl of
Guilford), 210 and n, 212, 241
North, Frederick, fifth Earl of Guilford,
199 and n, 210n, 212, 215, 241

Oltrocchi, Baldassare, letters of Lucretia
Borgia to Cardinal Bembo, 116
and n
O'Neil, Eliza, actress, 261 and n
Osborne, Thomas, 143
Ostend, 70 and n, 71 and n
Otway, Thomas, 131; 'Belvidera',
Venice Preserved, 203 and n
Ouchy, 81, 94–6
Oxberry, William, 72 and n

The Pamphleteer, 111 and n
Papadopoli, Signor, 197
Partridge, John, 176, 197
Paul, Prince of Würtemberg, 276 and n
Pausanias, *Description of Greece*, 74 and
n
Perry, James, ed. *Morning Chronicle*,
33–4, 176, 182, 194; defends B.,
58n
Petrarch, 213, 217
Petrotini, Signor, Italian censor, 255
Philips, Ambrose, attacked by Pope,
192n; *Contes Persans* (trans.), 192
and n

Phillips, Thomas, portraits of B., 28
and n, 106
Pictet, Marc-Auguste, Prof., 207 and n
Pindemonte, Ippolito, 233 and n, 234,
241, 293
Pius VII, Pope, 219, 224
Pliny, *Natural History*, 221n
Plutarch, Alcibiades and his dog, 185
and n; *Lives*, 238 and nn
Pole, Sacheverell Chandos, marriage of
his daughter, Elizabeth Mary, to
seventh Lord B., 39 and n
Pole, (William) Wellesley, 72 and n
Polidori, Dr. John William, personal
physician to B. while in Europe,
71n, 73 and n, 142, 161, 199, 207n,
295; illness, 76, 78; sprains his
ankle, 81, 82; B. gives him his
congé, 121, 122, 126, 295; in
trouble in Milan, 121–2, 124,
126–7, 295; to go to Brazil with
Danish Consul, 163, 183, 272;
B. recommends him to Murray,
163–4, 212, 240, 241, 265; with
Lord Guilford, 210, 212, 215, 241;
writes a tragedy, 258 and n, 296;
biog., 295–6; death, 296; *The
Vampyre*, 296
Ponsonby, Lady, 216
Pope, Alexander, 28 and n, 111n,
275n; B. on, 265; *Dunciad*, 267n;
Epistle to Dr. Arbuthnot, 107 and n,
192n; *Horace Imitated*, 86 and n;
*Memoirs of P. P., Clerk of this
Parish*, 67n; *The Rape of the Lock*,
118 and n
Porcius Latro, Marcus, 221n
Prepiani, Venetian miniaturist, port-
raits of B., 191 and n, 212
Pye, Henry James, *The Prior Claim*,
107n

Radcliffe, Mrs. Ann, 145
Rae, Alexander, joint manager, Drury
Lane, 135n
Ragusa, Duchess of, 111
Raphael, 218
Rawdon, Mrs. and Miss, 79 and n, 80,
226
Raymond, stage manager, Drury Lane,
sends B. a play, 67
Rhine, the, 76–7, 78
Riley, Mr., (unidentified), creditor of
B., 161 and n
Robinson, Henry Crabb, 13n